Assisted Death

Assisted Death

A Study in Ethics and Law

L.W. Sumner

OXFORD
UNIVERSITY PRESS

OXFORD
UNIVERSITY PRESS

Great Clarendon Street, Oxford OX2 6DP

Oxford University Press is a department of the University of Oxford.
It furthers the University's objective of excellence in research, scholarship,
and education by publishing worldwide in

Oxford New York

Auckland Cape Town Dar es Salaam Hong Kong Karachi
Kuala Lumpur Madrid Melbourne Mexico City Nairobi
New Delhi Shanghai Taipei Toronto

With offices in

Argentina Austria Brazil Chile Czech Republic France Greece
Guatemala Hungary Italy Japan Poland Portugal Singapore
South Korea Switzerland Thailand Turkey Ukraine Vietnam

Oxford is a registered trade mark of Oxford University Press
in the UK and in certain other countries

Published in the United States
by Oxford University Press Inc., New York

British Library Cataloguing in Publication Data

Data available

Library of Congress Cataloging in Publication Data

Data available

Typeset by SPI Publisher Services, Pondicherry, India
Printed in Great Britain
on acid-free paper by
MPG Books Group, Bodmin and King's Lynn

ISBN 978–0–19–960798–3

1 3 5 7 9 10 8 6 4 2

For Nicholas and Nathan
who will not need to face these issues for a long time

Preface

As I write these words I am in my seventieth year. When I was young I entertained the comforting supposition that I might never die. Of course, I knew the syllogism 'All humans are mortal, I am human, therefore . . .', but I thought that surely an exception could be made in my case. Now that I am increasingly feeling the effects of ageing, I know that there will be no exception. Consequently, I think about death—death in general, and mine in particular.

I was born just in advance of the post-war baby boom, but like the boomers that have lived through prosperous and largely peaceful times, I have become accustomed to making the larger decisions for my own life: where to live, what career to pursue, whom to marry, whether to have children, and so on. It therefore seems natural to me to want to be the one in charge of my dying, whenever that occurs. How do I want to go? Peacefully, in my sleep, never realizing that it happened? In some Hollywood *Love Story* fantasy, slipping away ever so calmly and gently with my loved ones gathered around my bed while violins play in the background? Fighting to the very end and railing against the injustice of it all? With a tube stuck in every orifice to make sure that good stuff gets into my body and bad stuff gets out?

The truth is that I don't know exactly how I want to go, but I do know that I want to be the one who decides. It is to be my way, up to me, executive functioning to the end. But if I am to choose among my own various end-of-life scenarios, then I want to know what my options will be. Some of them are in place already. If I manage to remain *compos mentis* to the end then I will be able to decide how aggressively to resist whatever disease is threatening to carry me off, calculating whether this extra bit of life is worth purchasing at the cost of these nasty side effects. If I am in good hands I will also be able to determine how much pain medication I need to keep the suffering below my threshold of toleration and whether nothing in the end will suffice but sedation to unconsciousness. If I want to hasten the end I will be able to do so by refusing food and water. If I am lucky I will also be able to decide to take myself home when death is near, so that I might at least expire in familiar, non-institutional, surroundings.

But suppose I want more control than this over my dying. Suppose I want to choose the time to go and to have my doctor speed me on my journey with a little medication specifically administered for that purpose. That option is currently unavailable in many countries, including mine. Will it be available by the time that I might want to avail myself of it? Should it be? Now we have arrived at the questions that this book is designed to answer. They are not really about my death, in so far as it might be distinctively different from yours. They are about the dying process itself and the proper limits of our control over it. They are about the end-of-life options that, in most places (though not all), still lie outside the limits of ethical and legal acceptability. Do they deserve to be beyond the pale in this way? Is there something inherently repugnant or objectionable about them? Would there be anything wrong with bringing them inside the circle, so that our sovereignty over our own dying might be thereby enhanced? Should such a step be taken, as a matter of social policy?

These are the issues up for discussion in the chapters to follow. They are very much on the public agenda these days in many jurisdictions, especially those in which the practices of assisted death are currently prohibited. They are very likely to stay on that agenda for some time yet. As matters of public debate, time is on their side. For one thing, the population of the more developed countries is slowly but inexorably ageing. In 2010 less than one-quarter of this population is aged sixty or more; by 2050 this figure is projected to have risen to one-third. It doesn't take rocket science to figure out that having more elderly people means having more people who will face end-of-life decisions. Furthermore, everyone who will be passing the age sixty mark during the next decade is one of those post-war baby boomers who, like me, has become accustomed to being in charge of their own lives. Many of them, like me, will take for granted that they will also be in charge of the last stage of their lives. Partly as a result of this demographic pressure, public opinion has gradually become more pro-choice on the subject of euthanasia and assisted suicide, just as over the past couple of decades it became more pro-choice on the subject of abortion. In both cases moral and religious objections have weakened in the face of such countervailing forces as compassion (for a cancer patient suffering through his last days or weeks, for a young working woman with an unwanted pregnancy) and respect for autonomy (his control over his dying, her control over her reproduction). Just as the winds have been blowing in favour of more liberal abortion laws, so now they are blowing in favour of more liberal restraints on assisted death.

There are, of course, counterpressures. Many people still think that suicide is a sin and many others equate euthanasia with murder. Even more worry that loosening the legal restrictions on assisted death will put vulnerable sectors of the population at risk: women, the elderly, the poor, persons with disabilities. And so in most of the developed countries the debate still hangs in the balance. But there are increasing efforts, both legislative and judicial, in favour of law reform, and the historical tendency is in that direction. In 1990 there were two jurisdictions in the world in which either assisted suicide or euthanasia was legal; twenty years on that total has increased to eight. In another twenty years' time it will almost certainly have risen again.

Of course, history can determine only what does happen, not what should happen. Even worldwide legalization of assisted death would not suffice to show that the practice is ethically or legally justified. Thus the need for books such as this one, which will argue the case on one side or the other. Before commending the rest of the book to you, dear reader, it is only fair to tell you on which side I will be arguing. The discussion to follow is not neutral; it is not an 'on the one hand, on the other hand' examination of the conflicting arguments, the sort of approach that would be appropriate to the undergraduate philosophy classroom. Instead, it is itself an extended argument to two conclusions, one ethical and one legal. The ethical conclusion is that, when all other factors are equal, assisted death is no more difficult to justify than other end-of-life measures that may also hasten death and that are already established legal and medical practice: the withholding or withdrawal of life-sustaining treatment and the administration of high doses of painkillers or sedatives. The legal conclusion is that, like these other measures, assisted death (under appropriate conditions) should itself be established legal and medical practice.

This book is therefore a partisan contribution to an ongoing ethical, social, political, and legal debate. Since the views it defends are highly contentious, it is safe to predict that not everyone will agree with them. What I hope everyone can agree on are the terms of the debate itself, especially the necessity of all participants observing three cardinal rules of fair play. The first rule is: *Be fair to your opponents.* Defending your favoured position on these issues, whatever it might be, will inevitably involve two distinct tasks: making a positive case for it and responding to the arguments on the other side of the question. In undertaking the second, and more defensive, task you will be tempted to cheat by ignoring or glossing over some of the more powerful objections, or dealing only with the more inept and refutable versions of them, or distorting what your opponents have to say. These temptations must be resisted. Instead, you must seek out your ablest antagonists, give their arguments a full and fair hearing, and then proceed to show why these arguments nonetheless fail (if they do).

The second rule is: *Be fair to your readers.* Every position on these issues will have its strengths—the questions to which it easily provides persuasive answers. But it will also have its weaknesses, where it must labour mightily to avoid delivering highly counter-intuitive results. In the process of articulating your position you will be tempted to carry on at great length about the former and to suppress or conceal the latter—to stay on message, as it were. This temptation too must be resisted. If your view has its warts—as it will—then you owe it to your readers to expose them to view and, if it comes to that, to confess frankly that you don't know how to remove them. In that case the best you will be able to do is to show that the blemishes on your rivals' views are even worse.

Finally, the third rule: *Be fair to the facts.* You don't have to be an ethical consequentialist to recognize that the right answers to these normative questions about assisted death are highly fact-dependent. In deciding whether there should be a place for assisted death within the practice of palliative medicine, for instance, one thing that matters is how effective the other available end-of-life measures are at preventing or alleviating patient suffering. That is a fact of the matter, and there is evidence on it that you have an obligation to consult. In deciding whether assisted death should be legally available within the framework of a regulatory regime it matters how such regimes in other jurisdictions have fared at preventing abuses and protecting vulnerable sectors of the population. That is another fact of the matter and again there is evidence (a lot of it). It won't do just to make bald assertions on these matters; the only views worth listening to will be solidly evidence-based. And by now it should be obvious that it also won't do to suppress or ignore the awkward evidence that conflicts with your own favoured view.

In what follows I have tried to play by all three of these rules. You, dear reader, will be able to decide whether I have succeeded.

No book is a solo effort. This one has been facilitated by a Research Grant from the Social Science and Humanities Research Council of Canada and by a Chancellor Jackman Research Fellowship in the Humanities from the University of Toronto. I am immensely grateful to both institutions for their continuing support of my work. For the extensive research demanded by this project I received outstanding assistance from Rachel Bryant, Esther Shubert, and Ryan Sosna, and expert translation of documents unavailable in English from Lara Pehar. Several colleagues were willing to take time out from their busy professional lives to comment on various chapters: Joseph Boyle, Victor Cellarius, Philip Clark, Tom Hurka, Larry Librach, Larry May, and Michael Stingl. They pointed out defects that I would not have found on my own and made constructive suggestions that opened up fruitful lines of enquiry; I am grateful to them all. I am also indebted to the two anonymous readers for Oxford University Press, whose many detailed suggestions, queries, challenges, and corrections resulted in innumerable improvements to the text. Finally, I want to acknowledge my appreciation to my editor, Peter Momtchiloff, for being so patient during the lengthy gestation period of this work and for always seeming to assume that one day it would be finished.

As always, however, my principal debt is to my wife Heather, who I know will be with me wherever the remainder of our journey may lead.

L.W.S

Toronto
October 2010

Contents

1

Prologue

Anita is fifty-three years old, a successful businesswoman with a loving husband and a devoted daughter in her early twenties. Six weeks ago she was diagnosed with an aggressive tumour in her colon which metastasized first into her bloodstream and lymph channels and eventually into her liver. Somewhat against her better judgement, but in order to calm the anxieties of her family, she agreed to a round of chemotherapy, which had to be terminated when she developed high fevers and constipation alternating with diarrhoea. Soon narcotics were necessary to deal with the pain caused by the growing liver metastases. A massive tumour developed in her pelvis and her legs became swollen when pressure from the tumour prevented the veins from draining fluid from them. A week ago she was admitted to a hospice with nausea, vomiting, diarrhoea, high fever, and pain from the liver and pelvic tumours. In an effort to control the pain Anita is now administered powerful tranquillizers as well as narcotics. Her physician tells her that she has at most a few weeks left before she succumbs to the cancer, during which time these symptoms will grow worse. While medication can control much of the pain she will experience, it cannot eliminate all of it, and there is little that can be done to alleviate the other symptoms. She tells her doctor, and her family, that she cannot tolerate living with these symptoms for those final weeks. Her husband and daughter, who have been with her throughout this ordeal, also want to see an end to her suffering.

Bill is forty-seven years old, a former real estate agent, now a single father with a ten-year-old son. Four years ago he was diagnosed with amyotrophic lateral sclerosis (ALS), a progressive degenerative disease of the central nervous system. Since that time he has gradually lost more and more motor control of his body, to the point where he now requires a wheelchair and constant assistance with such basic functions as bathing, eliminating, and eating. His speech is laboured and his words are slurred but he can still make himself understood. His mind is completely unaffected. The pain from his condition is worsening and now must be treated with narcotics. Most of the time Bill is bedridden. He knows that the disease will continue to shut down more and more of his body and that, if it is left unchecked, he will eventually die of asphyxia, probably in less than six months. He wants to continue living with his condition for a few weeks longer but, when it has become unbearable for him, he wants to be able to arrange relief from it.

Neither Anita nor Bill wants to wait for their illness to kill them. What options are available to them to enable them to minimize their suffering? What options should be available? These are the questions we are aiming to answer.

1.1 Matters of Life and Death

We will have much occasion in what follows to talk about death. But in order to ensure that we know what we are talking about, we need to resolve some conceptual and terminological ambiguities.[1] We can apply the concept of death to a person in at least three different ways. The first is what we have in mind when we say 'Mozart's death occurred at 1 a.m. on 5 December 1791', where this is equivalent to saying 'Mozart died at 1 a.m. on 5 December 1791'. Here death is reported as an event with a more or less precise temporal location ('Time of death was 1 a.m.'). Although the event of Mozart's death is obviously closely connected to Mozart's life, strictly speaking it is not an event *in* that life; it is therefore not an event, such as his completion of *Don Giovanni*. Rather, Mozart's death marks the end of his life, the temporal boundary that separates his being alive from his being dead. And that brings us to the second way in which we sometimes talk about death, where we say something like 'Mozart's fame in death was far greater than it was during his lifetime'. Here we speak of Mozart's death as though it were a stretch of time subsequent to his dying—that is, the state or condition of his being dead. His death (in the first sense) would then be the event that separates his life from his death (in the second sense). Finally, we can also say 'Mozart's death was a rather drawn-out affair accompanied by much suffering.' We are now speaking of his death in a third sense as the last stage of his life, a (more or less) extended period of time during which he is dying and that culminates in his death (in the first sense).

In order to disambiguate these three importantly different (though closely connected) notions, I will speak of *death* only as the discrete, datable event that terminates a person's life.[2] For the period following death I will speak of the person *being dead*, and for the period preceding death I will speak of the person *dying* or of the *dying process*.[3]

---

[1] In what follows I borrow heavily from Rosenbaum 1986. A similar (though somewhat more complicated) set of distinctions can be found in F. Feldman 1992: ch. 7.

[2] Saying that death (in this sense) is an *event*, which occurs at a (more or less precise) time, should not fool us into thinking that there is therefore a *moment* of death. Events can (usually do) have duration, and death may be no exception (cf. Nuland 1993: 42). If death takes some time to occur (usually or always) then this fact will blur somewhat the boundary between being alive and being dead, and also between the dying process and death.

[3] Providing a satisfactory conceptual analysis of the dying process is a surprisingly difficult matter; cf. F. Feldman 1992: ch. 5. I return to this issue in n. 13, below.

We therefore have three distinct concepts—death, being dead, and dying—which it will be important for us to keep separate. With this vocabulary in mind we can then ask what seems, on the surface at least, a simple and straightforward question: when does a person's death occur? When does a person stop being alive and start being dead? As a practical matter, answering this question used to be fairly straightforward: we would check the person for vital signs (heartbeat and breathing) and, if we found none and also concluded that there was no chance that they would return, then we would declare death. This way of proceeding implicitly invoked the *cardiopulmonary criterion* for the determination of death, so designated for its emphasis on heart and lung function:

CP: Death has occurred when circulation and respiration have irreversibly ceased.

This criterion served perfectly well for all practical purposes until the advent in the mid-twentieth century of mechanical ventilators capable of maintaining respiration after all brain functions had ceased. Formerly, when all brain functions shut down as the result of catastrophic head injury then heart and lung functions would cease as well and death could be declared. Once ventilators became capable of performing the role of the brainstem in maintaining respiration (and therefore also circulation) for patients in irreversible coma with no detectable brain activity, the question had to be faced whether such patients were alive or dead. The answer to this question was of obvious practical importance: to the healthcare team in making decisions about the patient's care, since once the patient has been declared dead no further medical treatment is appropriate, and to the patient's family, since death triggers various post-mortem activities, such as mourning, cremation or burial, transfer of property, etc. But it took on a further importance with the advent of widespread use of organs for transplant. An irreversibly comatose patient, maintained on a ventilator, could be an ideal source for such organs, but both ethics and law would condemn their removal while the patient was still alive. Since CP did not distinguish between spontaneous and artificially maintained respiratory function, it became imperative for medical practitioners, hospitals, and governments to develop a less ambiguous criterion for patients in irreversible coma. A significant step towards this goal was taken in 1968 when a special committee at the Harvard Medical School defined irreversible coma as the permanent loss of all brain functions—right down to the most primitive brainstem functions—and proposed procedures for diagnosing the condition.[4] More to our present purpose, it also proposed that physicians use these procedures in determining death, thereby endorsing the *whole-brain criterion*:

WB: Death has occurred when all brain functions, including brainstem functions, have irreversibly ceased.

WB was intended by its advocates as a disambiguation, rather than a revision, of CP. In their view CP had always implicitly assumed that persons should be declared dead

---

[4] Ad Hoc Committee of the Harvard Medical School 1968.

when they had irreversibly lost the capacity to breathe and circulate blood on their own, without mechanical assistance. On this interpretation CP was equivalent to the *spontaneous cardiopulmonary criterion*:

> SCP: Death has occurred when spontaneous circulation and respiration have irreversibly ceased.

Since patients in irreversible coma were incapable of supporting their own circulation and respiration, under SCP they could be declared dead.

By the 1990s most jurisdictions had adopted WB as the clinical and legal standard for determining death.[5] However, from the outset it has not been without its critics. Some have contended that WB does not go far enough. Just as the condition of irreversible coma forced a rethinking of CP, once artificial means of maintaining respiration became available, so, the critics argue, the condition of permanent vegetative state (PVS) should force a rethinking of WB. PVS differs from coma in that, while all 'higher-brain' functions (those supported by the cerebrum and especially the cortex) have ceased, 'lower-brain' (and especially brainstem) functions are still intact.[6] These differential outcomes can occur because the cerebrum is more sensitive than the brainstem to interruptions of circulation; a cut-off of oxygen supply to the brain of several minutes' duration might damage the cerebrum beyond repair while allowing the brainstem to resume functioning once circulation has been restored. Like coma patients, PVS patients lack all capacity for cognitive functions, external awareness, and purposeful movement. However, unlike coma patients, their eyes are open, they are capable of reflex movements (such as blinking and swallowing), and they have sleep–wake cycles. More important for present purposes, they are usually capable of breathing on their own, without mechanical assistance. As a result, according to WB (and SCP) they are alive. Some commentators, however, argue that since consciousness is

---

[5] In 1981 the Law Reform Commission of Canada recommended that federal legislation be amended to state that 'a person is dead when an irreversible cessation of all that person's brain functions has occurred' (Law Reform Commission of Canada 1981: 25). However, the LRC's model legislation also went on to stipulate that 'the irreversible cessation of brain functions can be determined by the prolonged absence of spontaneous circulatory and respiratory functions', thereby underlining the equivalence of WB and SCP. WB has since been adopted in every Canadian province and territory. In the same year in the United States the President's Commission proposed a Uniform Determination of Death Act as a model for state laws: 'An individual who has sustained either (1) irreversible cessation of circulatory and respiratory functions, or (2) irreversible cessation of all functions of the brain, including the brain stem, is dead' (President's Commission for the Study of Ethical Problems in Medicine and Biomedical and Behavioral Research 1981: 73). All American states have now adopted either WB or the UDDA disjunction of CP and WB as their standard. The United Kingdom, however, has preferred a formulation of WB that focuses exclusively on the irreversible cessation of brainstem functioning (Pallis 1983; Pallis and Harley 1996). By 2002 some version or other of WB had been adopted in at least eighty countries worldwide, including all first world nations (Wijdicks 2002).

[6] For clinical accounts of the condition see Multi-Society Task Force on PVS 1994*a*; Laureys 2005, 2007. 'PVS' is often, perhaps usually, taken to be the abbreviation of *persistent* vegetative state. But the condition is designated 'persistent' when it has lasted for one month after initial brain damage, and 'permanent' when it has lasted for at least a year and is considered irreversible. For doubts about the irreversibility diagnosis see Stone 2007.

irreversibly lost in both cases the distinction that WB draws between comatose patients and PVS patients is arbitrary; hence they advocate instead a *higher-brain criterion* for determining death:[7]

HB: Death has occurred when all higher-brain functions have irreversibly ceased.

Everyone declared dead by WB will also be declared dead by HB, but not vice versa (as we have seen for PVS patients). In this respect, WB is the more conservative criterion; while HB continues to have its philosophical defenders it has yet to be adopted by any legal jurisdiction.

More recently, some traditionalists have advocated a reinstatement of CP (which they do *not* interpret as equivalent to SCP).[8] They agree with the HB advocates that the line drawn by WB between coma and PVS is arbitrary, but they contend that both categories of patients should be deemed to be alive. Their principal argument is that there are many organic functions being carried out by the bodies of coma patients, despite their inability to breathe on their own. These functions include the exchange of oxygen and carbon dioxide, nutrition at the cellular level, homeostasis, elimination of cellular wastes, maintenance of body temperature, wound healing, and fighting of infection.[9] When coma patients display so many signs of self-maintained organic functioning, the argument goes, it is unwarranted to declare them dead just because their breathing must be mechanically assisted. If respiration and circulation continue (and continue to support all these further functions) then it should not matter whether they are spontaneous; the patient is alive in either case.

There remains therefore a lively debate over the adequacy of WB, despite its establishment as clinical and legal orthodoxy, a debate that reflects a deeper philosophical divide over the concept of death. It is well to keep in mind that WB and its various rivals are all criteria for determining death; their function is to suggest procedures and tests for ascertaining whether (and when) someone has died. They are not different concepts, or definitions, of death.[10] The function of a concept—or a conceptual analysis—of death is to reveal its nature: to tell us what it is, not just when it occurs.[11] Though a criterion is not a concept, different criteria for determining death may presuppose, or cohere with, different concepts of death. Put another way, the concept of death you have in mind may settle what will seem to you intuitively plausible as a criterion. So let us now turn from criteria to concepts.

It seems safe to say that death is the end of life—safe, but also unilluminating, because it simply invites the further question: what is life? We can perhaps take a small step forward by requiring that an adequate account of the (life and) death of a thing rest

---

[7] Veatch 1975; Engelhardt 1975; Green and Wikler 1980.

[8] David DeGrazia (2005: 147 ff.) offers a sophisticated defence of (an updated version of) CP.

[9] Shewmon 2001; Joffe 2010.

[10] Notwithstanding the title (*Defining Death*) of the President's Commission for the Study of Ethical Problems in Medicine and Biomedical and Behavioral Research 1981.

[11] For a fuller account of this concept/criterion distinction see F. Feldman 1992: 14–18.

on or reflect an adequate account of the nature of that thing. Since we are primarily interested in *our* death, that raises the question of how we are to understand our nature. Philosophers have tended to provide two different (though not mutually exclusive) answers to this question: we are animals (or, more broadly, organisms) and we are persons. As the former we share a nature with all other organisms and so it seems plausible to suppose that the best account of our death will apply to all of them as well. As the latter, we may be unique or we may share a nature with a relatively small set of other highly developed animals (depending on how the notion of a person is understood), and in that case we should expect the best account for us to be (more or less) species-specific. In any case, it looks as though there should be two quite different concepts of death that pertain to us, one for organisms and one for persons.[12]

Call the former concept *biological death*. We can work towards it by beginning with the assumption that the life of an organism consists of the integrated functioning of its several subsystems which are working together in a coordinated fashion so as to support the functioning of the organism as a whole. The particular subsystems in question will vary with the type of organism; in higher animals like us they will include the respiratory, circulatory, excretory, endocrine, homeostatic, immune, reproductive, and so on. It would follow that the death of an organism would consist in the irreversible cessation of this integrated functioning.[13] This concept of biological death has the advantage of being univocal across all living things; on this concept the death of a human is the same thing as the death of a frog or a tree or a bacterium (though, of course, the precise criteria for determining death will be species-specific).[14] It seems to be what we usually have in mind in saying that someone has died: the person is no longer breathing, his heart has stopped, his body is beginning to get cold and stiff, and eventually it starts to decompose. The biological concept also seems to be the one presupposed by CP, which purports to provide the appropriate criterion for determining death for the particular organisms that we are.

But we are not just organisms: we are also persons. What is required in order to count as a person has been much debated by philosophers, and the requirements have included such features as consciousness, self-consciousness, memory, language use, rationality, the capacity to construct a life narrative, and so on. We need not settle this issue here, since it is clear that all these features require a sophisticated mind (and therefore a complex brain capable of supporting such a mind). The concept of a person is therefore not bodily but psychological, and the end of a person would therefore be marked by the irreversible cessation of whatever psychological states or capacities are

---

[12] Cf. McMahan 2002: 423–6, 439.

[13] On this account biological death will mark the end of a process (whether gradual or sudden) during which the body's subsystems, and their integrated functioning, are failing. In this way the concept of biological death enables us to define somewhat more precisely the notion of the dying process (cf. n. 3, above). However, there are still complications (F. Feldman 1992: 80–6).

[14] Fred Feldman (ibid. 19–20) stresses this as a virtue in a concept of death.

taken to be essential to being a person. Call this *personal death*. Normally we should expect it to coincide with biological death; if the integrated functioning of the body ceases then the functioning of the brain will also cease, and since the brain is the substrate of the psychological states that constitute a person, the person will cease as well. But we now know that, while biological death is sufficient for personal death (barring a disembodied 'afterlife'), it is not necessary. PVS patients are not biologically dead, since their bodies remain capable of integrated functioning, but they have permanently lost all capacity for consciousness, which would seem to be the minimum requirement for being a person. In these cases, therefore, personal death has preceded biological death. Nancy Cruzan lapsed into PVS in January 1983 and the integrated functioning of her body ceased in December 1990 after her feeding tube was removed. Her personal death and her biological death were therefore nearly eight years apart.[15] Because HB yields the result that PVS patients are dead, it would seem to track the concept of personal, rather than biological, death.

Our two concepts of death are therefore the following:

Biological: Death is the irreversible cessation of the integrated functioning of the organism.

Personal: Death is the irreversible cessation of whatever psychological states or capacities are constitutive of a person.[16]

And our criteria for determining death seem to line up as follows: CP appears to presuppose biological death while HB appears to be appropriate for personal death.[17] It is an interesting, and important, result that these pairings seem to leave no room for WB, despite its near-universal adoption as the clinical and legal standard for determining death. WB is not a good fit with the personal concept of death since, while the cessation of all brain functions is sufficient for personal death, it is not necessary (as in PVS cases). But it is not a good fit with the biological concept either if, as its critics contend, many integrative bodily functions can survive the loss of all brain function.[18]

---

[15] Her family appeared to recognize both aspects of her death by engraving on her grave marker 'DEPARTED Jan 11, 1983 | AT PEACE Dec 26, 1990' (McMahan 2002: 423, citing Singer 1994: 62). For similar cases see Rachels 1986: 55. The fact that personal and biological death may occur at different times raises some difficult metaphysical issues, since it implies that the person and the organism cannot be identical; for sophisticated discussions of these issues see McMahan 2002: ch. 1, and DeGrazia 2005: chs. 2–4. The Cruzan case is discussed in more detail in §6.1, below.

[16] There are many questions to answer in both cases, since the cessation of both bodily and psychological functioning can be a matter of degree. How much functioning must be lost, in either case, for death to be declared? All of it? Most of it? I will happily ignore these complications.

[17] HB equates death with the irreversible cessation of all higher brain functions. Strictly speaking, the concept of personal death requires only something weaker: the cessation of whatever higher brain functions (such as memory and consciousness) are constitutive of a person. I owe this point to Larry May.

[18] For excellent presentations of the case against WB, see McMahan 2002: 426 ff.; DeGrazia 2005: 142 ff.; Joffe 2010.

Ironically, the best fit with the biological concept, at least as far as human organisms are concerned, seems to be the criterion that WB displaced, namely CP.[19]

Because biological and personal death normally coincide, CP and HB normally yield the same results. But when they diverge, as in PVS cases, which concept and which criterion should we prefer? The answer to that question is surely context-specific; it is, for instance, easy to imagine oneself in the position of Nancy Cruzan's parents when they take the view that they lost their daughter in 1983, not 1990. However, for clinical practice HB yields the desperately counterintuitive result that Nancy was dead throughout those eight years when she was breathing on her own, her heart was beating, her eyes were open, she was blinking and swallowing, etc. These are not things that corpses do and it seems too much to ask clinical staff to see Nancy, and other PVS patients, as dead. (It may be hard enough for clinical staff to see even comatose patients as dead.) It is also preposterous to suggest that normal postmortem activities (such as burial or cremation) could be initiated while she is still breathing, rather than waiting for her biological death. In dealing with the difficult ethical and legal issues concerning the withdrawal of life-sustaining treatment (especially nutrition and hydration) from PVS patients such as Nancy Cruzan and, more recently, Terri Schiavo, no court has ever taken the position that these patients are already dead. PVS cases therefore strongly suggest that HB is misconceived as a criterion for determining death. It may fare much better if it is taken to mark not the end of life but the end of everything that is valuable or worthwhile in life.[20] In that case it would still point to something important in the timeline of a life, even if it is not the transition from being alive to being dead.

Speaking of the value of life takes us to a further question about death: why is it such a bad thing? We normally assume that death, especially premature death, is one of the worst misfortunes that can befall us. We fear and dread our own death and, if necessary, take elaborate precautions to avoid it. If we suffer a life-threatening illness or injury we want the best care available in order to fend off the grim reaper. The worst-case scenario we can imagine is that moment in the doctor's office when we are told that there is nothing else that can be done and that death is imminent. We grieve and mourn the deaths of those close to us, not just for our loss of them but also for what they have lost. We find the deaths of others particularly unfortunate or tragic when they are struck down in their youth, or in the prime of life, before they have been able to realize their life's full potential. Many of us take comfort in religious belief which holds out the promise of an 'afterlife', thereby effectively denying the reality of death.

---

[19] It is ironic because the President's Commission based its case for WB on the biological concept: 'On this view, death is that moment at which the body's physiological system ceases to constitute an integrated whole' (President's Commission for the Study of Ethical Problems in Medicine and Biomedical and Behavioral Research 1981: 33). In retrospect, the Commission seems to have overstated the role of the brain in maintaining the body as an 'integrated whole'.

[20] This view is defended in §4.1, below.

Finally, the law treats homicide as the gravest of offences against the person, presumably because it judges the harm inflicted on the victim to be of a special seriousness.

And yet there are puzzles in trying to explain why it is a bad thing to die, or how it is that death harms us. These puzzles were famously expressed by Epicurus in his *Letter to Menoeceus*:

> Become accustomed to the belief that death is nothing to us. For all good and evil consists in sensation, but death is deprivation of sensation. And therefore a right understanding that death is nothing to us makes the mortality of life enjoyable, not because it adds to it an infinite span of time, but because it takes away the craving for immortality. For there is nothing terrible in life for the man who has truly comprehended that there is nothing terrible in not living.... So death, the most terrifying of ills, is nothing to us, since so long as we exist, death is not with us; but when death comes, then we do not exist. It does not then concern either the living or the dead, since for the former it is not, and the latter are no more.[21]

We do not know how Menoeceus responded to this piece of reasoning, but its conclusion will seem perverse to many of us (though in my experience a surprising number of undergraduates can easily be brought to endorse it). Among recent philosophers, Epicurus has had many critics, but also a few defenders.[22] Perhaps the direction of his argument is immediately obvious, but if not then some clarifications might help. First, when Epicurus speaks of 'death' in the foregoing passage he is best understood to be referring to what I have previously distinguished as *being dead*.[23] This reading makes the most sense of Epicurus's statement that 'death is deprivation of sensation', since the condition of being dead precludes all consciousness, and therefore all experience. It also works best for his claim that 'when death comes, then we do not exist', since he can then be construed as saying that death (the event) is the dividing line between being alive (existing) and being dead (no longer existing). This then brings us to a second point, namely, Epicurus's thesis that when we die we cease to exist. This thesis appears to be central to his argument, but it has seemed to some commentators to be very implausible.[24] They point out that it is not in general true that when living things die they cease to exist; a walk through a forest, for instance, will reveal many dead trees. So Epicurus's thesis does not fit the case of biological death—the death of organisms. But it may fare somewhat better for the death of persons, where we may be more comfortable saying that once someone has died then she is no longer with us. Certainly some contemporary philosophers,

---

[21] Epicurus 1940: 30–1. A similar argument was made by Epicurus's follower Lucretius: 'Death therefore to us is nothing, concerns us not a jot.... For he whom evil is to befall, must in his own person exist at the very time it comes, if the misery and suffering are haply to have any place at all; but since death precludes this, and forbids him to be, upon whom the ills can be brought, you may be sure that we have nothing to fear after death, and that he who exists not, cannot become miserable.' (Lucretius 1940: 131).

[22] Two recent critics: McMahan 1988; F. Feldman 1992: chs. 8 and 9. An influential defender: Rosenbaum 1986.

[23] Cf. Rosenbaum 1986: 218–19.

[24] Especially F. Feldman 1992: ch. 6.

by no means Epicureans, have agreed that personal death—the point at which we have permanently lost all capacity for psychological states—is the beginning of non-existence for us.[25] In any case, Epicurus's essential point about the condition of being dead appears to be that we will not be around to experience it, and that seems safe enough.

When Epicurus says that 'death is nothing to us' he appears to mean two things: that for us being dead is literally nothing (i.e. non-existence) and that it is nothing *to us* (i.e. not something we should concern ourselves about). It is this latter claim—that being dead is not bad for us, or is not a harm to us—that seems counterintuitive and paradoxical. Of course, Epicurus is not claiming that *dying* can't be bad for us, since it occurs while we are still living and might be attended by much suffering. Nor is he saying that *my* becoming dead can't be bad *for others*, since (unlike me) they will live to experience the loss of me. No, the crucial claim is that being dead can't be bad *for the one who dies*.[26] And the reason it can't seems to rest on the fact that once we are dead then we no longer exist (or at least are no longer capable of any form of experience).

Epicurus seems to be presupposing that all the evils in life are states or conditions that we experience.[27] The clearest case, of course, is physical suffering, but there are many others: depression, anxiety, frustration, disappointment, humiliation, loneliness, a sense of injustice or betrayal, and so on. What all these states have in common is that we experience them as *intrinsically* bad—that is, they are bad (for us) just in themselves and quite apart from any other states to which they might lead or with which they are connected. Then Epicurus's point about being dead is that the absence of all experience precludes all these evils—the dead are beyond being harmed.[28] If nothing bad can happen to us once we are dead then how, Epicurus would ask, can being dead be bad for us? Of course, by this point many of you will have spotted a possible flaw in his reasoning. If, as Epicurus is supposing, all the intrinsic evils in life are *experiential*, so are all the intrinsic goods: pleasure, enjoyment, happiness, love, a sense of accomplishment or success, peace of mind, wisdom, or whatever. Then if, as Epicurus is also supposing, being dead precludes all the experiential evils it equally wipes out all the experiential goods. From this vantage point being dead doesn't seem like such a good thing after all.

If Epicurus is insisting that being dead can't be intrinsically bad for us, we can concede him this point, but then we need to remind him that it cannot be intrinsically

---

[25] Jeff McMahan (2002: 423), for instance: 'Since the capacity for consciousness is the defining essential property of a mind, we must cease to exist when we lose the capacity for consciousness in a way that is in principle irreversible.' Or Woody Allen (1972: 99): 'It's not that I'm afraid to die, I just don't want to be there when it happens.'

[26] Epicurus is therefore denying the *prudential* disvalue of death; for an explication of the concept of prudential value, see Sumner 1996: §1.3.

[27] Epicurus himself was a hedonist, so for him the only (intrinsic) evil in life is pain or suffering (which is, of necessity, experienced). But we need not follow him in this.

[28] Whether posthumous harms (and benefits) are possible is a matter of much philosophical debate; see Sumner 1996: 126–7, and the further references there cited.

good for us either. This is not, however, sufficient to defeat his argument, since if being dead has neither intrinsic value nor intrinsic disvalue then it is still nothing for us and it is irrational to fear it. So we still lack an account of how death can be bad for us. The key to providing such an account lies in recognizing that not all goods (or evils) are intrinsic. Things can also be good or bad for us *extrinsically*—that is, by virtue of the states or conditions that they bring about or to which they are connected. The classic example of an extrinsic good is money: we seek and value it, not primarily for its own sake, but for the good things in life that it enables us to acquire. The same may be true of education, or job training, or regular workouts at the gym. On the negative side, most losses are extrinsic evils: the badness of the loss consists in whatever (intrinsically) good things one thereby forgoes. It seems that death (the event of death) can be either an extrinsic evil for us (since it deprives us of all intrinsic goods) or an extrinsic good (since it precludes all intrinsic evils). But in that case it will not be true, as Epicurus contends, that death is 'nothing' to us—that is, nothing we need concern ourselves about.

The mention, above, of losses as extrinsic evils suggests a fairly obvious (anti-Epicurean) way of thinking about the badness of death. It is a commonplace that death is the loss of life. But then it is a natural further thought that the disvalue of death lies in the value of the life thereby lost. This is the *deprivation account* of the badness of death: death is (extrinsically) bad for us by virtue of depriving us of the (intrinsic) goods of continued life.[29] On this account showing that dying now would be bad for you requires a comparison between two possible outcomes: the one in which you die now and the one in which you live on. Doubtless most stages of your life contain a mix of intrinsic goods and intrinsic evils.[30] But if the goods outweigh the evils over a particular stage of your life then that life-stage is overall (on balance) good for you. So suppose that the life you would have from now on would be (on balance) good for you until it reaches its terminus at some later time. In that case it would be better for you to continue living than to die now, and death therefore would be bad for you (since it would deprive you of this good future).

The deprivation account captures most people's intuitive thinking about the badness of death, and what seems perverse about Epicurus's argument is that he ignores or overlooks it. However, the deprivation account is not without its own puzzles.[31] For one thing, it seems to require an illegitimate value comparison between two possible futures for you: one in which you are alive and the other in which you are dead. This is, after all, the way in which we normally make comparisons between alternative futures for ourselves: if you have to decide whether to become a philosopher or a

---

[29] The deprivation account has had many recent philosophical defenders; see e.g. B. Williams 1973; Nagel 1979; McMahan 1988, 2002: ch. 2; F. Feldman 1992: chs. 8 and 9.

[30] The deprivation account does not depend on any particular view about what these goods and evils might be; I will therefore make the simplifying assumption that most of us agree (more or less) on these matters.

[31] In what follows I am indebted to F. Feldman 1992: ch. 9.

doctor then you will try to compare the overall value (for you) of the philosophical future with that of the medical future and choose accordingly. In retrospect, you will think that you chose wisely just in case you conclude that you fared better in your (actual) philosophical career than you would have in your (hypothetical) medical career. But if we assume that you cease to exist when you die, then your being dead can have no overall value (or disvalue) for you. In that case there is nothing to compare to the overall value of your continued life. Life–death value comparisons are incoherent.

Fortunately, the deprivation account does not require such comparisons. To see why, let us assume that your life up to now has, on balance, been good for you (this assumption is for convenience only; nothing changes if your life to this point has gone badly for you). Since the question is whether you die at this point or live on, there are two possible whole lives for you: the shorter one that stops now (because you die) and the longer one that continues for some time into the future (until you die later). Let us again make the optimistic assumption that the continued life stage would have a positive overall balance of value for you. Now we can compare the value of your two whole lives: the shorter one has only the accrued value to now and the longer one has that *plus* the value of the additional stage. Because the longer one is better for you than the shorter one, dying now would be bad for you. The relevant value comparison is 'life–life', not life–death.[32]

But this merely raises another question. Because the future is not (yet) determinate, there will be many possible continuations of your life from now to your later death, and different future life-stages will almost certainly have different overall values. Only one of these will be actual, but you don't know now which one; there is therefore no unique future life-stage whose value is to be added to the value of your life to now. So which possible future do we assume in making the life-life comparison? This is not a problem for a retrospective comparison, where you decide that it was (or, in the worst case, was not) a good thing that you did not die earlier, since by that point you know how that further life went for you. But what assumption do we make about the future in the case of a prospective comparison? The first thing that needs to be said is that this uncertainty problem afflicts all comparisons of possible future life-stages. In your earlier choice of philosophy over medicine there is, at the time of choice, no unique philosophical future for you and no unique medical future either. (Or if there are unique futures for the two choices, you have at that time no idea what they are.) In general, when planning for the future, we try to make the most accurate forecasts we can, based on all the information available to us. Usually we will at least be in a position to say that some possible futures are more likely than others and choose on that basis. In that case, from the prospective standpoint where the options are death now or

---

[32] Fred Feldman, who uses the notion of a 'life–life comparison' (1992: 153), attributes the phrase to Harry Silverstein (1980: 414).

continued life, you should estimate the (extrinsic) badness of death on the basis of the overall intrinsic value of the most probable continuation(s) of your life.[33]

We are not yet done with the puzzles raised by the deprivation account. Assume again, with Epicurus, that when we die we cease to exist. If the badness of death consists in the fact that it deprives you of the goods of (continued) life, then by the time that deprivation occurs you are no longer around. How then can *you* be the subject of the misfortune? How can that misfortune happen to you if you no longer exist? There seems, however, a straightforward answer to these questions. We are supposing that death is extrinsically bad if it results in the loss of a life-stage that would have been (on balance) intrinsically good. A particular death is extrinsically bad *for you* if (*a*) it happens to you and (*b*) the life-stage lost would have been yours. Since we can identify the person who died (you), we can identify the subject of the loss inflicted by death (you again). Things are different if we think instead of lives that never get started. Suppose that a couple is thinking of having a child, and that any child they have would lead a good life. If they change their minds and decide instead to remain childless then we might say that there is a loss of value to the world, but there is no one in particular who suffers that loss since there is no one in particular who was deprived of that life. By contrast, when someone dies there is someone in particular who suffers the loss of further life, and that is the person who bears the misfortune of death.[34]

On the deprivation account the (extrinsic) disvalue of death depends on the (intrinsic) value of the (further) life forgone. It would seem to follow then that *how bad* your death is for you will depend on how much value there would have been in your continued life. Now it seems plausible to think that the overall value of a life-stage will be a function of two basic factors: quality and quantity. Quality would be a matter of the net value of each of the component temporal parts of the life-stage (for convenience, let us assume net value per day); quantity would be the temporal duration of the life-stage (the number of days it contains). As long as net per diem quality continues to be positive then a longer life-stage will be better than a shorter one.[35] But that means that, *ceteris paribus*, how bad your death is for you will depend on how much life you thereby lose. This result seems intuitively correct in most cases, for we normally assume that (as long as life would continue to be good) it is worse to die younger than it is to die older—worse at sixty than at eighty, worse at forty than at sixty, worse at

---

[33] For a much fuller treatment of these issues see McMahan 2002: 103–17.

[34] There is a related, and less easily dismissed, problem about the *time* of the misfortune that is discussed in F. Feldman 1992: 153–4; Bradley 2004; Luper 2007. Because the business of this book does not require solving this problem, I here set it aside.

[35] It need not be positive *every day* (we can have bad days) as long as it continues to be a net positive overall. It should also be noted that we cannot assume, without argument, that the contribution made by a further life-stage to a person's overall lifetime value is strictly additive. If it is additive then as long as the further life-stage has positive net value then it will necessarily raise overall lifetime value. But some have argued that a further life-stage with positive (but lower) net value might actually decrease lifetime value by lowering its average (per diem) value; see the excellent discussion of these matters in Hurka 1993: ch. 6. I take no stand on this issue here; it is enough for my argument if continued life of positive quality is generally a good for a person.

twenty than at forty, and so on. We typically think that the deaths of youths, who still have so much life to live, are more tragic than the deaths of octogenarians, and the deprivation account supports this thought. However, if it is worse to die earlier than later (still assuming overall positive value for life) then it must be worst of all to die as an infant or a foetus. And our intuitions may not be quite as comfortable with those results.

Jeff McMahan has discussed this problem at length, and has developed a variant of the deprivation account—what he calls the time-relative interest account—that is designed precisely to block these (allegedly) counterintuitive results.[36] McMahan's variant is complex and dependent on his views about the importance of psychological connections between different stages of a person's life. It has been criticized on the ground that it has implications even more counterintuitive than the ones it is meant to avoid.[37] I will not enter into this controversy here, since it is tangential to the business of this book. At least for the most part, we will be dealing with life and death choices that occur late in life rather than early. And when we do come later (in §5.2) to deal with choices concerning infants, the hard cases will be ones in which the infant has little, if anything, to lose by dying, so that McMahan's concerns will not really apply.[38] However, I will say in passing that my intuitions are much less troubled by the implications of the straightforward life-comparison account than are McMahan's. Once we isolate the issue of the magnitude of the loss *for the person who suffers it* then it seems (to me at least) quite plausible to think that a child who dies in infancy, and whose life therefore barely gets started, loses more than someone who dies later (even later in childhood). This may not make the death of the infant more tragic than, say, the death of an adolescent, for there may be more to the tragedy of death than the amount of life lost. (It may, for instance, be more tragic for life plans to be interrupted in midstream than never to be formed in the first place, and also more tragic for parents to lose an adolescent in whom they have invested so much more than they have in an infant.) But it still seems worse *for the infant.*[39]

Finally, we should note the important implication of the deprivation account for the issues we will be discussing about assisted death. The implication has been obvious all along but it is nonetheless worth drawing out explicitly. If death is (extrinsically) bad when it deprives a person of a continued good life, then it is (extrinsically) good when it saves a person from a continued bad one (a life, let us say, that would be full of unavoidable suffering). On the deprivation account death is not always harmful or something to be feared; it can be beneficial or something to be embraced. Whether it

---

[36] McMahan 2002: 165 ff. David DeGrazia (2005: 189–92) endorses this account.

[37] See Broome 2004: 249–51; Bradley 2007, 2008.

[38] However, it is a major problem for McMahan's view that it has difficulty explaining what would be wrong with infanticide for perfectly normal babies; cf. his discussion of this issue in McMahan 2002: 338–62 (and also DeGrazia 2005: 289–93).

[39] Of course, the infant is not in a position to appreciate, in prospect, just how much he would lose by dying. But this seems to me irrelevant to the question of the prudential magnitude of the loss. I am quite confident that it would have been worse for me to die in infancy than to die at age twenty (it would have been twenty years worse).

harms or benefits depends on the circumstances of the person's life—and, in particular, on the expected quality (and duration) of the person's continued life. If someone's prospects are sufficiently bleak then death can be a welcome release.

1.2 Distinctions and Definitions

The preceding section concluded with an account of why death is a misfortune for the person to whom it occurs—and also when it might not be. In this section we turn our attention to ways in which death might occur—the causal pathways, as it were, which might lead us to the end of life. It will be immediately obvious that there are many such pathways, even if we describe each in the most generic way: accident, natural disaster, disease, negligence, the deliberate act of oneself or another, etc. Fortunately for our purposes in this discussion, we need not concern ourselves with most of these possible routes to death. Our topic of assisted death limits us to instances in which death comes about, in part at least, as a result of some end-of-life treatment decision(s). We are therefore presupposing a medical context in which one party (a patient) is under the care of another party (a healthcare provider, whom I will generally assume to be a physician). The treatment options available when a patient is in, or approaching, the final stage of life I will call *end-of-life measures*. The end-of-life measures with which we are specially concerned are those that have the potential to hasten the patient's death.

A number of important clarifications and qualifications are in order. For one thing, what we are calling an end-of-life measure may consist of administering some form of treatment to the patient, but it may equally consist of withholding or withdrawing treatment. Either of these options may have the effect of hastening death. (The 'may' here is epistemic: in some cases it is not possible to ascertain the cause(s) of death with enough certainty to be able to determine whether the treatment decision was implicated.) I speak here of 'hastening' rather than 'causing' death for two reasons. First, since the patient is going to die in any case (as are we all), the main causal impact of the treatment decision will be on the timing of death—whether it happens sooner or later.[40] Second, in most cases there will be several factors influencing the time of death, and singling out treatment (or non-treatment) as causing death might, misleadingly, suggest that no other causes were in play. It is also important to recognize that we are dealing only with instances in which the physician's actions are fully intentional—that is, she intends a certain outcome and pursues a course of action reliably expected to produce that outcome. We are not, therefore, dealing with tragic cases of medical mistake or negligence, in which a decision intended to have a quite different effect unintentionally hastens the patient's death. However, and this is important, while the

---

[40] Of course, treatment decisions affect other aspects of the dying process as well, such as the patient's comfort level. But our concern here is with their impact on the patient's death.

physician's actions are fully intentional in this sense, and while they may have the effect of hastening death, neither the physician nor the patient need intend that result. In some cases the patient's death may indeed be the intended outcome of the end-of-life measure, but in other cases a quite different outcome may be intended (relief of the patient's suffering, for instance) while the risk (or even certainty) of hastening death is foreseen but unintended. The category of end-of-life measures that may result in hastening death is meant to include these latter cases.

Identifying the generic category of end-of-life measures with which we are concerned is relatively uncontroversial. However, both academic and public debate over some of these measures is often at cross purposes due to lack of conceptual agreement on how they are to be defined. Consider euthanasia, for instance. There is widespread agreement that administering lethal medication with the intention of relieving a patient's suffering by hastening his death would be a paradigm instance of the concept. But do we apply the concept as well to withdrawing life support from the patient with exactly the same intention? Some are comfortable with distinguishing between 'active' and 'passive' euthanasia, while others reject the latter category, holding that euthanasia is necessarily 'active'.[41] Or consider suicide. Again a paradigm instance would be self-administering lethal medication with the intention of causing death, but what do we make of refusing life-support for the selfsame purpose?[42] Is this also suicide? I am not suggesting that there is a right answer to these—and other similar—questions. But I do insist that debate over the morality or legality of these practices will be productive only with some definitional exactness. So I will now proceed to explain my own conceptual choices, not because they are the only—or the best—possible but because they will be presupposed throughout the remainder of this book.

Because it is such a standard feature of this landscape, I might be expected to invoke the familiar 'active/passive' distinction. However, I will later argue that this distinction is both obscure and misleading (§4.3); I will therefore be resting much less on it, both in ethics and in law, than is normal in these debates. Instead, I will begin with a distinction that is simpler and more accessible: the intuitive difference between *administering medical treatment* and *withholding (or withdrawing) such treatment*. When we are speaking of end-of-life measures that may hasten death the paradigmatic instance of treatment is the administration of a lethal medication. On the other side, withholding treatment means not initiating it in the first place, while withdrawing it requires terminating it once initiated. (The boundaries between the two are not always clear, especially in cases where various treatment modalities have been tried over an extended period of time, but we can ignore this complication.) Either withholding or withdrawing treatment becomes particularly problematic in end-of-life scenarios where the treatment has some potential for sustaining or prolonging life.

---

[41] The reasons for my scare quotes will become evident later (§4.3).

[42] As we shall see later (§2.3), in an attempt to avoid the stigma associated with suicide, some right-to-die organizations reject the term even for (what I have called) the paradigm instance.

A 'do-not-resuscitate' (DNR) order, to be observed should the patient go into cardiac arrest, is a clear instance of the withholding of (potentially) life-sustaining treatment. Disconnecting a ventilator, or terminating chemotherapy or radiation treatment for an advanced cancer, are equally clear cases of withdrawing (potentially) life-sustaining treatment.

Both treatment and non-treatment may be either *voluntary* or *non-voluntary* on the patient's part. An end-of-life treatment measure is voluntary when it is the result of an informed choice by a competent patient. Likewise, when a competent patient makes the decision to terminate (or not initiate) treatment then we may speak of patient refusal of (potentially) life-sustaining treatment. At the other end of the spectrum both treatment and non-treatment will be non-voluntary when a patient lacks decisional capacity at the time the decision is made, the clearest instances being infants or young children.[43] These may still be cases of treatment request or refusal, but if so the decision-maker will be a proxy acting on the patient's behalf.

The voluntary/non-voluntary distinction is therefore orthogonal to the treatment/non-treatment distinction. In all these cases we can also raise questions about *intention*. When the decision has been made to administer a (potentially) life-shortening treatment we can ask what its aim or purpose is. One possibility is that the patient's death is intended (as a means of alleviating distress or suffering): this will invariably be the case when the treatment in question consists of the administration of a lethal dose of medication which has no therapeutic use other than to cause death (it is not, for instance, capable of alleviating suffering other than by causing death). Both assisted suicide and euthanasia fall into this category of hastening death by means of some treatment undertaken with this end in view. But there are other possibilities. Treatment known to have at least a significant risk of hastening death may be administered not in order to bring about this result but for some other therapeutic purpose, such as the relief of suffering. Administering strong analgesics (such as opioids) or sedatives (such as barbiturates) in doses large enough to risk hastening death may fall into this category, if the aim of both physician and patient is to alleviate suffering and they are willing to accept the risk of shortening life as a foreseen but unintended side effect.

The issue of intent can also divide non-treatment cases. In most instances in which (potentially) life-sustaining treatment is withheld or withdrawn the aim shared by patient and physician alike is to improve quality of life during the dying process and the shortening of life is accepted as a probable, or even inevitable, side effect. However, in some cases where the causal route from cessation of treatment to death is particularly direct—as in the withdrawal of a respirator or a feeding tube—the question of intent becomes more obscure. Whereas in most cases it is at least arguable

---

[43] There will be many intermediate cases on this spectrum, including both cases in which patient decisional capacity is in doubt and cases in which patients who clearly lack decisional capacity at the time of the treatment decision (due to unconsciousness or severe dementia, for instance) have recorded their refusal of treatment, through a device such as an advance directive, at an earlier stage of life when they were fully capable. Cf. §5.1, below.

that the patient dies from his underlying disease condition, that conclusion is harder to sustain when the cause of death appears to be anoxia (due to disconnecting the respirator) or dehydration (due to removing the feeding tube). Because these difficult issues about cause of death will be addressed later (§2.3), it would be premature to draw any conclusions at this point. But if withholding or withdrawing treatment does sometimes qualify as the (or, at any rate, a) cause of death, and if this outcome is known in advance to be certain, then the question of intention at least becomes a little more ambiguous. Furthermore, there may be clear cases in which the patient's aim in refusing treatment is to hasten death.

Finally, there is a potentially important distinction of *agency* specifically among treatment cases. If we assume the paradigm instance where death results from administration of a lethal medication intended (by patient and physician alike) to bring about this result, then we may still ask who did the administering. Where the medication was prescribed by the physician but self-administered by the patient (typically by ingesting an oral dose) we have a case of assisted suicide. Where it was administered by the physician (typically by injection) we have a case of euthanasia.[44]

So we have four important distinctions to keep in mind among treatment decisions that may hasten death. Being conscious that working through all of them can get rather complicated, I summarize them here as follows:

Modality: Administering treatment v. withholding or withdrawing it. Both assisted suicide and euthanasia belong in the former category.

Volition: Voluntary cases (request/refusal by a competent patient at the time of the treatment decision) v. non-voluntary ones. Both administering and withholding/withdrawing treatment can be either voluntary or non-voluntary.[45]

Intention: Cases in which death is intended (either as an end or, more likely, as a means to an intended end) v. those in which death is a foreseen but unintended side effect in the pursuit of some other aim. In both assisted suicide and euthanasia death is intended; in non-treatment cases the intended end may vary from case to case.

Agency: Lethal treatment administered by the physician v. self-administered treatment. This distinction separates assisted suicide from euthanasia.

We can now put these distinctions to work in order to define the concepts central to the primary themes of this book:

Assisted suicide is the self-administration by a patient of a lethal medication where (*a*) the patient intends the medication to cause his death as a means of relieving his

---

[44] The agency distinction can be applied to withdrawing treatment as well. If the physician must do something to discontinue the treatment (disconnect the respirator, remove the feeding tube, etc.) then her agency is involved. But patient refusal of treatment (chemotherapy, radiation, antibiotics, food and water) may require the physician to do nothing.

[45] See §2.1 for an outline of the conditions for voluntariness in the context of the Doctrine of Informed Consent.

suffering, (*b*) the patient's death is actually caused by the medication, and (*c*) the medication is provided by a physician for the purpose of facilitating the patient's suicide.

Euthanasia is the administration of a lethal medication to a patient by a physician where (*a*) the physician intends the medication to cause the patient's death as a means of relieving his suffering and (*b*) the patient's death is actually caused by the medication.

Assisted death is either assisted suicide or euthanasia.

The foregoing definitions presuppose that a physician is assisting the suicide of, or administering euthanasia to, a patient and that the means in either case is a lethal dose of medication (typically a barbiturate). It is, of course, possible for other parties, such as family members or friends, to act in either of these roles and for death to be induced by other means. However, the subject of this book is the ethics and legality of these practices in a medical setting; the definitions are therefore deliberately tailored to this purpose. They are not intended to have a wider application or to capture everything that we would commonly recognize as either assisted suicide or euthanasia. Unless otherwise indicated, the remainder of the book will deal only with *physician*-assisted suicide and *physician*-administered euthanasia, carried out in either case by means of a lethal medication.

A number of important implications of these definitions should be kept in mind in the discussions to follow. First, in terms of the common (though misleading) distinction, euthanasia is necessarily 'active' (since it requires the administration of a lethal medication); 'active euthanasia' is therefore redundant and 'passive euthanasia' is an oxymoron mistakenly applied to cases of withholding or withdrawing (potentially) life-sustaining treatment.[46] Second, in both assisted suicide and euthanasia death is necessarily intended (as a means of relieving suffering); in non-treatment cases the question of intention is left open and may depend on the particularities of the case. Third, in both assisted suicide and euthanasia the lethal medication administered is the cause of death; in non-treatment cases the question of cause of death is left open and may depend on the particularities of the case. Fourth, while physicians can, and do, perform many other services to assist their dying patients, I will speak of them assisting death only when they are parties to either assisted suicide or euthanasia. Finally, assisted suicide and euthanasia share a common end and a common cause of death

[46] I am aware that some (though now not many) commentators do prefer to speak of 'passive euthanasia' as a contrast to the 'active' variety. I have elected not to follow them in this for two reasons. First, this terminological preference rests more weight on the 'active/passive' distinction than it is capable of bearing (see §4.3, below). Second, it makes the term 'euthanasia' (unqualified) dangerously ambiguous. This ambiguity is particularly pernicious in public opinion surveys that ask respondents whether they think that 'euthanasia' should be legalized. There is a world of difference between interpreting an affirmative response as an endorsement of patient refusal of life-sustaining treatment (which is already legal) and 'active' euthanasia (which, in most places, is not). When we have the terminological resources to avoid this kind of ambiguity, it seems to me that we should use them.

and differ only in terms of the agent who administers the lethal treatment; whether this difference is of any ethical or legal significance remains to be seen.

1.3 Ethics and Law

We can now specify the subject matter of this book with more precision: we will be dealing with ethical and legal issues concerning assisted death. The ethical issues are all familiar ones. Is suicide a matter for moral evaluation? If so, can it be wrong (the violation of a duty)? A duty to whom? Do people have a right to determine when and how they will die? Can suicide be rational? Under what conditions? If suicide is morally permissible, is it also permissible for a second party to provide assistance? Does it make a difference if that second party is a doctor? Is there an ethical difference between assisting a suicide and administering euthanasia? Is euthanasia tantamount to murder? Do doctors have a role-specific duty not to kill their patients? Is there an ethical difference between euthanasia and withdrawing or withholding life-sustaining treatment? Under what conditions can either of these practices be justified?

The legal issues are equally familiar. Should attempting suicide be a criminal offence? If not, what is the rationale for the criminal prohibition of assisting a suicide? Should the law make exceptions to this prohibition? If so, under what circumstances and with what safeguards? Should the law make exceptions to the criminal prohibition of homicide to allow for voluntary euthanasia? If so, under what circumstances and with what safeguards? Is there a significant difference between legalizing assisted suicide and legalizing euthanasia? Is there a significant difference between legalizing either of these measures and decriminalizing them? Could either of them find a place in the standard practice of hospice palliative care? How could abuses of the law be prevented? How could the slide down a slippery slope to ethically unacceptable practices be prevented? Is non-voluntary euthanasia one of these practices? Could there be a case for legalizing it as well? What could we learn from jurisdictions in which one or more of these measures is legal? If such a policy is successful there could it be exported to other jurisdictions?

These are the questions this book sets out to answer, the ethical ones in Part I and the legal ones in Part II. But a preliminary word is in order about the relationship between the two sets of questions. It is tempting to think that the answers to the legal questions should be determined by the answers to the ethical ones. But this would, I think, be a mistake. The ethical status of practices of assisted death is neither necessary nor sufficient to determine their legal status. It is not inconsistent to think that some practice is morally impermissible but should be legally permitted. Commonplace examples concern small-scale wrongs, such as everyday lies or broken promises, which are just too trivial to be any concern of the law. But there are more interesting, and germane, examples as well. Some reasonable people believe that abortion is wrong—because a violation of a foetus's right to life—but also recognize that other equally reasonable people disagree on this point and, in the light of this recognition, accept that it would be improper for the law to enforce their particular moral view. They regard abortion as morally impermissible but think that it should be legally permitted. It would not be far-fetched to suppose that reasonable people might hold the same combination of views about such practices as assisted suicide or euthanasia. For one thing, when we shift from the ethical to the legal questions a host of factors come into play that are not germane to the ethical debate—factors concerning the enforceability of a law, the costs of its enforcement, the burden of its sanctions, etc. While one's own conscience might firmly reject any form of assisted death it might also require the law to respect the consciences of those who disagree. It is also not inconsistent to think that some practice is morally permissible but should not be legally permitted. Again this could be due to factors that are legally, but not ethically, salient. Perhaps no law can be crafted that would allow just the narrow set of morally permissible cases while excluding the impermissible ones. Perhaps there are strong pragmatic reasons to hold the line here, the cost of prohibiting some morally acceptable cases being necessary in order to prevent morally unacceptable ones. Many reasonable people take this view about assisted death. They concede that there are instances in which assisting a suicide or administering euthanasia can be the right thing to do but they do not trust the ability of any legal policy to discriminate these cases from the others in which it is wrong. They therefore believe that some ethically permissible practices should be legally impermissible.

Thus the separation in what follows of the ethical issues from the legal ones: I have not argued, and do not believe, that they are entirely independent of one another. Put better, I have not argued, and do not believe, that none of the factors relevant to settling the ethical issues are also relevant to settling the legal ones. But I have argued, and do believe, that even if we manage to arrive at a set of ethical conclusions about assisted death with which we are perfectly comfortable there will still be further issues to be resolved before deciding on a legal policy.

1.4 Last Words

This chapter began with some questions about Anita and Bill, who wish to avoid unnecessary suffering during the dying process. In the preceding sections we have developed some of the resources we need to begin answering those questions. We have two concepts of death—biological and personal—and two matching criteria for determining death—the cardiopulmonary and the higher brain. We also have an account of the (extrinsic) badness of death—the deprivation account—that makes room for circumstances (perhaps including those of Anita and Bill) in which death might not be a bad thing. Finally, we have working definitions of the various measures to hasten death that might be available, including assisted suicide and euthanasia. The business of the remainder of this book will be to explore the ethical and legal issues concerning these means of assisted death.

We will be turning first in Part I to the ethics of assisted death. The strategy of these chapters will be to work from relatively settled and uncontroversial territory towards the more disputed and contentious issues. We begin therefore (in Ch. 2) with the so-called 'passive' measures: the withholding or withdrawing of life-sustaining treatment as the result of its refusal by a competent patient. In Ch. 3 we turn to 'active' measures—the administration of high doses of painkillers or sedatives—which may have the effect of hastening death while not being intended to do so. At this point we will have exhausted our examination of end-of-life measures that, though they may hasten death, are conventionally accepted as ethically unobjectionable by most practitioners and analysts. We move onto more controversial ground in Ch. 4, which deals with assisted suicide and voluntary euthanasia. Finally, in Ch. 5 we turn to non-voluntary euthanasia, which is commonly regarded as occupying the very bottom of the ethical slippery slope.

In these chapters I will be employing two distinct argumentative strategies. One of them will be aimed against what I will call the Conventional View, which draws an ethical 'bright line' between assisted death, on the one hand, and all other end-of-life measures which may hasten death, on the other. What I mean by a 'bright line' is a sharp boundary between different measures, such that those on one side are ethically permissible while those on the other are impermissible. The Conventional View draws this line so as to isolate measures of assisted death as uniquely impermissible. By calling this view 'conventional' I do not mean to imply that it is held by most people who have thought about these issues. Far from it—I am confident that it represents the settled opinion of no more than a minority of people, at least in the developed countries with which we will primarily be dealing. However, the view is conventional in three other important respects. First, and perhaps foremost, it is embodied in the legal systems of Canada, the United Kingdom, and (with some significant exceptions) the United States.[47] Second, it represents the official view held by most of the major professional associations of healthcare providers in those same countries.[48] Third, it reflects standard clinical practice in those countries, which accepts withholding/withdrawing life-sustaining treatment and administering high doses of analgesics and sedatives, even though these measures may hasten death, while drawing the line against euthanasia and (in most instances) assisted suicide.

I will be arguing that the Conventional View is mistaken, since there is no way of drawing an ethical bright line just where that view locates it. I will consider a number of argumentative resources that have been used to justify that line—the intending/

---

[47] For an account of the state of the law in these jurisdictions, see §6.1, below.

[48] The policy statement of the British Medical Association is typical: 'Medical Treatment can legally and ethically be withdrawn when it is futile in that it cannot accomplish any improvement, when it would not be in the patient's best interest to continue treatment (because, for example, it is simply prolonging the dying process) or when the patient has refused further treatment.... Active and intentional termination of another person's life is morally and legally different to the withholding or withdrawal of treatment' (British Medical Association 2006: 2–3). Similar statements have been affirmed by the Canadian Medical Association (as recently as 2007) and the American Medical Association (1996).

foreseeing distinction, the doing/allowing distinction, the sanctity of life—and I will argue that all of them fail. This conclusion will go part way towards showing that assisted death is ethically permissible (under appropriate conditions). But not all the way, since it leaves open the possibility that a bright line might be located elsewhere, so as to include some other measures (besides assisted death) in the impermissible category. So my second argumentative strategy will be aimed against the very idea of such line-drawing. No attempt to locate a sharp ethical boundary can succeed, I will claim, since the best justification of the conventionally accepted practices will equally justify the rejected ones. From an ethical standpoint, the various end-of-life measures that can hasten death stand or fall together.

Before embarking on this journey one more preliminary note is in order. In the chapters to follow we will be asking, and answering, normative questions—first about assisted death itself and then about the best legal policy for dealing with it. These are questions that many people answer by reference to their religious convictions and on which most religious institutions have settled positions. Despite this, the arguments in this book will be resolutely secular. The reason for this exclusion of religious beliefs is most evident when we are trying to determine what the law governing assisted death should be. In a religiously pluralistic society, public policy governing the conduct of all cannot be justified by reference to faith-based premises shared only by some: to violate this constraint is to violate freedom of conscience.[49] Public debate about public policy must therefore be secular—that is, it must prescind from any views which can be defended only on religious grounds.[50] It may be less obvious why the inquiry into ethical matters will also be secular, but the reason is ultimately the same. The arguments of this book are aimed at all readers of good will regardless of their religious convictions. To base these arguments on any particular set of such convictions would be to limit the audience by excluding everyone who does not share them. There is a legitimate place for treatments of these issues that are aimed exclusively at a particular faith community, but this book is not one of them. Put another way, the arguments of this book are intended to appeal exclusively to the feature that unites people rather than dividing them—their common rationality. As such, they presuppose that complex and challenging ethical issues, on which people of good will take starkly opposing positions, are nonetheless capable of rational resolution. The subsequent chapters will go some way towards determining whether this presupposition is justified.

[49] Not just freedom of religious conscience. To be sure, imposing the religious beliefs of some on those of different faith denominations will violate the latters' freedom of religion. But the wrong is no less when the religious beliefs of some are imposed on those who have no such beliefs at all.

[50] That is not to say that public debate on these matters must be atheistic. To say that the debate prescinds from religious beliefs is to say that it takes no stand either way on the truth of such beliefs.

PART I
Ethics

2

Consent and Refusal

In the later chapters of Part I we will come to address ethical questions concerning assisted death that are the subject of heated and divisive debate. But that is not the place to begin. Although they are sometimes obscured by the very visible sites of disagreement, there are broad areas of unanimity concerning end-of-life measures, including measures that may hasten death. Since it seems only sensible to take advantage of this consensus, our order of analysis and argument will take us in discrete stages from settled to unsettled territory. And the most settled territory—the site of least disagreement—concerns the centrality in the clinical context of informed consent.

2.1 The Doctrine of Informed Consent

Informed consent to treatment is now such an established feature of the bioethical landscape that it is easy to overlook its relatively short history.[1] While some of its strands can be traced back to the early decades of the twentieth century,[2] the first definitive statement of the Doctrine of Informed Consent (DIC) was in the 1947 Nuremberg Code, formulated in response to the medical experiments carried out both in pre-war Nazi Germany and during the war in the concentration camps. The first clause of the Code stated that 'The voluntary consent of the human subject is absolutely essential. This means that the person involved should have legal capacity to give consent; should be so situated as to be able to exercise free power of choice, without the intervention of any element of force, fraud, deceit, duress, overreaching, or other ulterior form of constraint or coercion; and should have sufficient knowledge and comprehension of the elements of the subject matter involved as to enable him to

---

[1] For histories of the development of the Doctrine see Faden and Beauchamp 1986: chs. 3–6; Berg et al. 2001: ch. 3; Manson and O'Neill 2007: ch. 1.

[2] For example, in Justice Cardozo's statement of the common law in *Schloendorff* (1914), 129–30: 'Every human being of adult years and sound mind has a right to determine what shall be done with his own body; and a surgeon who performs an operation without his patient's consent commits an assault, for which he is liable in damages.'

make an understanding and enlightened decision.'[3] Although the Code was devised specifically to govern the use of human subjects in biomedical research, its basic principles were soon adapted to the clinical setting as well. Subsequent refinements of those principles have been shaped primarily by the courts, as they have adjudicated actions brought by patients against healthcare providers and hospitals.[4] In this respect the DIC is a legal doctrine partially defining the rights of patients and the responsibilities of caregivers.

While it is impossible to ignore the role of the courts in the evolution of the DIC, our concern here is with ethics rather than law, with moral rights (and responsibilities) rather than legal ones. As an ethical doctrine, informed consent has been a favourite topic of discussion and analysis in bioethics for decades and it continues to attract controversy and debate. I have no intention of making any original contribution to the now massive literature on the subject.[5] Instead, as much as possible I want to avoid the controversies by identifying the elements of the Doctrine—all of which are present in that first formulation of the Nuremberg Code—which would secure widespread, if not unanimous, agreement.[6] Under the DIC, as I shall understand it, there are four essential conditions for a patient to give valid consent to treatment by a healthcare provider:[7]

Assent. By means of some sign, the patient must agree to *this* treatment to be administered on *this* occasion by *this* provider. Depending on the circumstances, the sign may be oral, written, gestural, or whatever, as long as it is clear in the context that it is affirmative with respect to the treatment. The patient may take the initiative by actively requesting the treatment or, alternatively, may agree to it once it has been suggested or proposed by the provider. In some contexts, such as normal medical procedures during a routine check-up, tacit assent may be inferred from the mere fact that the patient has turned up for her appointment and is registering no objection to the examination. However this might be, what is crucial is that the assent is given *by the patient* and not on the patient's behalf by a substitute decision-maker.

Capacity.[8] The patient must be decisionally capable at the time with respect to the treatment options in question. Decisional capacity (or competence) is basically the

---

[3] Nuremberg Tribunal 1947.

[4] The phrase 'informed consent' was itself coined by a California court in *Salgo* (1957).

[5] A quick search of *MedLine* (in February 2009) turned up 2,362 entries with 'informed consent' in the title field alone, 209 of which were published in 2008. *MedLine* covers clinical ethics, but not philosophy; the *Philosopher's Index* lists 227 publications with the same title keywords. There have also been several book-length treatments of the subject (the most prominent being Faden and Beauchamp 1986; Berg et al. 2001; Manson and O'Neill 2007), as well as general treatises in bioethics that devote substantial attention to informed consent (such as Beauchamp and Childress 2009).

[6] In what follows I focus exclusively on informed consent in clinical, rather than research, settings.

[7] The first condition is the *consent*, while the other three are conditions of its *validity*; if any one of them fails then the assent is not valid. Alternatively, one might say that if any of the three further conditions fails then the assent is not *genuine*—that is, any affirmative sign given by the patient does not constitute consent. I prefer to distinguish the fact of assent from the conditions for its validity.

[8] Faden and Beauchamp 1986: ch. 8; Berg et al. 2001: ch. 5.

ability to make a reasoned decision whether to accept or reject a particular form of treatment. At a minimum it includes the ability to understand and appreciate the nature and consequences of both assenting to and declining a treatment option. Decisional capacity is the default presumption for adult patients. However, the presumption is rebuttable by evidence of some standing mental illness or disability serious enough to impair cognitive functioning. Alternatively, the impairment may be temporary and situational, where thinking is disordered by factors such as severe trauma, alcohol or drug intoxication, hysteria, etc. Young children, on the other hand, will be presumed to be decisionally incapable, though there will of course be a grey area located somewhere during adolescence (so-called 'mature minors').[9] It is important to note that the relevant decisional capacity for informed consent to treatment is the ability to make a reasoned decision concerning *this* treatment at *this* time. A person may be competent to make other personal decisions (such as financial ones) but not treatment decisions, may be competent to make some treatment decisions but not others, and may be competent to make particular treatment decisions at some times and not others.[10]

Many writers have emphasized the threshold or gatekeeping role of decisional capacity, since the outcome of this determination will settle whether decisional authority with respect to a particular treatment will be vested in the patient or in some surrogate.[11] The remaining two components of the DIC presuppose a decisionally capable patient.

Voluntariness.[12] The patient's giving of assent must be free of undue influence and coercion, whether by providers or by family or friends. It is recognized, of course, that our decision-making as patients will often be influenced by what others think or suggest or by our knowledge of what they want or would prefer. Since it would aim much too high to purge decision-making of all such influences, the issue of voluntariness will turn on when such influences are 'undue'—that is, when they rise to the level of 'force, fraud, deceit, duress, overreaching, or other ulterior form of constraint or coercion'. As with decisional capacity, there will inevitably be borderline cases in which the voluntariness of patient assent to treatment is uncertain.

Disclosure.[13] The patient must be provided with adequate information concerning the treatment option in question. This information will normally include the patient's diagnosis, prognosis in the absence of treatment (including any uncertainty attending either of these matters), the nature of each of the available treatment options, the probable outcome of each option, and the risks attached to each option. It may also include provider-specific information, such as HIV status (where relevant) and experience with the procedure(s) in question. The general rule for disclosure is that it

---

[9] Faden and Beauchamp 1986: 292–3; Berg et al. 2001: 97–8; Downie 2004: 80 ff.

[10] Allen Buchanan and Dan Brock (1989: 18–23) emphasize the decision-relativity of capacity.

[11] e.g. Faden and Beauchamp 1986: 287 ff; Buchanan and Brock 1989: 26–9.

[12] Faden and Beauchamp 1986: ch. 10; Berg et al. 2001: 67–70.

[13] Faden and Beauchamp 1986: ch. 9; Berg et al. 2001: 46 ff.

should include all the information that a reasonable person *in this particular patient's circumstances* would need in order to make a reasoned decision concerning the treatment in question. In order to facilitate this decision-making the information must therefore be communicated in a manner that the patient is capable of comprehending.

The Doctrine of Informed Consent is commonly assumed to confer a moral right on patients (and impose a corresponding moral duty on providers). While this assumption is basically correct, it is important to be clear about what kind of right (and duty) this is. Some rights—not all—are *claims* against others that they engage in (or forbear from) some specified course of action.[14] Familiar instances are contractual rights where each party has a claim against the other to some specific performance: if I sell you my computer for £100 then my claim against you is that you pay me the £100 and your claim against me is that I hand over my computer. In these cases the contents of the two claims specify the correlative duties: my claim against you just is your duty to me seen, as it were, from my point of view, and the same holds for your claim against me. Contractual claims may also be for specific non-performance by the other party: agreeing to pay blackmail has this structure. Contractual rights are therefore reciprocal pairs of matching claims and duties. However, claim-rights can also be held against everyone in general: your right not to be tortured is a claim against everyone not to torture you, which is in turn a duty belonging to everyone not to do so. Whether held against assignable others (as in the case of contract) or against the world at large (as in the case of security of the person), the defining feature of claim-rights remains the fact that at their core they require some act (or omission) by these others.

The right conferred on patients by the DIC begins as a claim-right, more specifically as a special case of the right to security, or integrity, of the person. The more general right is a claim against everyone that they refrain from the use of force or violence against one's person; paradigmatic violations, therefore, are such actions as assault, battery, rape, and homicide. Since most—not all—medical treatment is invasive of the body, it follows that healthcare providers, especially physicians, have a *pro tanto* duty not to administer such treatment. Were this the end of the normative story then medical treatment would be forbidden, much to our general detriment. But it is not the end of the story, since most (if not all) claim-rights have a further, very useful, feature: they can be *waived* by their holders in specific circumstances. Waiving a claim-right is a way of exercising a normative *power* over it, a power that enables one to limit or entirely extinguish one's claim. Again the contractual context provides the most familiar illustration: it is within my power to cancel my claim against you, and therefore your duty to me, by deciding to give you my computer rather than collecting the £100 you owe me for it. The same feature applies to non-contractual rights. Thus normally it would be a violation of my security of the person for you to deliberately put your shoulder into me in order to knock me over. But if we have

---

[14] For an explication of the concept of a claim, and of the related concepts of a power and a liberty, see Sumner 1987: §2.1.

agreed to play contact hockey then we have both waived this claim against one another; as a result, it is now permissible for you to bodycheck me (and vice versa).[15] The normative position of soldiers in a volunteer army can also be understood in this way: by signing up they have waived their right not to be aggressed against by enemy military personnel.

This power of waiver makes rights much more useful—because much more flexible—instruments for us. This is nowhere more evident than in the medical context. If I could not waive my right of personal security—held against every-one—then my physician would not be permitted to administer (invasive but benefi-cial) treatment to me. But this is where informed consent comes in: it is the mechanism whereby I waive my right against my physician that she not invade my body.[16] She has a duty not to administer treatment unless I have waived that duty by giving informed consent. In the absence of my consent her *pro tanto* duty not to treat me is also her final or *all things considered* duty. Normatively speaking, therefore, the default position is the physician's duty not to treat, which is altered by the patient's waiver/consent. That non-treatment is the default position is effectively obscured by the fact that, in the context of the physician–patient relationship, the waiver is the normal course of events: patients routinely agree to, or actively seek out, treatment by their physicians. Absence of waiver/consent, while it may be the normative baseline, is therefore statistically exceptional.[17] None of this alters the fact that physicians have a responsibility to obtain informed consent from patients before administering treat-ment, lest they be guilty of an assault or battery on their patients, nor the fact that this responsibility imposes affirmative duties on them (principally duties of disclosure).

So far informed consent implicates both a claim-right (to personal security) and the exercise of a power (of waiver) over that claim-right.[18] But one more ingredient is also needed in order fully to describe the patient's normative position. Everything we have said to this point is consistent with the patient having a duty not to exercise that power of waiver. If that were the case, then the normative situation would revert to the default position whereby administering treatment would be a violation of the phys-ician's duty. Since that result would be crazy we need to ensure that patients have the normative freedom to exercise their power of waiver. We do so by saying that the patient has a *liberty* to waive his claim-right, where that just means that he has no duty not to do so. Liberties define another class of rights—liberty-rights—which consists of the freedom to do, or not to do, something. Familiar instances include the basic political liberties of conscience, expression, and association; each of these defines a

---

[15] There are limits to the effect of the waiver, which is why some violence in hockey can lead to criminal charges.

[16] For convenience, I have assumed that the right in question is one of bodily integrity. But the right of personal security is broader than that, for it also forbids physicians from imposing non-invasive treatment (such as psychotherapy) on unconsenting patients.

[17] It is not really exceptional, of course, since each of us has consented to treatment by only a very small fraction of the world's healthcare providers. For all of the others, the normative default position holds.

[18] Cf. Otlowski 1997: 35–6.

normative space in which individuals are able to exercise freedom of choice. In the case of informed consent the patient has a liberty-right to choose whether to exercise his normative power to waive his claim-right to security of the person.

We can now see that the patient's right of informed consent is actually a layered set of distinguishable and interrelated normative components: a claim plus a power over that claim plus a liberty over the exercise of that power. From the amount of attention that informed consent has received in the bioethical literature we may assume that assigning this particular set of components to patients is a pretty important matter. Presumably its importance stems primarily from the stringency of the first-order claim-right to security of the person. But how stringent is it? Is it absolute? If not, under what circumstances may treatment be administered to an unconsenting patient? Under the DIC the exceptions to the requirement of obtaining informed consent are usually collected under the following headings:[19]

Emergency. Generally speaking, where treatment is urgently needed in order to prevent serious harm and where the patient is so incapacitated by her condition that she is unable to give consent, a physician may administer treatment without consent.[20] In these cases patient consent may be presumed, on the assumption that a reasonable person in this situation would agree to treatment, or the treatment may be justified on grounds of necessity as being in the patient's best interest.[21] Technically, this is not an exception to the DIC, which presupposes decisional capacity on the part of the patient. However, it is worth distinguishing emergency situations, in which the incapacity may be temporary, from cases of permanent incapacity in which consent must be sought from substitute decision-makers. In the emergency situation the physician may be answerable to the patient once capacity has been regained.

Harm to others. In certain cases, where the interests of third parties or society at large are at stake, treatment may be administered without the consent, or even despite the refusal, of a decisionally capable patient. Thus someone carrying an infectious disease may be subjected to compulsory quarantine, examination, and blood sampling in order to protect others against the spread of the infection, or a decisionally capable person with mental health problems may be subjected to involuntary confinement if found to be a danger to others. There are, however, limits to the 'harm to others' exception: a parent, even if a good match, cannot be compelled to donate a kidney, or even blood, to a child in need of it.[22]

Therapeutic privilege. Under this provision physicians may sometimes be permitted to withhold relevant information if disclosure would have a substantially adverse effect on

---

[19] See e.g. Berg et al. 2001: ch. 4.

[20] However, if there is time to obtain consent from a substitute decision-maker for the patient, then the physician may be obligated to do so.

[21] However, if it is known that the patient has a standing refusal of a certain form of treatment (as Jehovah's Witnesses do of blood transfusions) then the treatment may not be justified by either of these means.

[22] Downie 2004: 67.

the patient's condition. Although such situations may be extremely rare, one can at least imagine cases in which a patient with, say, an unstable cardiac arrhythmia, might be so upset by full disclosure of the gravity of his condition as to induce a full, and possibly fatal, seizure. Absent such (possibly only imaginary) situations, the exception of therapeutic privilege obviously needs to be very narrowly construed in order to prevent outright medical paternalism.

Waiver. We have already seen how the giving of informed consent is itself a waiver of a right of personal (or bodily) integrity. But just as rights can be waived, so can waivers of rights, and just as unconsenting patients cannot be compelled to submit to treatment, so unwilling patients cannot be compelled to make their own decisions about treatment. A decisionally capable patient may decline disclosure of the information needed to make an informed decision, or may abdicate decision-making altogether, leaving the matter to be determined by the physician or by a third party. In that case, the physician may be released from her normal duty of disclosure.

The Doctrine of Informed Consent is therefore a complex bundle of conditions for the valid waiver of the right to personal security and exceptions to the necessity of such a waiver. So far, however, we have only aimed to trace the main contours of the Doctrine; what remains is to seek its justification. The justification of a right usually looks to the values that it serves to promote or protect. What values, then, are served by the DIC? There are two prime candidates for this role: autonomy (or self-determination) and well-being.[23] Of the two, the former is the more intuitively obvious. As I shall understand it, exercising autonomy/self-determination is a matter of managing one's own life in accordance with one's own values and priorities.[24] It therefore requires being the one who makes the major decisions about how that life is

---

[23] Berg et al. 2001: 11: 'The ethical justification of informed consent stems from its promotion of autonomy and well-being (as individuals themselves define well-being).' Cf. 18: 'The primary goals of informed consent are the protection of patient or subject welfare and the promotion of autonomy'. See also Buchanan and Brock 1989: 29–41; Brock 1993: 24–36. There is, however, no consensus in the literature on this matter. One well-known 'theory' of informed consent grounds it in autonomy or self-determination alone (Faden and Beauchamp 1986: ch. 7), while a more recent revisionist account argues that 'appeals to individual autonomy, however conceived, are unlikely to provide convincing justifications for informed consent procedures' (Manson and O'Neill 2007: 22). In their influential general treatise on biomedical ethics, Tom Beauchamp and James Childress (2009: ch. 4) treat respect for autonomy as the primary justification for informed consent, but they do not deny that it may also be supported by considerations of beneficence or non-maleficence.

[24] Throughout this book I shall be using 'autonomy' and 'self-determination' interchangeably. The concept of autonomy has received a great deal of attention (arguably too much attention) in recent decades, resulting in a bewildering array of competing analyses, many of which have little or nothing to do with the decision-making context of informed consent. The more robust conceptions of autonomy require sophisticated capacities—for rational determination of the will or a high level of critical self-reflection—which no informed consent protocol demands. Under these interpretations most of us probably fail to be autonomous most of the time, and this will include patients making decisions about medical treatment. We can, with greater expectation of success, aim to ensure that these decisions are made in accordance with our own life goals and values. For the purposes of this discussion, that will suffice for being autonomous.

to go: what educational and career path to pursue, where to live, whether and whom to marry, whether to have children, how to spend leisure time, what social/political causes to support, and so on. The presumptive point of the requirement of informed consent is to provide us with the same managerial opportunity with respect to our healthcare. While many treatment decisions will be relatively trivial, some will have a profound impact on the course of our lives. In theory at least, the regime of informed consent is meant to ensure that no treatment goes forward unless or until we have signed off on it. No one else gets to make that final decision, no one else gets to determine how our therapeutic process will go—only we do.

The four major components of the DIC can all be seen as ensuring our status as self-determiners. Assent is the decisional act itself, which only the patient can perform. Capacity is meant to ensure that the patient has the decisional wherewithal to be a self-determiner; in the absence of capacity decisions will be made by others on the patient's behalf. Voluntariness in turn guarantees that the patient truly is the author of the decisional act, that it is an exercise of self-determination rather than determination by others. Disclosure provides the patient with the information necessary for rational and effective decision-making; while the healthcare provider can (and should) lay out a detailed road map of the options ahead, only the patient gets to determine which route to take. Finally, even the right of a patient to waive disclosure and decision-making authority requires an autonomous decision to abdicate autonomy.

Doubtless the foregoing picture of the patient as self-determining agent is a philosopher's ideal realized only imperfectly in actual practice. But it is appropriate for the justification of a practice to look to the ideal case, and the ideal theory of informed consent seems undeniably to link it closely to patient self-determination. However, this is clearly not the only value in play. While self-determination may be valuable in its own right—most of us want to be masters of our fate and captains of our souls—it is also an effective means whereby we are enabled to pursue our own well-being. A decisionally capable and well-informed agent is normally in a better position to act in his best interest than is any third party. This is especially so if well-being is interpreted subjectively, so that what is best for a person is ultimately determined by his own tastes, preferences, and values.[25] In that case, the goals that an agent freely chooses to pursue will normally coincide with, or constitute, his well-being. Giving the agent final authority over his healthcare decisions will then be an effective way of ensuring that those decisions are guided by his own conception of his good and not by someone else's. As John Stuart Mill put the matter: 'If a person possesses any tolerable amount of common sense and experience, his own mode of laying out his existence is the best, not because it is the best in itself, but because it is his own mode.'[26]

---

[25] I have argued for the subjectivity of well-being in Sumner 1996: ch. 2.
[26] Mill 1977: 270.

So autonomy and well-being will normally run together as the justifying values of the Doctrine of Informed Consent. Normally, but not necessarily. Free and fully informed self-determiners who surpass the threshold of decisional capability are nonetheless capable of making decisions to their own detriment. This can happen because they need not be egoists; they can, that is, have goals other than their own self-interest and may choose what is worse for themselves because it will be better for others. But it can also happen if their decision-making processes are distorted by self-deception, denial, phobias, traumatic memories, and the like. In cases such as these the twin justifying values of the DIC come apart: respecting autonomy will require acquiescence in the patient's decision while promoting health and well-being will urge disregarding it. In these cases the DIC tends to side with autonomy against well-being: as long as the patient in question is decisionally capable, fully informed, and free of the undue influence of others then in the absence of consent no treatment may be administered, whatever the adverse impact of non-treatment might be. In other respects, however, well-being may compete more successfully with self-determination. If there are genuine or legitimate cases of therapeutic privilege, for instance, then physician disclosure may be limited or compromised in the interest of patient health. Emergency situations may also be viewed as ones in which the immediate interests of the patient override the consent requirement; at any rate, to presume patient consent in such cases is to presume that, if consulted, the patient would agree to the course of action necessary to prevent grave harm or loss of life, that is, the course of action that would be best for him.[27] Finally, where treatment can be compelled to protect others then autonomy is clearly subordinated to well-being, albeit not that of the patient.

2.2 Refusal of Life-Sustaining Treatment

'The logical corollary of this doctrine of informed consent is that the patient generally has the right not to consent, that is the right to refuse treatment and to ask that it cease where it has already been begun.'[28] So wrote the judge in a Canadian legal case concerning the right to refuse life-sustaining treatment. In fact the relationship between consent and refusal is even closer than this talk of a 'corollary' suggests. In the previous section we established that an essential feature of informed consent is the

---

[27] Note that in at least some jurisdictions it is standard practice for hospital emergency wards to revive attempted suicides, notwithstanding the fact that they may have left notes specifically refusing this service. Cf. D'Oronzio 2002 (with accompanying commentaries) and Macauley 2007. In the recent English case of Kerrie Wooltorton, who had attempted suicide by swallowing anti-freeze, emergency physicians chose to honour her refusal of treatment ('Woman who swallowed anti-freeze dies after refusing treatment—because doctors feared "assault" claim if they saved her', *Daily Mail*, 17 October 2008). However, it is significant that when Ms Wooltorton arrived at hospital she was fully conscious and able to reaffirm her advance directive refusing treatment.

[28] *Nancy B.* (1992), 390. This case is discussed in §6.1, below.

patient's liberty-right to waive her claim against invasive treatment. But that liberty-right consists of two liberties: to waive the claim (by consenting to treatment) and not to waive it (by withholding consent). Without the liberty to withhold consent the 'right' to consent would be a duty, which would remove decision-making from the patient's hands altogether by making treatment mandatory. Since refusing treatment is the most emphatic way of withholding consent, the right of treatment refusal is an inextricable part of the Doctrine of Informed Consent.

Once the DIC has been accepted there is therefore no real normative issue concerning the right of decisionally capable patients to refuse treatment. Besides decisional capacity, we may assume that the further conditions of voluntariness and disclosure also apply to refusal just as they do to consent, so that we are speaking here of patients' free and informed refusal of medical treatment.[29] That leaves us with only two questions worthy of discussion: do matters stand differently if the treatment in question is necessary in order to sustain life? And what counts, in this context, as life-sustaining medical treatment?

While much medical treatment is routine, some is not. At the extreme, where initiation or continuation of treatment is necessary in order to sustain life, refusal of treatment becomes life-threatening. Even in these cases there is no real ethical or legal issue about the patient's right of refusal. It is well established in both ethics and law that even when the stakes are this high the free and informed refusal of treatment by a decisionally capable patient must be respected.[30] This is not the end of the story, however, since there is another way, short of overriding patient refusal, in which the higher stakes in life-and-death situations may be taken into account. Allen Buchanan and Dan Brock have proposed a sliding scale for determinations of decisional capacity (or, as they prefer, competence), arguing that 'a standard of competence should vary in significant part with the effects for the patient's well-being of accepting his or her choice'.[31] For routine, low-risk medical interventions the capacity threshold could be set at a correspondingly low level, while in the case of patient refusal of life-sustaining treatment, where the risk is the probability—or even certainty—of death, the threshold would be higher.[32] Buchanan and Brock see this as a way of balancing the two

---

[29] It may be that patient refusal of treatment must be respected even when it is uninformed. However, I shall continue to assume that we are speaking here of informed refusal.

[30] Otlowski 1997: 41–2: 'it is now a well-established common law principle that a patient who has the requisite decision-making capacity may refuse any treatment, including life-saving treatment'. See also President's Commission for the Study of Ethical Problems in Medicine and Biomedical and Behavioral Research 1987.

[31] Brock 1991: 105; cf. Buchanan and Brock 1989: 52–5. The sliding-scale approach is endorsed with minor variations in Beauchamp and Childress 2009: 116–17.

[32] To say that refusing life-sustaining treatment is a high-risk (or high-stakes) decision is, of course, not to say that its consequences are always, or even usually, bad for the patient. We have already seen (§1.1, above) that death can be a benefit rather than a harm, and many, perhaps most, scenarios in which patients wish to forgo life-sustaining treatment will fall into this category. Nonetheless, the finality of death—the foreclosing of any opportunity for later reconsideration—is by itself sufficient to make choosing it, or risking it, a high-stakes venture for which additional safeguards are appropriate. The higher thresholds of the sliding scale are meant to provide these safeguards.

fundamental values served by informed consent: patient autonomy and patient well-being. When the stakes are raised for the latter then a correspondingly higher standard will be applied for the former, in order to provide additional assurance that authority over the decision should properly be left in the hands of the patient. The effect of raising the threshold for decisional capacity is therefore to introduce a little more paternalism into the decision-making process: a higher protection of well-being at some cost to autonomy. But it remains the case that treatment decisions made by patients who surpass the higher threshold must be respected, whatever their cost to well-being.

The idea of a sliding scale for decisional capacity enjoys a good deal of common-sense support. Parents will standardly allow a young child some decisional authority over low-risk matters (what colour clothes to wear) but not high-risk ones (whether to play in the street). For the latter they will wait until the child is older and better able to appreciate the consequences of her actions. Applying the sliding-scale approach to medical decision-making will sometimes have the result of imposing a higher standard of capacity for refusal of a particular treatment than for consent to the very same treatment—in cases, for instance, where the treatment in question would clearly be beneficial and its omission would equally clearly be life-threatening.[33] But this does not seem anomalous, since the aim is to ensure that self-determination is most fully engaged when the consequences for well-being are most serious—and especially if they are irreversible.

One way to operationalize such a sliding scale would be to adopt a variable age of consent to (or refusal of) treatment. A 14-year-old girl might, for instance, be deemed decisionally capable with respect to relatively low-risk decisions (whether to use contraception or seek an abortion) but not high-risk ones (whether to embark on a round of chemotherapy for leukemia or continue renal dialysis). In general, younger adolescents who are capable of understanding the nature of the treatment in question and the consequences of accepting or rejecting it might meet the standard of decisional capacity for a broad range of treatment decisions, but not those in which either the acceptance or the rejection of the treatment carries with it a serious risk to life. For those decisions the age of consent/refusal might be set higher so as to require either parental endorsement of the decision or some independent evidence that it is in the patient's best interest.[34] Another sliding scale for decisional capacity might concern the

---

[33] Brock 1991: 111–12.

[34] This notion of a sliding scale of decisional capacity was applied by the Canadian Supreme Court in its decision in *A.C.* (2009). The case concerned a 14-year-old girl who was admitted to hospital, having suffered an episode of lower gastrointestinal bleeding as a result of Crohn's disease. A devout Jehovah's Witness, she refused blood transfusions that her attending physician determined were necessary in order to prevent the risk of death due to organ failure. These transfusions were subsequently administered by court order and A.C. recovered. In its treatment of the constitutional issues the Court endorsed 'a sliding scale of scrutiny, with the adolescent's views becoming increasingly determinative depending on his or her ability to exercise mature, independent judgment. The more serious the nature of the decision, and the more severe its potential impact on the life or health of the child, the greater the degree of scrutiny that will be required.'

absence of distorting factors, such as mental illness or depression, which are known to impair judgement. Where life-sustaining treatment is being refused it might some-times be advisable to refer a patient for psychological or psychiatric examination, if there is some initial suspicion that such factors are affecting his decision-making, whereas no similar referral would be appropriate for more routine decisions. We might similarly raise the bar for patients who are cognitively impaired, who might be deemed decisionally capable with respect to relatively minor therapeutic interventions but not life-or-death decisions.

The gatekeeping role of decisional capacity in the Doctrine of Informed Consent makes locating an appropriate risk-sensitive standard for capacity particularly import-ant, since we should be reluctant either to take decisional authority away from patients (at the cost of their autonomy) or to allow decisionally compromised patients to make catastrophic decisions (at the cost of their well-being). But the same sliding-scale idea can also be readily applied to the other conditions of valid consent/refusal. Where death is the expected outcome of treatment refusal it may be important to have a documentary record of the patient's decision—a signed refusal form. It would also seem appropriate to put in place a more rigorous procedure for ensuring that the patient's decision is fully voluntary and free of the undue influence of others, and that it represents the patient's stable and enduring will. This might be accomplished by interviewing the patient and family, by offering counselling, or, where appropriate, by asking the patient to reaffirm her decision over a suitable period of time. A more rigorous standard of disclosure might also be required where life is at stake in order to ensure that the patient fully understands the consequences of her decision. The effect of all of these higher standards—for assent, capacity, voluntariness, and disclosure—is to introduce additional safeguards of patient well-being where life is at risk because life-sustaining treatment is being refused. In these ways the peculiar urgency of these decisions can be acknowledged without threatening the normative heart of the DIC—that the free and informed refusal of a decisionally capable patient must be respected.

Our second question concerned what is to count as life-sustaining medical treat-ment. The general, and obvious, answer is: any form of treatment whose withholding or withdrawal would (probably or certainly) hasten death. There are many unprob-lematic instances, such as chemotherapy for cancer and renal dialysis for kidney failure. But other instances may seem less clear. Consider the case of a patient whose oesophageal cancer precludes both oral ingestion of food and water and its delivery by way of a nasogastric tube. Nutrition and hydration may still be provided to the patient through a gastrostomy tube introduced through the abdominal wall. There is little doubt that administering food and water in this way can be life-sustaining. The question that has been subject to some debate is whether it constitutes medical treatment or is instead just the same basic care that is provided to other patients when their meals are delivered on a tray.

Before proceeding any further it is important to note that the answer to this question is unimportant for decisionally capable patients, since these patients have the same right to refuse nutrition and hydration as they do to refuse medical treatment. In terms of the exercise of this right, it is a matter of indifference whether the patient is capable of taking food and water orally or must have it delivered artificially; forcefeeding the patient by mouth would be as much an invasion of his body as would implanting a tube against his will. Refusal of nutrition and hydration is therefore an ethical (and legal) end-of-life option available to decisionally capable patients, alongside refusal of treatment. Indeed, some writers have argued that the availability of this option makes legalization of any form of assisted death unnecessary.[35]

The question of the status of artificial feeding has therefore been debated largely for the case of decisionally incapable patients, principally those suffering from advanced dementia or permanent unconsciousness.[36] Some institutions, such as the Catholic Church, have taken the position that feeding tubes may not be removed from such patients, since artifically delivered nutrition and hydration constitutes basic care rather than medical treatment,[37] and the same view has had some defenders in the bioethical literature.[38] However, over the past couple of decades it has been decisively rejected by the courts and the major medical organizations in Canada, the United States, and the United Kingdom,[39] and it now represents a minority view among bioethicists.[40] This consensus notwithstanding, many clinicians and laypersons alike continue to think that there is something about withdrawing food and water from a patient that makes it significantly different from withdrawing chemotherapy or dialysis.

But what is the difference? It cannot consist in the fact that food and water are basic necessities of life, since oxygen is an even more basic necessity but no one denies that attaching a patient to a ventilator is a form of medical treatment. Might it have to do with cause of death? The orthodox view is that when a patient dies following withdrawal of life-sustaining treatment the cause of death is the patient's disease condition. Where food and water are withdrawn, however, death might be attributed instead to starvation (or, more properly, dehydration). This appears to be the thought that has led some to contend that withdrawal of nutrition and hydration is a form of euthanasia.[41] The causal issues involved here are complex and will be addressed in the next section. Meanwhile, it seems more likely that our discomfort about ceasing to

---

[35] Bernat, Gert, and Mogielnicki 1993; Gert, Culver, and Clouser 1998. I discuss this argument in §7.5, below.

[36] The ethics of withdrawing life-sustaining treatment—including nutrition and hydration—from decisionally incapable patients will be addressed in Ch. 5.

[37] This position was reaffirmed as recently as February 2009 by Rino Fisichella, President of the Pontifical Academy for Life, who was quoted as saying 'Thousands of doctors and scientists share our belief that food and water are not medical treatment but an essential requirement for life which can never be eliminated' (*Adnkronos International*, 17 February 2009).

[38] Siegler and Weisbard 1985; Rosner 1993.

[39] The leading legal cases are discussed in §6.1, below. The position of the American College of Physicians is typical: 'Artificial administration of nutrition and fluids is a life-prolonging treatment. As such, it is subject to the same principles for decisions as other treatments' (Slomka 2003: 549).

[40] The majority view is defended in Beauchamp and Childress 2009: 159–62, among many others.

[41] Siegler and Weisbard 1985.

feed a patient has something to do with the social meaning of food.[42] Eating and drinking together are important social events for us and providing food for another, especially a child, is an essential part of nurturing. (By contrast, we do not normally have to provide or administer oxygen; it's just there.) Ceasing to feed someone therefore runs against the grain for us in a way in which ceasing to administer chemotherapy or dialysis or even oxygen does not; most of us have no experience of providing these things for another in our daily life. It is not surprising, therefore, that the withdrawal of nutrition and hydration, however artificial its means of delivery might be, has a different feel for us. The fact remains, however, that the implantation of a gastrostomy (or nasogastric) tube is an invasive medical procedure—one, further-more, that carries with it a known risk of complications.[43] If a decisionally capable patient refuses to have the tube implanted, or requests that it be withdrawn once implanted, then he is refusing medical treatment, and this refusal has the same ethical and legal force as the refusal of any other form of bodily invasion.

2.3 Treatment Refusal and Suicide

Carol, who is seventy-one years old and a retired architect, has suffered total bodily paralysis since her spinal cord was severed two years ago when she was shot in the neck. Being unable to breathe on her own, she is now completely dependent on a mechanical ventilator, as well as a feeding tube. She is decisionally capable and well aware that, while she could live for at least a few more years with the ventilator, she will die quickly without it. Having reflected at length on her condition, she concludes that she no longer wishes to endure it and requests that the ventilator be removed. Her request is honoured and she dies shortly after. This is a classic instance of patient refusal of life-sustaining treatment. But can we also say that Carol committed suicide? If so, then by complying with her refusal did her physicians and the hospital assist her suicide?

The orthodox answer to both of these questions—the answer preferred by courts, professional associations, and healthcare institutions—is 'no'.[44] But this answer has come under attack by a number of philosophers, bioethicists, lawyers, and even some judges, who have argued that at least some cases of treatment refusal should be considered to be suicides.[45] How to settle this question? One obvious way would be to formulate a workable definition of suicide and then determine whether its elements

---

[42] Slomka 1995, 2003.

[43] Finucane, Christmas, and Travis 1999; Gillick 2000; Angus and Burakoff 2003.

[44] For a defence of this orthodoxy see Gert, Culver, and Clouser 1998: 191–2.

[45] Justice Scalia of the US Supreme Court in *Cruzan* (1990), 296–7: 'Starving oneself to death is no different from putting a gun to one's temple as far as the common law definition of suicide is concerned; the cause of death in both cases is the suicide's conscious decision to "pu[t] an end to his own existence".' See also Rachels 1986: ch. 5; Wreen 1988: 10–11; Beauchamp 1993: 83–5; Brock 1993: 165–6; Otlowski 1997: 61 ff.; Stell 1998; McMahan 2002: 455; G. Williams 2007: ch. 5.

are satisfied by any cases of treatment refusal. Standard definitions of suicide tend to isolate two separately necessary and jointly sufficient conditions:

Intention. The agent pursues some course of action for the purpose of bringing about her own death.

Causation. This course of action results in her death.[46]

If we adopt these conditions as our definition then the question is whether both of them can be satisfied in cases in which the 'course of action' in question consists not in jumping off a bridge or ingesting lethal medication but in refusing life-sustaining treatment.

It seems clear that the intention requirement will not be satisfied in all cases of treatment refusal, and perhaps not in most cases. Consider the case of Douglas, a seventy-six-year-old man with a diagnosis of pancreatic cancer. If left untreated the tumour will metastisize to other organs, resulting in death within three months to a year (depending on the organs affected). Chemotherapy will retard this process but will not arrest it; at best, it will extend his life by another six months or so. However, the side effects of the treatment are severe, and Douglas has decided that they are too much to bear for the additional weeks or months. He therefore declines chemotherapy, foreseeing that the (virtually certain) result of his decision will be to shorten his life. It would be quite mistaken to conclude that Douglas wants, or wishes, or intends to die; were his disease miraculously to go into spontaneous remission he would be delighted to get on with his life. His aim is not to die (or to die sooner) but to avoid unnecessary or fruitless suffering; furthermore, his death is not the means of achieving this aim but is rather a foreseen (and accepted) by-product of it. The same is true of a devout Jehovah's Witness who refuses a blood transfusion even when death will be the probable or certain result; her aim is not to die but rather to conform to (what she takes to be) her religious obligations.

However, while not all cases of treatment refusal leading to death will satisfy the intention requirement, one prominent class of cases will: patient refusal of nutrition and hydration. When a patient requests removal of a feeding tube, or simply refuses any further food or water by mouth, we cannot plausibly attribute any aim to her other than to die.[47] It makes no sense to say that if somehow it turned out to be possible for her to continue to live without food and water then she would happily accept that outcome; finding a relatively peaceful (and legal) route to death is her sole reason for taking this step. Similarly, what Carol means to accomplish by requesting removal of

---

[46] See e.g. McMahan 2002: 455: 'Let us say that an agent commits suicide if he dies as a consequence of acting with the intention of bringing about his own death.' Michael Wreen (1988) adds a couple of further conditions in order to deal with exotic counterexamples, but the intention and causation conditions remain the centrepiece of his definition. Tom Beauchamp (1993) requires additionally that the agent's act be uncoerced. However, it seems to me that history and literature present us with many examples of suicides committed under conditions of threat (Cato, Brutus, Mark Antony, Cleopatra).

[47] See e.g. the fact situation in *Bouvia* (1986).

the ventilator is the end of a life that she has come to regard as unbearable; her aim is to die and she sees that this is a means available to her of achieving it. Carol's ventilator is even more urgently necessary to keep her alive than a feeding tube and her refusal of it has only one purpose.

We seem therefore to have two classes of case: those in which the intention requirement is clearly satisfied and those in which it is equally clearly not.[48] Of course, real life can be, frequently is, more complicated than that and a patient's intentions in refusing life-sustaining treatment may be both multiple and ambiguous. Besides avoiding the burdens of futile treatment or hastening death, patients may aim to make things easier for their family, or 'let nature take its course', or place themselves in the hands of their god, or any combination of the foregoing. Or they may not be entirely clear, even in their own minds, as to their ultimate goal. None of these complications, however, threatens the fact that there are clear cases, like Carol's, in which the unambiguous aim of refusing treatment is death. In those cases the intention requirement does not distinguish between treatment refusal and suicide.[49]

Furthermore, there need be no meaningful distinction between the intention of Carol's physician in complying with her refusal and the intention of a physician in complying with a patient request for assistance with a suicide. In both cases it is open to the physician to say that she is not intending the death of her patient but is only respecting her patient's right to self-determination. Or she can say that, primarily or additionally, she is intending the death of her patient, believing it to be in the patient's best interest. Whatever her intentional stance might be, it can apply equally to terminating life-sustaining treatment and providing life-shortening treatment.

If treatment refusal cannot always be distinguished from suicide on the basis of patient (or physician) intention then perhaps causation will do the job. In a successful suicide it seems clear that some act on the part of the person in question—whether jumping off a bridge or ingesting a lethal medication—is the cause of death. On the other hand, courts have relied on a different causal story to distinguish suicide from treatment refusal: 'declining life-sustaining treatment may not properly be viewed as an attempt to commit suicide. Refusing medical intervention merely allows the disease to take its natural course: if death were eventually to occur, it would be the result, primarily, of the underlying disease, and not the result of a self-inflicted injury.'[50] So now our question is whether treatment refusal can be distinguished from suicide on the basis of cause of death. Not, it seems, if we rely on one familiar concept of causation. Suppose that someone intentionally kills herself by swallowing a lethal

---

[48] For a similar analysis and conclusion, see Brody 1995: 97–9.

[49] It is worth noting that intentions can be multiple and ambiguous in suicides as well. It is well known that 'suicide' attempts may be intended, primarily or additionally, as cries for help. Bernard Dickens once observed wrily that some acts we regard as successful suicides are actually failed suicide attempts—i.e. attempts that were meant only to send a distress message and that unexpectedly ended in death.

[50] *Conroy* (1985), 1224. Cf. *Quill* (1997), 2298: 'when a patient refuses life sustaining medical treatment, he dies from an underlying fatal disease or pathology; but if a patient ingests lethal medication prescribed by a physician, he is killed by that medication.'

dose of some medication. Then it seems clear that her act causes her death, since but for the act she would not have died. This concept of 'but for' (or *sine qua non*) causation plays an important role in the assignment of legal liability: the defendant's act cannot have caused the plaintiff's injury if the plaintiff would have suffered that injury even in the absence of the act.[51] But it is incapable in general of distinguishing between suicides and treatment refusals, since it is equally true in Carol's case that she would not have died but for her request to have the ventilator removed.[52] 'But for' causation will therefore yield the result that her refusal is a cause of her death.

Other cases may seem different. In Douglas's case it appears to make perfect sense to say, with the court, that when death comes its cause is the cancer rather than his refusal of chemotherapy. But even this appearance dissolves under closer analysis. Recall that death is a discrete, datable event—the boundary between being alive and being dead. As such, it always occurs at a (more or less) precise time. This enables us to ask a finer-grained question: not just what caused the patient's death but what caused his death *then*. If Douglas's treatment refusal hastened his death, then 'but for' the refusal he would have died later. In that case, it also appears to make perfect sense to cite it as a cause of his (earlier) death. We have to say 'a cause' here rather than 'the cause', since his cancer was also a 'but for' cause of his death happening *then*: were it not for the cancer then Douglas would have died at another time and in another way.

This result points to an important feature of 'but for' causation, namely, that on this conception all events will have multiple causes.[53] Besides Douglas's tumour and his refusal of chemotherapy, the causes of his death will include all the genetic and/or environmental factors necessary for the development of the tumour, all the previous actions by the patient and others necessary for exposure to these factors, the actions of his parents in conceiving and giving birth to him, all the factors that had to be in place in order for his parents to meet, and so on and on. The 'but for' causes of any event will stretch back in an endless chain of prior necessary conditions, each of which is *a* cause but none of which is *the* cause. By itself the concept of 'but for' causation is just too promiscuous to allow us to single out any prior event or condition as *the* cause of death. For that we need some other notion.

Let us say that being a 'but for' cause of death is necessary for being *the* cause of death, but it is not sufficient. However, we do often single out some factor as *the* cause of an event, including death. So how do we do this? The problem with 'but for' causation is that it is ruthlessly factual: it indiscriminately sweeps in all the empirically necessary conditions of an event. But not all our ordinary notions of causation are

---

[51] See Hart and Honoré 1985: ch. 5; Otlowski 1997: 16, 30. 'But for' causation is sometimes labelled 'empirical' or 'factual', to distinguish it from a normative or policy-driven conception; see Keyserlingk 1994: 711–13.

[52] Carol would, of course, have died at some later time and in some particular way (since we all do). But she would not have died *then* and in *that* way if she had not refused the ventilator. Likewise, the suicide victim would eventually have died as well, but not *then* and in *that* way.

[53] Cf. Kuhse and Singer 1985: 82–3; G. Williams 2007: 89–91.

purely factual. Others are *forensic*, meaning that we seek the cause of an event in order to answer some further question in which we have a particular interest. Since we might have many such interests there will doubtless be many different forensic notions of causation. I will mention only two of them for the particular case of seeking cause of death. The first we may label *pathological*, since it puts us in the position of a pathologist doing a post-mortem examination of the deceased.[54] The pathologist's question 'What was the cause of death?' is more or less the same as the question 'What evidence can I find in this body that could explain how the person died?' The kind of answer sought will be 'massive blunt trauma to the skull' or 'an aneurysm of the aorta' or (in Douglas's case) 'an aggressive tumour of the pancreas'. From the pathologist's standpoint whether Douglas had accepted or rejected chemotherapy is irrelevant: the tumour is still the cause of death. Likewise in Carol's case: the cause of her death is the shooting, or the paralysis resulting from it, and not her refusal of the ventilator. If the pathologist asks the same question about a suicide victim then the answer will be 'a lethal level of barbiturates' or 'massive internal injuries due to a fall', and therefore her own action, not some underlying condition over which she had little or no control. (This will be the answer even if she was driven to her act by chronic clinical depression.) So if we look at the cases from the standpoint of the pathologist we can indeed distinguish some cases of suicide from some cases of treatment refusal hastening death, and we can do it by settling on different factors as the cause of death. But what is the verdict to be when a patient with a chronic but not terminal condition dies after refusing food and water? From the pathologist's standpoint the cause of death would appear to be 'severe dehydration' (rather than the underlying condition), but this determination would then classify the case as a suicide.

In any case the pathologist's particular interests do not exhaust our forensic notions of cause of death. The second such notion we may call *normative*, since here our interest lies in allocating (legal or moral) responsibility for the death.[55] From this standpoint the main question is not 'What (substance or organic condition) caused this death?', though this will still be important, but 'Who should be held liable for this death?' Furthermore, knowing the pathological cause of death will not always identify the normative cause. To see this, compare two scenarios in each of which a physician disconnects Carol's ventilator. In the first scenario Carol's physician is complying with her request following a court decision that has upheld her right of refusal. In the second scenario she has made no such request but another physician, who happens to work in the same hospital, stands to inherit her estate upon her death.[56] The pathological cause of death is the same in both scenarios. However, in the first scenario the

---

[54] Cf. Benjamin 1976.

[55] 'Causality in law is, in the final analysis, a normative or policy choice' (Keyserlingk 1994: 712). Cf. Otlowski 1997: 16–18, 28–31; G. Williams 2007: 106–7.

[56] The two scenarios are adaptations of a pair of cases invented and discussed by Shelly Kagan (1989: 101–5). Kagan also considers the proposal that cause of death be assigned on normative grounds, as does Judith Thomson (1995: 107).

physician is not the normative cause of Carol's death, since he violates no (legal or moral) duty and is therefore not to be held liable for it. In the second scenario, on the other hand, because the physician is acting unlawfully (and immorally) he is the normative cause of her death. The important point about the notion of a normative cause is that its determination is posterior to, and not prior to, a determination of the agent's obligations. Thus under this conception the fact that one person has caused the death of another is not a reason for holding him (legally or morally) responsible for that death; rather, the fact that he was responsible for the death is a reason for concluding that he was the cause of it. Among the many agents who are 'but for' causes of a person's death the normative conception searches for the one who has committed a (legal or moral) wrong. One upshot of this approach is that in cases such as Douglas's in which no wrong has been committed the answer to the question 'who was the cause of death?' will be 'no one'. (The person who caused Carol's death in the first scenario is the person who shot her.) Furthermore, the same result may apply in the case of suicide. If suicide violates a (legal or moral) obligation then the suicide victim will be the cause of her own death, but if not then no one will be the cause of death. Likewise for physicians who assist a suicide: if doing so violates an obligation then they may be held liable as a cause of the patient's death, but not otherwise. Physicians in Oregon or Washington who provide legal suicide assistance are not the normative causes (though they may be 'but for' causes) of those deaths.

It should be obvious by now just how futile it is to try to distinguish suicide from treatment refusal on grounds of cause of death. If we confine ourselves to the strictly factual notion of 'but for' causation then there will inevitably be multiple causes in both cases, whereas if we shift to one or another forensic notion then our determination of cause of death will be driven by a particular interest or normative demand. In neither case do we get a clean, policy-neutral distinction. Moreover, the problems we encounter in working with the normative notion have a deeper lesson to teach. Our procedure has been to determine whether at least some cases of treatment refusal might also be cases of suicide by developing a workable definition of suicide and then applying it to those cases. But this procedure is bound to fail. For one thing, if we are trying to map our ordinary concept of suicide then there will inevitably be borderline cases in which our intuitions either conflict or yield no determinate result. Did Bobby Sands commit suicide when he died as a result of his hunger strike? Did Captain Oates commit suicide when he walked away from the Scott expedition into the blizzard? Did Socrates commit suicide when he drank the hemlock?[57] Reasonable people who, presumably, share the same common-sense concept of suicide may sharply disagree over the labelling of these cases.

Worse still, our intuitions about particular cases will also be driven by our moral feelings about suicide. The act carries with it a powerful moral stigma, due at least in part to centuries of condemnation by the world's major religions. Many people still

---

[57] For discussions of all these cases see Wreen 1988 and the further sources cited therein.

regard ending one's own life as cowardly, or associate suicide with acts of desperation by depressed teenagers. To avoid rumour and gossip families may conceal the fact that their loved one died by his own hand (how often do you see this acknowledged in a death notice?). On top of all this, reporting a death as a suicide may also have legal implications for important matters such as insurance. For these reasons our 'ordinary' concept of suicide is heavily morally freighted, so that we may reserve the label for the cases of which we most strongly disapprove. This tendency will doom to failure any neutral or purely factual distinction between suicide and treatment refusal. A family whose loved one has succumbed to cancer after declining life-sustaining treatment is unlikely to welcome the suggestion that she died by suicide, despite the fact that both the intention and causation conditions might be satisfied. Indeed, even in the most straightforward cases of assisted suicide, such as those occurring legally within the terms of the policy in place in Oregon, both families and advocacy groups have preferred the use of euphemisms such as 'death with dignity' or 'aid in dying'.[58] If the label 'suicide' cannot be applied even to these cases then it is not clear that it any longer has any acceptable application. Labelling someone a suicide now appears to be as politically incorrect as calling them a cripple or a retard.

For these reasons it may be fruitless to push the question whether Carol's refusal of treatment was also a suicide. However, the important issues are not terminological but substantive. Both intention and causation are widely thought to be highly salient in the ethical evaluation of medical decisions concerning end-of-life care. (Just how salient will be the subject of the next two chapters.) That is, many people take it to matter a great deal whether a patient's (or physician's) course of action in this context (*a*) was undertaken with the intention of bringing about the patient's death and (*b*) was at least a 'but for' cause of that death. These conditions are, of course, paradigmatically satisfied in cases of suicide (assisted or otherwise). If they are also satisfied in some cases of treatment refusal—such as Carol's—then it follows that *at least as far as intention and causation are concerned* there is no significant ethical difference between these cases and suicides.

2.4 Last Words

The Doctrine of Informed Consent entails that patients who are unwilling to submit to (further) medical treatment have both a legal and moral right to refuse that

---

[58] The Oregon Death with Dignity Act contains a clause stating that the practice authorized by its provisions does not constitute suicide or assisted suicide. The Annual Reports issued by the Department of Human Services for the first eight years of the Oregon policy nonetheless used the language of physician-assisted suicide. This practice was abandoned in 2006, largely at the behest of families and right-to-die organizations such as Compassion and Choices ('State Sidesteps "Suicide" in Report', Eugene *Register-Guard*, 23 October 2006). Barbara Coombs Lee, the Oregon-based president of Compassion and Choices, has been quoted as saying: 'Assisted suicide is irrational, the result of mental illness. Aid in dying is not mental illness. It's a courageous and prayerful inner dialogue on the meaning of life' (St Louis *Riverfront Times*, 8 April 2009).

treatment, even if doing so will (probably or certainly) hasten their death. Like Douglas, they may decline treatment simply because they judge its burdens to be too high a price to pay for a modest extension of life. Or, like Carol, they may decline treatment in order to die sooner. In the latter case the DIC permits patients to undertake a course of action that intentionally causes death.

At the beginning of Ch. 1 I introduced the cases of Anita, who has end-stage cancer, and Bill, who is afflicted with amyotrophic lateral sclerosis. Both Anita and Bill, I said then, wish to avoid what they regard as needless suffering during their dying process, and I asked what options are (or should be) available to them to enable them to achieve their aim. We now have a partial answer to that question: they can hasten their deaths by declining further treatment. However, this answer will be of scant comfort to Anita and Bill since, unlike Carol and Douglas, they are not currently undergoing any treatment whose purpose is to combat their disease condition. Instead, their treatment regimes have already reached the stage at which they are strictly palliative in nature, aimed exclusively at alleviating the symptoms of their conditions. The problem for both Anita and Bill is that this palliation is not, and cannot be, completely successful, with the result that they are left to endure symptoms they regard as intolerable. If, like Carol, they could hasten their deaths by declining further treatment they would do so. The only option of that sort available to them is to refuse nutrition and hydration (while continuing to accept comfort care) and wait to die of dehydration. Because neither of them is dependent on tube feeding, this option would involve declining food and water by mouth. However, though it would certainly hasten death, it may not be attractive to them. For one thing, death by this route will come slowly (usually in one to two weeks) and its timing will not be subject to their control. Perhaps more importantly, they may be uncertain whether the process of gradual dehydration over this period of time will itself add to their suffering, or to the distress of their families.[59] In any case, they may legitimately wonder whether there are (or should be) other means available to them of ending their lives in a comfortable and dignified manner. The question therefore remains whether this partial answer is also the whole answer.

---

[59] The evidence seems to suggest that the process need not be painful for the patient, at least when accompanied by good palliative care: 'Taken in toto, the anecdotal reports, laboratory studies, and the observations of nurses and physicians who care for terminally ill patients suggest that lack of hydration and nutrition does not cause unmanageable suffering in terminally ill patients and may even have an analgesic effect' (Bernat, Gert, and Mogielnicki 1993: 2726). Cf. Slomka 2003: 551; Ganzini et al. 2003; Jacobs 2003.

3

Indirect Death

The treatment options discussed in the previous chapter are frequently, though unhelpfully, classified as 'passive', since they involve withholding or withdrawing, rather than administering, treatment. We turn now to the so-called 'active' side and begin discussing forms of palliative treatment whose administration may hasten death. Euthanasia and assisted suicide fall into this category, of course, but they are controversial mainly because in both cases the hastening of death is intended as a means of relieving suffering. In line with our general approach we begin with less contentious measures that share the aim of relieving suffering but in which the hastening of death may not be a means to that end but instead an unintended side effect.

3.1 Relieving Suffering and Causing Death

The final stage of life need not go badly. In the best cases people die peacefully, without significant discomfort, in familiar surroundings, and in the company of their loved ones. Unfortunately, however, the final stage of life does not always live up to this ideal. In the developed world most people no longer die at home but in institutions where they are surrounded by strangers and vulnerable to fear, anxiety, and depression. For many the dying process is accompanied by such distressing physical symptoms as pain, shortness of breath, nausea, dizziness, agitation, or delirium. The World Health Organization defines palliative care as 'an approach that improves the quality of life of patients and their families facing the problem associated with life-threatening illness, through the prevention and relief of suffering by means of early identification and impeccable assessment and treatment of pain and other problems, physical, psychosocial and spiritual.' In pursuit of its aim to prevent and relieve suffering due to pain and other physical symptoms, palliative medicine has a wide variety of pharmacological resources at its disposal, of which the best known and most discussed are analgesics and sedatives. Most cancer patients, in the advanced stages of their disease, will experience pain severe enough to require treatment by means of analgesics. The World Health Organization has proposed the use of an 'analgesic ladder' in the treatment of cancer pain, beginning with a non-narcotic and progressing through weaker to stronger opioids.[1] Where patients request pain relief the physician is meant to ascend this ladder to the point where the analgesic of choice is sufficient either to eliminate the pain entirely or, failing that, to reduce it to a level that the patient finds tolerable. The location of this point will vary from case to case, but there is no question that for many patients only high doses of the strongest opioids, such as morphine, will suffice. In such cases it is standard clinical practice to increase the dosage or the frequency of morphine infusions as the severity of cancer pain increases. At every stage the aim is to provide the minimum dose necessary to control the pain: enough but not more than enough.

Most cancer pain can be successfully controlled in this way—most, but not all. A minority of patients at some stage of the dying process will experience pain (or other refractory physical symptoms) that cannot be adequately managed by administration of even the most sophisticated analgesics. Timothy Quill estimates this minority to be somewhere in the 2–5 per cent range; for these patients 'the dose of opioids and sedatives must sometimes be increased to the point where the patient loses conscious awareness of their suffering'.[2] While morphine infusions can be increased to the point where they induce unconsciousness, sedatives such as barbiturates or benzodiazepines are the pharmacological agents more commonly used for this purpose. Like analgesics, doses of sedatives can be titrated to achieve or maintain differing levels of diminished awareness, ranging from drowsiness to deep sleep. Where complete unconsciousness is the intended effect, it can be either intermittent—where the patient is brought back to wakefulness from time to time—or continuous. We will call sedation terminal when it is both deep and continuous to the point of death.[3] When they elect this option patients will frequently, though not invariably, also refuse artificial nutrition and hydration for the period of sedation.

Both high doses of opioids and terminal sedation are standard techniques in palliative medicine for the alleviation of refractory and intolerable symptoms during the dying process.[4] However, both have been subjects of controversy on the ground that in the process of relieving suffering they may also hasten death. Morphine in high doses has known side effects, the most serious of which is respiratory depression. Since

[1] Fohr 1998: 316.

[2] Quill 1998. Other sources estimate that 10–20 per cent of end-stage cancer patients may experience pain that cannot be controlled by the WHO 'analgesic ladder' (Twycross 1994: 2; Chater et al. 1998).

[3] While 'terminal sedation' is a widely used label for this form of treatment, it is not universally accepted; for some alternatives see Higgins and Altilio 2007: 4–8. It is important to note that the modifier 'terminal' connotes only that the sedation is maintained until the point of death, not that it is a cause of death; 'terminal sedation' therefore differs in this respect from 'terminal illness'. Also, to say that sedation is terminal does not imply that it is initiated shortly before time of death; in principle at least, terminal sedation can be maintained for weeks or months, as long as it is continued to the point of death.

[4] Pain is not the most common refractory symptom for which terminal sedation is indicated; it is more frequently used to alleviate otherwise untreatable delirium, agitation, or shortness of breath (De Graeff and Dean 2007).

depressed respiration can itself be a cause of death, there has been much concern that escalating doses of morphine might have the effect of shortening the patient's life, even if at each stage the dose is no more than the necessary minimum to control pain. Terminal sedation has been even more controversial in this respect, since there is a greater risk of respiratory depression when the patient is unconscious. Because we are dealing here with the administering of (potentially) life-shortening treatment, rather than the withholding or withdrawal of life-sustaining treatment, it is obvious that we are now on different ethical ground from that canvassed in the previous chapter. This difference notwithstanding, on the Conventional View these techniques for managing end-of-life suffering are also ethically permissible. So we need to ask: how are they to be justified? And how are they ethically distinct from assisted death?

The way in which they are standardly distinguished in the law was nicely summarized by Justice Sopinka in the landmark Canadian assisted suicide case: 'The administration of drugs designed for pain control in dosages which the physician knows will hasten death constitutes active contribution to death by any standard. However, the distinction drawn here is one based upon intention—in the case of palliative care the intention is to ease pain, which has the effect of hastening death, while in the case of assisted suicide [and euthanasia], the intention is undeniably to cause death.'[5] Sopinka here relies on a more general distinction between two different kinds of effect an action can have: one intended by the agent and one that is unintended though foreseen as probable (or even certain). The view that this distinction makes an ethical difference is codified in the Doctrine of Double Effect (DDE)—roughly, the principle that it may sometimes be permissible to bring about a harm as an unintended but foreseen side effect of one's action when it would be impermissible to bring about the same harm as an intended effect. The death of the patient is an intended effect of euthanasia but only (we may assume) an unintended (though foreseen) side effect of aggressive pain management or terminal sedation, whose intended effect is the relief of suffering.[6] Whereas euthanasia is impermissible, so the view goes, the administration of analgesics or sedatives, where necessary to control refractory symptoms, may be permissible even when it has the effect of hastening death.

Philosophical discussions of the DDE standardly cite the administration of opioids or sedatives in order to control end-of-life suffering as a real-life example of its application.[7] In this philosophers accept the factual assumption that these palliative

[5] *Rodriguez* (1993*b*), 607. Cf. *Quill* (1997), 2298–9: 'in some cases, painkilling drugs may hasten a patient's death, but the physician's purpose and intent is, or may be, only to ease his patient's pain. A doctor who assists a suicide, however, "must, necessarily and indubitably, intend primarily that the patient be made dead"' (citation omitted).

[6] David Orentlicher (1998: 305) has argued that this distinction cannot be maintained for terminal sedation: 'Just as a physician performing euthanasia must necessarily intend the patient's death because the patient will certainly die, so must a physician providing terminal sedation intend the patient's death when the sedation is accompanied by the withholding of nutrition and hydration. In such cases the patient will surely die.'

[7] See e.g., Frey 1975: 261; Brock 1993: 173; Beauchamp 1996*a*: 11–12; Boyle 2004; Cavanaugh 2006: 183–90; Beauchamp and Childress 2009: 162; McIntyre 2009.

measures may also have the effect of hastening death. That assumption has tended to pervade the empirical literature as well. In 1990 the Dutch government struck a commission of inquiry to investigate various practices that it collected under the general heading of Medical Decisions concerning the End of Life (MDELs). The Commission was headed by Professor Jan Remmelink, who was at that time Attorney General of the High Council of the Netherlands; its report, which was issued in 1991, is therefore generally referred to as the Remmelink Report.[8] The Commission's definition of an MDEL was meant to cover 'all decisions by physicians concerning courses of action aimed at hastening the end of life of the patient or courses of action for which the physician takes into account the probability that the end of life of the patient is hastened'.[9] Although the principal focus of the report was on euthanasia and assisted suicide, it also provided data on the incidence of end-of-life pain management practices, which it defined as the 'intensifying of alleviation of pain and/or symptoms taking into account the probability that this action will hasten the end of life or in part with the purpose of hastening the end of life of the patient'.[10] It is obvious from this definition that the Commission was working with the assumption that at least in some cases large doses of analgesics were being administered to patients either with the intention of hastening death or, failing that, in full knowledge of the risk of hastening death. This is confirmed by the preamble to the section of the questionnaire sent to Dutch physicians concerning this clinical practice: 'I should like to ask a separate question about the alleviation of pain and symptoms. It happens from time to time that, in serious cases, pain and other symptoms can only be treated with high doses of morphine or morphine-like drugs. This can also shorten life.'[11] The physicians responding to the questionnaire were therefore primed to report on cases in which their administration of analgesics had (probably or certainly) caused the death of their patient, either with or without their intent to do so.

In that light, what is startling about the Remmelink Commission's findings is the number of reported cases. To put this in context, the Commission concluded that approximately 2,300 cases of euthanasia and 400 cases of assisted suicide had occurred during 1990, making up 1.8 and 0.3 per cent respectively of all deaths in the Netherlands for that year. By contrast, its figure for 'the alleviation of pain and/or symptoms, at least taking into account a probable shortening of life' was 22,500 (17.5 per cent of all deaths). In other words, by the Commission's reckoning cases in which the administration of analgesics at least probably caused the death of the patient outnumbered euthanasia cases by roughly a factor of ten.

This reported incidence, furthermore, is very much in line with the results of other empirical studies utilizing the Remmelink methodology. In the Netherlands

---

[8]   For the English version of the full report see van der Maas, van Delden, and Pijnenborg 1992. A short summary of the report's findings was published in van der Maas et al. 1991. The report's findings are discussed in more detail in §7.4, below.

[9]   Van der Maas, van Delden, and Pijnenborg 1992: 19–20.

[10]   Ibid. 127.   [11]   Ibid. 71.

follow-up studies were carried out for the years 1995, 2001, and 2005. During that period the incidence of euthanasia declined from 2.4 per cent of all deaths in 1995 to 1.7 per cent in 2005, while the comparable figures for 'alleviation of pain and other symptoms with possible life-shortening effects' rose from 19.1 per cent (1995) to 24.7 per cent (2005).[12] A 1997 survey of Australian physicians that defined 'alleviation of pain and symptoms with opioids' as 'the administration of doses large enough so that there was a probable life-shortening effect' concluded that 30.9 per cent of all Australian deaths for the period under investigation fell into this category (as compared with 1.8 per cent for euthanasia and 0.1 per cent for assisted suicide).[13] Other studies utilizing the Remmelink methodology reported similar results for Belgium (18.5%) and the United Kingdom (32.8%).[14] Finally, in a 2003 survey of physicians in six European countries (Belgium, Denmark, Italy, the Netherlands, Sweden, and Switzerland) the share of total deaths for the period in question attributed to 'alleviation of pain and symptoms with possible life-shortening effect' varied from 19 per cent in Italy to 26 per cent in Denmark.[15]

The questionnaire used in a 1996 survey of end-of-life experiences and attitudes on the part of Danish physicians invited responses to seven scenarios, all of them variations of the same fact situation of an end-stage cancer patient whose pain is being treated with morphine.[16] One of the scenarios, labelled 'pain relieving lethal morphine (no informed consent)', was described as follows: 'In order to relieve pain morphine is given in such quantities that it is obvious that the patient's life will be shortened by the treatment. This happens without the informed consent of the patient. The patient dies from the treatment.' Another scenario was identical to this, except that patient consent was obtained. Of respondents, 53 per cent reported that they had acted as the staff did in the first scenario, 80 per cent for the second—this despite the fact that in both instances they were being instructed to report only cases in which the morphine infusion was the *obvious* cause of death.

Both the methodology and the reported results of these various studies are therefore based on the assumption that the administration of high doses of opioids can have life-shortening effects. However, this assumption is open to question. After an extensive review of the available evidence on opioid use, Susan Fohr drew the following conclusion:

It is important to emphasize that there is no debate among specialists in palliative care and pain control on this issue. There is a broad consensus that when used appropriately, respiratory depression from opioid analgesics is a rarely occurring side effect. The belief that palliative care hastens death is counter to the experience of physicians with the most experience in this area.

---

[12] Van der Maas et al. 1996; Onwuteaka-Philipsen et al. 2003; van der Heide et al. 2007.

[13] Kuhse et al. 1997.

[14] Deliens et al. 2000; Seale 2006. The UK figure may be unrealistically high; a subsequent, and more finely grained, study (Seale 2009a) found the incidence to be 17.1 per cent, which would be more in line with the other European results.

[15] van der Heide et al. 2003.   [16] Folker et al. 1996.

No studies have shown that patients' lives have been shortened through the administration of appropriate pain medication.[17]

On the contrary, Fohr argued, 'the correct use of morphine is more likely to prolong a patient's life . . . because he is more rested and pain-free'.[18] While the administration of opioids does carry a known risk of respiratory depression, the risk is highest when opioids are first begun. Thereafter, pain acts as a natural antagonist to this effect and as the level of pain increases so does tolerance to the effect.[19] Increasing doses of morphine, therefore, need not raise the risk of causing death by depressing respiration.

If Fohr's conclusion is correct then the 'appropriate' use of high-dose opioids is seldom, if ever, a ('but for') cause of death. But then how can we reconcile her conclusion with the survey results that purport to show a high incidence of life-shortening administration of analgesics? One possible explanation is that these results are largely an artefact of the survey methodology employed in the studies. In the surveys utilizing the Remmelink methodology respondent physicians were asked to report instances of the administration of opioids in large enough doses to 'possibly' or 'probably' hasten death. Because the actual cause of death is left ambiguous by this wording, it is possible that physicians simply reported all cases in which high doses of opioids had been administered in order to control severe pain (or other symptoms). If so, then there is no reason to conclude that death in all these cases was actually caused by the narcotic, as opposed to the disease condition (typically cancer). The respondent physicians may not even have believed that opioid adminstration was the cause of death in all cases they reported; it would have been enough that they could not conclusively rule out this possibility.

The Danish study, however, was not ambiguous on this point, since the relevant scenarios were labelled 'lethal morphine' and physicians were told that 'it is obvious that the patient's life will be shortened by the treatment'. Perversely, the high percentage of respondents who reported having engaged in this clinical practice (with or without patient consent) may be partly due to this very disambiguation. That is, many physicians would have had the experience of administering high doses of opioids to manage severe pain. Since the presented scenarios seem to presuppose that such doses hasten death, physicians may have concluded that this *must* have happened in the cases they recall from their own experience. They therefore report these cases as ones in which the morphine infusion was the cause of death.

This interpretation of the various survey results is, of course, speculative, but it is reinforced by the gap between myth and reality that was Fohr's principal concern. There is, Fohr contends, a widespread belief among physicians that large doses of opioids will hasten the deaths of their patients, despite the lack of clinical evidence for this effect. This belief may lead physicians to overreport (supposed) cases of 'alleviation

---

[17] Fohr 1998: 319. Cf. Ashby 1997; Morita et al. 2001; Sykes and Thorns 2003. For a sceptical view see Allmark et al. 2010: 172.

[18] Fohr 1998: 317.   [19] Ibid. 316.

of pain and symptoms with possible life-shortening effect' by encouraging them to assume that every case of the aggressive treatment of severe pain must fall into this category.

However this might be, it is in any case no easy matter to determine cause of death in the kinds of end-of-life situations we are now envisaging. Doses of morphine large enough to risk side effects such as respiratory depression will normally be used to relieve only the most severe pain. Timothy Quill reports that 'some dying patients experience a "crescendo" of pain just prior to dying, requiring rapidly escalating doses of analgesics'.[20] In the various surveys cited above physicians who reported having administered possibly lethal doses of opioids were asked to estimate the time by which life had thereby been shortened. When offered the option, between a third and half of respondents typically said that it had not been shortened at all, while 15–25 per cent replied 'unknown'. Of the remainder, nearly all respondents estimated less than one week and about half of that group opted for less than twenty-four hours. It seems likely, therefore, that many patients die shortly after having been administered 'rapidly escalating doses', but it does not of course follow that they died because of them. In many such cases the analgesic will not be a ('but for') cause of death, while in others it will be simply impossible to determine cause of death with any degree of certainty.[21]

There is, of course, another possible explanation for the apparent disparity between the clinical evidence, as Fohr summarizes it, and the survey results. That evidence pertains exclusively to what Fohr calls 'the administration of appropriate pain medication'. By 'appropriate' she means 'the minimum dose necessary to achieve pain control'.[22] She readily concedes that 'an excessive dose can, of course, cause respiratory depression'. It is also possible, therefore, that at least some respondents to the surveys were reporting the administration of 'inappropriate' doses above the necessary minimum. It would be less surprising in these latter cases if the opioids administered did in fact hasten death.

The incidence of terminal sedation has been less frequently studied than that of opioid administration, probably because this measure has only more recently achieved the status of standard palliative practice. Most of the studies cited earlier did not identify terminal sedation as a distinct end-of-life measure. However, in the survey of six European countries physicians were also asked about this practice and those results were reported separately.[23] The percentage of all deaths preceded by terminal sedation ranged from a low of 2.5 per cent in Denmark to a high of 8.5 per cent in Italy. However, a recent survey conducted in the United Kingdom reported a much higher figure of 16.5 per cent.[24] In the Netherlands the two most recent studies found an incidence of 7.1 per cent of all deaths for the year 2005.[25] This figure locates terminal sedation in the middle ground between the incidence of euthanasia (1.7% for

---

[20] Quill 1998: 334.
[21] As Allmark et al. 2010 have pointed out, randomized clinical trials are impossible in this context.
[22] Fohr 1998: 316.   [23] Miccinesi et al. 2006.
[24] Seale 2009*a*.   [25] van der Heide et al. 2007; Rietjens et al. 2008.

the same year) and high doses of opioids (24.7%). Interestingly, in the five-year period from 2001 to 2005 the incidence of euthanasia in the Netherlands declined (from 2.6% to 1.7%) while that of terminal sedation increased (from 5.6% to 7.1%).[26] This trend may signal not only that terminal sedation is becoming an increasingly common practice in palliative medicine but also that it is coming to be preferred to euthanasia even in a jurisdiction in which the latter is legal.[27] If so, then this fact will only strengthen suspicions that terminal sedation is increasingly being practised as 'slow euthanasia'.[28]

Like opioid use, terminal sedation is widely believed by physicians to be a cause of death. In one survey of Dutch physicians who had administered this palliative treatment some 60 per cent reported that the life of the patient had been shortened by periods ranging from a day to more than a month.[29] However, there is a crucial distinction to keep in mind here. As noted earlier, terminal sedation is frequently, though not invariably, accompanied by withholding or withdrawing artificial nutrition and hydration. In the European study roughly one-third (Italy) to two-thirds (Denmark) of all reported cases fell into this category. Since patient refusal of nutrition and hydration is a recognized ('but for') cause of death, it is important to disentangle this effect from the possible life-shortening impact of the sedation itself.[30] But when we do so, there may not be much residual impact left. A number of studies have cast doubt on the likelihood that sedatives prescribed at levels appropriate for symptom control at the end of life, up to and including deep continuous sedation, will shorten patients' lives.[31]

The widespread assumption that the administration of 'appropriate' levels of opioids and sedatives will hasten death is therefore at least open to question, in which case these measures do not furnish ideal instances to illustrate the operation of the Doctrine of Double Effect. If the assumption is false then our discussion of these measures could stop right here. However, there are good reasons to keep it going. For one thing, the facts of the matter are at least unclear. It may not be safe to assume, as most discussants have, that high-dose opioids or sedatives hasten death, but it also may not be safe to assume that they do not. Furthermore, the causal issue depends on being able to distinguish 'appropriate' dose levels of these medications (which may not hasten death) from 'inappropriate' ones (which do). But in clinical settings this will be a very blurry

[26]   Rietjens et al. 2008. The incidence of terminal sedation has also increased sharply—from 8.2 per cent of all deaths in 2001 to 14.5 per cent in 2007—in Belgium, where euthanasia has been legal since 2002 (Bilsen et al. 2009).

[27]   The incidence of euthanasia in the Netherlands has increased somewhat since 2005, rising to 2 per cent of all deaths in 2009. I know of no comparable figures for terminal sedation for this period.

[28]   Billings and Block 1996. Cf. Orentlicher 1998.

[29]   Rietjens et al. 2004. For later studies with similar results see Rietjens et al. 2006; Rietjens et al. 2008; Claessens et al. 2008; Rurup et al. 2009.

[30]   Since I am still dealing in this chapter with voluntary measures, I will assume that in cases of terminal sedation artificial nutrition and hydration are being withheld/withdrawn at the request of the patient. Non-voluntary cases will be considered later (in Ch. 5).

[31]   Chater et al. 1998; Morita et al. 2001; Sykes and Thorns 2003a, 2003b; Maltoni et al. 2009.

distinction at best, complicated by the fact that the pathological cause of death may in many cases be impossible to determine. Finally, whether these measures actually hasten death or not, they are at least widely believed to do so and are standardly justified in the face of that belief. For these reasons, when we are addressing the ethical issues raised by them it is best to proceed on the basis of the most conservative assumption—that is, to ask whether (and how) they can be ethically justified *if* they do indeed hasten death. Those who have made that assumption have relied on the DDE as their justifying device. It is therefore appropriate to ask whether it is capable of bearing this argumentative weight.

3.2 The Doctrine of Double Effect

At this point it is time to revisit Anita, the fifty-three-year-old businesswoman whose metastasized colon cancer can no longer be treated with chemotherapy. Anita is experiencing considerable pain which cannot be completely relieved even by administering high doses of opioids. There is also little that can be done for her other physical symptoms, which include nausea, vomiting, and diarrhoea. Her doctor has told her that she has at most a few more weeks left, during which time all these symptoms will grow worse. Anita has told her doctor, and her family, that she does not want to endure those final weeks. Let us now extend the story by supposing that her doctor offers her the option of deep, continuous sedation, to be maintained to the point of death. For the sake of the argument we will stipulate that the sedation will hasten Anita's death, by some hours or days, by depressing her respiration. Her doctor informs her of this expected outcome but also makes it very clear to her that his aim in offering this palliative treatment is not to shorten her life but rather to make it possible for her to avoid any further suffering. He also explains that Anita has the option of forgoing artificial nutrition and hydration during the period of sedation. After discussion with her family, Anita agrees to be sedated but requests that she be given food and water, since she does not wish to die of dehydration. Like her physician, her aim in giving consent is not to hasten her death but merely to avoid further suffering. When Anita's death subsequently occurs, respiratory depression is one of its ('but for') causes (as is her cancer). The Doctrine of Double Effect tells us that under these circumstances the terminal sedation is justified. The question is: how does it reach this conclusion?

The origins of the DDE are usually traced back to Thomas Aquinas's analysis of justifiable homicide in self-defence.[32] By the sixteenth century it had become an established feature of Catholic moral thinking, but more recently it has broadened out to secular philosophy as well in its application to a wide range of moral problems including abortion, the use of lethal force against civilians in wartime, and the use of

---

[32] For comprehensive histories of the Doctrine see Mangan 1949 and Cavanaugh 2006: ch. 1.

analgesics or sedatives to relieve suffering. Given the lengthy history of the DDE, it is surprisingly difficult to find a canonical formulation of it.[33] Rather than attempt a general formulation, I will outline the DDE as it applies specifically to the case of Anita's terminal sedation. Whether this version can be extrapolated successfully to all the other problems to which the Doctrine has been applied is an open question, especially since commentators have suggested that at least some of these applications are dubious or downright mistaken.[34]

Anita's physician has a treatment option available to him (terminal sedation) which (we are assuming) will have two effects: it will relieve Anita's suffering (by rendering her unconscious) and it will hasten her death (by depressing her respiration). In order for the DDE to have application in this scenario we must further assume that one of these effects (relief of suffering) is good, the other (death) bad. The DDE then tells us that the treatment is permissible only if three conditions are satisfied:[35]

Intention. In administering the treatment the physician's aim is the good effect rather than the bad effect.

Causation. The bad effect is not a ('but for') cause of the good effect.

Proportionality. There is a proportionately serious reason for bringing about the bad effect.

Before we go any further, there are several features of the DDE that are worthy of note. The first is that while these three conditions may be individually necessary in order for terminal sedation to be permissible, they are not jointly sufficient, since they omit other equally necessary conditions.[36] In Anita's case one of these conditions stands out: obtaining her informed consent (or that of her substitute decision-maker) to the sedation. As we have constructed the case, this condition is also satisfied, but it is no part of the DDE.

---

[33] Various versions of the Doctrine can be found in Mangan 1949; Boyle 1980; Quinn 1989a: 334 n. 3; Marquis 1991; Bennett 1995: 196–7; McIntyre 2004; Cavanaugh 2006: 26 ff.

[34] See e.g. McIntyre 2001: esp. 243 ff. Warren Quinn (1989a: 343 n. 17) has argued that the Doctrine does not apply to the administration of analgesics (and, by implication, sedatives) since in this case there is no conflict between the rights or interests of different persons.

[35] The DDE is often formulated with a fourth condition as well: the action in itself must not be bad (or wrong or impermissible)—see e.g. Mangan 1949: 43, 60; McIntyre 2004. I have omitted this condition in part because of notorious difficulties in identifying what an action is 'in itself'—that is, apart from its consequences (Bennett 1995). In the sedation case if the physician's action is described as 'administering a sedative' then this fourth condition would appear to be readily satisfied; likewise, if it is described as 'relieving Anita's suffering'. But what if we describe it as 'hastening Anita's death'? It would not be a happy result if the DDE's justification of the physician's action were to depend on the particular description chosen. This problem could be circumvented if there were some rubric for identifying the pertinent act-description(s). However, the rubric generally favoured by deontologists relies on the agent's intention(s). For instance, Joseph Mangan's formulation of this fourth condition requires that 'the action itself *from its very object* be good or at least indifferent' (Mangan 1949: 43, emphasis added). If by 'object' Mangan means 'intended end' then the character of 'the action itself' is determined by the agent's intention(s). But in that case the fourth condition is redundant, since on its most plausible reading it turns out to be entailed by the intention condition (cf. Boyle 1980: 530–2).

[36] Joseph Boyle (1980: 532) formulates the DDE as providing both necessary and sufficient conditions for justification, but I think that this cannot be correct.

Next, the Doctrine presupposes a deontological ethic with a strong 'sanctity-of-life' principle which generally prohibits killing (or at least killing humans). Within such an ethic the Doctrine functions to define a justifiable exception to this general prohibition. It makes no sense, and has no place, within a straightforward consequentialist ethic that would determine when causing death is justified by means of a case-by-case harm/benefit comparison.[37] Consequentialists would therefore have no reason to embrace either the intention or the causation condition for its own sake—that is, unless these factors had some bearing on the resultant balance of harms and benefits. (Depending on how it is interpreted, consequentialists may accept some version of the proportionality condition—more on this below.) So if you are attracted by the consequentialist treatment of these cases, you will have no use for the DDE; under appropriate circumstances (such as Anita's) terminal sedation will be justifiable without it.

The sanctity-of-life principle presupposed by the DDE may, but need not, be absolute. It might be formulated as a prohibition on the taking of human life with other exceptions—the death penalty, killing of enemy combatants, killing in self-defence—which (*pace* Aquinas on the last case) are not justified by means of the Doctrine. Or it might be formulated as a prohibition on the taking of *innocent* human life for which the (generalized version of the) DDE defines the sole class of exceptions. For our purposes it does not matter which of these deontological backgrounds is in place.

The other assumption that is necessary in order to apply the DDE to the sedation case is its value assignments to the two effects in question. One of these assignments is not controversial: we will all agree that the relief of Anita's suffering is a good thing. But the other is: why should we agree that Anita's death is a bad thing, thus that hastening it is a bad thing? Earlier (§1.1) I argued that the best explanation of the badness of death is provided by the deprivation account, according to which death is (extrinsically) bad to the extent that it deprives us of the (intrinsic) goods of life. In that discussion I noted the obvious implication of this account: 'On the deprivation account death is not always harmful or something to be feared; it can be beneficial or something to be embraced. Whether it harms or benefits depends on the circumstances of the person's life—and, in particular, on the expected quality (and duration) of the person's continued life. If someone's prospects are sufficiently bleak then death can be a welcome release.' This implication would appear to apply to Anita, whose prospects are bleak if anyone's are. Her suffering has reached the point where she sees no value in her continued life for the weeks she has remaining. Under these circumstances it is difficult to see how hastening Anita's death *harms* her, thus why it would be extrinsically bad, since it is hard to see how it deprives her of anything that would be

---

[37] As one defender of the DDE has said, it is 'simply a non-consequentialist way of thinking about hard cases' (Cavanaugh 2006: 185).

intrinsically good for her.[38] But if we reject this valuation of Anita's death then the Doctrine will have no application to this case.[39]

Defenders of the DDE may object that the wrong comparison is being made in the foregoing analysis. The deprivation account invites us to compare two future lives for Anita: a longer one, which contains more suffering (with no counterbalancing goods), and a shorter one with less suffering. On that comparison the shorter one looks better, since it minimizes suffering, which yields the result that hastening Anita's death would be a net benefit to her. But this comparison ignores the fact that, *ex hypothesi*, Anita will be rendered unconscious by the terminal sedation and thus will not be suffering. The relevant comparison, the defenders will urge, is between sedation that hastens death and sedation that does not hasten death, thus between a shorter period of unconsciousness and a longer one. This, however, does little to help, since it still fails to explain why dying sooner would be worse for Anita. From Anita's standpoint the shorter and longer lives would appear to be of equal value, since she is continuously unconscious in both cases, while for the DDE to have purchase the shorter one must be worse. It is hard to see how this might be so—that is, what the added value would be for Anita of a few more hours or days of unconsciousness. Of course, defenders of the Doctrine might believe that merely being alive has intrinsic value on its own, quite apart from any goods that the life might contain, but this view seems to have little to recommend it.[40]

The deontological defenders of the Doctrine might be better advised to reject the assumption, implicit in the foregoing argument, that the extrinsic badness of hastening death derives in this way from the badness of the resultant condition of being dead. Perhaps conceding this assumption is already starting to play the consequentialist's game. If this route is taken, then deontologists will owe us an explanation of why hastening death is bad (or wrong or impermissible) independently of the harm it does its victim. We will explore the options available to them more fully later (§4.1) when we discuss the ethics of killing, but we can anticipate that discussion by noting that one of them is closed off in the case of Anita. Generally speaking, one might seek the

---

[38] The DDE borders on incoherence here. On the one hand, it treats relief of Anita's suffering as a good thing, which presupposes that her suffering is a bad thing. On the other hand, though Anita's death would relieve her suffering, the Doctrine treats it as a bad thing.

[39] The ethical irrelevance of the DDE in situations such as Anita's has been argued in Allmark et al. 2010: 175–6. It is worth noting, however, that an extended version of the DDE might still apply in these cases. The standard version holds that it is worse to intend a harm to someone than to bring it about as an unintended but foreseen side effect of one's action. Where benefits are concerned, rather than harms, we might expect the opposite to hold: it is better to intend a benefit to someone than to bring it about as an unintended but foreseen side effect. If so, then the extended version of the DDE, applying to both harms and benefits, would imply that, other factors equal, intentionally hastening Anita's death, in order to prevent her suffering, would actually be better than doing something that foreseeably brings it about. Jeff McMahan (2002: 461) makes a point similar to this for the doing/allowing distinction.

[40] Patients in a persistent vegetative state, due to oxygen deprivation or severe head trauma, may survive for years in that condition. However, it is difficult to see how these additional years are of any benefit to them, or how their absence would be any loss. This issue is discussed at greater length in §4.1, below.

wrongness of killing in either (or both) of two directions: the harm done to the victim (through loss of life) or the violation of the victim's autonomy. Both factors are in play in standard scenarios of unlawful killing, such as murder. But neither is in play for Anita who, it appears, will not be harmed by her death and who has consented to the terminal sedation despite having been informed that it will shorten her life. When both harm and autonomy violation are subtracted from the picture, it is hard to see what remains that might explain why causing death is assumed to be a bad thing in this instance. It might remain for the deontologist to insist that no explanation is needed: causing the death of a person just is intrinsically bad (or wrong or impermissible) even though there is nothing bad about it. But that seems a desperate *ad hoc* resort. In general, it never seems out of place to ask for the bad-making characteristics of bad actions.

We now have a reason to question the applicability of the DDE to Anita's terminal sedation, even if we assume that the treatment will hasten her death. However, it will still be worthwhile to take a closer look at the Doctrine's three conditions. For reasons that will eventually become clear, I will consider them in reverse order. The proportionality condition requires that there be a 'proportionately serious reason' for bringing about the bad effect.[41] It is easy to see why some version of this condition is necessary, since otherwise the DDE might justify terminally sedating Anita in order to save her from some relatively minor suffering (the pain of unrequited love perhaps). But the proportionality condition as stated raises unavoidable questions: how do we measure the seriousness of reasons? And when is a reason sufficiently serious to justify causing Anita's death? One answer to these questions is provided by the consequentialist, who would measure the seriousness of the reason in terms of the value of the good effect (relieving Anita's suffering) and require only that this value outweigh the disvalue of the bad effect.[42] Although this interpretation of proportionality has some support in the double effect literature,[43] the straightforward consequentialist balancing it calls for seems too weak to be a good fit with the deontological presuppositions of the Doctrine. Deontologists hold that agents have at least a *pro tanto* duty not to harm others, a duty that is particularly stringent when the harm in question is death. The function of the first two conditions is to rebut the presumption that terminal sedation violates this duty (since, *ex hypothesi*, it causes death) and it is natural to expect the third condition to behave in the same way. But in order for it to do so, it must surely set a higher threshold for justification than a mere positive balance of benefit over harm; at the very least it must require that the benefit substantially or significantly outweigh the harm.[44]

---

[41] Joseph Boyle (1980: 528) speaks of a 'grave reason' or 'sufficiently serious moral reasons' (1991: 476). Anyone who thinks that it should be a comparatively simple matter to provide an intuitively satisfactory interpretation of the proportionality condition should look at Kagan 1989: 151 ff.

[42] In Anita's case this condition would appear to be trivially satisfied, since for the consequentialist the 'bad' effect (death) will have no disvalue.

[43] See e.g. Donagan 1977: 161, and the sources cited in McIntyre 2001: 222.

[44] This approach would bring the proportionality condition into line with Judith Thomson's 'thresholds for rights'; see Thomson 1990: ch. 6, and the discussion in Brennan 1995.

So one reading of the proportionality condition would go something like this: in the terminal sedation scenario there is a proportionately serious reason for causing death just in case the disvalue of death will be substantially outweighed by the value of relief of suffering. But this still does not capture everything that should matter to the deontologist. To see why, it will help to take a brief look at the way proportionality conditions function in other settings. Consider self-defence, for instance, which is another classic exception to the general *pro tanto* duty not to cause injury or death to another. Proportionality here requires that the harm done to the attacker not significantly outweigh the harm prevented by averting the attack (I am not permitted to kill you to prevent you from stepping on my toes).[45] But it additionally requires that the harm done to the attacker be no more than is necessary in order to repel the attack (I may not shoot you to save my life if I know that yelling at you would work just as well).[46] It is this further necessity requirement that we have so far not captured in the Doctrine's proportionality condition. A similar requirement appears in just war theory, as one of the limitations on the use of lethal force, especially against non-combatants, in pursuit of legitimate military objectives.[47] It turns up as well in the rubric used by the Canadian Supreme Court to determine when legislation infringing a right secured by the *Charter of Rights and Freedoms* is 'demonstrably justified in a free and democratic society'.[48] This rubric includes a proportionality condition, one of whose components is 'minimal impairment': roughly speaking, the requirement that the law not limit the right to a greater extent than is necessary in order to achieve its objective.[49] So the DDE's proportionality condition must at least be modified somewhat thus: there is a proportionately serious reason for causing death just in case the disvalue of death will be substantially outweighed by the value of relief of suffering and there is no less harmful means available for relieving suffering. Satisfaction of this further requirement was built in to Anita's terminal sedation scenario, but it is nonetheless worth noting how the requirement is an indispensable element of the proportionality condition.[50]

---

[45] Notice that in self-defence the harm prevented may actually be less than the harm inflicted: I may be justified in killing an attacker who is threatening to put out my eyes. In double effect scenarios, by contrast, the good to be done (or harm to be prevented) is usually required to be greater than the harm inflicted. This asymmetry may be a reason for thinking that (Aquinas notwithstanding) the DDE is not the best vehicle for justifying self-defence.

[46] In the Canadian *Criminal Code* (s. 34) one condition necessary for justifying the infliction of death or grievous bodily harm on an assailant is that the victim 'believes, on reasonable grounds, that he cannot otherwise preserve himself from death or grievous bodily harm'.

[47] Proportionality plays a dual role in just war theory, as a part of both *jus ad bello* and *jus in bellum*. See e.g. Hurka 2005.

[48] The rubric was first formulated in *Oakes* (1986).

[49] For a fuller account, see Sumner 2004: ch. 3.

[50] Tom Hurka (2005, 2008) has pointed out that in just war theory the necessity requirement is usually treated as standing on its own rather than as part of the proportionality condition. On the other hand, when it is mentioned at all by defenders of the DDE it is usually treated as one aspect of proportionality (e.g. by Cavanaugh 2006: 32–3). I take no stand on this issue: the important point is that some such condition is indispensable to the Doctrine. (Hurka does allow that proportionality in just war theory can be interpreted so as to include necessity.)

Even as modified, however, the proportionality condition is still not a good fit for the deontologist, since it accepts the consequentialist's view that the seriousness of moral reasons (for or against actions) derives entirely from outcomes: in this case, from the value of relief of suffering and disvalue of death. But no deontologist should accept this view, since it attaches no independent moral weight to such deontic factors as duties, obligations, and rights. There is no reason to think, the deontologist should say, that the comparative values of the two effects exhaust the reasons in play, even when we add the further necessity condition.[51] For one thing, as we have already seen, the stringency of the duty not to cause death may be thought to be a function of factors other than the badness of death. Furthermore, there could be other relevant deontological factors in the terminal sedation scenario. Anita's physician has role-specific obligations to her, which will include the obligation to respect her wishes and also the obligation to minimize her suffering (in each case, consistent with other duties or obligations). Additionally, he may have promised her to do whatever he can to ease her dying (with the same proviso) or he may have made similar promises to her family. For the deontologist all these non-consequentialist considerations have to be in play as well in deciding when there is a 'proportionately serious reason' for going ahead with the terminal sedation. Putting all these pieces together, T. A. Cavanaugh formulates the proportionality condition thus: 'the agent has proportionately grave reasons for acting, addressing his relevant obligations, comparing the consequences, and, considering the necessity of the evil, exercising due care to eliminate or mitigate it'.[52] This compendious formulation has the advantage of inclusiveness but the disadvantage of indeterminacy. If this is the way to understand the proportionality condition, then there will be no algorithm or decision procedure for deciding when, all things considered, the balance of reasons in favour of the sedation is serious enough.[53]

Since proportionality, in one form or another, has a role to play in a broad range of ethical and legal contexts, it does not mark out the DDE as a distinctive justificatory rubric for the deontologist. Whatever is unique about the Doctrine must therefore be contributed by the other two conditions. Causation, as we have seen, requires that the bad effect (death) not be a ('but for') cause of the good effect (relief of suffering). In this respect the causal structure of terminal sedation is meant to be distinguished from that of euthanasia. In plotting the following causal sequences we continue to assume that terminal sedation involves administering no more medication (whether a barbiturate or a benzodiazepine) than is necessary to induce deep, continuous unconsciousness, while euthanasia involves administering enough medication (a barbiturate or muscle relaxant) to cause virtually immediate death.

---

[51] This point is made in Cavanaugh 2006: 31 ff.

[52] Ibid. 36.

[53] This point is made in McIntyre 2001: 223. It is not fatal to the DDE since any pluralist moderate deontology must face the problem of how to weigh conflicting *pro tanto* duties and reach an 'all things considered' conclusion.

	Action	Consequences
TS:	Administer medication → Unconsciousness → Relief of suffering
	↘ Respiratory depression → Death
E:	Administer medication → Death → Relief of suffering

In this diagram the solid arrows represent causal relations. Thus the immediate consequence of the sedation is to render Anita unconscious, which in turn relieves her suffering. By contrast, the immediate consequence of the lethal medication used in euthanasia is Anita's death and it is by virtue of that consequence that her suffering is relieved. However, we are assuming that the sedation also causes respiratory depression which in turn hastens Anita's death. The important feature of the causal structure of terminal sedation, as far as the DDE is concerned, is that there is no arrow from Anita's death to relief of her suffering. Her suffering is relieved by means of her loss of consciousness, not by means of her death. (Once she is unconscious her death provides no *further* relief.) Her death is therefore a side effect relative to relief of her suffering, by virtue of the fact that they have a common cause.

Assuming that we have a clear causal distinction here, we can ask why it should be thought to be ethically relevant. Presumably for the consequentialist there is nothing to choose between these two causal sequences, at least as long as there is no more suffering for Anita in one than in the other and no collateral effects on others that differentiate them. Why, then, should the DDE entail that the terminal sedation sequence is permissible and the euthanasia one not? The standard answer in the double effect literature is that in the latter sequence the good effect is being produced *by means of* the bad one.[54] But this 'by means of' is not merely causal; it is also intentional. The intentional structures of the two treatment options are therefore as follows:

	Action	Means	End
TS:	Administer medication ⇨ Induce unconsciousness ⇨ Relieve suffering
E:	Administer medication ⇨ Hasten death ⇨	Relieve suffering

In this diagram the open arrows represent the intentional relation 'in order to'. The problem, as the Doctrine sees it, is the agent's means–end reasoning in the euthanasia case: in inducing Anita's death in order to relieve her suffering the physician violates the injunction that 'evil not be done that good may come of it'.[55] And the problem with violating that injunction is that, by virtue of being utilized as a means to an intended good effect, the bad effect is also intended. By contrast, in the terminal sedation sequence the bad effect is not an intended means to the good.[56] The relevant

---

[54] See e.g. Mangan 1949: 43.   [55] Romans 3: 8.

[56] There are complications here, since if the sedation is certain to hasten Anita's death and if there is no other way to relieve her suffering (both of which we have assumed) then it is causally impossible to relieve her suffering without causing her death. This makes her death a necessary ('but for') condition of relief of her suffering. I will ignore these complications and assume that there is a perspicuous way of showing why death is a ('but for') cause of relief of suffering in euthanasia but not in terminal sedation.

difference between the two scenarios is therefore one of intention, not causation.[57] This, then, takes us finally to the first condition, which requires that the physician aim only at the good effect and not the bad one.

The contention that lies at the heart of the Doctrine of Double Effect is that 'it is sometimes permissible to bring about a harm as a merely foreseen side effect of an action aimed at some good end, even though it would have been impermissible to bring about the same harm as a means to that end'.[58] This contention in turn rests on the distinction between intending an effect of one's action and (merely) foreseeing it.[59] It is said to make a significant ethical difference whether, in offering Anita terminal sedation, her physician intends both to relieve her suffering and to hasten her death or intends only the former while foreseeing the latter.[60]

Relying on the intending/foreseeing distinction in this context is complicated by the ambiguity of physicians' reported intentions when they administer opioids or sedatives.[61] For one thing, it is far from clear that all, or even most, doctors fully understand the difference between intending an outcome and foreseeing it as certain. Even after considerable prompting by an interviewer, physicians who have adminis- tered terminal sedation are either unwilling or unable to clarify whether the patient's death was an intended or a merely foreseen outcome.[62] When they do, there is evidence that they resist the dichotomizing 'intended/foreseen', preferring to speak instead of partial, or ambiguous, or multi-layered intentions, or to assume a continuum whose extremes are marked by something like 'fully intended' and 'merely foreseen' but which admits of a grey area between them.[63] These ambiguities and complications concerning intention may not show that it is impossible to draw a clear intending/ foreseeing distinction, but they do establish that there is not a clearly understood distinction out there in the clinical setting. In that case, the DDE may not mark any unambiguous distinction between permissible and impermissible end-of-life measures.

Even if we put this complication to one side, however, and assume that the DDE is capable of drawing a bright line, there seems to be no way for it to draw the line where the Conventional View locates it. Death is clearly the intended outcome of euthanasia, but it is equally clearly the intended outcome in some cases of treatment refusal, such as the removal of a ventilator or a feeding tube.[64] In that case the DDE will locate these 'passive' cases on the 'wrong' side of the line for the purposes of the Conventional

---

[57] Jonathan Bennett (1995: § 61) reaches the same conclusion. The causation condition is not entirely redundant, since it explains why in terminal sedation the bad effect need not be intended. But it is subsidiary: it is not where the ethical action is.

[58] McIntyre 2001: 219.

[59] We need the qualifier 'merely' here, since presumably intended effects are also foreseen.

[60] Whatever his intentional stance is towards hastening Anita's death, he clearly intends to relieve her suffering by rendering her unconscious. Thus the issue is whether he also intends the other effect.

[61] This ambiguity can apply equally to more 'active' interventions, such as physician-assisted suicide. Timothy Quill (1993) has detailed the multiple intentions that attended his prescription of barbiturates to his patient Diane, who subsequently used them to end her life (Quill 1991).

[62] Douglas, Kerridge, and Ankeny 2008: 393.

[63] Quill 1993; Quill, Dresser, and Brock 1997; Douglas, Kerridge, and Ankeny 2008.

[64] Cf. the discussion in §2.3, above.

View. Put another way, if the DDE supports the conclusion that euthanasia is impermissible then it will equally support the conclusion that (in at least some cases) the removal of a ventilator or feeding tube is impermissible. And these results do not serve the needs of the Conventional View.

The deployment of the intending/foreseeing distinction in this context can also be challenged from a different direction. We are working here with the assumption that the hastening of death is a certain, and therefore predictable, outcome of deep, continuous sedation. It might reasonably be wondered whether it is possible to foresee an outcome of one's action as certain and *not* intend it. Here is a non-medical case to test our intuitions. Alphonse is a revolutionary who wishes to topple the monarchy of Ruritania and usher in a democracy. In furtherance of this goal he plans to assassinate the Grand Duke by tossing a bomb into his carriage as it passes during a procession. Alphonse knows that the Grand Duchess will also be in the carriage. Assassinating her is not necessary for the success of his plan, since she has no real power in the realm. Alphonse succeeds in tossing the bomb into the carriage and killing both the Duke and the Duchess. He clearly intended to kill the Duke, but did he also intend to kill the Duchess?

It seems to me that we are likely to be of two minds in answering this question (at least I am). On the one hand, Alphonse tossed the bomb knowing full well that it would kill the Duchess. Once he learned that the Duchess would also be in the carriage he could have decided to wait for another opportunity to kill the Duke, one that would not also put her in harm's way, but he did not. We therefore cannot say that killing her was unintentional, as though it was the result of some accident or mistake. But if it was not unintentional then he must have intended it. On the other hand, the death of the Duchess was also clearly a by-product or side effect of the death of the Duke. Had she not been in the carriage no part of Alphonse's plan would have been affected and he would still have tossed the bomb, whereas had the Duke not been there he would have refrained. There is therefore some significant difference between the two deaths as far as Alphonse's planning is concerned and it seems appropriate to mark this by saying that he intended the one while (merely) foreseeing the other.

If we are to resolve this question one way or the other some disambiguation of the notion of intention will be required. We do seem to have a broad sense of intention that inclines us towards saying that Alphonse did intend to kill the Duchess, a sense in which an agent will be said to intend all the consequences of his action that he foresees as certain or even probable.[65] Clearly this sense is ill-suited to the Doctrine of Double

---

[65] Henry Sidgwick defended this broad sense in arguing that 'for purposes of exact moral or jural discussion, it is best to include under the term "intention" all the consequences of an act that are foreseen as certain or probable' (Sidgwick 1907: 202). However, the context makes it clear that Sidgwick favoured this interpretation primarily in order to ensure that agents such as Alphonse are held responsible for the foreseeable collateral damage that they cause in pursuit of their plans (Sidgwick discusses a scenario similar to Alphonse's in a footnote). This connection between intention and responsibility also explains the familiar legal doctrine that agents will be held to have intended 'the natural and foreseeable consequences' of their actions. For lawyerly discussions of this doctrine see Pedain 2003; Kaveny 2004; G. Williams 2007: ch. 1.

Effect, since it entails that Anita's physician must have intended to hasten her death. But we also have a narrower sense in which intending some outcome is related to wanting or desiring or welcoming it. Alphonse had a reason to want the Duke dead, but not the Duchess, so while his death was intended hers was an unwanted, therefore unintended, side effect. While this seems close to the distinction we are looking for, it is still not quite right. To say that Alphonse wanted the Duke dead may suggest that this outcome was positively valenced for him, one he would be pleased to accomplish. But for all we know Alphonse might be deeply repulsed by the act of killing the Duke; for him it might be a repugnant, but regrettably necessary, means to the end (toppling the monarchy) which he clearly does want. Where some action or state of affairs is intended as a means to an adopted end, it is better to say that for the agent it was sought as a necessary element in a larger plan. Alphonse's plan was something like this: topple the monarchy by killing the Grand Duke, kill the Duke by tossing the bomb into his carriage. In this deliberative sequence killing the Duke figures as a necessary step in carrying out the plan, while killing the Duchess does not. So we have a reason for saying that Alphonse intends to kill the Duke while (merely) foreseeing that he will also kill the Duchess.

This narrower account of intention locates it within the concept of a plan.[66] It presupposes that human agents are planning creatures and that plans typically include both an end or goal and some conception of the steps to be taken to achieve it. Clearly the agent's end is intended, but so are the various intermediate steps that are taken in order to achieve it. So we say that Alphonse intends to (1) bomb the carriage, in order to (2) kill the Duke, in order to (3) topple the monarchy. Since we don't find 'kill the Duchess' in this intentional sequence then we can conclude that killing her was no part of Alphonse's plan, thus that it was unintended. There are other ways of putting essentially the same point. Once Alphonse decides that assassinating the Duke is necessary in order to topple the monarchy, and therefore adopts this as a subsidiary end, various further planning steps come into play: he must decide whether to use a gun or a bomb; if a bomb, he must decide how to deliver it; if the carriage is the most accessible site then he must find out the route it will take, and so on. In all of this further planning tracking the movements of the Duke is crucial, while tracking those of the Duchess is entirely immaterial. The steps Alphonse takes are guided by the movements of the Duke, not those of the Duchess. We may also say, with Jonathan Bennett, that of the two deaths caused by the bombing, only one is part of the explanation of why it happened; the answer to the question 'Why did Alphonse bomb the carriage?' will refer to the death of the Duke, not that of the Duchess.[67]

I conclude therefore that we do have a narrower, more focused concept of intention that enables us to distinguish an intended effect from a (merely) foreseen effect, even in the case in which the latter is foreseen as certain. This intending/foreseeing distinction

---

[66] For development of this idea see Bratman 1987: chs. 2 and 3.
[67] See Bennett 1995: sec. 62.

applies readily to the terminal sedation scenario. As we have constructed the case there is a treatment plan in place that has been agreed to by both Anita and her physician (call this Plan A). The goal of the plan is to relieve Anita's suffering and the steps to be taken to achieve this goal are (1) administer a sedative, in order to (2) render her unconscious. Anita's death is no part of this plan and the fact that the sedation will hasten her death is no part of the explanation of why it is initiated. The specific dosage of sedative used is calculated to achieve and maintain unconsciousness for Anita, not death. Should the sedation unexpectedly not result in deep, continuous unconsciousness for Anita then it would have failed to achieve its aim, since it would have failed to relieve her suffering. But, once it has achieved this aim, should it unexpectedly not hasten her death it would not have failed in any respect.

Contrast this with Plan B, an alternative regime on which Anita and her physician might have agreed. Recall that Anita wants to avoid pointless suffering; suppose then that terminal sedation becomes attractive to her because it provides two distinct means of relieving her suffering: rendering her unconscious *and* hastening her death. She still requests that she be given food and water while sedated, since she does not want to die of dehydration. But the prospect of dying sooner from respiratory depression is now positively attractive to her, since she prefers to have her suffering ended by death sooner rather than later (she doesn't want to linger on any longer than necessary). Her physician agrees to the plan, as long as it is clear that he will still be administering no more of the sedative than is necessary to maintain deep and continuous unconsciousness. The intentional structures of the two terminal sedation plans therefore differ as follows:

Action	Means	End
TS(A): Administer medication ⇨	Induce unconsciousness ⇨	Relieve suffering
TS(B): Administer medication ⇨	Induce unconsciousness ⇨	Relieve suffering
	⇲ Hasten death ⇨	Relieve suffering

As before, the open arrows represent the intentional relation 'in order to'. Unlike Plan A, hastening Anita's death is now within the scope of Plan B; the fact that the sedation will, *inter alia*, hasten her death is now part of the explanation of why it is chosen. We have been making the causal assumption that there is no available means of relieving Anita's suffering except a treatment option that also hastens her death. But if there were—if, for instance, there were a way of sedating her without hastening her death—then it would be dispreferred *on that ground* by both Anita and her physician. Whereas under Plan A Anita's death is foreseen but not intended, under Plan B it is intended.

The intention condition in the DDE therefore rests on an intelligible distinction between what Anita's physician might intend as a means and what he might merely foresee as a side effect. The remaining question is whether this distinction has any ethical significance. To put the question succinctly: Plan B would be different from Plan A but, from an ethical standpoint, would it be worse? It certainly could not be found worse on the ground of its motive, since in electing either plan Anita's physician is motivated solely by compassion for her suffering and respect for her wishes. Nor on the ground of its outcome, since the outcomes of both plans are identical: in both cases Anita experiences exactly the same amount of suffering, is unconscious for exactly the same duration, and dies at exactly the same time. Since the two plans differ only in their intentional structure, it must be something about the fact that death is intended in Plan B, but not in Plan A, that makes the ethical difference. But why? What is it about the fact that Anita's death is intended in Plan B that makes it ethically suspect?

The normative significance of the intending/foreseeing distinction lies at the heart of the Doctrine of Double Effect. In the light of that fact it is surprising how few defenders of the Doctrine have attempted to justify that significance. One notable exception is Thomas Nagel, who writes:

The difference [between intending an effect and merely foreseeing it] is that action intentionally aimed at a goal is guided by that goal. Whether the goal is an end in itself or only a means, action aimed at it must follow it and be prepared to adjust its pursuit if deflected by altered circumstances—whereas an act that merely produces an effect does not follow it, is not *guided* by it, even if the effect is foreseen.[68]

So far, Nagel might be pointing to the fact that, other factors equal, intending harm makes an agent more of a risk to others than merely foreseeing it. If I have incorporated harming you into my plan, whether as an end or as a means, then I am targeting and pursuing you. Nagel's image of the guidance system is apt here: once I am locked in on you then I will take such countermeasures as are necessary to defeat your evasions and defences. By contrast, if you are not my target then you may still end up as collateral damage by being in the wrong place at the wrong time. But if I am forced to alter my plan then you may escape harm altogether, for I am not tracking you. All of this seems entirely correct—it recapitulates the distinction between the Grand Duke and the Grand Duchess in the earlier Alphonse example—but it points at best to an extrinsic difference between intention and foresight. In general, harm may be more likely to ensue when aimed at than when anticipated and accepted as a side effect (though there will, of course, be cases in which the opposite is true). But none of this has any application to Anita's case, since her death (which we are assuming for the sake of the argument to be a harm) is equally certain under both plans. And it is not Nagel's point; he wants to locate not an extrinsic but an intrinsic normative difference between intention and foresight.

He continues the foregoing passage thus:

What does this mean? It means that to aim at evil, even as a means, is to have one's action guided by evil. . . . But the essence of evil is that it should *repel* us. If something is evil, our actions should be guided, if they are guided by it at all, toward its elimination rather than toward its

---

[68] Nagel 1986: 181 (emphasis in the original).

maintenance. That is what evil *means*. So when we aim at evil we are swimming head-on against the normative current. Our action is guided by the goal at every point in the direction diametrically opposite to that in which the value of that goal points.

Now it is obvious what Nagel's point is: what is (intrinsically) wrong with intending evil—whether as an end or a means—is that one must take an inappropriate attitude towards the evil; instead of avoiding or preventing it one must seek and pursue it.

The example Nagel discusses involves causing a child pain (by twisting his arm) as part of a plan to save the lives of some friends badly injured in an auto accident. One can appreciate in this case what he is driving at, since deliberately hurting a child should surely repel us, if anything should. However, it makes a significant ethical difference that in Nagel's example the pain is sought as a means and not as an end. In a case in which a child is tortured for sadistic pleasure the agent is in no way repelled by the pain; on the contrary, he is attracted or aroused by it. This seems a straightforward case of 'swimming head-on against the normative current'. But in the case Nagel describes it is possible for the agent both to choose to hurt the child and to be repelled by doing so. If he comes to the conclusion that twisting the child's arm is necessary in order to save the lives of his friends then he may overcome his inhibition against causing pain to a child in order to prevent a greater evil. In that case, unlike the sadist, he is repelled by the evil he is causing, but his repulsion is overcome by the more powerful attraction of saving lives. Indeed, what is there to the structure of this case except the weighing of competing evils? It is a commonplace of means–end reasoning that greater evils may sometimes be prevented only by causing lesser ones. Pointing out in such cases that we should be repelled by the means does not really settle the issue of whether it is nonetheless justified by the end.[69]

Nagel's diagnosis therefore seems much more applicable to evils sought as ends than to those inflicted as means (at least where proportionality is satisfied). There is, however, another factor at work in Nagel's example that might be thought to make a difference. The child is an innocent bystander who, we might plausibly think, is being *used* against his will to secure benefits for others. If the child has a right not to be used in this way, then it might be this interpersonal dimension of the case that explains why it is wrong to hurt him.[70] I will not pursue this issue further, since this dimension is entirely absent from the scenario of Anita's sedation. In that scenario both of the effects (relief of suffering and death) belong to her. Rather than being used in the service of someone else's good, she is a fully consenting participant in decisions about her own good.[71] Of course, this is not the only respect in which the terminal sedation case differs from Nagel's example. No one would doubt that the pain caused to the

---

[69] Shelly Kagan (1989: 167–9) makes a similar point about Nagel's argument.

[70] Shelly Kagan (ibid. 173 ff.) explores this line of defence for the intending/foreseeing distinction.

[71] Perhaps, then, Warren Quinn (1989a: 343 n. 17) was right to contend that the DDE applies only to interpersonal cases in which rights are at stake.

child, considered just in itself, is an evil. However, as noted earlier, it is far less obvious that Anita's death is an evil, thus that intending it involves swimming against any normative current.

In any case the crucial question for the DDE in this scenario is whether the intending/foreseeing distinction marks a significant ethical difference between Plans A and B. Recall that the two plans are identical in the following ethically salient respects: motive (compassion and respect in both cases) and outcome (unconsciousness—and therefore relief from suffering—followed by death). The difference between them lies solely in the fact that in Plan B Anita's death is one of the intended effects while in Plan A it is merely foreseen. Try as I might, I cannot see that this difference is capable of drawing a bright line between the two plans, so that Plan A is permissible and Plan B impermissible.[72] Both plans appear to me to be justified by the same weighing of outcomes: relieving Anita's suffering by rendering her unconscious and (thereby) hastening her death is better than allowing her to suffer. It seems to me to make no difference in this case whether the hastening of her death is an intended or merely foreseen effect of the sedation. If it is better for Anita to be sedated and thereby to die sooner (which it surely is), then it is pursuit of her overall good that equally justifies both plans.

Having surveyed all three components of the Doctrine of Double Effect—intention, causation, proportionality—we can now ask ourselves which ones matter in the terminal sedation scenario. Earlier we determined that causation matters only for the way in which it feeds into intention. Now we have concluded that intention as well does not matter in its own right. So that leaves us with proportionality as the only factor driving our moral thinking about this case. Proportionality requires that there be a sufficiently serious reason for initiating a treatment plan that will (intentionally or foreseeably) hasten death. When we ask whether terminal sedation is justified in Anita's case two questions dominate all others: what will be best for her? What does she want? The aim of palliative care must be to ease the dying process for Anita as much as possible while respecting her right of informed consent/refusal. Terminal sedation prevents unnecessary suffering both by rendering her unconscious and (we are assuming) by hastening her death. If the latter result is also comprehended in the treatment plan, thus in the aims of both Anita and her physicians, that appears to make little difference. What matters is that Anita's suffering is severe enough to make either unconsciousness or death a better option for her.

I said earlier that the Doctrine of Double Effect has come to be applied to a wide range of moral problems. We have been considering its application only to one such

---

[72] For an argument to a similar conclusion (but about a quite different scenario) see Thomson 1999: 514–16. Interestingly, there is neurological evidence to suggest that we think differently about intended v. unintended harms, even when presented with moral scenarios that are similar in other relevant respects. Functional magnetic resonance imaging (fMRI) shows that neural areas associated with emotion are more in play when harm is intended as a means while those associated with cognition are more active when harm is anticipated as a side effect (Schaich Borg et al. 2006). Perhaps these results show that our emotions become engaged when we feel that we are swimming against Nagel's 'normative current'.

problem: the choice of end-of-life treatment regimes. It needs to be emphasized that rejecting the ethical relevance of the intending/foreseeing distinction in this context does not entail rejecting it in other contexts. This is so because the end-of-life scenario is distinctive in a number of ethically salient respects: (1) the effect that may be either intended or foreseen (death) is not a harm or an evil in this case, (2) both the 'double' effects (death and relief of suffering) picked out by the DDE belong to the same person, and (3) this person has consented to both of these effects. It is the presence of these factors, I contend, that drives our intuitive judgement that the distinction in this case between intending death and merely foreseeing it makes no ethical difference. Where one or more of these factors is absent, therefore, the intending/foreseeing distinction may still mark an ethically significant boundary.[73]

3.3 Last Words

The administration of analgesics and sedatives, at levels necessary to control intractable symptoms at the end of life, has become a standard technique of palliative medicine. It has also come to provide a standard illustration of the operation of the Doctrine of Double Effect. However, the DDE may be misapplied in these end-of-life scenarios, since it requires the assumption that death is a harm, an assumption there is no reason to accept. Furthermore, the ambiguity of intention makes it difficult for the DDE to draw a bright line between different end-of-life measures, and if it is capable of doing so it will draw it in the wrong place for the purpose of the Conventional View. Most importantly, in these scenarios it seems to make no ethical difference whether death is an intended means to relieving suffering or a foreseen and tolerated side effect. The factors that do appear to matter include the severity and expected duration of the patient's suffering, the available means for mitigating or eliminating it, and the patient's informed choice. Decision-making in this context is understandably, and justifiably, dominated by the aim of ensuring that the patient does not suffer more than is necessary and that her autonomy is respected. Against the imperative of achieving this aim, the intending/foreseeing distinction appears to have no weight.

It needs to be emphasized again that this result for the Doctrine of Double Effect is specific to these end-of-life scenarios and is not a general case against the Doctrine. The cases we have discussed are distinctive in at least three ethically significant respects: the absence of a bad effect, the absence of interpersonal conflict, and patient consent. The DDE may be much more defensible in other contexts that do not share these features. Still, our concern here is with end-of-life treatment options that (actually or possibly) hasten death. If the DDE has no useful application to these cases of 'indirect death' that is still a significant result. But it may also have an even

---

[73] All the foregoing factors are absent in some of the classic cases in which the application of the DDE seems intuitively most plausible, such as the distinction between strategic bombing and terror bombing.

more important implication. The side-by-side comparison of treatment options in the previous section involved two variants of terminal sedation, one in which death was intended and one in which it was not. No comparison was made of either option with euthanasia. Nonetheless, the outcome of the previous argument—especially the centrality of proportionality and the weighing of goods and evils—does suggest an approach to the ethics of euthanasia as well. How that approach might fare is the business of the next chapter.

4

Death by Request

The main business of this book is to answer two related questions: under what conditions, if any, can assisted death be ethically justified? Under what conditions, if any, should it be legally permitted? In this chapter we turn to the first of these questions. We know from our earlier discussion (§1.2) that assisted death can take either of two forms: assisted suicide or euthanasia. In an assisted suicide a patient self-administers a lethal medication with the intention of causing death in order to relieve suffering, the role of the physician being limited to providing the medication (with the intention of thereby offering the patient the choice of a safe and certain suicide). For our purposes, therefore, assisted suicide is necessarily *physician-assisted* suicide, though I will usually not bother to mention this qualifier explicitly. Euthanasia, on the other hand, involves a physician administering a lethal medication to a patient in order to cause the patient's death and thereby relieve his suffering. I am therefore assuming that euthanasia is *physician-administered* euthanasia, though once again the cumbersome qualifier will usually be omitted.

So characterized, assisted suicide and euthanasia share two important features. First, both are forms of treatment administered to (or self-administered by) a patient. It is this common feature that distinguishes them from withholding or withdrawing treatment and that has led them to be labelled (misleadingly, as we shall see) as 'active' rather than 'passive'. It is also a feature they share with the methods of 'indirect death' discussed in the previous chapter. Second, in both cases the hastening of the patient's death is the intended aim of the treatment, not just an unintended (though possibly foreseen) side effect. This is the feature that distinguishes assisted death from the other 'active' measures we have so far discussed: in all of them the death of the patient may be an intended outcome but it need not, whereas hastening death is necessarily the aim of assisted suicide or euthanasia.

The two forms of assisted death are distinguished by the dimension of agency. Whereas assisted suicide requires self-administration by the patient of lethal medication (usually by oral dose), in euthanasia the medication is administered by the physician (typically by injection). This distinction notwithstanding, in the course of this chapter I will be arguing that the ethical issues involved in assisted suicide and voluntary euthanasia are essentially the same.[1] However, for the purpose of exposition it will be convenient to work from the former to the latter. The scenario with which we are dealing initially, therefore, is one in which a physician intentionally assists a patient to commit suicide by providing the patient with the means to do so (let us say a prescription for a lethal dose of a barbiturate).[2] Is it wrong of the physician to do this? It seems plausible to think that an answer to this question will depend, at least in part, on the answer to a prior question: is it wrong of the patient to commit suicide? If the suicide itself is wrong then intentionally assisting it must surely also be wrong.[3] So we begin with the ethics of suicide.

4.1 Suicide and the Sanctity of Life

The best-known and most influential arguments for the impermissibility of suicide begin with theistic premises. Life is a gift from God, one of the familiar arguments runs, and so should not be destroyed. Or: it is up to God, and not to us, to decide when we quit this life. However, theistic arguments of this sort are beyond the scope of this book, since, being faith-based, they are not susceptible of rational refutation and cannot serve as the ethical basis of public policy.[4] So our question must be: can any persuasive secular argument be made for the wrongness of suicide?

The prospects of any such argument might appear bleak. Suicide is an intentional taking of human life, with the peculiar feature that perpetrator and victim are the same. If you want to make a case that it is impermissible, then the obvious argumentative strategy would be to include it within the scope of broader ethical principles prohibiting homicide. Leaving aside special justifications, such as self-defence, we all think that it is wrong to kill another person—wrong, say, to commit murder. But what is wrong with it? Two wrong-making features of murder immediately come to mind. The first is the harm or injury it does to the victim. What makes murder the most serious offence against the person seems to lie in the special seriousness of the harm—the deprivation of life—that it inflicts on the person. The second wrong-making feature is the violation of the victim's self-determination or autonomy. By taking the life of another without her consent the murderer denies the victim sovereignty over her own life; instead of respecting her status as the active manager of her life, he substitutes his will for hers, thereby demoting her to the status of subordinate or chattel.

---

[1] The further issues raised by non-voluntary euthanasia will be addressed in the next chapter.

[2] To keep the issues clear, we are to assume also that the physician is not assisting the suicide in any other way, including counselling or encouraging it.

[3] The converse need not hold: there is at least logical space for holding that, while the suicide would not itself be wrong, it would be wrong for a second party to assist it. I return to this question in §4.2, below.

[4] The standard theistic arguments are not terribly convincing even in their own terms (Baelz 1980; Battin 1994: ch. 11).

Suppose that this is (more or less) the right account of the wrongness of homicide. The problem with extrapolating it to suicide is then glaringly obvious: neither of these wrong-making features seems to apply. Taking them in reverse order, when someone kills himself that appears to be an exercise of autonomy, not a usurpation of it. Of course, in the case of many (perhaps most) suicides we may legitimately doubt that the agent is genuinely self-determining. We are focusing in this book on a narrow range of possible suicides—those contemplated by competent patients at the end of life as a means of escaping intolerable suffering. But suicide is a much wider social phenomenon than that. In Canada, for instance, some 3,700 deaths by suicide occur every year, which is approximately the total of deaths by homicide and vehicular accidents combined. Studies have shown that more than 90 per cent of these suicide victims have a diagnosable psychiatric illness.[5] The most common psychiatric conditions associated with suicide are mood disorders, such as bipolar disorder and unipolar depression, but others include schizophrenia, alcoholism, substance abuse, and personality disorders, such as borderline or antisocial personality disorder. The principal effect of depression is to focus the person's attention exclusively on everything that is going wrong in his life, with an accompanying sense of hopelessness that it could ever be better in the future. Personality disorders, on the other hand, are characterized by increased aggression and impulsivity, thereby increasing the risk of sudden action on the basis of powerful feelings. It is important not to oversimplify the causes of suicide, which are usually multiple and complex. In particular, although suicide is generally a complication of a psychiatric disorder, most persons with such disorders never attempt suicide.[6] Suicide attempters appear to differ from non-attempters with the same disorder in two salient respects: they experience a higher degree of depression and hopelessness and they have a greater tendency towards impulsiveness.[7]

If this overview is accurate, it supports the generalization that most suicides are irrational in at least one important respect—the subject's deliberative process is either distorted by an overly negative view of his present situation and future prospects or it is truncated by a sudden and impulsive response to a current overwhelming feeling.[8] For this reason, we may be reluctant to dignify these suicides as exercises of autonomy, since there seems to be no self-determining agent in charge here. But for the same reason these are the suicides least likely to attract moral condemnation, because of the agent's diminished responsibility for his decision and his action.

In any case, suicides need not be irrational in this way.[9] To reassure ourselves on this point, we need only consider Anita, the end-stage cancer patient who contemplated terminal sedation in the previous chapter. Though her current situation and future prospects are grim, Anita is not clinically depressed, nor does she manifest any other

[5] Mann 2002; Joiner 2010: 188–9.   [6] Mann 2002: 303.
[7] Ibid. 304.
[8] Richard Brandt (1975: 69–72) details the effects of severe depression on the suicidal person's thought processes.
[9] Cf. Lester 2006: 519 ff.

psychiatric disorder. She is fully informed of the future course of her illness and has a clear view of the suffering it will occasion. She has made a considered and stable decision that she does not wish to endure the final few weeks before she dies of the cancer, a decision fully supported by her family. It was this determination to avoid needless suffering that led her to request terminal sedation. If the reasoning process which brought Anita to this decision was not in any way impaired or distorted, then it would be no less rational were it to eventuate in a choice of suicide as the optimal way out. Anita's suicide would be a last resort response to an intolerable exigent situation, a means of avoiding immediate and pointless suffering. For a somewhat different scenario let us revisit Bill, whose amyotrophic lateral sclerosis has progressed to the point where he has lost motor control over much of his body, including speech, though his mind remains entirely unaffected. Bill knows that the disease will continue to shut down more and more of his body and that, if it is left unchecked, he will eventually die of asphyxia, probably in less than six months. He wants to continue living with his condition for a few weeks longer but, when it has become unbearable for him, he then wants to be able to choose the time, and the means, of his death. Bill is already on opioids for pain control and could, if his condition becomes intolerable at a later date, opt for terminal sedation. Like Anita, he is fully informed concerning his future prospects and, though he is despairing of his situation, he has no diagnosable psychiatric disorder. There is no reason to think that a later decision for terminal sedation would fail to be deliberatively rational. Suppose instead that Bill decides to stockpile enough narcotics to be able to end his life at the point where he considers the further course of his illness to be nothing but a burden to him. Presumably, that decision would be equally rational.

There seems no serious reason to doubt that a decision to commit suicide could be an exercise of autonomy for Anita or Bill. In that case, one of the grounds for the moral condemnation of homicide would not apply to their act. What about the other? We have already determined (§1.1) that the harm of death lies in the value of the life thereby foregone, so the question becomes whether suicide is self-harming in this way. Once again the answer for most suicides may well be in the affirmative. A suicide that is deliberatively irrational, in the sense delineated above, is very likely also to miscalculate the person's own future interests. While the person himself feels nothing but hopelessness, from a more objective standpoint there may well be good reason to anticipate future improvement in the conditions of his life. It is from this perspective that we may say of someone's suicide that it is irrational in a further sense: senseless, crazy, a tragic waste. Suicides that are irrational in this second respect are self-harming by virtue of depriving the person of a continued life that has the potential, under appropriate conditions, to be worth living.

However, not all suicides are self-harming. If we think that terminal sedation would be best for Anita, because the experience of her remaining weeks would only detract from the overall value of her life for her, then we must draw the same conclusion about suicide. In short, Anita's suicide could be both procedurally rational—in its deliberative process—and substantively rational—in its outcome. And so could Bill's. Suicide therefore may, but need not, be self-harming. What then about harm to others? There is no doubt that suicide can be devastating for surviving family and friends who, besides having to cope with the loss of a loved one, are left to wonder whether there was something they might have done to avert the tragedy. Under normal circumstances, doing something this hurtful to others would be ample ground for moral judgement.[10] If this is not our usual reaction in the case of suicide, the most likely explanation is that our attention is dominated by the even greater loss that the perpetrator/victim has inflicted on himself. Hearing of someone's suicide is likely to evoke not moral condemnation but sorrow, both for the one who has been driven to such tragic lengths and for surviving loved ones. However, there are exceptions.[11] Some suicides are clearly calculated to punish the survivors, a message conveyed either in the manner of the act or in an accompanying note or manifesto. In those cases our sympathy for the survivors—who are themselves victims—may well induce condemnation of the perpetrator.

However, just as suicide need not be self-harming, it also need not harm others. In choosing suicide Anita would not be harming herself, nor, since her family is fully onside, would she be harming anyone else. Bill's situation is somewhat more complicated due to the fact that he is the single father of a ten-year-old boy. Some provision obviously needs to be made for his son, but Bill is already unable to care for him and will die before long in any case. It may actually be better for the boy not to have to watch his father go through his last stages of decline.

So far we have noted two wrong-making features of homicide: the harm done to the victim and the violation of the victim's autonomy. Since at least some suicides will display neither feature, we do not yet have an argument from the (general) impermissibility of homicide to the impermissibility of suicide. Any such argument will need to identify some further wrong-making feature that we have not yet considered. It should be obvious by now that no consequentialist principle will be capable of meeting this need, since there will inevitably be cases (such as Anita's and Bill's) in which suicide is both better for the patient and better (or at least not worse) for others. The most promising option would therefore seem to lie in some form of deontological sanctity-of-life principle that would provide grounds for the impermissibility of homicide and suicide alike. We briefly encountered such principles previously (§3.2) in the context of the Doctrine of Double Effect, but now we need to take a closer look at them.

As noted in the earlier discussion, such a principle need not be exceptionless; it can allow that some cases of both homicide (e.g. killing in self-defence) and suicide (e.g. heroic self-sacrifice) are justifiable. But in order to make a case against assisted suicide (and euthanasia) the principle will have to be pretty strict; in particular, it will have to condemn suicides such as those of Anita and Bill that are undertaken for the sole

---

[10] Cf. D. Feldman 2006.

[11] I leave aside here the most obvious kind of exception, namely suicide bombings.

purpose of escaping future suffering. The common idea that unites all forms of sanctity-of-life principle is that human life is 'sacred'—that is, it has some form of value or status weighty enough to rule out most cases of the intentional taking of life, whether one's own or that of another. There may be some cases in which intentional killing does not engage this value, or in which it is outweighed by an even weightier competing value, but these cases will be rare and exceptional. They will not include Anita or Bill.

There are two forms of deontology that share this common idea but interpret it in radically different ways. Following Alan Donagan, I will call them Thomistic and Kantian.[12] According to both theories the wrong-making feature of suicide lies in its violation of a kind of respect that we owe to everyone, including ourselves. The theories part company, however, on the precise object or target of this respect. For the Thomists respect is owed to the fundamental goods that constitute a person's well-being or human fulfilment, whereas for the Kantians it is owed to the person herself. The two deontological traditions converge over most (though possibly not all) of their practical implications, including the condemnation of suicide, but they reach this common ground from quite different starting points.

The Thomistic (or natural law) tradition begins with a conception of human well-being as consisting in a plurality of goods, such as knowledge, aesthetic experience, and friendship.[13] Each of these goods is independent of and irreducible to the others and each makes an intrinsic, and not merely instrumental, contribution to human fulfilment or flourishing. Morality then enters the picture in the form of an injunction to respect each of these goods in every act, where this is interpreted to mean that one must never 'choose directly against a basic good' or 'choose to destroy, damage, or impede some instance of a basic good for the sake of an ulterior end'.[14] On this view respect for a person consists in respect for the fundamental goods that constitute that person's well-being.[15] This respect is owed equally to the goods of all persons, including one's own. The theory therefore makes room for the idea of duties to oneself, consisting in duties not to 'destroy, damage, or impede' any of one's own fundamental goods. The prohibition of both homicide and suicide is then entailed by the fact that life itself is one of those fundamental goods.[16] Any intentional taking of life, whether one's own or that of another, will constitute the choice to destroy a fundamental good and is forbidden for that reason.[17]

---

[12] Donagan 1977: 63–5. John Finnis draws a similar distinction in Finnis 1983: ch. 5. I will not deal with either theory in its original version, but only in the versions now defended by the ablest advocates.

[13] Finnis 1980: chs. 3 and 4; Finnis, Boyle, and Grisez 1987: ch. 10; Gorsuch 2006: ch. 9.

[14] Finnis 1980: 118–25, Finnis 1983: 125–32; Finnis, Boyle, and Grisez 1987: 283–7.

[15] Finnis 1983: 125–6; Finnis, Boyle, and Grisez 1987: 278.

[16] Finnis 1980: 86–7; Finnis, Boyle, and Grisez 1987: 304–9.

[17] The Thomistic theory justifies killing in self-defence by means of the Doctrine of Double Effect: the death of the attacker is not a means to protecting oneself against the attack but an unintended (though possibly foreseeable) side effect; see Finnis 1983: 132; Finnis, Boyle, and Grisez 1987: 312. It is less easy to justify the death penalty unless the prohibition of homicide is limited to the killing of innocent persons; see ibid. 317–18.

The case this theory builds against suicide obviously rests in part on the claim that life itself is a fundamental aspect of human well-being. So we are entitled to ask what is here meant by life. Earlier in this book (§1.1) I distinguished two concepts of life: biological and personal. Biological life consists in the integrated functioning of the organism and is possible after the irreversible cessation of all capacity for consciousness or experience. Personal life, by contrast, requires the capacity for whatever psychological states are constitutive of a person. For human beings the two normally go hand in hand, but they can diverge in pathological conditions such as permanent vegetative state. So is it biological or personal life that, on the Thomistic view, is a fundamental human good? In some contexts it seems to be a robust version of the latter. Thus John Finnis writes: 'The term "life" here signifies every aspect of the vitality (*vita*, life) which puts a human being in good shape for self-determination. Hence, life here includes bodily (including cerebral) health, and freedom from the pain that betokens organic malfunctioning or injury.'[18] But it seems obvious that this cannot be the conception of life that will support an absolute (or near-absolute) prohibition of suicide. Neither Anita nor Bill enjoys a life in this sense, and so their death (and therefore their suicide) would not destroy a fundamental good for them. More generally, on this conception of life it would be difficult, if not impossible, to condemn any suicide undertaken to escape serious suffering.

This unwelcome implication has been duly noted by the proponents of the Thomistic theory, who have come to defend the view that mere biological life, in the absence of all capacity for personal life, is still a basic human good.[19] Since every suicide necessarily destroys biological life, then every suicide will qualify as choosing directly against a basic good. This contention—that biological life is in itself an intrinsic good for a person—plays an indispensable role in the Thomistic/natural law view concerning the treatment of persons in a permanent vegetative state.[20] Critics, however, have found the contention deeply implausible. Jonathan Glover, for instance, has written:

I have no way of refuting someone who holds that being alive, even though unconscious, is intrinsically valuable. But it is a view that will seem unattractive to those of us who, in our own case, see a life of permanent coma as in no way preferable to death. From the subjective point of view there is nothing to choose between the two. . . . For permanently comatose existence is

---

[18] Finnis 1980: 86. Cf. Finnis 1983: 40: 'there is this good that consists not merely in my being a human being of a certain sort but in my being and continuing to be who I am. The goods that are (so far as possible) thrown away in suicide include that good.' Presumably, 'continuing to be who I am' requires personal as well as biological life. See also Finnis, Boyle, and Grisez 1987: 279: 'Life itself—its maintenance and transmission—health, and safety are one form of basic human good.'

[19] Finnis, Boyle, and Grisez 1987: 305–6; Boyle 1995: 192–4; Finnis 1995: 32–3.

[20] It may not be indispensable to the Thomistic condemnation of suicide, since virtually anyone capable of suicide has a personal, as well as a biological, life to lose. It should be noted that Finnis rejects the distinction between biological and personal life as unacceptably dualistic, saying about permanent vegetative state that 'human bodily life is the life of a person' (Finnis 1995: 32).

subjectively indistinguishable from death, and unlikely often to be thought intrinsically preferable to it by people thinking of their own future.[21]

The view that Glover finds much more plausible is that the value of biological (and personal) life lies not in the fact that it matters for its own right but in the fact that it is a necessary condition of everything that does matter: 'If life is worth preserving only because it is the vehicle for consciousness, and consciousness is of value only because it is necessary for something else, then that "something else" is the heart of this particular objection to killing. It is what is meant by a "life worth living" or a "worth-while life".'[22] Proponents of the Thomistic theory have recognized that they must hold the line on this point; if life has value only as a condition of whatever else is prudentially valuable then the case against suicide undertaken to end serious suffering will collapse.[23] However, it seems to me that both Glover's negative point (against the intrinsic value of merely biological life) and his positive proposal enjoy a great deal of support from common sense. Try as I may, I cannot discern any value in the life of a permanently comatose patient *for that patient*—any contribution that her life is making to her well-being. Like Glover, I cannot disprove the Thomistic claim to the contrary, but I find it deeply implausible.

Suppose, however, that the claim is true. Suppose, that is, that bare life (whether biological or personal) is an intrinsic prudential good regardless of any other goods it might contain or make possible. The impermissibility of suicide will not follow from this claim alone. For it might be that the value of bare life is comparatively slight compared to the value of the other goods, so that a life that lacked all of these other goods would itself be of only slight value.[24] Furthermore, if that life contained serious suffering then the disvalue of the suffering might exceed the value of being alive, so that on balance the person's (continued) life would not be worth living. Since this is arguably the condition of Anita and Bill, then their suicides might be justifiable after all as being in their overall best interest. The Thomistic theory blocks this conclusion by virtue of its principle that one must never 'choose to destroy, damage, or impede some instance of a basic good for the sake of an ulterior end'. If Anita or Bill were to choose suicide they would be choosing to destroy one basic good (life) for the sake of another (freedom from suffering). So now we need to ask why, on the Thomistic view, it is always wrong to intentionally 'destroy, damage, or impede' one fundamental good for the sake of pursuing another. Friendship and knowledge are two such goods, but it seems that, for the sake of my own well-being, I might rationally choose to damage or impede the former for the sake of the latter—for instance, by cutting ties with my friends in order to make time for important research. Any deontological principle that

---

[21] Glover 1977: 45–6. Cf. Buchanan and Brock 1989: 109.

[22] Glover 1977: 52.

[23] Finnis, Boyle, and Grisez 1987: 301–3.

[24] 'In the life of the person in an irreversible coma or irreversibly persistent vegetative state, the good of human life is really but very inadequately instantiated' (Finnis 1995: 33). Cf. Joseph Boyle's view that continued life has only 'limited benefits' for PVS patients (Boyle 1995: 197).

rules out these trade-offs would appear to be unreasonably rigoristic. But if trade-offs are permissible why would it necessarily be wrong to give up the slight value of life in order to achieve the much greater value of putting an end to suffering?

The Thomistic prohibition of trade-offs that sacrifice one good for the sake of another is one of the theory's bulwarks against consequentialism.[25] The theory shares with consequentialism a commitment to the priority of the good: both theories begin with an axiology (a menu of intrinsic goods) and then define duties (and rights) in terms of these goods. However, because consequentialists allow trade-offs among different goods (if they are value pluralists) or among different instances of the same good (if they are not) they can direct agents to choose the outcome with the greatest overall value.[26] By contrast, every deontological theory will hold that it is at least sometimes wrong to do what is best on the whole. Thomists block the consequentialist move by denying the legitimacy of trade-offs. But that seems much too strong, especially because it blocks trade-offs within a single life (for instance, friendship for knowledge) as well as across different lives. Furthermore, it seems unmotivated: what exactly is wrong with trading fundamental goods off against one another? The Thomists' final answer to this question is that trade-offs are not so much impermissible as unintelligible, since the various fundamental goods are incommensurable with one another.[27] Incommensurability here must mean incomparability: no instance of one good can be judged to be better than, equal in value to, or worse than any instance of another good.[28] In particular, because the goods of life and freedom from suffering are incomparable,[29] the value of the latter, however great, can never be judged to outweigh the value of the former, however slight. A decision to end one's life in order to prevent further suffering can therefore never be defended on the ground that it is in one's overall best interest. Indeed, it can never even be rational, since it must rest on a comparison of goods (or evils) that is in principle impossible to make. Nor could any other calculation of one's overall best interest be rational, if it involves balancing the value of different fundamental goods. So it would make no sense for me to say, for example, that my overall well-being is better served by my deep personal relationships than by my knowledge of the team batting average of the 1937 Detroit Tigers.[30]

---

[25] Judging by the amount of space the Thomists allocate to refuting consequentialism, they must regard it as the main rival to their own theory.

[26] For a fuller characterization of consequentialism, see Sumner 1987: §6.1.

[27] Finnis 1980: 111–24; Finnis 1983: 86–93; Finnis, Boyle, and Grisez 1987: ch. 9.

[28] 'Thus, it is unreasonable to choose to destroy, damage, or impede some instance of a basic good for the sake of an ulterior end. In doing this, one does not have the reason of maximizing good or minimizing evil—there is no such *reason*, for the goods at stake in choosable options are not rationally commensurable' (Finnis, Boyle, and Grisez 1987: 286–7). For analyses of the notion of incomparability among values, see Griffin 1986: ch. 5, §3; Raz 1986: ch. 13; Chang 1997.

[29] Finnis 1983: 107.

[30] The Tigers' .292 average led the major leagues that year.

It should be clear that these implications for rational prudential choice are a high price to pay for excluding trade-offs among fundamental goods in our ethical decision-making. However, this exclusion appears to be necessary for the Thomistic prohibition of suicide—even if we allow that bare (biological or personal) life has prudential value in its own right. The problem for the Thomistic theory seems to stem from the fact that it starts with a list of fundamental human goods and then interprets respect for persons as respect for these goods. In order to avoid these unpalatable results a different deontological conception of respect is needed. Alan Donagan, who is acutely aware of the Thomistic tradition, has contrasted its idea of respecting basic human goods with the Kantian idea of respecting human nature as an end in itself, and has argued for the superiority of the latter.[31] Donagan defends the fundamental principle that 'It is impermissible not to respect every human being, oneself or any other, as a rational creature.'[32] The injunction that we are to respect ourselves as rational creatures makes room in Donagan's deontology for a category of duties to oneself. Chief among these are duties not to injure or hurt ourselves. Since 'the worst physical injury anybody can do to himself is to kill himself, that is, to commit suicide',[33] it follows on Donagan's version of a Kantian theory that suicide is (at least normally) impermissible.[34]

Actually, this conclusion follows only when suicide is self-harming. Since we have reason to think that this is not always so (and would not be so for Anita or Bill), Donagan's Kantian case for the impermissibility of suicide is seriously incomplete. It is incomplete in another way as well, since Donagan never makes it very clear what it is to fail to respect oneself (or another) as a rational creature, and thus leaves it equally unclear why suicide (at least normally) manifests such a failure. Some further account is clearly needed, both of the Kantian notion of respect in general and of its application to suicide in particular. One influential account, proposed by David Velleman, turns on a distinction between two different kinds of value pertaining to persons.[35] The first is the value of a person's life *for that person,* which is identical to her well-being. It is this value we have in mind when we say that Anita's life is going badly for her, or Bill's for him, by virtue of the suffering that they are currently enduring and the further suffering in prospect for them. Following my own accustomed usage, I will continue to call this kind of value *prudential*; its identifying feature (which is marked out by the *good/bad for* locution) is that it is *subject-relative.*[36] The second kind of value belongs to

---

[31] Donagan 1977: §2.4.   [32] Ibid. 66–7.   [33] Ibid. 76.

[34] In line with the Judaeo-Christian 'common morality' he is attempting to interpret, and also with Kant's treatment of the question, Donagan allows that there are some instances in which suicide is permissible (such as thereby preventing harm to others). But he does not countenance the legitimacy of suicide simply to avoid suffering.

[35] Velleman 1999.

[36] A fuller account of the nature of prudential value, and its distinction from other kinds of value that lives can have, can be found in Sumner 1996: §1.3. Velleman characterizes this kind of value as 'interest-relative'; since I believe that he means by this exactly what I mean by 'subject-relative', I will continue to use my own preferred terminology.

all persons by virtue of their rational nature; following Kant, Velleman calls this *dignity*, and it is for him the secular version of the sanctity of human life. What morality requires, Velleman claims, is that we respect the dignity of persons, which includes respecting our own dignity. Suicide may well be best for Anita and Bill, if their lives have irretrievably lost all prudential value. But deciding for suicide just on this basis would be immoral, Velleman argues, since it would disrespect their dignity as persons.[37]

It is not much clearer in Velleman's account than in Donagan's just *why* a decision for suicide in order to avoid great suffering manifests disrespect for one's dignity as a person. He compares it to the decision to sell oneself into slavery,[38] which is objectionable presumably because the person thereby demotes his status from that of a free agent to that of a chattel. Here the transition from dignity to indignity is intelligible, but how does that apply to the decision to end one's life? Is the condition of being dead undignified? Leaving this question aside, Velleman's Kantian case against (most) suicide turns on his claim that, by virtue of their rational nature, persons have this special kind of (non-subject-relative) value. Velleman does not defend this claim by appeal to intuition; instead, he has an argument for it: 'what's good for a person is worth caring about only out of concern for the person, and hence only insofar as he is worth caring about. A person's good has only hypothetical or conditional value, which depends on the value of the person himself.'[39] So the case for dignity as a distinct value inhering in persons is that it is presupposed, and thus entailed, by the prudential value of persons' lives.

In addressing this argument we might begin by asking: why the exclusive focus on persons? And why is the possession of a rational nature necessary for dignity? On Velleman's view we start by noting that personal well-being matters and then see that this could be the case only if persons matter. But many people, myself included, think that the well-being of other creatures—sentient animals, for instance—also matters. Are we just mistaken in this? If we are not mistaken then is the prudential value of the lives of these creatures also conditional on the logically prior value of the creatures themselves? If so, do they also have dignity or, failing to be rational, do they have instead some lesser kind of (non-subject-relative) value? When we expand the scope of well-being or prudential value beyond persons, it becomes clearer that Velleman has

---

[37] Velleman allows that there may be other grounds for suicide compatible with respect for personal dignity; his objection is to suicide chosen solely on the ground that death would be best for the person in question. Presumably this objection would hold equally strongly for the decision to refuse life-sustaining treatment on the same ground. Velleman (1999: 618) also allows that suffering can rise to the level at which it can justify suicide, but only if (and because) it undermines the capacity for rational agency. This is a particularly perverse result, since it means that by the time a patient's suffering has reached the point where an assisted suicide would be justified he has also lost the capacity for rational agency and so cannot autonomously request it. Some might regard this as a *reductio* of the view.

[38] Ibid. 615.

[39] Ibid. 611. Cf. 615: 'we cannot avoid presupposing the existence of this value...since it's needed to account for the importance of interest-relative values'.

got the order of explanation between his two values reversed. It's not that the welfare of animals matters because the animals matter but the other way around: animals matter because they have a welfare—that is, because they can be harmed or benefited. That is why they matter in their own right and rocks and mountains do not.[40] The same holds for people, whose moral status is likewise dependent on the fact that they have lives that can go well or badly for them. That moral status—dignity, if you like— is not independent of and logically prior to the prudential value of their lives; it is instead conditional on that value. Velleman's case against suicide rests on the claim that where dignity and well-being conflict, the former takes precedence; otherwise, suicide to escape severe suffering might be justified, all things considered, even though it came at the cost of dignity. The priority of dignity in turn seems to rest for Velleman on its unconditional status. If it loses this status, then there seems no way for Velleman to support a strong prohibition of suicide.

In any case, if Anita or Bill opts for suicide in order to escape further suffering there seems no reason to think that they are thereby disrespecting themselves as persons or rational beings. In so far as their rationality is an issue at all, their decision can be seen as an expression of their rational nature rather than a denigration of it. As we have already seen, that decision can be rational both in its deliberative process, if it is not distorted by depression or truncated by impulsivity, and in its outcome, if it is in their best interest. Furthermore, when freely elected by Anita or Bill it would also be an exercise of her or his autonomy or self-determination in a way that does no harm to any other persons. It seems to me that there should be much for a Kantian to like in such a decision.

In any case, we still lack a convincing case against suicide on sanctity-of-life grounds. We have not, of course, canvassed all imaginable ways of interpreting this idea and thus we cannot rule out the possibility that a convincing case can be made. But the two interpretations of the sanctity of life that we have considered—Thomistic and Kantian—have been by far the most prominent and influential among deontologists who wish to defend the impermissibility of suicide. If neither of them is sufficient to deliver that result, then we are entitled to assume, at least for the purpose of further argument, that suicide can be both rational and ethical.

4.2 The Ethics of Assisted Death

In that case what are we to say about the ethics of assisting a suicide? To keep matters as uncomplicated as possible, suppose that physician-assisted suicide is legal in Anita's and Bill's jurisdiction. They ask their physicians to provide them with a prescription for a

---

[40] Do non-sentient animals and plants matter in the same way? That is a disputed issue in environmental ethics, but it turns on the (equally disputed) question whether they have a good (a welfare) of their own; for discussion, see Sumner 1996: §3.4.

lethal dose of barbiturates, to be taken orally at the time and place of their choosing. If they do no wrong by choosing suicide, do their physicians do any wrong by assisting them in this way? We must be careful not to answer too quickly. The two acts in question—suicide and assistance with suicide—are different, and there is no simple entailment relation between the moral status of the first and that of the second.[41] To make the obvious point, in committing suicide the patient causes her own death while in assisting the physician enables, and therefore to that extent causes, the death of another. While suicide remains within personal boundaries (leaving aside spillover effects on others), assistance crosses those boundaries: it is action not by a person on herself but by one person upon another. Therefore, at least in principle there is room here for an ethical distinction. However, in practice it is difficult to see what the ground of the distinction might be. We are imagining that the decision for suicide is entirely Anita's and Bill's, with no undue influence from any other parties, including their physicians. The role of the latter is limited to providing the means for Anita and Bill to do something that is itself ethically unproblematic. It is unclear, therefore, how there could be anything ethically problematic about them playing this role.[42] The real ethical burden of justifying assistance with suicide seems to be discharged by justifying suicide itself.

The next step is to ask how matters would stand with voluntary euthanasia. Recall the difference in the physician's role, between providing lethal medication for the patient to ingest and administering it to the patient. Does this difference make an ethical difference? Again, in principle it could: instead of the patient killing himself he is now being killed by another; instead of suicide we are dealing with homicide.[43] While this moves us into a distinct ethical domain, it is once again difficult to see how the verdict might be different if all other factors remain constant. If Anita or Bill makes a rational, considered, stable request to hasten death, and if that request is in her or his best interest, how can it matter how the agency of the physician figures in the scenario? If the physician would be justified in assisting her or his suicide, how could she not be equally justified in administering euthanasia in response to her or his request?

There is an argument, based on the right to life, that purports to show that agency does matter. The concept of a right to life is a much contested one, but whatever else it might be thought to entail it surely includes, at a minimum, the right not to be killed by another. Under this interpretation my right to life is a claim-right in which my claim against you (and everyone else) that you do not kill me is identical to a duty imposed on you (and everyone else) not to kill me.[44] Murdering me would, of course,

---

[41] More generally, from the fact that it is permissible for an agent to do something it does not follow that it would be permissible for someone else to assist him; see McMahan 2002: 458–9. However, the entailment does seem to hold for impermissibility: if the act would be wrong then it would be wrong to assist it.

[42] We will consider later (§7.5) the contention that assistance with suicide compromises the professional role of the physician or the physician–patient relationship.

[43] Though, of course, not necessarily *culpable* homicide.

[44] Cf. the earlier discussion of claim-rights (§2.1). Joel Feinberg (1978: 104–10) considers another possible interpretation of the right to life as a liberty-right. If it includes a full liberty to live or not to live,

violate that right, but, the argument goes, so would administering euthanasia to me. This construal of a right to life distinguishes between euthanasia and (assisted) suicide, since it appeals to a duty not to kill which is imposed on others, not on oneself. On this view I would not violate my right to life by killing myself, nor would you violate it by assisting me to kill myself, but you would violate it by killing me.

The effect of this argument is to deny the salience of one of the distinctions between voluntary euthanasia and murder. If you murder me then you kill me against my will, whereas euthanasia involves ending my life with my consent, or at my request. If my right to life imposes on you a duty not to kill me, then you violate that duty if you kill me, whether I have consented or not. However, this argument for the impermissibility of voluntary euthanasia depends on a hidden premiss: that the right to life is, in an important sense, inalienable. Joel Feinberg has distinguished two different ways in which the right to life (interpreted as above) might be alienated: by *relinquishing* it or by *waiving* it.[45] Each of these ways would involve exercising a power over the right: the power to cancel or annul the duty it imposes on others. If I relinquish the right then I give it up irrevocably or abandon it, so that no one in future would have any duty not to kill me. Since that would leave my life bereft of all protection against others, there is good reason to deny that the right to life includes the power to relinquish that right. On the other hand, if I waive the right then I annul the duty imposed on a particular other on a particular occasion. Recall from our earlier discussion of informed consent (§2.1) that most claim-rights have the useful feature that they can be waived by their holders in circumstances in which doing so will be beneficial. It is this power of waiver, exercised by informed consent, that permits physicians to treat their patients. Consenting to, or requesting, euthanasia is another exercise of this power; since it cancels the physician's duty not to kill, then the physician does no wrong in administering this particular treatment.

The argument from the right to life to the impermissibility of euthanasia therefore requires that the right be inalienable in this second way—i.e. that it cannot be waived. But this step in the argument runs up against the fact that, for patients such as Anita and Bill, waiving the right would be both in their best interest and an exercise of their autonomy. Whereas there might be a convincing case to be made against the power to relinquish one's right to life, there seems no similar case against the power to waive it (under certain conditions).[46] Indeed, denying the power of waiver seems inconsistent with the very function of rights. There are two basic theories about this function, one that rights protect choices, the other that they protect interests.[47] Since the effect of

---

as one wishes, then it is (in his language) a *discretionary* right that is fully compatible with requesting assisted death. But if it includes only a liberty to live, but no liberty not to live, then it is a *mandatory* right. A mandatory right to live is equivalent to a duty to live. This cannot be the interpretation of the right to life relevant to the assisted death issue, since it would equally rule out refusal of life-sustaining treatment.

[45] Ibid. 114 ff.

[46] This is Feinberg's (1978) conclusion. Philippa Foot (1977: 105–6) argues to the same conclusion.

[47] For discussion of these rival theories, see Sumner 1987: §2.2.

the power of waiver is to expand the rightholder's options, denial that the right to life is waivable is barely intelligible on the first theory. But it does not fare much better on the second, if the power of waiver is denied in situations in which it would be in the right-holder's interest to be able to exercise it. If, as we are assuming, requesting euthanasia would be both beneficial for Anita and Bill and an exercise of their autonomy, then it would be perverse to insist that the inalienability of their right to life prevents them from doing so.

We therefore seem to have an ethical continuum that runs from suicide through assisted suicide to voluntary euthanasia: when the first step in this sequence is justified then each of the further steps would also be justified *under the same circumstances*. And the reason that this extensionist argument goes through is that at each step the act in question is justified by reference to the same two basic values: patient well-being and patient autonomy. It is these two values that enable us to construct the two principal arguments for the ethical justifiability of assisted death.[48]

The argument from well-being is based on a simple, basic proposition: suffering is intrinsically bad and is therefore something to be prevented or relieved. Both Anita and Bill are suffering and are faced with an immediate future in which that suffering will get worse. The relief of suffering during the dying process is one of the principal aims of palliative medicine. Short of terminal sedation, none of the standard palliative treatment options will eliminate Anita's or Bill's suffering. Like terminal sedation, assisted death will eliminate their suffering without imposing a comparable cost on anyone else. There is therefore a strong ethical case in favour of this option. •

Before looking more closely at this argument it would be well to clarify somewhat the concept of suffering. Clearly one of the issues for both Anita and Bill is pain, and much of palliative medicine quite understandably focuses on providing adequate pain control. However, besides the fact that not all pain can be effectively controlled, it is important to understand that not all suffering is due to pain. The concepts of pain and suffering, though related, are quite distinct.[49] Pain is best understood as a certain distinctive feeling or sensation, to which we are normally (though not necessarily) averse.[50] Pain normally causes us to suffer, but so do many other physical sensations

[48] What I am calling the arguments from well-being and autonomy are the ones standardly employed by philosophers or bioethicists who wish to justify assisted death (e.g. Battin 2005: ch. 1; ch. 4, 89–93) and standardly opposed by those who wish to condemn it (e.g. Marquis 1998). But they are equally prominent in public discussions of the issues. The arguments were nicely summarized in an opinion piece by a physician which appeared in *The Times* (Tallis 2009): 'Unbearable suffering, prolonged by medical care, and inflicted on a dying patient who wishes to die, is unequivocally a bad thing. And respect for individual autonomy–the right to have one's choices supported by others, to determine one's own best interest, when one is of sound mind–is a sovereign principle. Nobody else's personal views should override this.'

[49] I discuss the concepts of pain and suffering at some length in Sumner 1996: 99–106. See also Mayerfeld 1999: 23–9.

[50] Indifference to, or even enjoyment of, pain seems to be psychologically (and therefore conceptually) possible (Sumner 1996: 100–2). However, it may not be possible in the case of very intense pain. In any case, for practical purposes I shall assume that patients in the dying process have an aversive reaction to the pain they are experiencing.

that we find disagreeable: nausea, dizziness, itching, fatigue, shortness of breath, and so on. None of these is quite the same as pain, but each can be a component of suffering. Furthermore, while most—perhaps all—pain has an organic basis, many of the most familiar forms of suffering are psychological: anxiety, depression, despair, hopelessness, abandonment, rejection, humiliation, indignity, and so on. Suffering is therefore best understood broadly as encompassing any experience or condition of life to which we are averse.[51] It is the aversiveness of suffering—the fact that we hate it and want to be rid of it—that makes suffering bad for us. And it is the fact that suffering is bad for the one who experiences it that makes it intrinsically bad and thereby gives us all an ethical reason for wanting to prevent or relieve it.[52]

No one seriously disputes that Anita's or Bill's suffering is intrinsically bad and therefore something to be prevented or relieved, if possible. The whole enterprise of palliative care is organized around the assumption that patient suffering calls for a response and, where possible, intervention for the purpose of amelioration. Affirming the intrinsic badness of suffering need not lead us to deny that it can sometimes be extrinsically good. We can learn by suffering, not least about our own resources for coping with it. On the other hand, extravagant claims are sometimes made to the effect that suffering builds character or that we need to suffer in order to appreciate the good things in life. There may be some measure of truth to these claims, but it would be cruel to bring them into play for patients who are suffering through the dying process. For them there will be no future goods to compensate for the present evil. Because their suffering will be of no extrinsic value to them, and thus entirely pointless, they are left just with the intrinsic badness of it.

The argument from well-being to the justifiability of assisted death can take a number of different forms. It might be consequentialist, resting simply on the fact that, given their circumstances, assisted death would be best for Anita and Bill, since it would avoid a great evil for them. This would not, of course, be sufficient to show that it would have the best overall consequences, since it might adversely affect the interests of others. If friends and family have no desire to see their loved ones suffer, and if they agree that hastening death would be best in these circumstances, then it seems unlikely that any harms to others could be found which would outweigh the great harm to Anita and Bill of continued suffering. We can hold this remote possibility open by saying that, for the consequentialist, the avoidance of further suffering for Anita and Bill provides a strong *pro tanto* reason in favour of assisted death. However, in their circumstances that reason is virtually certain also to be conclusive.

---

[51] Cf. Mayerfeld 1999: 14–19. Some may wish to confine suffering to experiences or conditions to which we are *strongly* averse, thereby ruling out the possibility of mild suffering. I take no stand on this, since the instances of suffering with which we will be dealing—the ones to which assisted death could be a rational response—will all be serious.

[52] I am therefore assuming that suffering is *agent-neutrally* bad. For the classic treatment of this issue—for pain, rather than suffering—see Nagel 1986: 156–62.

But the argument need not be consequentialist. Deontologists can posit a duty to relieve suffering. This duty might be role-specific, attaching to physicians (and other healthcare providers) as part of their more general duty of care for their patients. Or it might be quite general, applying to anyone who is in a position to prevent or relieve serious suffering.[53] In either case, the duty need be no more than *pro tanto*, to leave open the possibility that some ways of acting on it might be prohibited by other (role-specific or general) duties.[54] In the absence of such countervailing considerations, it would be conclusive.

One ethically salient fact about Anita and Bill is that they are suffering, and that further suffering can be prevented. But it is not the only one: it is equally salient that each wants to prevent that further suffering by hastening her or his death. Each will die anyway in the foreseeable future, but each wishes to die sooner, by medically assisted means, rather than wait to have the disease dictate the time and manner of death. Both are fully informed of their current condition and prognosis and fully competent to make their own treatment decisions. For Anita and Bill, therefore, a request for assisted death is an exercise of their autonomy. The value of autonomy grounds the second important argument for the justifiability of assisted death. As explicated earlier (§2.1), autonomy (or self-determination) is a matter of being the active manager of one's life in accordance with one's deeply held goals and values. In that earlier discussion, autonomy (along with well-being) was one of the values served by informed consent to treatment (and therefore also informed refusal of treatment). But being the active manager of one's dying process may require requests for treatment as well as refusals. We have seen this already with respect to the treatment modalities discussed in the previous chapter. If the suffering of a competent patient reaches intolerable levels and she makes an informed request for either high-dose opioids or terminal sedation, then respecting that request serves both the patient's well-being and her autonomy, even though it may also hasten her death. The same holds for a request for assisted suicide or voluntary euthanasia.

As we have seen, the most familiar form of the argument from well-being is consequentialist: where assisted death would be in the best interest of the patient, by preventing further suffering, then providing it would have the best consequences. But it can also take a deontological form, working from a duty of care to the patient or a duty not to inflict or permit avoidable suffering. Likewise, the argument from autonomy can also take either form. On the one hand, we can say that where acceding to a patient request for assisted death serves both her best interest and her autonomy then we have even more reason to think that it would be best on the whole. But for this argument the more common form is deontological, resting on a right

---

[53] Jamie Mayerfeld (1999: ch. 5) argues for a duty of this sort.

[54] Mayerfeld's duty to relieve suffering is *pro tanto* in this way. For the argument that role-specific duties prohibit physicians from assisting the deaths of their patients see §7.5, below. Sanctity-of-life arguments, of the sort discussed in the previous section, are attempts to ground a general duty not to assist death.

to self-determination. As we saw earlier (§2.1), the requirement of informed consent to treatment, and the honouring of informed refusal of treatment, are usually justified by reference to such a right: how things are to go with her body and her life is a matter for the patient to decide. But the right of self-determination is also engaged by treatment requests, such as analgesics or terminal sedation. And again this will hold equally if the request is for assisted death.[55]

The arguments from well-being and autonomy provide the basic justificatory framework for assisted suicide and voluntary euthanasia. However, they do not, and cannot, show that these practices are always justified. On the contrary, appeals to these values are capable of justifying the practices only under appropriate conditions. What remains is to outline those conditions. My substantive claim is that assisted suicide and voluntary euthanasia are justified when the following five conditions are satisfied:[56]

Request. Because both treatment options are voluntary, they must be requested by the patient and not on the patient's behalf by a substitute decision-maker.

Capacity. The patient must be decisionally capable at the time with respect to the treatment option in question. Decisional capacity includes the ability to understand and appreciate the nature and consequences of requesting a therapeutic intervention that is intended to cause death. While decisional capacity must be the default presumption for adult patients, it is rebuttable by evidence of either some standing mental illness or disability or some situational factors serious enough to impair cognitive functioning. The relevant decisional capacity for assisted death is the ability to make reasoned decisions *with respect to this kind of treatment*. A person may be competent to make other personal decisions (such as financial ones), or even other treatment decisions, but not this one.

Voluntariness. The patient's request must be free of undue influence and coercion, whether by providers or by family or friends. It is recognized, of course, that our decision-making as patients will often be influenced by what others think or suggest or by our knowledge of what they want or would prefer. Since it would aim much too high to purge decision-making of all such influences, the issue of voluntariness will turn on when such influences are 'undue'—that is, when they rise to the level of fraud, deceit, duress, or any other form of coercion. As with decisional capacity, there will inevitably be borderline cases in which the voluntariness of a patient request for assisted death is uncertain.

Disclosure. The patient must be provided with adequate information concerning the treatment options in question. This information will normally include the patient's diagnosis and prognosis in the absence of treatment (including any uncertainty attending these matters), the nature of each of the available treatment options, the probable outcome of each option, and the risks attached to each option. The general rule for

---

[55] This is not to deny that there is a significant asymmetry between treatment refusals and treatment requests. For discussion of this issue see §4.3, below.

[56] Satisfaction of all of these conditions is sufficient for justification. I do not argue that it is necessary.

disclosure is that it should include all the information a reasonable person *in this particular patient's circumstances* would need in order to make a reasoned decision concerning the treatment in question.

Diagnosis. The patient must be diagnosed with a medical condition (an illness or disability) serious enough to warrant consideration of treatment options that will hasten death. The condition may, but need not, itself be terminal. The patient must be experiencing a degree of suffering that he regards as intolerable and which cannot be alleviated to the patient's satisfaction by any treatment option that will not also have the effect of hastening death.

Of these five conditions, the first four simply replicate the standard conditions for informed consent to treatment enumerated earlier (§2.1). The fifth, however, is specific to treatment decisions that will hasten death. It has, of course, been formulated here so as to apply to requests for either assisted suicide or voluntary euthanasia. However, it should also be applied to requests for high-dose opioids or terminal sedation (on the assumption that these methods of treatment also have the potential to hasten death). The reason for requiring that other treatment options have first been exhausted, or that they have been refused by the patient, is straightforward: hastening death is final and irreversible, precluding all further opportunity for rethinking one's choice. There is a mild degree of paternalism at work here—some privileging of patient well-being over autonomy—in ensuring that assisted death is not requested prematurely or unnecessarily. This condition of intolerable and intractable suffering is specific to requests for treatment methods that hasten death (whether intentionally or not). It has no counterpart for treatment refusals, even if they will also hasten death, reflecting the fact that the right to refuse treatment is weightier than the right to request it. The reasons for this asymmetry will be explored in the next section.

4.3 The Doctrine of Doing and Allowing

The previous section defended an argument by extension: from the justifiability of suicide through that of assisted suicide to voluntary euthanasia. What the extensionist argument claims is that there is no significant ethical difference between the various measures in this sequence *when all other relevant factors are equal.* So for Anita and Bill it makes no ethical difference whether they forestall further suffering by ending their lives on their own, ending them with the assistance of their physicians, or requesting that their physicians end them: if suicide is justified in their cases then so is assisted suicide and if that is justified then so is euthanasia. And the reason this extensionist argument goes through is that at each stage the practice in question can be justified by reference to the same two basic values.

But this is only the latter stage of a longer extensionist argument that has been running through the last three chapters, from the justifiability of refusing life-sustaining treatment, to that of administering high-dose opioids or sedatives, to assisted suicide and (voluntary) euthanasia. The argument of this book is that if the first treatment decision in this sequence is justified then so are all the others *when all other relevant factors are equal*. There are no ethical bright lines between the first and last measures in the sequence: if treatment refusal is permissible in principle then so is euthanasia.[57] And again the reason the extensionist argument goes through is that at each stage the measure in question can be justified by reference to the same two basic values.

There are, however, two well-established and widely influential ways of resisting this argument. The first attempts to block the step from the administration of high-dose analgesics and sedatives to assisted death by invoking the ethical significance of the intending/foreseeing distinction. I have already argued (in §3.2) that the Doctrine of Double Effect does not succeed in drawing an ethical bright line between measures in which death is merely foreseen and those in which it is intended *when all other relevant factors are equal*, and I will not repeat that argument here.

The second means of resistance attempts to block the transition from refusal of treatment to assisted death by invoking the ethical significance of the doing/allowing distinction. This distinction turns on the fact that there can be two different ways of bringing about the same effect—by making it happen (doing) or by letting it happen (allowing). In the case of a bad, or harmful, effect the Doctrine of Doing and Allowing (DDA) holds that it may sometimes be permissible to let it happen, though it would be impermissible to make it happen. Obviously, this Doctrine has a very wide range of potential applications, including any decision situation in which we can compare these two ways of bringing about the same harm or injury, and it argues for a significant ethical distinction running through all these situations. As such, it has attracted a quite sizeable literature.[58] Since I have no intention of adding to that literature, I will confine myself to the DDA's implications for end-of-life decisions. In this context it is standardly used to support the Conventional View, which draws an ethical bright line between two means of hastening death: 'active' (euthanasia) and 'passive' (withholding or withdrawing life-sustaining treatment).[59] My question is whether it is up to this task.

---

[57] This claim is subject to one important qualification, to be discussed later in this section, having to do with the asymmetry between treatment refusals and requests. Healthcare providers may be obligated to respect a patient's refusal of treatment regardless of whether doing so will be in the patient's best interest. But they may have no obligation to respect a request for euthanasia (or assisted suicide or opioids or sedatives) if this treatment will be of no medical benefit to the patient (e.g. by providing relief from suffering). Thus the need for an appropriate diagnosis among the justifying conditions for assisted death. None of this, however, threatens the justification of euthanasia.

[58] A few of the more prominent contributions: Glover 1977: ch. 7; Foot 1984; Quinn 1989*b*; Kagan 1989: ch. 3; Bennett 1995: chs. 4–8.

[59] Assisted suicide will count as an 'active' means as well. However, in this case the main 'activity' is carried out by the patient who self-administers a lethal dose, the role of the physician being limited to facilitating the act by prescribing the medication. In discussing 'active' means I will focus instead on euthanasia, where the physician is the primary agent.

Although the Doctrine of Doing and Allowing has some superficial similarities with the Doctrine of Double Effect, the two are quite distinct. As Shelly Kagan has pointed out, the distinctions invoked by the two doctrines (doing/allowing, intending/foreseeing) are orthogonal to one another.[60] Among 'active' measures death is the intended outcome of euthanasia but it may be an unintended side effect of terminal sedation (assuming that this measure does indeed hasten death). All treatment refusals are conventionally classified as 'passive', but they divide between those in which death may be the intended outcome (e.g. refusal of a ventilator or of food and water) and those in which it is not (e.g. refusal of further chemotherapy).[61] We therefore have this matrix of possible combinations:

	Doing	Allowing
Intending	Euthanasia	Some treatment refusals
Foreseeing	Terminal sedation	Some treatment refusals

Rejecting the ethical significance of the intending/foreseeing distinction (at least as it pertains to these different treatment decisions) therefore tells us nothing about the significance (if any) of the doing/allowing distinction. That remains to be determined.

As conventionally understood, the 'active/passive' distinction sorts all cases of euthanasia to the 'active' side and all cases of withholding/withdrawing treatment to the 'passive' side. As the quotation marks. I have been continually putting around 'active' and 'passive' are meant to suggest, I do not find these terms perspicuous for capturing the distinction in question. The terms suggest that it consists in the distinction between doing something and doing nothing, or between acts and omissions. Administering euthanasia undeniably requires the physician to do something, and there are certainly cases, such as complying with a 'do-not-resuscitate' order, in which withholding treatment requires the physician to do nothing. But there are also many cases, such as disconnecting a ventilator or removing a feeding tube, in which withdrawing treatment requires activity on the part of the physician. The 'active/passive' distinction therefore cannot be understood in terms of the act/omission distinction.[62]

The obvious alternative is to construe it in terms of the doing/allowing distinction. We can then say that it concerns two different ways in which death can be brought about—'active' when it is *made* to happen, 'passive' when it is *allowed* to happen. Since euthanasia makes death happen it counts as killing the patient; since withholding/withdrawing treatment merely allows death to happen it counts as letting the patient

---

[60] Kagan 1989: 83–9. Ralph Wedgwood (2009) has suggested that the two distinctions mark two different dimensions of 'agential involvement' in an act: intentional and causal. Wedgwood claims that, other things equal, someone's degree of agential involvement in bringing about a state of affairs is greater if either (1) she intends it (as opposed to merely foreseeing it) or (2) she actively causes it to happen (as opposed to failing to prevent it).

[61] See the discussion in §2.3, above.

[62] For a critique of the use of the act/omission distinction in the law, see G. Williams 2007: ch. 3.

die. On this proposal, therefore, the 'active/passive' distinction is the killing/letting die distinction. By itself, however, this proposal does not much advance our understanding. Administering a lethal injection to a patient certainly looks like a clear case of killing the patient (at least if we can bracket all of the pejorative implications of 'killing') and discontinuing chemotherapy when it will have no therapeutic benefit looks like a clear case of letting the patient die of her cancer. But what are we to make of the action of a physician who removes a patient's ventilator, leading to her death minutes later by anoxia? Is this a case of letting death happen or making it happen, letting the patient die or killing her? To answer these questions we need to dig deeper, to determine what the killing/letting die distinction is gesturing towards.

We know that it cannot be a difference of intention. Nor, it seems, can it be a matter of causation. In euthanasia it seems plausible to consider the lethal medication as the cause of death. But identifying the cause of death when life-sustaining treatment is withheld or withdrawn is much more problematic.[63] In one perfectly good sense ('but for' causation) the physician's removal of the ventilator is a cause of the patient's death (had the ventilator not been removed the patient would not have died *then* and *in that way*). That makes removing the ventilator appear to be making death happen. If we seek a means of avoiding this conclusion by saying that the cause of death in this case is the patient's underlying condition, and not the removal of the ventilator, then we may need to resort to a normative concept that determines cause of death on the basis of a prior determination of whether the physician's action was justifiable.[64] If that is the way in which the killing/letting die (or 'active/passive') distinction is being drawn, then it cannot serve as the basis of differential ethical judgements about the two categories, since it will presuppose such judgements.

It is by no means obvious, therefore, that there is any coherent non-normative basis for the 'active/passive' (killing/letting die) distinction. In that case, the Doctrine of Doing and Allowing may not mark any unambiguous distinction between permissible and impermissible end-of-life measures. Even if we put this complication to one side, however, and assume that the DDA is capable of drawing a bright line, there seems to be no way for it to draw the line where the Conventional View locates it. If we make the (plausible) assumption that the administration of a lethal medication is the cause of death in the case of euthanasia, then there will be no way to avoid the (equally plausible) conclusion that the administration of sedatives can be the cause of death in the case of terminal sedation or that the removal of a feeding tube can be the cause of death when a patient has refused nutrition and hydration. But in that case the DDA will locate terminal sedation and (some cases of) treatment refusal on the 'wrong' side

---

[63] As we saw earlier (§2.3, above).

[64] Recall the two scenarios (discussed earlier in §2.3) in which a physician removes a patient's ventilator: in the first he is complying with the patient's refusal of treatment and in the second he is attempting to inherit her estate upon her death. If we wish to say that the physician's action is the cause of death in the second scenario, but not the first, this is presumably because we believe that he is (morally and legally) responsible for her death in this case.

of the line for the purposes of the Conventional View. Put another way, if the DDA supports the conclusion that euthanasia is impermissible then it will equally support the conclusion that terminal sedation, the administration of high-dose opioids, and the removal of a feeding tube or a ventilator are impermissible. And these results do not serve the needs of the Conventional View.

Leaving aside the question of where the DDA draws its line, we can still ask whether that line is ethically significant. To have a reasonably concrete situation with which to work, I will reintroduce Douglas, who is dying of pancreatic cancer. Chemotherapy holds out the possibility of slowing the dying process somewhat but the side-effects of the treatment are severe; without it Douglas will soon die from his cancer. Let us say that Douglas has two means of managing his dying process: refusing treatment (letting death happen) and requesting euthanasia (making death happen). So as to keep other factors equal, as much as possible, we will assume that euthanasia is legal in Douglas's jurisdiction, that he would satisfy the criteria for it, and that his physician is willing to administer it. Furthermore, we will stipulate that Douglas will experience no more suffering by refusing treatment than by requesting euthanasia. Douglas is indifferent between the two options: he will give informed refusal to chemotherapy and informed consent to euthanasia. What, then, does the DDA tell us about these options?

It will tell us nothing unless it makes the assumption that, regardless of the way it comes about, Douglas's death will be a harm to him. However, as with the Double Effect in our earlier discussion (§3.2), there is no reason to accept this assumption. If under the circumstances death would be a benefit for Douglas, rather than a harm, then the DDA has nothing to say about the choice between treatment refusal and euthanasia.[65] We will need to ignore this complication in order to address the doing/ allowing issue straight on. So we now ask: Is there an ethically significant difference between the 'active' and the 'passive' means of bringing about Douglas's death?

In a much-discussed article James Rachels has argued that there is not.[66] He asks us to consider this pair of cases:

Smith stands to gain a large inheritance if anything should happen to his six-year-old cousin. One evening while the child is taking his bath, Smith sneaks into the bathroom and drowns the child, and then arranges things so that it will look like an accident. No one is the wiser and Smith gets his inheritance.

Jones also stands to gain if anything should happen to his six-year-old cousin. Like Smith, Jones sneaks in planning to drown the child in his bath. However, just as he enters the bathroom Jones sees the child slip, hit his head, and fall face down in the water. Jones is delighted; he stands by, ready to push the child's head back under if necessary, but it is not necessary. With only a

---

[65] Jeff McMahan (2002: 461) has argued that (an extended version of) the Doctrine should have something to say: 'If doing harm is worse than allowing harm to occur, actively *benefiting* someone should, in general, be *better* than merely allowing someone to be benefited, even when all other things (such as motive, intention, cost to the agent, and so on) are equal.' I am agnostic on this point.

[66] Rachels 1975; cf. his 1986: ch. 7.

little thrashing about, the child drowns all by himself, 'accidentally', as Jones watches and does nothing. No one is the wiser, and Jones gets his inheritance.[67]

Rachels argues that these two cases are equivalent in all relevant respects: the agents' motive, intention, and the consequences of their action (or inaction). The 'bare difference' in these cases that the one is a killing and the other a letting die does not, he urges, make an ethical difference. Rachels concludes from this that in general this bare difference does not make a difference, thus that, other factors equal, 'active' means are no worse (and no better) than 'passive' ones.

Shelly Kagan has argued that Rachels is unjustified in drawing a general conclusion from his particular pair of cases.[68] Kagan contends that Rachels must assume the 'ubiquity thesis': if variation in a particular factor makes a moral difference anywhere, then it must make a difference everywhere (and thus, if it does not make a difference everywhere then it must not make a difference anywhere). But this thesis, Kagan contends, is false, since the difference a factor makes may not be independent of the other factors with which it is combined in particular cases. Thus, if the doing/allowing distinction makes no moral difference (between Smith's conduct and Jones's) in Rachels' cases, it does not follow that it makes no difference in end-of-life cases.[69]

Assuming that Kagan is correct in this, we should test the DDA by addressing the case of Douglas directly, rather than by relying on extrapolation from other cases. So let us assume that all other relevant ethical factors are equal for the two measures in question. We are left, then, with the 'bare difference' between an 'active' means (euthanasia) and a 'passive' one (treatment refusal). Does this difference make an ethical difference? I suggest that the grounds for saying that it does are no more persuasive here than they are in Rachels' cases.

Even if this is correct, it is still a conclusion about one particular pair of cases. Of course, that conclusion is itself enough to defeat the application of the DDA to these cases, since it would imply the wrong result. But, heeding Kagan, we should still be wary of generalizing this result to all end-of-life scenarios in which two means of bringing about death differ only along this killing/letting die dimension. However, two observations are in order. One is that Kagan does allow for a more moderate conclusion to be drawn from a particular pair of cases: if a factor makes no difference in these cases then this fact at least creates a rebuttable presumption that it will make no difference in other similar cases.[70] What counts as a similar case? In general, where

---

[67] Rachels 1986: 112.

[68] Kagan 1988. For other examples of the overgeneralization objection, see Trammell 1975: 132; Foot 1977: 101–2; Bennett 1995: 77–8.

[69] It could also be said that the relevant difference in the Smith–Jones cases is between doing something (act) and doing nothing (omission). But, as pointed out above, most 'passive' withdrawals of treatment are not omissions in this sense. This provides a further reason for distrusting the generalization from this pair of cases to the 'active/passive' distinction.

[70] I have adapted this conclusion from Kagan 1988: 30. Kagan's own conclusion is formulated in terms of factors that do make a difference.

'active' and 'passive' means to the same end are being contemplated in end-of-life decision-making, cases are similar when all the factors that were equal in Douglas's case are equal, including (especially) patient consent and patient benefit. In these cases there would appear to be no other factors in play that might rebut the presumption that the bare 'active/passive' difference makes no difference, in which case we may conclude that (even on the assumption that death is a harm) the DDA fails in its application to end-of-life options.[71] The second observation slightly, but significantly, corrects the generalization from Douglas's case to other end-of-life cases. The case of Douglas was selected precisely to keep all (other) factors equal, including the upshot of the two measures in terms of relief of suffering. Among other things, this required specifying a 'passive' means (refusing chemotherapy) which would be as quick and painless as euthanasia. But few cases are like this. Much more typical is Anita's situation, where discontinuation of all cancer treatment will result in weeks of further suffering. In this case all (other) relevant factors are decidedly not equal—in particular, the consequences of the two measures. But where this is the case then euthanasia seems obviously the better option.[72]

The DDA therefore provides no ground for drawing an ethical bright line between assisted death and conventionally accepted end-of-life measures. This is, of course, the same conclusion reached earlier (§3.2) for the Doctrine of Double Effect. So we now have the following result: neither the intending/foreseeing distinction nor the doing/allowing distinction, taken by itself, is capable of drawing the line required by the Conventional View. But might the combination of these two distinctions not be more successful?[73] Might it not be the case that euthanasia is, after all, ethically unique, since it is the only measure in which death is *both* intended and caused? We already know the answer to this question. If we continue to make the plausible assumptions that in refusing a ventilator or a feeding tube a patient can be intending to die, and that the removal of the device is the cause of death, then some instances of treatment refusal will share the two features that death is both intended and caused.

The Doctrine of Doing and Allowing is one standard means of identifying a moral asymmetry between 'active' and 'passive' means. But it is not the only one. We know that the measures conventionally classified as 'active' all involve administering treatment (which causes death), while those classified as 'passive' involve withholding or withdrawing treatment (which may hasten death).[74] It may seem unlikely that this

---

[71] It may well be much more persuasive in its application to other types of cases, such as comparisons between killings and failures to rescue. As in the case of the Doctrine of Double Effect, my aim is not to undercut it across the board, but only to show that it cannot justify a differential ethical evaluation of 'active' and 'passive' measures hastening death in end-of-life scenarios.

[72] It is better in another important respect as well, since it would allow Anita (and Douglas) to determine the time and circumstance of their deaths. It would therefore be superior to waiting to be killed by the cancer in terms of both patient well-being and patient self-determination.

[73] I owe this question to Tom Hurka.

[74] The treatment/non-treatment distinction will, of course, place the administration of high-dose opioids and terminal sedation in the 'active' category (whether or not they hasten death). But this is as it ought to be: on any reasonable account they are not 'passive'.

treatment/non-treatment distinction has any ethical significance in itself, not least because the latter category is so heterogeneous. It includes cases in which treatment refusal is intended to hasten death and cases in which it is not, and it includes cases in which treatment refusal is itself a cause of death and cases in which it is not. How could all these cases possibly be normatively unified? And how could there be a significant normative difference between them and the 'active' cases?

One answer to these questions looks at the rights that are engaged by the two categories of cases. We have already discussed (§2.2) the way in which the patient's right to refuse treatment engages the Doctrine of Informed Consent, which is in turn based on the patient's claim-right to security, or integrity, of the person. This claim-right imposes on others a duty not to use force or violence against one's person. Since most—not all—medical treatment is invasive of the body, it follows that physicians have a *pro tanto* duty not to administer such treatment, a duty that the patient can waive by giving informed consent to treatment. This negative duty (*not* to use force or violence) is normally taken to be very stringent: it is the basis of the major legal offences against the person, such as assault, rape, and homicide. With the exception of some extreme situations, such as emergencies, the duty forbids physicians from administering any treatment that the patient has refused. In the so-called 'passive' cases, therefore, physicians are not merely *permitted* to withhold or withdraw treatment, even though doing so may hasten the patient's death, they are *required* to do so. And within this general rule it is irrelevant whether the patient's (or physician's) intention is to hasten death or whether the cessation of treatment will be the (plausible) cause of death. The 'passive' cases are unified, not by any of these further features, but just by being instances of the patient's exercise of the right to security, or integrity, of the person.

There is, therefore, an important normative asymmetry between the 'passive' and 'active' cases, between refusals of treatment and requests for treatment.[75] When the patient has requested, or at least consented to, treatment her claim-right to security or integrity of the person is not engaged in the same way. However, this is not to say that it is not engaged at all, or that no other rights are engaged. Patients may also have a claim-right to aid or assistance from others which will include a right to medical treatment (under appropriate circumstances). This right imposes, not a negative, but a positive duty on others: a duty to provide such aid or assistance. However, in general positive duties are usually taken to be less stringent than negative ones, in part at least because they impose a greater burden on duty-bearers. It is very easy for me to fulfil my negative duty not to assault, rape, or murder anyone: all I have to do is refrain from these acts. It would be much more difficult to fulfil my positive duty to aid or assist everyone, since the many opportunities for providing such aid or assistance would be overwhelming. It is for this reason that legal systems are reluctant to impose positive

---

[75] The view that this refusal/request distinction marks the important moral difference between 'active' and 'passive' means is defended by Gert, Culver, and Clouser 1998. The more general point, that the doing/ allowing or killing/letting die distinction rests on the normative distinction between negative and positive rights (or duties), has been made by Foot 1984 and Quinn 1989*b*.

'good Samaritan' obligations on citizens, while insisting that they not violate their negative obligations not to harm. In the medical context 'active' cases (of euthanasia) are obviously requests for the administration of treatment rather than refusals of treatment. As such, they engage a right to request treatment that is weaker than the right to refuse it. While (competent) patients have a blanket right to refuse any treatment they do not want, they do not have an analogous blanket right to request any treatment they want. Just to make the most obvious point, the treatment in question must be clinically indicated—it must, that is, have a reasonable prospect of conferring a medical benefit on the patient. But, in addition, there may be relevant considerations of scarcity or expense. The general point is that a positive right to treatment imposes significantly greater burdens on others than a negative right to non-treatment; it is, therefore, correspondingly weaker.

'Weaker', however, does not mean negligible or non-existent. Doctors do, after all, have positive duties towards their patients, above all the duty to respect their auton-omy and the duty to promote their well-being. The latter includes the duty to relieve their patients' suffering, when they have the means to do so. It is this duty whose fulfilment has led palliative medicine to embrace the 'analgesic ladder' and to practise terminal sedation. There is no reason, in principle, why it should not lead to the practice of assisted suicide or euthanasia as well. The fact that a patient who wishes to prevent further suffering has a weaker right to request treatment (for this end) than to refuse it may imply that the physician is not *required* to administer euthanasia upon request, but it gives no reason to think that she is not *permitted* to. There is therefore no argument from this asymmetry of rights (and duties) to the impermissibility of euthanasia.[76]

4.4 Last Words

This chapter has laid out a constructive argument for the justifiability of assisted death that appeals to the two basic values of patient well-being and patient autonomy. That argument can be expressed in either consequentialist or deontological form—the former if it urges that (under appropriate conditions) assisted death will have the best overall consequences because it will best serve these two values, the latter if it appeals either to the physician's duty to relieve suffering or to the patient's right of self-determination. In either form, the argument makes a strong presumptive case that making assisted death available to patients (under appropriate conditions) will be at least morally permissible, if not obligatory. However, there are well-known counter-arguments that attempt to rebut this presumption, especially those that appeal to the sanctity of life, the inalienable right to life, or the doing/allowing distinction. All these

---

[76] Philippa Foot (1977) argues to the same conclusion from a similar asymmetry between duties of justice and duties of charity.

counterarguments have been analysed and found wanting. The presumptive case therefore stands.

The conclusion drawn in the foregoing discussion is that *when all relevant factors are equal* assisted death is not worse than either withholding/withdrawing treatment or the administration of opioids or sedative at dose levels that may hasten death. However, there is an important sense in which this conclusion is much weaker than the constructive argument will support. In discussing the doing/allowing distinction I focused on a particular case—that of Douglas—in which all *other* ethically relevant factors were held constant so as to isolate just the 'active/passive' distinction. However, that case had to be carefully constructed so that all other factors *were* equal. In particular, the consequences of the two treatment decisions—to administer euthanasia or withhold chemotherapy—had to be identical in terms of both Douglas's autonomy and his well-being. Thus it had to be specified that (*a*) he would be equally willing to choose either way of proceeding and (*b*) his suffering would be equally relieved by either. These factors will not be equal whenever a patient prefers euthanasia (or assisted suicide) to any alternative means of dealing with his suffering, and thus specifically requests it, or whenever this measure will be most effective at minimizing that suffering. But these latter conditions will frequently be satisfied, since assisted death has significant advantages for many patients over the other options available to them. In terms of self-determination, choosing assisted suicide or euthanasia enables the patient to determine the time, place, and manner of her own death, thereby enabling her to be the active manager of her dying process. By contrast, refusal of treatment allows these matters to be determined by the patient's disease condition. And in terms of well-being, death seldom follows treatment withdrawal as quickly and painlessly as it was stipulated to do in Douglas's case. Much more typical is Anita, who would face weeks of further suffering from her cancer following cessation of all therapeutic treatment. Under these very common circumstances we can say not only that assisted death would be no worse than the other available end-of-life options, but that it would be better.

5

Deciding for Others

The previous three chapters have explored the ethical significance (if any) of a number of dimensions along which end-of-life measures can differ: whether they are requests for treatment or refusals, whether death is intended or merely foreseen, whether death is made to happen or allowed to happen. Despite their many differences, however, all the measures so far discussed share one important feature in common: they are all voluntary. To say that an end-of-life measure is voluntary is to say (roughly) that it is freely chosen by the patient at the time at which the measure is put into effect. The decision made by the patient may take the form of a request or a refusal, but in either case the patient is giving (or withholding) contemporaneous consent to treatment. Voluntariness therefore presupposes contemporaneous decisional capacity on the part of the patient, a presupposition that frequently fails in end-of-life scenarios. We will say that an end-of-life treatment decision is nonvoluntary whenever the patient is not decisionally capable at the time it is put into effect.[1] The ethics of nonvoluntary measures is the subject of this chapter.

At least on the face of it, the voluntary/nonvoluntary distinction appears to be ethically salient. The case for the justifiability of all end-of-life measures so far discussed, including assisted death, has appealed to the same pair of values: well-being and autonomy. Since each of these values appears to matter a great deal by itself in ethical decision-making, any argument that is able to draw on both of them will be very powerful. When a treatment decision is nonvoluntary appeal can still be made to the patient's best interest, but the absence of decisional capacity will preclude at least the normal kind of appeal to patient self-determination. It is therefore an open question whether measures that can be justified when voluntary can also be defended

---

[1] Nonvoluntary measures are therefore distinct from involuntary ones—i.e. those imposed on a decisionally capable patient against her will. No justification will be offered for involuntary measures. It should be noted, however, that there is at least one type of scenario in which treatment is often imposed on a patient who has antecedently refused it—namely, when the patient's condition is the result of an unsuccessful suicide attempt and his refusal is in the form of a suicide note. For discussion of these issues see D'Oronzio 2002 (with accompanying commentaries) and Macauley 2007.

when nonvoluntary. In attempting to answer this question our main focus will be on euthanasia, but it will be well to keep in mind that it applies with equal force to every other form of end-of-life treatment (or nontreatment).[2]

5.1 The Formerly Competent

If we make the assumption that a patient is either decisionally capable or not at the time of the treatment decision, then the voluntary/nonvoluntary distinction is mutually exclusive.[3] However, it conceals an important distinction among the nonvoluntary cases. A patient who lacks current capacity may or may not have had capacity at an earlier time. We will say that a patient who has had such capacity, and subsequently lost it, is *formerly competent*, while a patient who has never had capacity is *never competent*. The importance of this distinction lies in the fact that patients in the former category, but not the latter, may have made an end-of-life treatment decision in advance of the time when it is to be put into effect. If so, then self-determination may still be in play for them as a factor in justifying the later decision either to administer or to withhold/ withdraw treatment. We might think of these cases not as purely nonvoluntary but rather as quasi-voluntary and we will discuss them first.

While there are many conditions under which decisional capacity may be irretrievably lost, in what follows I will focus on just two of them: advanced dementia and permanent (irreversible) unconsciousness. Treatment decisions will frequently need to be made for patients in one or the other of these conditions, and yet the patients themselves will be unable to register contemporaneous consent to (or refusal of) treatment. In that case, (two questions immediately present themselves: Who should make the treatment decision? On what basis should the decision be made?)

Both questions are answered, in principle at least, by the standard model of advance care planning. The basic idea behind this model is simple. While you will not be capable of informed consent/refusal should you become severely demented or permanently unconscious, at an earlier stage in your life, when you are still decisionally capable, you can anticipate that you may later find yourself in one or the other of these conditions. If you wish to be able to exercise some degree of control over your later treatment then the obvious mechanism is to register your treatment decisions in advance, ideally in a written instrument. These will be now-for-then decisions, as opposed to the normal contemporaneous now-for-now decisions. But because they are made by a decisionally capable patient, though applicable only in the event of incapacity, they will still count as the exercise of (diachronic rather than synchronic) self-determination.

---

[2] Except, perhaps, assisted suicide, which appears to be necessarily voluntary.

[3] Decisional capacity surely admits of degrees, but it must still be determined whether *this* patient surmounts the threshold of capacity and is therefore to be recognized as the decision-maker for *this* treatment at *this* time. And that will be a yes/no determination.

There are two types of instrument available for advance care planning.[4] Instruction directives (also known as living wills) allow persons to stipulate which modes of treatment they accept, and which they reject, under particular conditions of incapacity (such as advanced dementia and permanent unconsciousness). In effect, they provide the opportunity to register *now* the decisions the person would make *then*, if capable of doing so. Proxy directives (also known as durable powers of attorney) appoint someone else to serve as substitute decision-maker for the (later) incapacitated patient. Most advance directives include both types of instrument,[5] in which case they provide answers to both the foregoing questions: treatment decisions for the incapacitated patient should be made by whomever the patient has designated in advance as her proxy, and they should be made on the basis of the patient's advance instructions.

So understood, advance care planning is a logical extension of the Doctrine of Informed Consent. Just as the requirement of informed consent safeguards the individual's autonomy in contemporaneous treatment (or nontreatment) decisions, so the requirement that advance directives be respected safeguards the individual's autonomy over such decisions at later stages of her life.[6] Furthermore, if we continue to assume that autonomous individuals are normally the best judges of their own interests then respecting treatment (or nontreatment) decisions registered in advance will have the added justification that it is also protective of patient well-being.

The standard model of advance care planning therefore appears to provide a straightforward means whereby formerly competent patients may exercise some degree of control over their end-of-life care. That control can take the form either of requesting or refusing familiar modes of treatment: resuscitation, tube feeding, ventilation, administration of antibiotics, sedation, etc. And so we might now ask the logical further question: Is there any reason not to extend it to requests for euthanasia? Alas, however, these matters are not as simple as they might seem. From the outset critics have raised a number of concerns about reliance on advance directives for decision-making on behalf of formerly competent patients. Some of these concerns turn on issues that are specific to cases of advanced dementia or permanent unconsciousness, and we will come to them shortly when we discuss these conditions in more detail. But some of them are more general, challenging the efficacy of advance care planning, and we will deal with them first. To keep matters as uncomplicated as possible, for the moment we will focus on advance refusals of treatment, postponing the issue of advance requests until later.

Over the past couple of decades Rebecca Dresser has been the most persistent critic of this model of advance care planning. Most of her objections have been broadly practical in nature, pointing to various respects in which advance treatment refusals are

    [4] Buchanan and Brock 1989: ch. 6; Cantor 1993: ch. 4; Olick 2001: 98 ff.

    [5] Model advance directives (combining both instruments) abound; for one influential version see Emanuel and Emanuel 1989.

    [6] The view that the principal rationale of advance care planning lies in its extension of patient autonomy is defended in Buchanan and Brock 1989: 95; Cantor 1993: ch. 2; Olick 2001: chs. 2 and 3.

less reliable than contemporaneous ones as expressions of patient self-determination. Although she does not sort them in this way, I will divide the issues she has raised into two categories: problems of information and problems of vagueness.[7]

The informational deficiencies of advance directives are best appreciated by contrasting them with contemporaneous care decisions. Recall (from §2.1) that one of the core elements of the Doctrine of Informed Consent is the requirement of disclosure, whose general rule is that the patient must be provided with all the information that a reasonable person in her particular circumstances would need in order to make a reasoned decision concerning the treatment in question. This information will normally include the patient's diagnosis and prognosis in the absence of treatment (including any uncertainty attending these matters), the nature of each of the available treatment options, the probable outcome of each option, and the risks attached to each option. The requirement of disclosure requires communication, preferably face to face, between the patient and her healthcare providers, with the attendant opportunity for both questioning and discussion. Furthermore, it must be emphasized that the information is specific to *this* treatment for *this* condition and *this* patient. It can therefore be as full and detailed as the patient requires and the circumstances permit. In principle at least, contemporaneous decision-making can live up to the highest ideals of informed choice.

Contrast this rosy picture with treatment decisions made years, even decades, before the onset of incapacity and the need for treatment. Not only are there many types, and degrees, of incapacity (including dementia and unconsciousness), there are even more conditions for which an incapacitated patient might require life-sustaining treatment. To try to anticipate all these future contingencies in detail, and to decide for each of them whether to accept or decline a particular form of treatment, is a practical impossibility. By contrast, therefore, with the specificity of contemporaneous consent/refusal, advance decision-making is necessarily more general: for this *kind* of condition I accept/refuse this *kind* of treatment. It is also, by its nature, less susceptible to the give-and-take of direct communication with one's healthcare provider. General scenarios can, of course, be discussed in advance as hypotheticals, but doing so is far less informative than a specific treatment consultation. Finally, contemporaneous decision-making also has the advantage that the information provided is up to date. While it may not be possible to anticipate further discoveries or treatment modalities that would be relevant to the patient's decision, at least the current state of both knowledge

---

[7] Dresser sometimes also cites the fact that, even in developed societies with an educated populace, only a relatively small minority of people (usually reported as being 10–25 per cent) ever complete an advance directive. (Dresser 1994; 2003: 1829) However, this fact has no obvious bearing on the question of whether we should respect the treatment refusals (or requests) that have been registered by members of that minority. As Dresser herself notes, executing a written instrument recording treatment decisions years or decades in advance of the time when they might become operational is both time-consuming and psychologically challenging. In the light of these obstacles it seems reasonable to assume that the minority who have persisted with this task must be particularly determined to have a say over their own future care. In that case, perhaps they have a particularly strong claim to have their choices respected.

and art can be fully communicated. By contrast, treatment decisions registered far in advance might be rendered obsolete or redundant by subsequent medical developments. Even if these decisions were as informed as possible *then*, they may not reflect the options available to the incapacitated patient *now*. For that reason they also may not reflect the informed choices the patient would make now, were she capable of such choices.[8]

The informational deficiencies canvassed in the previous paragraph are all factual in nature. But it is equally possible for a person's values to shift with the passage of time, so that a decision autonomously made earlier in one's life ceases to have that status later.[9] Advance directives can, of course, be modified, or renounced entirely, in response to changes of heart. But for various practical reasons this may not happen, with the result that the treatment decisions recorded in the written directive are now uninformed, not about factual matters, but about the subject's own preferences. Furthermore, it is often difficult, or even impossible, to anticipate in advance what it would be like to be in the various conditions for which one is trying to plan. As an active able-bodied person you might imagine full body paralysis, or 'locked-in' syndrome, to be unendurable. When it occurs you might discover that it still makes a meaningful life possible, but if you are unable to communicate treatment decisions at the time you might find yourself bound by your own earlier, uninformed, preferences.

The vagueness problem for advance directives is a corollary of the foregoing informational impediments.[10] Whereas contemporaneous refusal is specific as to both treatment and occasion, advance instructions must attempt to anticipate a wide variety of treatment options and circumstances.[11] While one might attempt to respond to each of these possible scenarios with detailed and precise directions concerning forms of treatment to be withheld or withdrawn, there is a strong tendency towards broader and more general directions such as 'No resuscitation if I become terminally ill' or 'No life-sustaining measures whose burdens would outweigh their benefits'. Instructions as vague as these cannot be applied mechanically to later treatment decisions and therefore require interpretation by substitute decision-makers: does the DNR order apply when resuscitation would make possible six more months of meaningful life? How do we decide when the burdens of further life have become great enough to outweigh the benefits? Indeed, instruction directives can be vaguer still, simply recording the subject's values or priorities for her life: 'I believe that life should have dignity' or 'I don't want to be too much of a burden on others'. In these

---

[8] Dresser 1986: 376, 394; 2003: 1833 ff. Linda Emanuel (1994) has argued that advance directives 'must meet criteria for real-time informed consent'; for a critique of this view see Olick 2001: 103 ff.

[9] Dresser 1986: 379.

[10] Dresser 2003: 1830 ff. For an argument that instruction directives are inherently flawed and confusing, see Stone 1994: 225–34.

[11] The treatment-specific advance directive in Emanuel and Emanuel 1989 is intended to overcome the problem of vagueness. Completing it requires indicating acceptance or refusal of twelve different forms of treatment for each of four 'paradigmatic scenarios' of incapacity involving unconsciousness or dementia. For critiques of this approach, see Cantor 1993: 59 ff; Olick 2001: 103 ff.

cases advance care planning loses much of its utility in determining treatment decisions for (later) incompetent patients.

Uninformed and vague directives both raise the same basic kind of worry: that the instructions the person recorded *then*, while competent, do not adequately specify the choices she would make *now*, when incompetent. Of course, her current lack of capacity (we are assuming) makes it impossible for her to make an autonomous, informed decision about her care. But we can still ask what she would decide now *were she capable of doing so*. If we have reason to think that her current (hypothetical) decision might be different from, or just underdetermined by, her former (actual) decision then we have a problem: once again, on what basis are treatment decisions for incompetent (but formerly competent) patients to be made?

Broadly speaking, there appear to be three ways of answering this question, each of which has something to be said for it.[12] The first is the one we have already been considering: when a formerly competent patient has executed an instruction directive, then the proxy decision-maker should follow the directions recorded therein. This approach will not help us in the case of any patient who has neglected to complete such a directive, though it might be extended to some whose wishes have been communicated by other, less formal, means. But the practical problems noted by Dresser are sufficient to render straightforward reliance on advance directives problematic in a broad range of cases. We need a different way of proceeding where there is no directive, or where the directive is too vague to be of much use, or where it is based on obsolete information, or where we have reason to believe that the patient's preferences have subsequently changed, or where.... If our primary concern is to respect patient self-determination then the logical next step is to the *substituted judgement standard*: the proxy should attempt to make the treatment decision that the patient herself would make *if she were capable*.[13] The thought experiment required by this standard might seem odd, even incoherent. Here we have a patient who, *ex hypothesi*, is decisionally incapable due to some condition such as advanced dementia or permanent vegetative state. Any treatment decisions made for such a patient must, presumably, take into account her current condition. Yet we are asked to imagine what decision she would make *were she decisionally capable*—that is, *were she not in this condition*. Under those circumstances she would presumably have no reason to forgo life-sustaining treatment, but what does that tell us about her wishes for her actual condition? Perhaps the way around this conundrum is something like the following. We are to imagine that, miraculously, this demented/unconscious person has been restored to temporary lucidity, during which time we can ask her how she wishes to be treated once she lapses back into her demented/unconscious state.[14] Then the

---

[12] I follow here the three 'guidance principles' articulated in Buchanan and Brock 1989: 94 ff.

[13] Dresser 1986: 376–9; Buchanan and Brock 1989: 112–22; Cantor 1993: 30; Olick 2001: 14 ff.

[14] This version of the thought experiment is suggested in Cantor 1993: 30, following judicial guidelines in *Quinlan* (1976), 663; *Saikewicz* (1977), 431; and *Spring* (1980), 119. For a rather different proposal see Davis 2002: 124–5.

substituted judgement standard tells the proxy decision-maker to follow the directions the patient would provide under such conditions.

If we adopt this standard for all treatment decisions on behalf of incompetent (but formerly competent) patients, including those with written directives, then the role of advance directives becomes essentially evidentiary: a subject's directive gives us evidence—more or less reliable, depending on the circumstances, but rarely conclusive—concerning the decisions she would now make if capable. This is not the only role such a directive could have. As we saw earlier (§2.1) the giving of informed consent to treatment is a normative act, since it waives the subject's claim-right against having her bodily security invaded by another. It follows that informed refusal is also a normative act, one that leaves that claim-right intact and obligates the healthcare provider not to administer treatment. In principle, an advance refusal could be accorded the same normative status.[15] In that case, an earlier explicit written refusal of a specific treatment would not be evidence that the patient would now refuse that treatment; instead, it would be a normative act of refusal that would render administration of the treatment a violation of the patient's rights.

The problems of information and vagueness pressed by Dresser are sufficient to challenge this picture of advance directives as normatively authoritative. But they are not sufficient to undermine their evidentiary role on a substituted judgement standard. Even a vaguely worded directive provides some insight into a person's deeply held values and her goals for the end-stage of her life.[16] If our aim is to respect her autonomy over her treatment decisions then a written directive must be given serious evidentiary weight. At the same time, the evidence that it provides concerning her current (hypothetical) decision must also be rebuttable—by reasons for thinking that her recorded refusal of treatment was based on misapprehensions about her current condition, by subsequent indications that her values may have changed, by new and salient information about treatment options, or whatever.

Advance directives therefore have an important role to play—albeit an evidentiary one—under a regime of substituted judgement. We have not yet, however, dealt with the full force of Dresser's critique of reliance on directives, which is not (merely) practical but normative. Dresser's principal concern is with cases in which following a patient's advance directive would conflict with that patient's own present interests. Competent individuals are, of course, entitled to refuse treatment when doing so will be worse for them: Jehovah's Witnesses may do this when they decline blood transfusions, and anyone can decline treatment on altruistic grounds (for example, so

---

[15] Cf. Buchanan and Brock 1989: 116–17.

[16] The information provided to one's proxy decision-makers about one's values and life goals need not be vague. Norman Cantor has argued that an instruction directive should aim to define 'the kind of existence which the declarant deems intolerable' and his own directive does just that, at some length and in some detail (Cantor 1993: 60 and app. A). Cf. Olick 2001: 102: 'Instructions should focus on desired outcomes with or without aggressive medical interventions, rather than the nature of the medical procedures themselves.' Along these lines, Cantor has also provided a template for a 'values profile' to guide substitute decision-makers (Cantor 1993: app. D).

as not to unduly burden their family). When we honour these refusals, as we often must, we effectively side with patient autonomy over patient well-being. Since the point of the substituted judgement standard is also to respect patient autonomy, there is so far no obvious reason why we should not equally honour advance refusals that conflict with present interests. But Dresser argues that there are special problems in the case of an advance refusal by a (formerly) competent person that, if respected, would be contrary to the best interest of the (later) incompetent patient. In such cases, she urges, we should reject substituted judgement in favour of the *best interest standard*: the proxy decision-maker should attempt to make the treatment decision that is in the patient's best interest.[17] On this standard, advance directives diminish even further in significance as guides to decision-making for incompetent patients, though they may still tell us something about how the patient views—or once viewed—her interests.

Dresser has argued her point primarily for patients suffering from dementia and so we now turn to these cases. In order to assess her view it will be helpful to work with the example introduced and discussed by Ronald Dworkin:

When Andrew Firlik was a medical student, he met a fifty-four-year-old Alzheimer's victim whom he called Margo, and he began to visit her daily in her apartment, where she was cared for by an attendant. The apartment had many locks to keep Margo from slipping out at night and wandering in the park in a nightgown, which she had done before. Margo said she knew who Firlik was each time he arrived, but she never used his name, and he suspected that this was just politeness. She said she was reading mysteries, but Firlik 'noticed that her place in the book jumps randomly from day to day; dozens of pages are dog-eared at any given moment.... Maybe she feels good just sitting and humming to herself, rocking back and forth slowly, nodding off liberally, occasionally turning to a fresh page'. Margo attended an art class for Alzheimer's victims—they all, including her, painted pretty much the same picture every time, except near the end, just before death, when the pictures became more primitive. Firlik was confused, he said, by the fact that 'despite her illness, or maybe somehow because of it, Margo is undeniably one of the happiest people I have ever known.' He reports, particularly, her pleasure at eating peanut-butter-and-jelly sandwiches.[18]

Dworkin invites us to imagine that years before, when she was fully competent, Margo gave considerable thought to the overall course of her life and reached the settled conviction that she never wanted to live as a demented person; perhaps she regarded such a life, however happy it might be, as undignified or demeaning. (If we wish, we can also imagine that Margo's assessment of such a life was informed by her experience of her mother's final years.) Acting on this conviction, she executed an instruction directive declining all life-sustaining treatment in the event that she should reach the advanced stages of Alzheimer's. Now she has acquired an infection easily treatable by antibiotics but fatal if left untreated. Should her earlier refusal of treatment be respected, allowing her to die despite the evident fact that she is now quite happy?

---

[17] Buchanan and Brock 1989: 122 ff.; Dresser 1986: 383 ff.; 2003: 1842–4.
[18] R. Dworkin 1993: 220–1, citing Firlik 1991.

Dworkin contends that it should, on grounds of both Margo's autonomy and her well-being. He argues that, due to her dementia, Margo is no longer capable of making autonomous decisions about how her life should go. But she was once capable of such decisions—indeed, made just such a decision—and respect for her precedent autonomy requires doing now what she then directed. Thus far, we might seem to have another case of conflict between autonomy and well-being: respect for Margo's autonomy will require us to do what is worse for her, namely, allow her to die. But Dworkin resists this construal of the situation, arguing that honouring Margo's advance refusal may also be in her overall best interest. He supports this contention with a distinction between two types of interest, which he calls *experiential* and *critical*. Our experiential interests consist of the pleasure or enjoyment we take in things that we do or that happen to us.[19] Margo has always had experiential interests and still does, since she gives every sign of enjoying her mystery book, her art class, and her peanut-butter-and-jelly sandwiches. Allowing her to die would be contrary to her current experiential interests. Critical interests, on the other hand, are based on a person's convictions of how her life should go and the goods it should contain. Margo's critical interests, Dworkin argues, were formed by her past convictions about the overall course of her life, including her wish not to finish it as a demented person. Margo is now unable to form critical interests, Dworkin claims, since she now lacks the capacity to think about the overall course of her life, but she retains the critical interests she formed while previously competent. Postponing her death by giving her life-sustaining treatment would be contrary to those interests. Since Dworkin considers that, in case of conflict, critical interests should be given priority over experiential interests, he concludes that, all things considered, honouring Margo's advance refusal would best serve her well-being (as well as her autonomy).

Dresser disagrees with Dworkin in two important respects. First, because she advocates a best-interest standard of decision-making for patients such as Margo, she rejects the contention that we are bound to respect Margo's (precedent) autonomy. Second, she argues that in applying the best-interest standard only Margo's current experiential interests should be considered, in which case the decision should be made to prolong her life, at least as long as she continues to be happy. Clearly this second claim is crucial to her view, since if she were to acknowledge that Margo's critical interests are also in play, then the best interest standard she favours might entail complying with Margo's advance refusal of life-sustaining treatment. Dresser puts her point in this way: 'Happy and contented Margo will experience clear harm from the decision that purports to advance the critical interests she no longer cares about. This seems to me justification for a policy against . . . withholding effective, nonburdensome treatments, such as antibiotics, from dementia patients whose lives offer them

---

[19] Dworkin's experiential interests are essentially identical to Epicurus's experiential goods (and evils), which figure prominently in his argument against the badness of death (§1.1).

the sorts of pleasures and satisfactions Margo enjoys.'[20] Presumably, the decision to withhold treatment will cause Margo 'clear harm' only regarding her experiential interests. Why, then, are we not also to consider her critical interests? Dresser's answer to this question is—and must be—that they no longer matter because 'she no longer cares about' them. She develops this point at greater length in a later discussion:

If a patient can no longer appreciate the values that motivated the [advance] choice, treatment decisions should take into account what now matters to the patient. When the capacity to appreciate critical interests is lost, experiential interests should take priority. Competent persons are free to elevate their critical interests above experiential interests. But after they lose decisional capacity, they have a different set of concerns. Experiential interests become central to their lives. Experiential interests should also be central to decisions about their life-sustaining treatment.[21]

In other words: if you are no longer capable of caring about your critical interests then those interests no longer count.

Dresser provides no real defence for this contention and it is difficult to see how it could be defended.[22] If you once accept Dworkin's notion of critical interests—which Dresser does—and if these interests include a person's settled conviction about how the end-stage of her life should go, what reason could there be for discounting these interests simply because the person has later lost the capacity to endorse, or even understand, them? It would be a different matter if, at some stage before or during the gradual onset of her dementia, Margo had reconsidered and disaffirmed her earlier disparagement of life in a demented condition. In that case there would be no reason to consider her earlier view of the matter still authoritative as an expression either of her autonomy or of her interests. But we are to suppose that she neither reconsidered nor disaffirmed her refusal of treatment when she was still capable of doing so. Now that she has lost this capacity her earlier directions remain our only evidence of where her current critical interests lie.[23] Indeed, disregarding these interests because she has

---

[20] Dresser 1995: 36.

[21] Dresser 2003: 1840 (footnotes omitted).

[22] In an influential discussion, Agnieska Jaworska (1999: 111) rejects Dresser's claim: 'The fact that the demented patient no longer affirms critical interests in no way implies that he does not have critical interests. Since such interests are not inherently time-specific, the prudential importance of satisfying them may survive the person's unawareness of their satisfaction, whether due to unconsciousness, dementia, or even death. Thus, a demented person who cannot generate contemporaneous critical interests may still have some of the same critical interests he professed when he was healthy.' However, Jaworska also defends the view that many demented persons are capable of generating critical interests, since they are capable of valuing.

[23] John Davis (2002: 120) has suggested a hypothetical reaffirmation test for determining when a person's previously stated (and never disaffirmed) preferences about his life remain current once he has lost capacity: 'If the agent is unable to form a preference in his actual circumstances, then his preference in those circumstances is whatever he earlier preferred, provided he would reaffirm that preference in hypothetical circumstances just like his current circumstances (except for having the mental capacity to affirm or reject the earlier preference).' The resemblance to the substituted judgement standard (discussed above) is obvious. However, presumably the only reason we could have for thinking that an agent would not now reaffirm an earlier preference would be either some new and relevant information or some evidence of a later change of heart.

now lost the capacity to appreciate them would seem to undermine the whole point of advance care planning. If I execute an instruction directive while competent then my aim in doing so is to direct my care when I become incompetent. It would be perverse to disregard my earlier directions simply because I am now in the very condition of incapacity I anticipated in recording them.

This point becomes even clearer if we move beyond the case of Margo and dementia to persons who have become permanently unconscious. As discussed earlier (§1.1), permanent vegetative state (PVS) is a condition in which all 'higher-brain' functions (those supported by the cerebrum and especially the cortex) have ceased while 'lower-brain' (and especially brainstem) functions are still intact. PVS patients lack all capacity for cognitive functions, external awareness, and purposeful movement; however, they are usually capable of breathing on their own, without mechanical assistance, and can remain in this condition for many years as long as they are sustained by nutrition and hydration delivered through a feeding tube (since they are unable to swallow on their own). In the next chapter (§6.1) I discuss some high-profile cases in the United States and United Kingdom in which substitute decision-makers have petitioned the courts for permission to withdraw artificial nutrition and hydration, with the inevitable result that death will occur within approximately two weeks. In none of these real-life cases had the patient executed an instruction directive explicitly refusing such care. But suppose one of them—we will call her Nancy— had done so, based on her settled view that she did not want to be a person whose final years were spent lying unconscious on a bed. Then that directive would stand as an expression both of her self-determination and, in Dworkin's terms, of her critical interests. Once unconscious, she is, of course, completely unable to care about or appreciate those critical interests. But how could that be a reason for disregarding them?

In one important respect permanent unconsciousness provides a simpler case than dementia for advance refusals of treatment. While Margo undeniably has (in Dworkin's terms) experiential interests while in her demented condition, Nancy has none. In Margo's case we have a conflict of interest, with her experiential interests providing a reason for, and her critical interests providing a reason against, prolonging her life. There is no such conflict of interest for Nancy, and so her family and healthcare providers need not feel similarly conflicted about acting on her wishes.[24] However,

---

[24] However, the situation is complicated by the fact that 'disorders of consciousness' are difficult to diagnose with certainty, with the result that in a small minority of instances patients mistakenly diagnosed as PVS subsequently regain consciousness (Multi-Society Task Force on PVS 1994b; Stone 2007: 85–6; Schnakers et al. 2009). Jim Stone argues that, as long as there is a non-zero probability of the patient recovering consciousness, then her best interest requires sustaining her life; she cannot be worse off that way (since, subjectively, unconsciousness and death are indistinguishable for her) and she might be better off (since she might recover consciousness). However, this argument assumes that we are to consult only her experiential interests. Just to complicate matters even further, fMRI imaging of PVS patients has shown that a small percentage of them have some capacity for awareness and cognition and, in some cases, even communication by means of brain activity (Monti et al. 2010). This last, fascinating, result opens up the

despite the differences between the two cases, we should not lose sight of the important factor they have in common: if we accept Dworkin's framework, then in each case we have at least a *pro tanto* reason, based on respect for both patient autonomy and patient well-being, for complying with the advance directive.[25]

Whether this reason is conclusive will depend on a number of factors. For one thing, the various practical problems raised by Dresser should lead us to treat a written directive as a presumptive indication of the subject's settled convictions about her care, subject to rebuttal by evidence of informational deficits, later change of heart, etc. For another, as discussed above, where other factors are equal the reason for compliance will be stronger when patient incapacity is the result of unconsciousness rather than dementia, due to the absence of countervailing experiential interests. But there are other complicating factors in the dementia scenario as well. Agnieska Jaworska has argued, persuasively to my mind, that at least mid-stage dementia patients (such as Margo) are capable of both having and, to a lesser extent, acting on values, and that this capacity for valuing is all that is necessary in order to have both critical interests and a rudimentary form of autonomy.[26] If Jaworska is right then the decision to comply with Margo's advance refusal of treatment is not, as Dworkin argued, settled by respecting her precedent autonomy and her critical interests. Instead, there will be both critical interests and expressions of autonomy manifested during her dementia that must also be part of the equation. In that case, her proxy decision-makers will need to decide whether to attach more weight to her earlier (fuller) autonomy and (more autonomous) critical interests or her later (diminished) autonomy and (less autonomous) critical interests, as well as determining how to balance all these factors against her current experiential interests. It would be entirely understandable if, rather than attempting to sort out these deep philosophical questions, they simply opted to continue life support for Margo as long as she remained happy.

Let us recapitulate the argument to this point. We began with a simple and straightforward case in favour of advance care planning as a means of extending patient self-determination over periods of incapacity. We then considered Rebecca Dresser's practical objections to advance directives, followed by her more philosophical arguments that in deciding on behalf of incompetent patients (*a*) we should reject the substituted judgement standard in favour of the best-interest standard and (*b*) in applying this standard we should confine our attention to current experiential interests. Though, taken together, these two contentions would effectively negate the authority of advance refusals of treatment, we did not find reason to accept either of them.

intriguing possibility of consulting some PVS patients concerning their care. However, it should be stressed that this seems to apply only to a very small minority of 'permanently unconscious' patients with traumatic brain injury and not at all to such cases as those of Nancy Cruzan and Terri Schiavo whose unconsciousness was precipitated by oxygen deprivation to the brain.

[25] For similar conclusions see Cantor 1993: 79–82, 101–9; Olick 2001: 57 ff.

[26] Jaworska 1999.

Dresser, however, has one more card to play. The rationale behind advance care planning is based on the assumption that the (earlier) competent person who executes the directive is the same as the (later) incompetent person whose care it directs. However, this assumption is open to question. On the psychological view of personal identity, two person-stages belong to one and the same person if and only if enough relations of connectedness and continuity hold between their mental states (especially forward-looking states such as intention and backward-looking states such as memory).[27] However, it can be argued that in cases of severe dementia these relations fail to hold, since the demented person is capable neither of carrying out any plans made by the competent person nor of remembering anything about that person. In that case, according to the psychological view we may be dealing, not with different stages of the same person, but with two different persons. Dresser then asks the obvious question: 'why should a patient who is now a different person be burdened by a treatment decision consistent with the former person's preferences? Compelling justification is lacking for according greater respect to the wishes of the earlier person (no longer in existence) than to the interests of the existing one.'[28]

If we consider pre-demented Margo and now-demented Margo to be two different persons then there is surely no reason to think that decisions made by the former should have any authority over the latter. This case against advance care planning—what David DeGrazia has nicely labelled 'the someone else problem'—has been much discussed in the literature.[29] While it is not possible to summarize all the argumentative moves that have been made to date, I think it is fair to say that the case has not been satisfactorily made out.[30] For one thing, not everyone is persuaded that the psychological account of personal identity is correct, and at least some rival accounts will not support the conclusion that the two Margos are numerically different.[31] For another, even on the psychological view there may be enough continuity between the two Margos to consider them the same person, especially if the onset of dementia is slow and gradual.[32] Finally, the implications that Dresser attempts to draw from the psychological account, if taken literally, are massively counterintuitive. Margo's daughter, who (let us say) is now her substitute decision-maker, does not really doubt that this woman who is reading her book and enjoying her sandwiches is the same woman who was born in Brooklyn in 1931, grew up in Cleveland, married at the age of 27, had three children, etc. If she is mistaken on this point, if this is not her mother, then why is she being accorded the status of substitute decision-maker, since she has no right to make such decisions on behalf of a stranger? Furthermore, why is

---

[27] See Parfit 1984: sect. 78.

[28] Dresser 1986: 381; cf. 1989: 157 ff.

[29] Besides Dresser, see Buchanan and Brock 1989: ch. 3; Cantor 1993: ch. 6; Kuhse 1999: Olick 2001: ch. 4; DeGrazia 2005: ch. 5; Wrigley 2007.

[30] It is noteworthy that Dresser herself has come to make less and less use of this particular objection to advance care planning, to the point where it has virtually disappeared by the time of Dresser 2003.

[31] See e.g. McMahan 2002: chs. 1 and 5; DeGrazia 2005: chs. 2–5.

[32] Buchanan and Brock 1989: 159 ff.

this Margo still being treated as the legal owner of that property in Florida and these investment certificates? If the previous, competent Margo no longer exists, where did she go? Did she die? If so, why did no one notice? How did this Margo come into existence? And why is she even called Margo?

The personal identity problem (if it is one) is even more acute for permanently unconscious patients who are arguably no longer persons at all; instead of 'the someone else problem' we would have 'the no one at all problem'. In real-life cases, like that of Nancy Cruzan, there is indeed some temptation for the family to think that the sister and daughter they once knew vanished when she became irreversibly unconscious.[33] However, in the view of the courts there is no doubt that the person lying unconscious in that hospital bed is the same person who was involved in the automobile accident, and that these people before the court have decision-making rights with respect to her because she is their daughter. For all practical purposes, philosophical theories do not prevent families, friends, healthcare providers, hospitals, and courts from assuming continuity of identity between the previously competent person and the currently incapacitated one. Perhaps in this instance it is better to fit theory to practice rather than the other way around.

To this point we have been assuming that advance directives take the form of selective refusal of various life-sustaining procedures. But, of course, they can and often do include treatment requests as well. Indeed, a model instruction directive might take the form 'under these circumstances, this I accept, this I decline'. Most requests, therefore, will be either for life-sustaining procedures (resuscitation, ventilation, the use of antibiotics for infections, tube feeding) or for palliative measures (adequate pain control, sedation). As outlined previously (§4.3), treatment requests raise somewhat different issues from refusals, since they engage the patient's positive right to assistance, rather than her negative right to bodily security. Positive rights generally impose greater burdens on healthcare providers than negative rights, since they require providers to initiate or sustain treatment rather than withhold or discontinue it. They also impose greater burdens on a healthcare system, since the administration of treatment will usually consume (often scarce) resources. However, having said all this, in a context of care the patient has the right to expect her healthcare providers to offer any form of treatment with a reasonable expectation of medical benefit, or at least to balance the expected benefits of treatment against its costs. Most advance requests for treatment will therefore be unproblematic; issues are likely to arise only when providers take the view that the requested measure will be of no medical benefit to the patient.[34]

If life-prolonging treatments can be requested in advance then, in principle at least, so can life-shortening ones, including euthanasia.[35] The argument of the previous

---

[33] As noted in §1.1, above, her grave marker read 'DEPARTED Jan 11, 1983 | AT PEACE Dec 26, 1990' (McMahan 2002: 423, citing Singer 1994: 62).

[34] For discussion of some of the legal issues involved in cases of 'medical futility', see §6.1, below.

[35] For the purposes of the discussion, I will assume that euthanasia is legal in the jurisdiction in question.

chapter concluded that *when all relevant factors are equal* voluntary euthanasia is no less defensible than other end-of-life measures that are already widely accepted, including the administration of opioids or sedatives at dose levels that may hasten death. It follows that if it is legitimate to request these measures in advance then it is equally legitimate to request euthanasia, in which case advance euthanasia directives should have the same authority for substitute decision-makers and healthcare providers as any other directives.[36]

Suppose, then, that (in the foregoing scenarios) either Margo or Nancy had made such a request, to be carried out in the event that she became severely demented/permanently unconscious. In Margo's case we would have to decide whether to honour this expression of precedent autonomy or, if we chose to work with the substituted judgement standard, whether her advance request constituted credible evidence of her current hypothetical choice. If we put Margo's interests in play, under a best interest standard, then we will once again have to balance her critical against her experiential interests. But we had to engage all these issues when her instruction directive took the form of refusing life-sustaining treatment. Nothing of ethical significance changes when, instead, it takes the form of requesting life-terminating treatment. Actually, that is not quite true: ending Margo's life quickly and painlessly by means of a lethal injection might be better for her, and those who care about her, than allowing her to die by an untreated infection.[37]

Can we actually imagine administering euthanasia to happy and contented Margo? The foregoing argument yields only a comparative judgement: if honouring Margo's advance refusal of life-sustaining treatment is justifiable then so is honouring her advance request for euthanasia. Euthanasia directives therefore introduce no novel entries into the ethical balance sheet. But perhaps, like Dresser, we cannot imagine ourselves acting on either directive in the face of Margo's current contentment with her (diminished) life. Our reluctance to do so might just be perspectival error: we are confronted daily by Margo's current experiential enjoyments, whereas her previous disparagement of the life she is now living seems barely visible in the distant past. If we wish to give our reluctance some philosophical support then the obvious means would be to agree with Dresser in rejecting Dworkin's privileging of critical over experiential interests. As a general thesis, it is hard to see how one might argue that current pleasures and enjoyments, under conditions of diminished or non-existent autonomy,

---

[36] A 'conscience clause' might exempt healthcare providers who conscientiously object to euthanasia from the obligation to administer it. But the same could also apply to the withdrawal of a feeding tube from a PVS patient.

[37] The Netherlands and Belgium are the only jurisdictions to explicitly permit advance euthanasia directives (see §6.2, below), though there appear to have been only a few cases to date of euthanasia under the terms of these provisions. For discussion of the merits of euthanasia directives, specifically with respect to patients with advanced dementia, see van Delden 2004; Hertogh et al. 2007; Beaufort 2007; Goering 2007; Woien 2007; Hertogh 2009; Gastmans and de Lepelere 2010. Belgium restricts its provision to permanently unconscious patients.

always take precedence over previous, fully autonomous, expressions of one's deepest and most enduring values. However this might be, it is well to keep in mind that Margo is the easiest case for Dresser's rejection of advance directives and the hardest case for Dworkin's defence of them. Mid-stage Alzheimer's is seldom as rosy as Margo's day-to-day experience, and the end-stages of the disease never are. As patients slide further and further into dementia it is far more common for their lives to be marked by disorientation, irritability, and episodes of aggression or rage. In these cases current experiential interests no longer speak so unequivocally in favour of prolonging life, and the case for acting on an advance refusal/request becomes stronger. In order to dismiss reliance on advance directives altogether for patients with dementia, Dresser would have to contend that we could never have a sufficient reason for honouring a directive, however distressed the person had become. No such sweeping claim seems at all plausible.

The situation is essentially similar for Nancy and for other permanently unconscious patients. If it is ethically acceptable to discontinue artificial nutrition and hydration, on the basis of Nancy's advance refusal of this measure, then it would be equally acceptable to end her life by means of a lethal injection, on the basis of her advance request for this measure. However, we should note two material differences between the dementia and PVS scenarios. The first is that Nancy has no experiential interests, positive or negative, to complicate the application of a best-interest standard. If any of Nancy's interests survive the onset of permanent unconsciousness, then they will be critical interests and, *ex hypothesi*, they favour assisted death. The second difference is that death by dehydration, though it will be accompanied by no suffering, takes longer (typically ten to fourteen days) than death by untreated infection or cardiac arrest. As far as her subjective experience is concerned, a quick and immediate death by lethal injection will be no better (or worse) for Nancy, but it might be significantly preferable for her loved ones who must otherwise maintain a vigil during her prolonged dying process.

There therefore appears to be no ethical problem, at least in principle, with the making or honouring of advance euthanasia requests, thus with the idea of quasi-voluntary euthanasia. But we have so far neglected the most common cases, namely, those in which the now incompetent patient has left no advance written instructions regarding treatment—neither refusals nor requests. So let us now imagine that we are the substitute decision-makers for either Margo or Nancy and that we must decide whether to initiate (in Margo's case) or continue (in Nancy's case) life-sustaining treatment. In the absence of a written directive, we will need to fall back on either a substituted judgement or best-interest standard. There will be less difference between the application of these two standards than might appear, since in either case we will need essentially the same information about the person's preferences, values, 'philosophy of life', religious convictions (if any), and so on. If we can use this information to determine what Margo or Nancy would decide for herself, were she able, then it will serve equally well to settle where her critical interests lie.[38] In Margo's case this process will be more or less speculative, depending on what we know, from past experience, of her views about these matters. But in any case the best and most reliable information we have will concern her current experiential interests, which (taken by themselves) speak unequivocally in favour of prolonging her life. If it is unlikely that the decision to decline treatment would be taken even when Margo had registered an explicit advance refusal, it is much less likely to be taken in the absence of such a refusal.[39]

Nancy's case is both simpler and more complicated: simpler because she has no experiential interests speaking in favour of prolonging her unconscious life, more complicated because we must therefore decide the question on the basis of either substituted judgement or best interest.[40] I will not attempt to predict the outcome of that decision process except to say that, if we have sufficiently reliable evidence concerning Nancy's own values and priorities, it is not unthinkable on either standard that the decision will be taken to terminate life support by removing Nancy's feeding tube. Despite the reliance on Nancy's hypothetical decision under the substituted judgement standard, it would be a stretch to consider this anything other than a nonvoluntary 'making death happen'. The argument of this section yields the result that a decision for euthanasia would be equally justified, if it were equally supported by what we know of Nancy's own values and convictions.[41] In that case, euthanasia would no longer be even quasi-voluntary but just flat out nonvoluntary. However, it would not be less justifiable for that.

5.2 The Never Competent

As noted at the beginning of this chapter, end-of-life decisions that hasten death are easiest to justify when the twin values of self-determination and well-being are both in play. This is paradigmatically the case when these measures are fully voluntary, the outcome of the patient's contemporaneous informed consent. However, there remains room for appeal to both values in the case of a patient who, while currently

---

[38] Unless, that is, the patient's (hypothetical) decision would be based, at least in part, on non-self-interested considerations (such as not wishing to be a burden to others). For the role of patients' 'altruistic' interests in a substituted judgement standard see Berger 2005.

[39] Margo is still some considerable distance from the end stage of Alzheimer's. For patients with more advanced dementia the decision must sometimes be faced of whether to initiate tube feeding once the patient has become either unwilling or unable to swallow food and water. However, there appears to be little clinical evidence that tube feeding in these cases is of therapeutic benefit (Finucane, Christmas, and Travis 1999; Gillick 2000).

[40] The real-life Nancy Cruzan had no advance directive; nonetheless, the decision to remove her feeding tube was reached under a standard of substituted judgement together with anecdotal evidence of her previously stated wishes. See the discussion of this case in §6.1, below.

[41] In the absence of a written directive, evidence of someone's views about what they would want done (or not done) in the event of permanent unconsciousness is likely to come from informal discussions with friends or family. These discussions are frequently stimulated by high-profile real-life cases, such as those of Nancy Cruzan, Anthony Bland, or (more recently) Terri Schiavo (§6.1, below).

incompetent, has previously had decisional capacity, since reference back to her earlier values and preferences (with or without an explicit advance directive) can help us to determine both what she would now choose, were she able, and what would now be in her best interest. These important pieces of evidence are, however, entirely absent in cases where the patient has never had decisional capacity. These are, accordingly, the cases in which treatment (or nontreatment) decisions hastening death are hardest to justify.

Some persons lead lives, often lengthy ones, during which they never manifest decisional capacity. One such was Joseph Saikewicz, who had a lifelong IQ of 10 and a mental age of approximately 2 years and 8 months. When Mr Saikewicz was 67 years old he was diagnosed with acute myeloblastic monocytic leukemia, which is invariably fatal and which if left untreated would lead to death in a matter of weeks or months. Administration of chemotherapy would offer some hope of temporary remission, at best only a few months, and would be accompanied by severe adverse side effects. The decision was made by his court-appointed guardian not to initiate this treatment. A more dramatic case of permanent incapacity was that of Tracy Latimer, who suffered from a severe form of cerebral palsy caused by neurological damage at the time of her birth. She was quadriplegic, had the mental capacity of a 4-month-old baby, suffered frequent seizures, and experienced considerable pain as her spine and joints were distorted by the gradual but inexorable tightening of her muscles. She underwent numerous surgeries intended to correct these problems. When she was 12 years old and scheduled for further surgery to deal with a dislocated hip, her father killed her by means of carbon monoxide poisoning in order, he said, to spare her further suffering.[42]

In both of these cases a decision was made that had the effect (and, at least in the latter case, was made with the intent) of hastening death, yet in neither of them could this decision be justified by any reference back to the person's earlier, competent wishes. So we need to ask how, if at all, these decisions could be justified. This is exactly the kind of question on the table in this section, but I do not plan to pursue it for either the Saikewicz or the Latimer case. Instead, I want to turn attention to a different class of cases which are, if anything, even more difficult: life and death decisions for infants.

Unlike Joseph Saikewicz, most of us are decisionally capable through most, if not all, of our adult lives. However, we do not achieve this capacity *tout d'un coup*; instead, it is developed gradually, the expectation being that (except in pathological cases such as Tracy Latimer's) its more or less mature form will be in place by the age of majority. This gradual process leaves us with a lengthy grey area, extending roughly from the age of 11 or 12 to 18 or 19, during which decisional capacity may be neither clearly present nor clearly absent. These cases of so-called 'mature minors' can raise complex questions that need to be resolved on a case-by-case basis: to what extent is *this* person

---

[42]   The legal aspects of both the Saikewicz and Latimer cases are addressed in §6.1, below. For discussion of the ethics of Robert Latimer's action and a defence of nonvoluntary euthanasia see Brown 2010.

competent to consent to, or refuse, *this* treatment?[43] However they are to be decided, everyone agrees that there is a lower age limit to even partial, or underdeveloped, competence. When treatment decisions need to be made for young children (below the age of 10, let us say) then the normal mechanisms of informed consent/refusal are inapplicable. On this sliding scale infants, and especially newborns, represent the extreme case.

Most newborns do not present difficult treatment decisions: either they require no treatment at all (aside from standard care), or what they need is routine and trivial, or it is more serious but there is no legitimate reason not to proceed with it. However, some infants are born with disabilities, ranging from moderate to severe, that raise more challenging questions concerning their care. A severely disabled newborn may require intervention in order to sustain life, ranging from aggressive (surgery, intubation) to more routine (resuscitation, antibiotics). Decisions must therefore be made whether to initiate, withhold, continue, or withdraw any of these forms of treatment. With respect to those decisions, we can reiterate the two questions raised in the previous section: Who should make the decision? On what basis should it be made?

On the face of it, there is a simple and obvious answer to each of these questions. Since the infant is incapable of making healthcare decisions, the task must fall to one or more substitute decision-makers. And since the infant is also incapable of appointing a proxy, the substitute decision-makers will normally be the next of kin—i.e. the parents. The basis for their decision cannot be either an advance directive or the substituted judgement standard, since there is no expression of precedent autonomy, formal or informal, on which the decision-makers can rely. They must therefore fall back on the best-interest standard—more particularly, they must aim to make the treatment decision that is in the best interest of the child.[44]

Each of these answers is at least partially correct. But the issues raised by the two questions are more complicated than these simple answers would suggest. We will postpone further exploration of the 'who decides?' question until later in order to come to grips first with the difficult issue of determining the best interest of a newborn. Let us start with a normal, healthy baby and ask why continuing to live would be good for him—or, alternatively, why dying would be bad for him. The obvious answer is given by the deprivation account of the badness of death: dying would deprive the infant of a life worth living.[45] If we are asked what makes a life worth living, we can help ourselves again to Ronald Dworkin's distinction between experiential and critical

---

[43] Cf. §§2.1 and 2.2, above. For discussion of the ethical issues raised by mature minors, see Buchanan and Brock 1989: 216 ff.

[44] Later I will consider the role to be played in the best-interest standard by the parents' (or, more broadly, the family's) interests.

[45] This answer cannot be given by Jeff McMahan's time-relative interest account of the badness of death (§1.1), since a newborn infant is only weakly connected, if at all, to his future interests. McMahan therefore has considerable difficulty in explaining why infanticide would be wrong for perfectly normal babies (see his 2002: 338–62).

interests. The former include goods such as pleasure and enjoyment (and presumably also the avoidance of bads such as pain and suffering). The latter include the formation of personal values and the pursuit and achievement of life goals and ambitions (and presumably also the avoidance of disappointments and frustrations). Because the infant is sentient he already has experiential interests, though they are currently limited to such basic matters as food, warmth, rest, and the avoidance of pain. However, as he matures he will develop other, more complex, experiential interests, as well as critical interests. If he is even moderately fortunate the resultant goods in his life will outweigh the bads, so as to render it, on the whole, worth living. Death will deprive him of this worthwhile life—ergo, allowing him to die (or killing him) would be bad for him and sustaining his life is good for him.

The normal, healthy infant is, of course, the easy case; here we do not hesitate to offer life-sustaining treatment, if we are able. Many of the most difficult treatment/non-treatment dilemmas arise for extremely premature babies (those born before the end of the second trimester), because of the difficulty of determining the infant's prognosis (survival with only mild to moderate disabilities/survival with severe disabilities/death). However, I will not deal with these cases but will instead focus on three of the more frequently discussed disorders that may afflict full-term infants.

Anencephaly is a neural tube defect that results in the absence of all higher-brain regions including the cerebrum, which is responsible for thinking and coordination. Infants born with anencephaly are usually blind, deaf, and unconscious. Although some individuals with anencephaly may be born with a rudimentary brainstem, the lack of a functioning cerebrum permanently rules out the possibility of ever gaining consciousness. Most newborns with anencephaly do not survive infancy; if not stillborn, then the infant will usually die within a few hours or days of birth. The anencephalic infant occupies the opposite end of the spectrum from the normal infant; by virtue of being irreversibly unconscious he has no current experiential interests and no prospect of developing any future interests, whether experiential or critical. Except for lacking precedent autonomy, and therefore critical interests, the anencephalic infant is in the same condition as the PVS patient. Although his life contains no bads, it also contains no (present or future) goods; subjectively, it is indistinguishable from being dead. Since recovery of consciousness in this case is impossible, it cannot be contrary to the infant's interest to die. Death cannot be worse for him than continued life and may be better for the anguished family. In this case, therefore, there is no point in undertaking any measures to preserve life; instead, it may be that the sooner death occurs the better.

All the hard cases lie between these extremes of normality and anencephaly. Actually, some of them are not that hard. Down's (or Down) syndrome is a chromosomal disorder caused by the inheritance of an extra twenty-first chromosome. Individuals with the syndrome have a characteristic set of facial features, various other physical anomalies, and lower than average cognitive ability. During the 1970s and into the 1980s there were a number of highly publicized incidents of Down's syndrome infants being 'allowed to die' by means of withholding treatment.[46] Most Down's infants require no more neonatal care than their chromosomally normal fellows. However, in some cases the syndrome is accompanied by a physical anomaly such as a congenital heart defect or a blockage somewhere in the gastrointestinal tract. Normally these defects are easily correctable by surgery, but they would be fatal if left uncorrected. Undertaking the corrective surgery would be a routine decision in the case of a normal infant. However, in the case of some Down's infants the needed surgery has been refused by the parents, either in accordance with or contrary to medical advice. In those instances the babies were given only comfort care, including pain medication, and left to die of starvation or dehydration.

One of the foregoing cases, that of 'Baby Doe', ignited a political battle in the United States that led to regulations governing the care of disabled newborns.[47] We need not pursue the complex history of that particular affair, but we do need to acknowledge that many people were outraged that Down's infants were being treated (or, better, left untreated) in this manner. Down's syndrome is a broad spectrum disorder, with the resulting degree of cognitive impairment ranging from mild to severe and with an array of possible further complications including hearing deficits, cataracts, thyroid dysfunctions, and skeletal problems. The severity of any of these problems, including the cognitive impairment, is impossible to forecast at birth. However, what is known is that the syndrome does not result in any significant degree of suffering, save for the social stigmatization that inevitably results from looking and acting 'different'. In fact, the vast majority of Down's infants, children, adolescents, and adults are markedly happy and content, perhaps more so than the general population. High-functioning Down's adults are capable of gainful employment and living fairly independent lives. In Dworkin's terms, they definitely have experiential interests and, if we accept Jaworska's threshold for having values and exercising autonomy, they have critical interests as well. No serious case can be made that their lives are not, on balance, worth living. Accordingly, if treatment decisions are to be based on the best interest of the child, there can be no justification for withholding from Down's infants any treatment that would be offered to a chromosomally normal baby.

However, we have assumed to this point that the only interests implicated by the best-interest standard are those of the patient—in this case, the infant. But what of the interests of the parents or, more broadly, of the family (if other siblings are involved)? Many, perhaps most, Down's children are integrated into loving families who are happy to have them. But raising a Down's child undeniably imposes additional burdens on the family, especially when the degree of physical and mental disability is severe. The additional burdens of care, which will tend to fall largely on the mother, can lead to fatigue and burn-out and can also strain the family's financial resources.

[46] For three of these cases see Kuhse and Singer 1985: chs. 1 and 4.
[47] For a summary history of the development of these regulations see ibid. ch. 2.

Parents of disabled children have a higher rate of marital break-up and the siblings of such children are more likely to be behaviourally disturbed, the incidence of disturbance correlating with the degree of the disability.[48] Down's syndrome can, of course, be diagnosed prenatally through procedures such as amniocentesis, and the vast majority of couples who receive the diagnosis will then elect abortion. What, then, are we to make of parents who discover only at birth that their infant has the condition and conclude that they will just not be able to handle the burdens of raising a Down's child or that it will place too much of a strain on their other children? To what extent should these interests also be considered when applying the best-interest standard? On the one hand, no parents can be compelled to raise a disabled child against their will; any such compulsion would scarcely be in the interest of the child. On the other hand, the rights of the parents extend only as far as refusing to take on the responsibility of caring for the child; they do not include refusing treatment necessary to sustain the child's life.[49] What this means, then, is that if the parents of a Down's infant elect to abandon the child then some other arrangement—fostering, adoption, institutionalization, or whatever—must be found for him. While the interests of the parents will inevitably have a profound effect on the child's future circumstances, in the treatment decision itself the best interests of the child must be paramount. Since a Down's infant will have a life worth living, there can be no justification for allowing him to die of neglect.

These matters become considerably more complicated when we turn to spina bifida, a developmental birth defect caused by the incomplete closure of the embryonic neural tube. Like Down's syndrome, spina bifida encompasses a wide range of disorders. In its mildest form its physical manifestations may be virtually unnoticeable and it will result in no cognitive impairment. However, in its most severe (myelomeningocele) manifestation the spinal cord is exposed, with the result that spinal fluid leaks through the opening and the baby is prone to life-threatening infections. In these cases there will inevitably be some degree of paralysis and loss of sensation below the level of the spinal cord defect—the higher the level of the defect the more severe the associated nerve dysfunction and resultant paralysis. In addition, bladder and bowel function may be lost and intense pain may occur, originating in the lower back and continuing down the leg. Most infants born with myelomeningocele will also have hydrocephalus, which consists of excessive accumulation of cerebrospinal fluid in the ventricles of the brain. The build-up of fluid puts damaging pressure on the brain, causing moderate to severe cognitive impairment. Like Down's syndrome, spina bifida

---

[48] Ibid. 146 ff.; Rodrigue, Morgan, and Geffken 1990; Cuskelly and Dadds 1992; Cuskelly and Gunn 1993.

[49] 'It is one thing to say that parents may *responsibly* divest themselves of the duty to care for their infant in order to insure that they can pursue their own legitimate interests or those of their other children. It is quite another to say that they may disregard the infant's basic interests while refusing to divest themselves of decision-making authority, terminating the infant's life *in order* to terminate their obligations' (Buchanan and Brock 1989: 259).

is readily diagnosable at birth and reasonably reliable estimates can be made of the expected degree of physical—but not mental—impairment.

During the 1960s and 1970s a lively debate was waged among paediatricians and paediatric surgeons over the appropriate treatment of newborns diagnosed with spina bifida.[50] Some defended the view that active treatment to repair the physical defects should be undertaken for all such infants. At a minimum the corrective surgery involved would include closing the spinal column and inserting a shunt to drain the excess fluid from the brain; additional surgeries might also be needed to deal with further orthopaedic anomalies, such as dislocation of the hips. The case for this treatment regime rested on the seemingly reasonable principle that every child deserved the best care available, despite the degree of its disability. The problems with it came to light when follow-up studies were done of a population of infants all of whom had been aggressively treated in this manner.[51] What was discovered was that only about half these children survived, most of the other half dying in their first year, and that most of the surviving children were severely physically disabled. Many also experienced moderate to severe mental retardation. In the light of these results some physicians began to advocate a more selective approach in which infants born with the most severe disabilities would be left untreated. The aim of this regime was to reserve corrective treatment exclusively for those spina bifida infants whose prognosis was that they would suffer no worse than moderate handicap. Children who were denied treatment were offered ordinary feeding, but nothing else: no incubators, no oxygen, no tube feeding, no antibiotics.[52] All these children would die within six months.

The logic underlying the selective treatment regime was that spina bifida infants who present at birth with the worst physical anomalies are very likely to die in their first year of life even with maximal treatment, in which case treatment should be regarded as futile. Worse, not only would corrective treatment be of no benefit to the child, but the additional suffering caused by the required surgical interventions would arguably be a harm to him. The ethical justification for the selective approach was therefore that it would enable parents and physicians alike to identify the cases in which initiating treatment would not be in the best interest of the child. Implementing it, of course, required developing criteria for determining which infants would be denied treatment. These criteria would look to such matters as 'the size and location of the opening over the spine, the existence of severe paralysis or spinal deformity, very bad hydrocephalus, and other major defects or brain damage'.[53] The precise formulation of these criteria can no doubt be a matter of legitimate disagreement, especially since they must be applied in the first days of the infant's life, but that is a conversation that must be left to the specialists.

---

[50] See Kuhse and Singer 1985: ch. 3.   [51] See e.g. Lorber 1975.

[52] For a recent defence of withholding artificial nutrition and hydration from severely compromised newborns, see Porta and Frader 2007.

[53] Kuhse and Singer 1985: 57.

In the years that have followed this debate the selective treatment regime has become the norm for newborns presenting with severe disabilities.[54] It is intended to answer one important question concerning these infants: is this an instance in which initiating (or continuing) treatment would not be in the best interest of the child, since it would have little or no chance of gaining the child a life worth living? We have seen already that the answer to this question is 'yes' for anencephalic infants, and I will henceforth assume that it is also 'yes' for some spina bifida (but not Down's syndrome) infants. However, the first question inevitably leads to a second: what is to be done with the infants who are denied treatment? Until recently, there has been only one possible answer to this question: the infants will be given comfort care (food, water, pain medication if necessary) but no other measures will be undertaken to prolong their lives. In other words, they will be left to die. But now, at least in one jurisdiction, there is another possibility.

In 2002 physicians at the University Medical Centre in Groningen, the Netherlands, developed a protocol for end-of-life decision-making for seriously compromised newborns.[55] In many respects the Groningen Protocol resembles the earlier criteria used to decide when to withhold/withdraw treatment; the factors it takes to be determinative include 'extremely poor quality of life (suffering) in terms of functional disability, pain, discomfort, poor prognosis, and hopelessness'.[56] But there is one important difference: infants selected for non-treatment are not left to die but rather have their lives ended by euthanasia. Largely because of this additional feature, the Protocol has been very controversial.[57] However, there has been something quite remarkable about this controversy. The critics have focused almost exclusively on the criteria embedded in the Protocol, especially the required judgement of poor quality of life and intractable suffering. One of them has concluded, after some discussion of the nature of suffering, that 'it is unreasonable to believe that either a physician or parent can accurately judge whether the burdens of an infant's life outweigh the benefits of living *for that child*'.[58] This claim can, of course, be contested.[59] But what makes it remarkable is that it is so beside the point. The innovation in the Protocol is not that it requires judgement calls about the prospects of severely compromised newborns; as we have seen, the necessity of making such calls has been accepted since the 1970s. What is novel in the Protocol is the use of euthanasia for infants selected for nontreatment instead of waiting for them to die of their condition.[60] The

---

[54]   See e.g. Nuffield Council on Bioethics 2006. A recent overview of non-treatment decision-making for newborns can be found in Pinter 2008.

[55]   The Protocol is discussed in more detail in §6.2, below.

[56]   Verhagen and Sauer 2005.

[57]   Critics of the Protocol include Chernevak, McCullough, and Arabin 2006; Kon 2007, 2008 Jotkowitz, Glick, and Gesundheit 2008. It has been defended by Manninen 2006, 2008; de Vries and Verhagen 2008; Woien 2008; Lindemann and Verkerk 2008.

[58]   Kon 2007: 457 (emphasis in original); cf. Kon 2008.

[59]   As it has been by de Vries and Verhagen 2008; Woien 2008; Manninen 2008.

[60]   To be fair, some of the critics (Kon 2007; Jotkowitz, Glick, and Gesundheit 2008) do also object to the Protocol on the ground that it crosses the 'killing/letting die' boundary, but they offer no reason for thinking that, in the case of the infants in question, waiting for them to die is better than killing them.

main points the critics make could just as easily be directed against the criteria for nontreatment that have been in place for more than thirty years now. From the point of view of the interests of the child, there may be a case against euthanasia rather than waiting for the infant to die, since it precludes the possibility of an unexpectedly positive outcome. But this case would have to be weighed against the advantage of euthanasia in preventing any further suffering by the child (and, one might add, the parents). In the end the best course of action for a particular infant will have to be determined by the particular circumstances of the case. But it should be clear by now that, once the decision has been made that this infant's life is not to be rescued, there can be no objection in principle to ending the life by means of a lethal injection rather than waiting for the baby to die over a period of weeks or months. In many instances, if not all, this will be the most humane thing to do.

In the case of severely disabled newborns, the best-interest standard can therefore lead to the result that (a) no corrective treatment will be undertaken for the infant's condition and (b) euthanasia will instead be administered. In short, it can justify nonvoluntary euthanasia as an outcome. Our only remaining question is the one we set aside earlier in this discussion: who decides whether or not this baby will live? By now the broad outline of an answer to this question has already emerged. The parents are the default substitute decision-makers for the child, with the authority to consent to or refuse treatment on the child's behalf.[61] However, in the kinds of hard cases we have been discussing, parents will be dependent on the neonatal intensive care unit for expert medical opinion and advice. This dependency will inevitably result in a collaborative decision-making process between the parents and the attending physicians. When they are in agreement there will normally be no reason to overrule their mutual decision, unless (as in some of the earlier Down's syndrome cases) an infant with clear prospects of a worthwhile life is being left to die. In the event that they disagree, matters become more complicated. Typically the disagreement takes one of two forms: either the parents are refusing treatment that the healthcare team thinks will be of medical benefit to the infant or they are demanding treatment that the team judges to be futile. These two possible scenarios are illustrated by two recent Canadian cases.

One of them involved a baby girl named Phebe who, following severe complications during her birth, was placed on a ventilator and had a feeding tube inserted. When the parents were advised that the infant had little chance of survival they decided in consultation with the doctors to discontinue all life support. However, once the ventilator was removed it was discovered that Phebe could breathe on her own. The hospital ethics committee then overruled the parents' decision to have the feeding tube removed. At the time of writing Phebe is two years old and, in the light of what they regard as her poor quality of life, her parents continue to request that

---

[61] For a study of parental attitudes towards intentionally hastening the death of a child with end-stage cancer, see Dussel et al. 2010.

artificial nutrition and hydration be discontinued.[62] The other case concerned a baby boy named Isaiah who suffered serious brain damage during the birth process. After three months the neonatal intensive care unit sought to disconnect the ventilator that was keeping the baby alive, on the ground that his brain damage was profound and irreversible and would preclude him from achieving any meaningful functioning. The parents, however, insisted on the continuation of life support and secured a court order to prevent the disconnection of the ventilator until they could obtain a second, independent medical assessment. When that assessment confirmed the baby's poor prognosis they agreed to the removal of life support, and Isaiah died shortly thereafter.[63]

In these cases of stalemate between parents and physicians (or hospital) there may be no recourse other than reference to some decision-making body—perhaps a hospital ethics committee in the first instance and, if the disagreement persists, ultimately a court. (Both of the foregoing cases went before the courts.) If the parents' refusal of treatment is found to be clearly contrary to the interests of the child, then decision-making authority may need to be transferred to a neutral party (a child services agency, a guardian appointed by the court, etc.). As mentioned earlier, parents cannot be compelled to raise a seriously (or even mildly) disabled child against their will, but their refusal to care for the child cannot be a reason to deny it treatment that is judged to be clearly beneficial to it. On the other hand, if the parents are demanding life-sustaining measures that will have the effect merely of prolonging the baby's hopeless condition, then at some point the medical team may no longer have any obligation to comply with their wishes. Each case will, of course, feature its own peculiar set of circumstances, so that generalizations about outcomes would be foolhardy. All that can be said with certainty in these cases is that the best interest of the child must remain paramount. Tragically, as we have seen, that interest is not always best served by continued life.

5.3 Last Words

Euthanasia is easiest to justify when it is voluntary, hardest when it is not. But 'hard' here does not mean 'impossible'. There are circumstances under which nonvoluntary euthanasia offers the best outcome for decisionally incapable persons in the dying process. Where the person has decisional capacity in her past then we have a point of reference for determining both what she would now choose for herself (were she able) and what would be in her best interest. If we have this information then we—or, rather, the person's substitute decision-makers—should use it. It will sometimes justify 'active' measures rather than merely 'passive ones'—the pharmaceutical hastening of

---

[62] 'Legal fight has child's life in the balance', *Globe and Mail*, 27 January 2010.

[63] 'Baby Isaiah dies in parents' arms', *Globe and Mail*, 12 March 2010. For a British case similar to Isaiah's, see Brazier 2004.

death rather than letting it happen on its own timetable. The harder cases are the ones in which there is no precedent autonomy on which to base our current decision. But even then euthanasia can satisfy the best-interest standard, at least as well as, and more commonly better than, waiting for the patient to die after withholding or withdrawing treatment. The argument from well-being remains a powerful one and it will often favour the gentler and speedier end.

We have now reached the final destination of our ethical journey, which began with unanimity concerning patient refusal of life-sustaining treatment and ended with bitter division over the euthanasia of newborns. Without attempting to summarize all the intervening argument, three dominating themes can be seen running through it. The first is that essentially the same case—appealing to both patient well-being and patient autonomy—can be made for the justifiability of all of the voluntary measures we have considered. Though these measures may differ in a number of respects they are unified by virtue of their justificatory foundation. The second is that the appeal to well-being alone—or in tandem with an attenuated appeal to autonomy—is still capable of justifying some nonvoluntary measures, including euthanasia. The third is that none of the attempts to draw ethical bright lines in this spectrum of end-of-life options is successful. Neither the intending/foreseeing distinction nor the doing/allowing distinction is capable of showing that assisted death differs in an ethically salient way from already accepted practices, such as terminal sedation and treatment withdrawal. Nor is their combination capable of yielding this result. Appeals to the sanctity of life or to the right to life are no more successful. We conclude, therefore, that there are no such bright lines, that essentially the same kind of justification is available for all the measures we have canvassed, and that the decision as to which would be best in a particular case must be based on the peculiar circumstances of the case.

We began the ethical inquiry with Anita, our terminal cancer patient, and Bill, who is in the latter stages of ALS. Neither wants to wait for their illness to kill them; each wants to find some way of forestalling further needless suffering. We asked then which end-of-life options should be available to them. We now have an answer: as far as the ethics of these measures goes, Anita and Bill should be able to choose any treatment plan they want, from the least interventionist—refusing food and water—to the most aggressive—assisted suicide or euthanasia. There is no ethical case against any of these options; the right one for them is whatever they settle on as the outcome of their process of informed choice.

However, this is only a partial answer. It tells us whether Anita and Bill, and their healthcare providers, would be violating any ethical constraints if they opted for assisted death. But it does not tell us whether this option should be legally available to them. The outcome of our ethical inquiry takes us partway towards settling the legal question, but not all the way. It does suffice to clear away one very common ground of objection to the legalization of assisted death, namely that the law should not permit the morally impermissible. If there is a case against legalization, it cannot take this form. However, there are other grounds of objection that we have not yet considered, because they raise issues that are not germane to the ethical status of assisted death. Furthermore, these issues are the most important ones in the debate over public policy: they constitute the strongest reasons for declining to make assisted death legally permissible even after it has been shown to be morally permissible. Dealing with them takes us into Part II of this book.

PART II
Law

6

The Legal Landscape

To get to where the law should be we need to start from where it is. Every legal jurisdiction has two basic options with respect to euthanasia and assisted suicide: prohibition (both practices are unlawful) and regulation (at least one of them is lawful under stipulated conditions).[1] In this chapter we take a look at jurisdictions in both categories. Since the vast majority of countries remain prohibitionist on assisted death, our survey of that category cannot be comprehensive. Instead, in the first section we will focus exclusively on three common law jurisdictions: Canada, the United States, and the United Kingdom.[2] We will then turn in the second section to the eight current regulatory regimes.

6.1 Prohibition

The three common law jurisdictions all attempt to maintain a bright line between assisted death and all other end-of-life measures that may have the effect of hastening death. On the one side of that line the most firmly established treatment principle, both at law and in standard medical practice, is the Doctrine of Informed Consent. With the exception of special situations—such as emergencies—initiation or continuation of medical treatment without the consent of the patient will constitute either a tort or a crime. As courts in all three jurisdictions have recognized, the consent requirement confers upon competent adults the right to refuse treatment, even when doing so is certain to hasten death. This right was explicitly affirmed for the refusal of nutrition and hydration in the American case of *Bouvia* (1986). Elizabeth Bouvia was a twenty-eight-year-old woman who was quadriplegic as a result of severe cerebral palsy. Except for a few fingers of one hand and some slight head and facial movements

---

[1] I am assuming here that no jurisdiction will wish to legalize either of these measures and then leave it entirely unregulated. However, see n. 122, below.

[2] With apologies to readers in Australia and New Zealand; no disrespect intended but the line had to be drawn somewhere.

she was completely immobile and confined to a bed in a hospital. She was also in continual pain from degenerative and severely crippling arthritis, not all of which was being relieved by periodic doses of morphine. Despite her physical disabilities, she was intelligent and fully mentally competent. She was capable of being spoonfed, but the hospital medical staff determined that she could not—or would not—take in enough nutrition by this means to keep her weight from falling to dangerously low levels. They therefore inserted a nasogastric feeding tube against her will and contrary to her express written instructions. Her petition for removal of the tube was denied by the trial court but was then upheld by the California Court of Appeal, which affirmed her right to refuse this life-sustaining treatment.[3]

The appellate court simply asserted, without argument, that the provision of food and water by means of a nasogastric tube constituted medical treatment. However, it did devote some attention to the question of whether, in refusing the tube feeding, Ms Bouvia was seeking to commit suicide. Despite evidence that she had earlier expressed a wish to die, and had indeed attempted to starve herself to death, the court held that in petitioning for removal of the tube she was not intending to die but rather accepting an earlier death as a foreseeable outcome of her decision.[4] In removing the tube, therefore, her physicians would not be assisting her suicide.

In Canada the right of a competent patient to refuse life-sustaining treatment was affirmed in *Nancy B* (1992).[5] The plaintiff in that case was a twenty-five-year-old woman suffering from Guillain-Barré syndrome, an irreversible neurological disorder that had left her incapable of movement and dependent on a ventilator. Her intellectual capacity was unaffected by the disease. After two and a half years in this condition she requested removal of the respiratory support in order to escape the suffering caused by her immobility. With the ventilator she could potentially have lived for a long time; without it she would die quickly. While her decision was not opposed either by her healthcare providers or by the hospital, it was unclear whether under Canadian law disconnecting her from the ventilator would constitute criminal negligence causing death (a culpable homicide). Justice Dufour, who heard the case in the Quebec Superior Court, affirmed Nancy B's legal right to refuse continued use of the ventilator, even though such refusal would precipitate her death. The cause of death, Dufour argued, would be the disease, not the removal of the ventilator. He therefore concluded that Nancy B could not be considered to be committing suicide

---

[3] Interestingly, after receiving this ruling in her favour, Ms Bouvia decided that she wanted to continue to live; at last report she was still alive.

[4] The majority of the court went so far as to assert that in refusing food and water she would be allowing nature to take its course. They were taken to task for this tortured reasoning in a concurring opinion by Justice Compton, who claimed that it was clear that her intention was to die.

[5] The legal obligation of healthcare providers to respect treatment refusals recorded in advance directives had been affirmed by the Ontario Court of Appeal two years earlier in *Malette* (1990). However, 'the Court of Appeal explicitly rejected the extension of the reasoning in this case to cases involving patients who have been diagnosed as terminally or incurably ill or patients in a persistent vegetative state' (Downie 2004: 21 n. 19).

by refusing artificial respiration, even though she would certainly die without it, and that her physicians could not be liable for assisting a suicide. Five weeks after the judgment her attending physician induced Nancy B into a coma and removed the ventilator; she died comfortably in her sleep.[6]

A year after *Nancy B* the Supreme Court of Canada canonized the right to refuse life-sustaining treatment in *Rodriguez* (1993). Writing for the majority, Justice Sopinka stated that 'Canadian courts have recognized a common law right of patients to refuse consent to medical treatment, or to demand that treatment, once commenced, be withdrawn or discontinued. . . . This right has been specifically recognized to exist even if the withdrawal from or refusal of treatment may result in death.'[7] *Nancy B* dealt specifically with artificial respiration, but there is little doubt that the courts would take the same view of nutrition and hydration artificially administered by means of a feeding tube. Indeed, in determining whether placing a patient on a ventilator is a form of medical treatment Justice Dufour reasoned as follows: 'Of course it is a technique of the same nature as feeding a patient. One cannot therefore make a distinction between artificial feeding and other essential life-sustaining techniques.'[8] No Canadian case has specifically addressed the withdrawal of a feeding tube, but in affirming the patient's right of refusal Justice Sopinka referred approvingly to the leading American and British cases on this question, each of which involved removing the feeding tube of a patient in a permanent vegetative state.[9] Since Nancy B was presumably being given food and water by artificial means, then by Justice Dufour's reasoning she could equally have refused this treatment. However, her dependence on the ventilator meant that death would come much more quickly following its withdrawal.

It is obvious that withholding or withdrawing life-sustaining treatment will in most cases result in hastening death, though the cause of death will normally be recorded as the underlying disease condition rather than the (non-)treatment decision. But there are other ways in which physicians may legally hasten death, including the administration of narcotics, such as morphine, in order to control pain. As we saw earlier (§3.1), it is at least widely believed that if the pain is severe enough then the dosage of medication necessary to bring it down to acceptable levels may also be sufficient to cause death. In such cases it can (and will) be argued that death is not the intended effect of the treatment; rather, the intended effect is pain relief and hastening death is merely foreseen as a possible, or probable, side effect. No charges have ever been laid in Canada in so-called 'double effect' cases involving the administration of possibly lethal doses of pain medication.[10] Furthermore, in his majority judgement in *Rodriguez*

---

[6] Lemmens and Dickens 2001: 144. An English case, *Ms B* (2002), which raised essentially the same issues and reached the same conclusion, was heard ten years later; see McLean and Williamson 2007: 142 ff.

[7] *Rodriguez* (1993*b*), 598 (case citations omitted, including *Nancy B*).

[8] *Nancy B* (1992), 391.

[9] *Cruzan* (1990); *Bland* (1993). These cases will be discussed later in this section.

[10] Downie 2004: 30–2. For the legal experience in the UK (and its problems) see Huxtable 2007: ch. 4.

Justice Sopinka addressed this practice in order to distinguish it from assisted suicide (or euthanasia): 'The administration of drugs designed for pain control in dosages which the physician knows will hasten death constitutes active contribution to death by any standard. However, the distinction drawn here is one based upon intention—in the case of palliative care the intention is to ease pain, which has the effect of hastening death, while in the case of assisted suicide, the intention is undeniably to cause death.... In my view, distinctions based upon intent are important, and in fact form the basis of our criminal law.'[11] Notwithstanding these remarks, however, there may still be some potential for legal liability. The Canadian Criminal Code defines criminal negligence, in part, as 'doing anything' that 'shows wanton or reckless disregard for the lives or safety of other persons'. In the event that a case came to legal attention, therefore, physicians would need to show that in administering potentially life-shortening medication they were not displaying such disregard for the life of their patient. Presumably they could do so by establishing (a) that the medication in question had a legitimate therapeutic function, such as pain relief, (b) that no more of it was administered than was necessary in order to achieve this result, and (c) that no other means was available of producing the same result without also hastening death.

Finally, as noted earlier (§3.1), terminal sedation is often also assumed to have the effect of hastening death. However this might be, patients who request it may also execute an advance directive refusing all other treatment, including nutrition and hydration, while sedated. The combined effect of this treatment request and refusal would then be to shorten life. Since each of these components can be perfectly lawful, as long as the usual conditions for informed consent and refusal are satisfied, their conjunction is presumptively lawful as well.[12] Terminal sedation is therefore a standard, if extreme, measure available to patients and physicians in palliative care settings without risk of legal liability.[13]

Though it might seem but a short ethical step from terminal sedation to euthanasia, at law they are poles apart. In the United Kingdom euthanasia is a form of homicide (murder or manslaughter, depending on the circumstances) under the Homicide Act 1957. Dr Nigel Cox was a consultant rheumatologist at Royal Hampshire County

---

[11] *Rodriguez* (1993b), 607. Cf. Law Reform Commission of Canada 1983: 23; Special Senate Committee on Euthanasia and Assisted Suicide 1995: 26–32. In the United Kingdom Lord Goff reached a similar conclusion in *Bland* (1993) by relying on the principle that the physician must act in the best interests of the patient: 'It is this principle too which, in my opinion, underlies the established rule that a doctor may, when caring for a patient who is, for example, dying of cancer, lawfully administer painkilling drugs despite the fact that he knows that an incidental effect of that application will be to abbreviate the patient's life. Such a decision may properly be made as part of the care of the living patient, in his best interests; and, on this basis, the treatment will be lawful. Moreover, where the doctor's treatment of his patient is lawful, the patient's death will be regarded in law as exclusively caused by the injury or disease to which his condition is attributable' (868).

[12] Special Senate Committee on Euthanasia and Assisted Suicide 1995, 33–6. I know of no case in which the lawfulness of terminal sedation has been challenged in court.

[13] However, in a recent case in England physicians refused a terminally ill patient's request for total sedation on the ground that providing it would be tantamount to assisting her suicide ('Allow me to die, terminally ill woman urges court', *The Guardian*, 13 February 2007).

Hospital in Winchester who by 1991 had been caring for Lillian Boyes for thirteen years. In August of that year, at the age of seventy, Ms Boyes was in such acute pain from rheumatoid arthritis that 'she couldn't bear to be touched, and, according to one of her nurses, screamed like a wounded dog'.[14] When the pain persisted despite huge doses of painkillers, including heroin, and after Ms Boyes begged him to put her out of her agony, Dr Cox administered potassium chloride in order to stop her heart. His act was reported by a nurse who read Ms Boyes's medical record and Dr Cox was subsequently charged with attempted murder. (The charge was attempted murder, rather than outright murder, because by the time the case was investigated Ms Boyes had been cremated; it could therefore not be proven that the cause of death was the potassium chloride, as opposed to her illness.) He was convicted in 1992 but given only a twelve-month suspended sentence.[15] The professional conduct committee of the General Medical Council, the body regulating physicians in the United Kingdom, decided that no further action was necessary and Dr Cox then resumed his practice. Dr Cox had the strong support of his patient's family throughout this entire incident. To this day Dr Cox remains the only UK physician convicted of a euthanasia-related offence.[16]

The Criminal Code of Canada makes no special mention of euthanasia, though it docs specifically exclude the consent of the victim as a defence against a charge of homicide. A case of 'mercy killing' is therefore considered to be a culpable homicide: either murder (first or second degree) or manslaughter, depending on the circumstances and the discretion of police or Crown prosecutors. Homicide charges in such cases have, however, been rare, especially where the party held responsible for the death is a healthcare provider (a physician or nurse). Where charges have been laid they have tended to be for a lesser offence, such as 'administering a noxious thing'.[17] The reluctance of both the Crown and the courts to pursue homicide charges is perhaps best illustrated by the case of Dr Nancy Morrison.[18] In November 1996, while on staff at the Queen Elizabeth II Health Sciences Centre in Halifax, Nova Scotia, she administered a lethal dose of potassium chloride to a patient named Paul Mills. Mr Mills was sixty-five years old and was suffering from an incurable chest wall infection

[14] *Independent on Sunday*, 10 April 2005.
[15] *Cox* (1992). See also the summaries of this case in Dworkin 1993: 184–5; Huxtable 2007: 106 ff.; McLean 2007: 142–3.
[16] For a brief account of other UK cases see McLean 2007: 141–4.
[17] Two Ontario cases during the 1990s provide examples of this outcome. In *Mataya* (1992), Scott Mataya, a Toronto nurse, administered a lethal dose of potassium chloride to an elderly patient who was suffering acute respiratory distress while dying of kidney, liver, and lung failure. After an initial charge of first-degree murder the Crown agreed to a guilty plea to the lesser offence and Mataya was placed on probation for three years. In *de la Rocha* (1993) a lethal dose of the same medication was administered by Alberto de la Rocha, a Timmins physician, to an elderly patient dying of cancer of the mouth, cheek, and lungs. Dr de la Rocha was charged with second-degree murder but allowed to plead guilty to the lesser offence; he also received a three-year term of probation. Both cases were cited in *Latimer* (1997); for further details on these cases see Sneiderman and Deutscher 2002.
[18] For full accounts of the facts of this case, see Downie and Anthony 1998; Sneiderman and Deutscher 2002. I have borrowed extensively from these accounts in my brief summary.

stemming from cancer of the oesophagus. Both his family and his thoracic surgeon had come to the conclusion, following multiple surgeries, that any further interventions would be futile and that the time had come for him to die. A 'do not resuscitate' (DNR) order was entered on his chart, antibiotics and tubefeeding were stopped, and he was removed from his ventilator in the expectation that death would follow shortly. However, he did not die as anticipated and instead began to exhibit extreme respiratory distress, continually gasping for air. In an effort to relieve this distress massive amounts of narcotics were administered over the ensuing eight-hour period, which appeared to have little or no effect. The intensive care unit nurse who attended Mr Mills during his last two days, and who had eleven years of ICU experience, stated afterward that 'it was beyond a shadow of a doubt the worst death I have ever witnessed'.[19] It was at this point that Dr Morrison, the attending physician at the ICU, injected the potassium chloride, which has no analgesic or sedative properties and whose function is to stop the heart.[20] Within a minute all electrical activity in Mr Mills's heart had ceased. After an internal review Dr Morrison's hospital privileges were suspended for three months. However, the hospital did not report the incident to the police; that step was instead taken six months later by another physician who, having seen the internal review, concluded that Mr Mills had been the victim of euthanasia. The police responded by charging Dr Morrison with first-degree murder.

In December 1997 a preliminary inquiry was held to determine whether the case should go to trial.[21] At the inquiry doubts were raised by the defence about the cause of Mr Mills's death. One possible explanation for the fact that the unusually high doses of narcotics had had no effect was that the intravenous line through which they had been administered had slipped out of the artery, in which case the drugs were not reaching his bloodstream. But if that were the case then the potassium chloride administered by Dr Morrison might also not have reached Mr Mills's heart in time to kill him. Judge Randall of the Nova Scotia Provincial Court, who presided over the inquiry, accepted this defence argument and ruled that there was no case to go to trial for murder or any other offence. When the Crown's appeal of this decision was denied in the Nova Scotia Supreme Court,[22] no further legal action was taken against Dr Morrison.[23]

A case similar in many important respects to that of Dr Morrison unfolded in the United States at just about exactly the same time. Dr Ernesto Pinzon-Reyes was on staff at Highlands Regional Medical Center in Sebring, Florida, when he admitted seventy-nine-year-old Rosario Gurrieri in October 1996. Over the previous year Mr Gurrieri had been suffering from congestive heart failure, pulmonary congestion, high blood

---

[19]   *Morrison* (1998*a*), 320.

[20]   Dr Morrison could therefore not have used the 'double effect' argument that Mr Mills's death was merely a foreseen but unintended consequence of her action.

[21]   *Morrison* (1998*a*).

[22]   *Morrison* (1998*b*).

[23]   In 1999 she received a reprimand from the Nova Scotia College of Physicians and Surgeons.

pressure, shortness of breath, and irregular heartbeat. But what brought him to the hospital on this occasion was something new and different: acute pain due to terminal metastatic lung cancer. After a few days of hospitalization Mr Gurrieri's condition worsened: the pain became more severe and he began to suffer as well from respiratory distress. Over a period of about twenty-four hours Dr Pinzon-Reyes administered ever-increasing dosages of narcotics in an attempt to get the pain under control. Eventually he managed to get Mr Gurrieri sedated but the patient was still struggling to breathe and sweating profusely with an elevated heart rate. Everyone agreed that by this time Mr Gurrieri was within hours of death. Dr Pinzon-Reyes then administered potassium chloride, evidently with the intent of bringing Mr Gurrieri's heart rate down. The patient died about forty minutes later. Shortly after Mr Gurrieri's death Dr Pinzon-Reyes was charged with first-degree murder. He was acquitted of this charge in June 1997, in part because of reasonable doubt about the cause of death, based on the fact that when potassium chloride is lethal it kills within three to five minutes and not forty minutes later.[24] At the time of the initial murder charge the Florida State Medical Board suspended Dr Pinzon-Reyes's medical licence. At the hearing for reinstatement of the licence following his acquittal, the Board found that the cause of Mr Gurrieri's death had been 'multi-organ failure and the tumor burden imposed on his body by pervasive cancer' rather than the dose of potassium chloride.[25] It concluded that no further disciplinary action against Dr Pinzon-Reyes was warranted.

The best-known conviction of a physician for the practice of euthanasia was that of Dr Jack Kevorkian, who was trained as a pathologist and became an advocate for the legalization of assisted death. Between 1990 and 1998 Dr Kevorkian assisted the suicides of more than one hundred clients who sought out his services. During this time he was prosecuted on several occasions in Michigan but never convicted. However, in September 1998 he administered (voluntary) euthanasia to a fifty-two-year-old man who was in the final stages of amyotrophic lateral sclerosis. Dr Kevorkian then allowed a videotape he had made of this episode to be aired on the CBS news-magazine *60 Minutes*, during which he dared the authorities to prosecute him. He got his wish in March 1999 when he was charged with first-degree murder and the delivery of a controlled substance (administering a lethal injection). The law of homicide being much more settled in the state of Michigan than that of assisted suicide, he was convicted of second-degree murder and sentenced to a period of ten to twenty-five years in prison. In June 2007 he was paroled for good behaviour. He has vowed to continue his campaign for the legalization of assisted death, but only by lawful means.

Unlike euthanasia, assisting a suicide is a specific offence in Canada, the United Kingdom, and the majority of American states.[26] Over the past twenty years or so

---

[24] *Pinzon-Reyes* (1997*a*).   [25] *Pinzon-Reyes* (1997*b*).

[26] In the remaining states, with the exception of Oregon, Washington, and Montana, it is an offence under a different statute, usually murder or manslaughter. The exceptions are discussed in §6.2, below.

several Canadian cases have come to light, with outcomes varying widely from no charges laid to conviction and imprisonment.[27] In 1993 the Canadian law was challenged on constitutional grounds by Sue Rodriguez, who was diagnosed with amyotrophic lateral sclerosis (ALS). Foreseeing that the relentless progress of the disease would eventually render her unable to swallow, speak, move, or breathe on her own, she wished to choose the time and manner of her death by a lethal dose of medication. However, she knew that when that time arrived she would need the assistance of a physician. Unwilling to ask any physician to commit an unlawful act, she decided to challenge the law on the ground that it violated her rights to equality, and to life, liberty, and security of the person, under the Canadian Charter of Rights and Freedoms. Her challenge was unsuccessful in both the trial court and the British Columbia Court of Appeal (though in the latter venue she lost by a 2–1 majority, with the Chief Justice dissenting).[28] On further appeal, the Supreme Court was deeply divided on the case, with a narrow majority of 5–4 finding against the challenge.[29]

Needless to say, the Supreme Court decision was a personal disappointment for Ms Rodriguez. However, it did not prevent her from carrying out her wishes in 1994, with the assistance of an anonymous physician. No charges were laid in the case, either against the physician or against Svend Robinson, the Member of Parliament who supported her and was with her at her death. Subsequently, the British Columbia Attorney-General developed prosecutorial guidelines for such cases that were similar in some respects to those in place in the Netherlands prior to 2002, when legislation explicitly legalizing assisted suicide and euthanasia came into force (see §6.2, below).[30]

---

[27] A sampling of cases: *No charges laid*: David Lewis, Vancouver, 1990—helped eight friends with HIV/AIDS to end their lives (*Vancouver Sun*, 7 July 1990); Svend Robinson, Victoria, 1994—present during assisted suicide (or euthanasia) of Sue Rodriguez (*Globe and Mail*, 14 February 1994); Eric MacDonald, Windsor, Nova Scotia, 2007—accompanied his wife to Zurich where she died of an assisted suicide provided by the Swiss organization Dignitas (*Halifax Chronicle-Herald*, 26 June 2007). *Charges laid but dropped*: Bert Doerksen, Winnipeg, 1997—suspected of helping his wife kill herself by carbon monoxide (*Winnipeg Free Press*, 29 July 2000). *Acquittal*: Wayne Hussey, New Dundee, Ontario, 1999—test-fired the gun with which his father killed himself (*Toronto Star*, 27 April 2000); Evelyn Martens, Duncan, BC, 2002—provided companionship during two suicides (*Globe and Mail*, 5 November 2004); Stéphan Dufour, Alma, Quebec, 2008—set up rope and dog collar with which his uncle hanged himself (*Globe and Mail*, 13 December 2008). *Conviction on lesser charge*: Robert Cashin, Edmonton, 1994—provided a large dose of sedatives to his mother who was dying of cancer, convicted of administering a noxious thing, sentenced to two years probation (*Toronto Star*, 9 April 1995). *Conviction for assisting suicide*: Mary Jane Fogarty, Halifax, 1994—wrote out the suicide note of a friend and provided her with a syringe, sentenced to three years probation and 300 hours of community service (*Halifax Chronicle-Herald*, 19 December 1995); Dr Maurice Genereux, Toronto, 1996—prescribed barbiturates for two HIV-positive patients who used them for suicide attempts, sentenced to two years imprisonment (*Globe and Mail*, 14 May 1998); Marielle Houle, Montreal, 2004—helped her son who suffered from multiple sclerosis commit suicide, sentence suspended (*Montreal Gazette*, 28 January 2006); Dr Ramesh Kumar Sharma, Vernon, BC, 2006—provided a potentially lethal supply of medication to a ninety-three-year-old patient with congestive heart failure, two year conditional sentence (*Vancouver Province*, 14 June 2007). For American cases in which charges were downgraded or dropped see Pugliese 1993.

[28] *Rodriguez* (1993a).

[29] *Rodriguez* (1993b).

[30] Lemmens and Dickens 2001: 138. The guidelines are reproduced in Special Senate Committee on Euthanasia and Assisted Suicide 1995: A59–A63 and in Downie 2004: 145 ff.

Since 1993 there has been no further legal challenge in Canada to the assisted suicide law. The Canadian Senate, however, set up a Special Committee to examine the question of both euthanasia and assisted suicide. In its 1995 Report the Committee divided on the legalization issue in much the way the Supreme Court had done two years earlier.[31] A majority on the Committee favoured retaining the existing laws prohibiting both practices, but with a less severe penalty for homicide where the element of compassion could be proved. The minority advocated legalizing voluntary euthanasia and assisted suicide with clearly defined safeguards for each. Both sides agreed that nonvoluntary euthanasia should remain a criminal offence, but with a reduced penalty. No action was taken by the government on any of these recommended changes. In recent years a Member of Parliament from Quebec has tabled a series of private member's bills aiming to reform the law, but none has come close to passing.[32]

Later in the 1990s the laws prohibiting assisted suicide in the states of Washington and New York were challenged in cases that reached the US Supreme Court.[33] In *Glucksberg* (1997) the Court ruled that the right to assistance in suicide is not a fundamental liberty interest protected by the Due Process Clause of the US Constitution's Fourteenth Amendment. Furthermore, it found that Washington's ban on assisting a suicide was rationally related to various important state interests, including the preservation of life and the protection of vulnerable groups, and that legalizing assisted suicide would set the law on a 'slippery slope' towards the legalization of euthanasia. In the companion case of *Quill* (1997) the Court determined that the New York law did not offend against the Equal Protection Clause of the Fourteenth Amendment by drawing an arbitrary distinction between assistance in suicide and refusal of life-sustaining treatment.

In the United Kingdom a similar challenge against the Suicide Act was launched in 2001 by Dianne Pretty who was suffering from motor neurone disease, a progressive degenerative condition from which she had no hope of recovery. Ms Pretty was fully competent and wished to be able to end her life at a time of her own choosing. Being physically incapable of carrying out this wish on her own, she needed the assistance of her husband, who was willing to provide it. However, she did not want to leave him vulnerable to criminal prosecution and therefore appealed to the Director of Public Prosecutions for an undertaking that he would not be charged. When that undertaking was refused she argued that the prohibition on assisting a suicide contravened her rights under various articles of the European Convention on Human Rights. When these arguments were rejected by the House of Lords,[34] Ms Pretty appealed to the

---

[31] Special Senate Committee on Euthanasia and Assisted Suicide 1995.
[32] Her most recent effort ended in a 228–59 defeat in a free vote on second reading of the bill in the House of Commons on 21 April 2010.
[33] Rosenfeld 2004: 33–8; Tucker 2004: 264–7; Gorsuch 2006: ch. 2.
[34] *Pretty* (2001).

European Court of Human Rights which also found unanimously against her.[35] Shortly after that decision she died from complications brought on by her condition.

The Director of Public Prosecutions has more recently been involved in a closely related assisted suicide issue. Because assisting a suicide is unlawful in the UK, a number of British citizens have chosen to travel to Zurich to end their lives with the help of the Swiss organization Dignitas.[36] In most cases they have been accompanied by a family member or close friend. However, it has never been clear whether rendering this service might constitute 'aiding, abetting, counselling, or procuring' a suicide under the terms of the Suicide Act. Although no returning friends or relatives have yet been prosecuted, many have been questioned by the police and have had to wait several months to see whether charges would be laid.[37] Debbie Purdy is an Englishwoman with multiple sclerosis who plans to avail herself of the services of Dignitas when she deems her suffering to be too much to bear. She wants to be accompanied on that journey by her husband but does not wish to expose him to any risk of prosecution. She appealed to the Director of Public Prosecutions to reveal the policy of the Crown Prosecution Service on prosecution for the offence of assisting a suicide but was refused. In June 2008 she obtained permission to bring a High Court challenge of this refusal, in an attempt to obtain clarification of the circumstances under which people could be prosecuted for helping their loved ones to die. However, in October 2008 the High Court judges denied her challenge, arguing that what she was asking for would involve a change in the assisted suicide law, which could only be brought about by Parliament. This decision was upheld on appeal, but Ms Purdy then appealed it further to the Law Lords.

In the midst of this judicial process Keir Starmer, who had taken office as the new Director of Public Prosecutions, issued a statement that the Crown Prosecution Service would not be initiating a prosecution against the parents of twenty-three-year-old Daniel James, who in March 2007 sustained a serious spinal injury resulting in tetraplegia in a rugby accident.[38] In September 2008 Mr James was accompanied by his parents to Zurich, where his suicide was assisted by Dignitas. In his decision in the case Mr Starmer stated that, while there was sufficient evidence to prosecute the parents for assisting a suicide, such a prosecution would not be in the public interest. That decision was, of course, specific to this particular case, but it nonetheless provided some degree of assurance to others who planned to travel to Zurich with their loved ones that they also would not be prosecuted, as long as the circumstances of their case are relevantly similar.

[35] *Pretty* (2002). Cf. McLean 2007: 87–92.

[36] For an account of the operations of Dignitas, and of Swiss law concerning assisted suicide, see §6.2. To date approximately 140 Britons have availed themselves of the services of Dignitas.

[37] The same has been true in Canada. In June 2007 Elizabeth MacDonald, a Nova Scotia woman with multiple sclerosis, travelled to Zurich to die, accompanied by her husband Eric, a retired Anglican priest. At the request of a Canadian anti-euthanasia group, the RCMP launched an investigation into the circumstances of Ms MacDonald's death but concluded that Mr MacDonald's role had broken no Canadian law.

[38] Crown Prosecution Service 2008.

The decision of the Law Lords in July 2009 constituted a significant victory for Ms Purdy.[39] The Lords found that the unclarity in the application of the Suicide Act constituted an interference with Ms Purdy's right to 'respect for her private and family life' under Article 8(1) of the European Convention on Human Rights and that this interference failed the Article 8(2) requirement that it be 'in accordance with the law'. They therefore ordered the Director of Public Prosecutions to formulate a policy identifying the facts and circumstances that would be taken into account in deciding whether to proceed with a prosecution in situations relevantly similar to Ms Purdy's. Mr Starmer complied with this order in September 2009 by releasing an interim policy intended for public consultation.[40] After receiving nearly 5,000 responses, he then published the final policy in February 2010.[41]

The policy does not change the Suicide Act and does not guarantee immunity from prosecution for assisting a suicide. However, it does attempt to clarify when proceeding with a prosecution would (or would not) be in the public interest.[42] To this end, the policy lists a number of factors that would tend to favour prosecution (e.g. that the 'victim' was a minor or was not decisionally capable) and a further list of factors telling against prosecution (e.g. that the decision by the 'victim' to commit suicide was 'voluntary, clear, settled, and informed'). The policy applies to assistance (of any kind) that is provided (at least in part) in the United Kingdom, whether the suicide occurs there or abroad. It is therefore of much broader application than the cases of friends or relatives accompanying loved ones to Zurich.[43]

This step taken by the Director of Public Prosecutions has some echoes of the situations in both the Netherlands and Switzerland (to be discussed in the next section). As in the former case, the door has been opened to legal assistance with suicide not by a change in the law but by the development of prosecutorial guidelines. As we will see, both euthanasia and assisted suicide were *de facto* legal in the Netherlands for decades before the law was finally amended to reflect this reality. However, the resulting policy is actually rather closer to the Swiss model. For one thing, it rests a great deal of weight on the motive of the party providing the assistance: a prosecution will be more likely if that person is thought to have been motivated by the prospect of personal gain, less likely if the motive was wholly compassionate. This feature resembles the provision in the Swiss law whereby assisting a suicide is unlawful only if done from 'selfish motives'. More importantly, the UK policy draws a distinction among those providing assistance between family members or friends on the one hand and

---

[39] *Purdy* (2009). For a dissenting opinion on this decision see Greasley 2010.

[40] Crown Prosecution Service 2009.

[41] Crown Prosecution Service 2010. The policy applies only in England and Wales, not Scotland or Northern Ireland. However, a similar policy has been developed for Northern Ireland.

[42] The 'public interest' question arises only when there is sufficient evidence to support a charge; where such evidence is lacking the case proceeds no further.

[43] Four months after the final policy was published the Crown Prosecution Service ruled that it would not be in the public interest to prosecute a Yorkshire man for assisting his wife's suicide by fitting a bag over her head as she ended her life by inhaling helium (*Yorkshire Post*, 24 May 2010).

healthcare professionals on the other, prosecution being more likely in the latter case.[44] In this respect it is very different from the Dutch policy, which has always presupposed that suicide assistance (or euthanasia) is to be provided solely by physicians, and closer to the Swiss practice in which the service is offered by non-medical organizations such as Dignitas (though physicians are still involved, since they alone have the legal authority to prescribe the needed medication). It also seems, perversely, to encourage prosecution of those best able to assist a suicide efficiently and safely.

To repeat: the publication of this prosecutorial policy has not changed the law in the UK. As far as legislative action is concerned, for a number of years a member of the House of Lords has introduced bills designed to legalize either voluntary euthanasia or assisted suicide under stipulated conditions.[45] The first attempt by Lord Joffe—the Patient (Assisted Dying) Bill—was debated in the Lords in June 2003 but proceeded no further. He then introduced the Assisted Dying for the Terminally Ill Bill, which would have authorized physicians to provide both euthanasia and assisted suicide to their patients. This bill was remitted in March 2004 to a Select Committee who reported in April 2005, recommending, inter alia, that any future bill on this issue distinguish clearly between these two measures.[46] Accordingly, in his next version of the bill, introduced in November 2005, Lord Joffe restricted the physician's options to making available the means for a patient to end his/her own life, with no provision for euthanasia. However, to this day the Lords has yet to pass any bill legalizing either assisted suicide or euthanasia. Bills aiming to reform the law have from time to time also been tabled in the House of Commons and the Scottish Parliament, but equally without success.[47]

Turning now from voluntary to nonvoluntary measures, all the common law jurisdictions have specific provisions governing the making and application of advance directives. Among other things, these provisions allow substitute decision-makers to refuse treatment—including life-sustaining treatment—on behalf of (formerly competent but currently) incompetent patients. In the event of such refusal healthcare providers are under a duty not to administer such treatment and are protected from liability for withholding or withdrawing it. Matters are somewhat less cut and dried

---

[44] In April 2010, just two months after the prosecutorial policy was published, Dr Michael Irwin, a retired general practitioner, openly invited prosecution by disclosing that three years earlier he had accompanied pancreatic cancer sufferer Raymond Cutkelvin to Zurich for an assisted suicide. Despite the fact that Mr Cutkelvin was previously unknown to Dr Irwin, and that Dr Irwin had personally paid some of his expenses with Dignitas, the Crown Prosecution Service ruled in June that it would not be in the public interest to prosecute him. It remains unclear whether a prosecution would ever be undertaken against a physician as long as it could be established that his/her role in an assisted suicide was motivated solely by compassion (*BBC News*, 25 June 2010).

[45] Cf. McLean 2007: 146 ff.

[46] Select Committee on the Assisted Dying for the Terminally Ill Bill 2004.

[47] In January 2010 Margo MacDonald introduced her End of Life Assistance (Scotland) Bill in the Scottish Parliament. At the time of writing the bill, which would legalize both assisted suicide and (voluntary) euthanasia, was still at the committee stage. A similar bill that she introduced two years earlier failed to attract sufficient support to pass.

when the formerly competent patient has not executed a written directive. The first high-profile case in which the American courts had to face this issue was that of Karen Quinlan, who was twenty-one when she lapsed into a permanent vegetative state in April 1975, after ingesting a combination of alcohol and tranquillizers.[48] She was placed on a ventilator and fed through a nasogastric tube. After several months during which she remained unresponsive, her family requested that the ventilator be removed. Hospital officials refused to comply, taking the view that this step would be tantamount to killing her. Their refusal was upheld in Morris County Court on the ground that disconnecting the ventilator would not be in Ms Quinlan's best interest. However, this decision was overturned on appeal to the New Jersey Supreme Court, which cited her constitutional right to privacy.[49] Ms Quinlan's ventilator was removed in May 1976, but she proved to be capable of breathing on her own. She remained in a permanent vegetative state until her death in June 1985.

The Quinlan decision was not appealed beyond the New Jersey courts, but a similar case reached the US Supreme Court in *Cruzan* (1990).[50] Nancy Cruzan lapsed into a permanent vegetative state in 1983 as a result of oxygen deprivation to the brain following an automobile accident. Ms Cruzan could receive nutrition and hydration only through a feeding tube implanted in her stomach. After she had remained in this condition for several years her parents sought and received permission from the trial court in Missouri to withdraw the feeding tube. This decision was then reversed in the Missouri Supreme Court.[51] The court recognized a patient's right to refuse life-sustaining treatment through the device of an advance directive. However, Ms Cruzan had executed no written directive; instead the trial court had heard testimony from her room-mate concerning whether she would want to live or die under certain conditions. The court ruled that this testimony did not meet the standard of 'clear and convincing evidence' set out in the Missouri Living Will statute. Under the substituted judgement standard Ms Cruzan's surrogate decision-makers were obliged to base their treatment decisions on her previously expressed wishes, in so far as these could be known. Where the evidence concerning these wishes was inconclusive or equivocal they were not entitled to refuse life-sustaining treatment on her behalf.

When this decision was appealed to the Supreme Court the narrow issue to be adjudicated was whether the Missouri requirement of 'clear and convincing evidence' was consistent with the Due Process Clause of the Fourteenth Amendment. A divided court held that it was. Following this decision Ms Cruzan's parents went back to the trial court with new evidence concerning their daughter's treatment wishes, which the court accepted as meeting the evidentiary standard. The feeding tube was removed and Ms Cruzan died in December 1990. Leaving the evidentiary issue aside, the *Cruzan* decision clearly affirms the right of an incompetent patient to refuse life-sustaining treatment by means of directions registered in advance, and the right of

---

[48] Rosenfeld 2004: 29–31.   [49] *Quinlan* (1976).
[50] Rosenfeld 2004: 31–3.   [51] *Cruzan* (1988).

substitute decision-makers to give effect to this refusal.[52] However, it is also worth noting Justice Scalia's concurring opinion in the case in which he argued that patient refusal of food and water amounted to a form of suicide.[53] Scalia's claim has not generally found favour in the courts. We have seen Justice Dufour's conclusion on this issue in the *Nancy B* case, which was then implicitly accepted by the Canadian Supreme Court in *Rodriguez*.

The leading English case on the withdrawal of life-sustaining treatment from a decisionally incapable patient is *Bland* (1993). The facts in *Bland* are very similar to those in *Cruzan*. Anthony Bland was seventeen years old when he suffered a severe crushed chest injury in the disaster at the Hillsborough football ground in April 1989. As a result of loss of oxygen to his brain, he too lapsed into a permanent vegetative state. In his case, however, the initiative to withdraw his feeding tube came not from his parents (though they evidently agreed with this course of action) but from his attending physician, who took the view that, since there was no hope of Mr Bland's recovery, continued treatment could be of no benefit to him. The hospital sought a declaration from the court that withdrawal of life-sustaining treatment would be lawful. This declaration was issued by the lower court and affirmed by the Court of Appeal. Upon further appeal to the House of Lords the five Law Lords who submitted written opinions converged on the same conclusion, based on a best-interest rather than a substituted judgement standard. The feeding tube was subsequently withdrawn and Mr Bland died in March 1993.

In his judgement in the case the issue of whether refusal of life support was tantamount to suicide was addressed by Lord Goff of Chieveley in these terms:

I wish to add that, in cases of this kind [where the patient has refused consent], there is no question of the patient having committed suicide, nor therefore of the doctor having aided or abetted him in doing so. It is simply that the patient has, as he is entitled to do, declined to consent to treatment which might or would have the effect of prolonging his life, and the doctor has, in accordance with his duty, complied with his patient's wishes.[54]

Implicit in the foregoing is acceptance of the view that the artificial delivery of nutrition and hydration (for example, through a feeding tube) is a form of medical treatment on a par, for legal purposes, with other forms of life-sustaining treatment (such as a ventilator). This view was also explicitly affirmed by Lord Goff:

There is overwhelming evidence that, in the medical profession, artificial feeding is regarded as a form of medical treatment; and, even if it is not strictly medical treatment, it must form part of the medical care of the patient. Indeed, the function of artificial feeding in the case of Anthony,

---

[52] Every US state now makes some legislative provision for either instruction or proxy directives (or both) and several states explicitly recognize coma or permanent vegetative state as a condition that can justify withdrawal of treatment in compliance with the terms of an advance directive (Lemmens and Dickens 2001: 146).

[53] *Cruzan* (1990), 292 ff.   [54] *Bland* (1993), 866.

by means of a nasogastric tube, is to provide a form of life support analogous to that provided by a ventilator which artificially breathes air in and out of the lungs of a patient incapable of breathing normally, thereby enabling oxygen to reach the bloodstream. The same principles must apply in either case.[55]

The Law Lords also felt obliged to pronounce on one other issue. In *Cruzan* Justice Scalia had stated that: 'Starving oneself to death is no different from putting a gun to one's temple as far as the common law definition of suicide is concerned; the cause of death in both cases is the suicide's conscious decision to "pu[t] an end to his own existence".'[56] There are two related ideas here: that the patient who refuses food and water intends to die and that his refusal is the cause of his death. Since Anthony Bland was irreversibly unconscious, and since the court was not relying on his prior refusal of treatment, no question arose in that case concerning patient intent. However, the Law Lords did address the other issue: if artificial nutrition and hydration are terminated and Anthony Bland subsequently dies, what are we to say is the cause of his death? Is it starvation (or, more properly, dehydration) or is it his pre-existing condition (the injuries he suffered in the Hillsborough disaster)? The naive among us might think that the lawfulness of removing Mr Bland's feeding tube might depend (at least in part) on the answer to this causal question; Scalia's analysis seems to presuppose this ordering of the issues. But the Law Lords who addressed this question reversed the ordering, so that the cause of death depended on the lawfulness of the physicians' actions. Thus Lord Mustill: 'In one form the argument presented to the House asserts that for the purpose of both civil and criminal liability the cause of Anthony Bland's death, if and when it takes place, will be the Hillsborough disaster. As a matter of the criminal law of causation this may well be right, once it is assumed that the conduct is lawful. . . . If the declarations are wrong and the proposed conduct is unlawful it is in my judgement perfectly obvious that the conduct will be, as it is intended to be, the cause of death.'[57]

The two foregoing cases both involved treatment refusals by substitute decision-makers on behalf of formerly competent patients. But decision-makers can also make treatment requests. Of course, healthcare providers have no legal duty to accede to requests by competent patients for any form of treatment—such as euthanasia and assisted suicide—which it would be unlawful for them to administer. In the prohibitionist jurisdictions a patient request for such treatment in an advance directive is therefore of no force or effect. But the situation is somewhat murkier where requests for life-sustaining treatment are concerned, whether such requests come from competent patients or substitute decision-makers. No problem arises in cases in which there is at least some likelihood of therapeutic benefit from the treatment. The difficult

---

[55] *Bland* (1993), 871. Cf. the opinion of Lord Keith of Kinkel at 861.

[56] *Cruzan* (1990), 296–7. Scalia is quoting Blackstone's definition of suicide.

[57] *Bland* (1993), 893. Cf. Lord Goff at 867–8. This is therefore a clear case of the judges utilizing what was identified earlier (§2.3) as a normative conception of causation.

cases are those of 'medical futility', where there is no realistic prospect of any such benefit but the patient—or, more likely, the family of the patient—is demanding that treatment be initiated or continued.[58] The leading American case on this question is that of Helga Wanglie, an eighty-seven-year-old woman in a permanent vegetative state who by May 1991 had been maintained for about a year on a ventilator. Her physicians came to the conclusion that further ventilation would be of no medical benefit to Ms Wanglie, but her husband refused to agree to its removal. When the issue went to District Court, Mr Wanglie was confirmed as his wife's substitute decision-maker with the power to request continued treatment.[59] Ventilation was duly continued but Ms Wanglie nonetheless died shortly thereafter.

In Canada there is some legal basis for thinking that healthcare practitioners may override the treatment request in such cases and unilaterally withhold or withdraw life-sustaining treatment, but the law on this issue remains somewhat unsettled.[60] For a while it appeared that it might be clarified by the case of Samuel Golubchuk, an eighty-four-year-old man who by June 2008 had been under critical care in a Winnipeg hospital for several months, suffering from pneumonia and kidney failure. Mr Golubchuk was only minimally responsive and dependent on a ventilator and feeding tube, both of which the attending physicians wished to withdraw on the ground that the patient had no realistic chance of recovery. The family, however, argued that detaching life support would be contrary to Mr Golubchuk's Orthodox Jewish beliefs and requested that every possible measure be taken to prolong his life. After the family obtained a court order compelling treatment three doctors in the hospital intensive care unit refused further shifts, arguing that continuing treatment would be both cruel and futile. Mr Golubchuk's case was scheduled for a court hearing in the autumn of 2008, but he died before the hearing could take place.[61]

Karen Quinlan, Nancy Cruzan, Anthony Bland, Helga Wanglie, and Samuel Golubchuk were all formerly competent persons who subsequently lost decisional

---

[58] This issue was not tested in the *Bland* case since the family concurred with the physicians' judgement that the feeding tube should be removed on grounds of medical futility. The issue appeared to be at stake in the more recent case of *Burke* (2004), in which a patient suffering from a progressive degenerative disease was concerned that at a further point in the course of his illness doctors might decide to remove his feeding tube, contrary to his wishes, on the ground of their judgement of his poor quality of life. However, when the case went to appeal in *Burke* (2005) the court found that Mr Burke was likely to remain decisionally capable until very near his death, that there was no conflict in prospect between his request for treatment and his best interest, and that therefore his wish to continue artificial nutrition and hydration was determinative.

[59] *Wanglie* (1991). For discussion of this case see Miles 1991; Angell 1991; Capron 1991.

[60] Cf. *R.L.* (1997); *Sawatsky* (1998). Both cases involved 'do not resuscitate' (DNR) orders that were regarded as medically appropriate by physicians and resisted by the families.

[61] 'Man's ICU death ends legal fight', *Globe and Mail*, 26 June 2008. The College of Physicians and Surgeons of Manitoba issued a statement at about the same time claiming that physicians could unilaterally withhold or withdraw life-sustaining treatment when its 'minimum goal' could not be achieved. The minimum goal was defined as 'the maintenance of or recovery to a level of cerebral function that enables the patient to achieve awareness of self, achieve awareness of environment, and experience his/her own existence' (College of Physicians and Surgeons of Manitoba 2007: 15-S3).

capacity. But substitute decision-makers must also make treatment decisions for persons who have never had that capacity. The leading American case for a never-competent adult is *Saikewicz* (1977), in which the Supreme Judicial Court of Massachusetts ruled that potentially life-sustaining treatment could be withheld from a sixty-seven-year-old profoundly retarded man who had lived in state institutions for more than forty years. In April 1976 Joseph Saikewicz was diagnosed with an invariably fatal form of leukaemia. The guardian for Mr Saikewicz who had been appointed by the probate court concluded that the initiation of chemotherapy would not be in his best interest, since the illness was incurable, the treatment would have significant adverse side effects, and Mr Saikewicz would be unable to understand the reason for this discomfort. The probate court agreed with the guardian on this point and ordered that no treatment be administered. Mr Saikewicz died in September of the same year of bronchial pneumonia, a complication of the leukaemia. The decision to withhold treatment was then affirmed by the Supreme Judicial Court on the basis of a substituted judgement standard, which the court interpreted thus: 'In short, the decision in cases such as this should be that which would be made by the incompetent person, if that person were competent, but taking into account the present and future incompetency of the individual as one of the factors which would necessarily enter into the decision-making process of the competent person.'[62]

In the previous chapter (§5.2) we briefly noted the 'Baby Doe' regulations, mandated by the US federal government in the 1980s, which at least initially seemed to require maximal treatment for all severely handicapped newborns.[63] However, the regulations as finally formulated in legislation allowed that treatment need not be initiated or continued for neonates when it would merely prolong the dying process or otherwise be medically futile. As a result, selective (non-)treatment regimes, based on the best interest of the child, are now standard practice in all three common law jurisdictions.[64] Needless to say, none of these jurisdictions has authorized euthanasia in such cases.

The best-known Canadian prosecution and conviction for nonvoluntary euthanasia concerned not a physician but a private citizen. Robert Latimer is a Saskatchewan farmer who in 1993 took the life of his twelve-year-old daughter Tracy by placing her in the cab of his pick-up truck, inserting a hose from the truck's exhaust pipe into the cab, and running the engine until she succumbed from carbon monoxide poisoning. Tracy had suffered from a severe form of cerebral palsy caused by neurological damage at the time of her birth. She was quadriplegic, had the mental capacity of a four-month-old baby, suffered frequent seizures, and was completely dependent on others for her

[62] *Saikewicz* (1977), 431. The use of the substituted judgement standard in the case of a patient who was never decisionally capable is, to say the least, odd. An English court would almost certainly have reached the same resolution of the case, but on the basis of the best-interest standard.
[63] Cf. Kuhse and Singer 1985: ch. 2.
[64] See Elliston 2007: ch. 4, for instance, for the current situation in the UK.

care. More to the point, perhaps, she experienced considerable pain as her spine and joints were distorted by the gradual but inexorable tightening of her muscles. She underwent numerous surgeries intended to correct these problems and was scheduled for further surgery, to deal with a dislocated hip, at the time of her death. For the management of the pain she was given only minor analgesics, since it was believed that more effective painkillers would conflict with her anti-seizure medication and cause her difficulty in swallowing, the latter problem then requiring the insertion of a feeding tube. Robert Latimer was by all accounts a loving and attentive father to Tracy, but he had come to the conclusion that the further suffering that would be caused by the scheduled surgery was cruel and pointless. Thus his decision to end her life. He acted on his own without the knowledge of other family members but has been supported throughout by his wife.[65]

The police autopsy on Tracy's body revealed carbon monoxide in her blood. While Mr Latimer at first maintained that Tracy had passed away in her sleep, he soon confessed to having taken her life and re-enacted the event for the police. He was charged with first-degree murder and convicted by a jury of second-degree murder.[66] This conviction was, however, overturned by the Supreme Court of Canada, due to interference by the prosecutor with the jury selection process.[67] At Mr Latimer's second trial, before Judge Noble of the Saskatchewan Court of Queen's Bench, he was once again convicted of second degree murder. Despite the mandatory sentence for the offence (at least ten years' imprisonment before parole eligibility), the jury in that trial recommended a penalty of one year's imprisonment before parole. Judge Noble then granted Mr Latimer a constitutional exemption from the mandatory sentence, which he held to be 'grossly disproportionate' to the circumstances of the offence. Instead, he sentenced him to one year of imprisonment and one year on probation, to be spent confined to his farm.[68] This sentence was then overturned by the Saskatchewan Court of Appeal which imposed the mandatory minimum.[69] Upon Mr Latimer's further appeal the Supreme Court unanimously confirmed the longer sentence though it also pointedly referred to the availability of the royal prerogative of mercy, which can be exercised only by the executive and not by the courts.[70]

---

[65] For a fuller account of the background to Tracy Latimer's death, see Hutchinson 1995 and Brown 2010.

[66] There was ample evidence entered at trial that Latimer's act was 'planned and deliberate', which would meet the requirement for first degree murder in Canadian law. That the jury failed to convict on this charge is probably due to the fact that they regarded the penalty (life imprisonment with no possibility of parole before a minimum of twenty-five years served) as unduly harsh for this particular offence. The minimum period before parole eligibility for second-degree murder is ten years.

[67] *Latimer* (1997a).

[68] *Latimer* (1997b).

[69] *Latimer* (1998).

[70] *Latimer* (2001). The royal prerogative of mercy is found in the Criminal Code, s. 749. Successive governments since 2001 have declined to exercise this prerogative. To this day Mr Latimer continues to maintain that he was justified in killing Tracy. In December 2007, seven years after beginning his term of imprisonment, he was denied day parole on the ground that he showed no remorse for his act. However, this decision was overturned on appeal in February 2008. Mr Latimer remains in custody as of this writing.

6.2 Regulation

The Netherlands was the first jurisdiction in the world to legalize any form of assisted death.[71] The process by which this occurred was uniquely Dutch, extending as it did over a period of some thirty years before the law was formally amended to permit both euthanasia and assisted suicide (under stipulated conditions).[72] Both killing another at that person's own request and assisting the suicide of another had been expressly forbidden in articles 293 and 294 of the Dutch Criminal Code adopted in 1886. However, the former statute was put in question in 1973 by the case of Dr Geertruida Postma, who administered a lethal dose of morphine to her seventy-eight-year-old mother who was deaf, partially paralysed, and confined to a wheelchair, and who had pleaded with her daughter to end her suffering by ending her life. Dr Postma alerted the authorities of her action and was prosecuted under article 293. At her trial she invoked the defence of necessity, arguing that she was faced with a conflict between her duty to preserve her mother's life and her duty to relieve her suffering.[73] Because the morphine she had administered was an analgesic that could legitimately be used to relieve suffering in her mother's circumstances, she was also able to appeal to the Doctrine of Double Effect. Although her arguments were largely accepted by the court, she was nonetheless convicted on the ground that the morphine dose she administered exceeded the level necessary to control her mother's suffering. She received a conditional jail sentence of one week plus one year's probation.

The *Postma* case ignited a lively debate in the Netherlands concerning the conditions under which euthanasia might be justified. The subsequent course of that debate, and of the development of Dutch policy on assisted death, was shaped primarily by three influences: standards of medical practice developed by the Royal Dutch Medical Association (RDMA), recommendations of official government commissions, and further court decisions. As early as 1975 the RDMA adopted the position that, under certain circumstances, voluntary euthanasia could be considered to be standard medical practice. That position then played an important role in the *Schoonheim* case in the early 1980s. In July 1982 Dr Schoonheim administered a lethal injection to Caroline B, a ninety-five-year-old patient who was chronically, though not terminally, ill and who wished to die before developing further problems which would impair her

---

[71] Although the Dutch law explicitly permitting assisted death was not enacted until 2002, both euthanasia and assisted suicide were effectively legal decades before this date. Both practices were briefly legal during 1996–7 in the Northern Territory of Australia, before the law was overturned by the Australian Parliament (Lewis 2007: 157–8).

[72] There are several good histories of the development of the Dutch euthanasia policy: Griffiths, Bood, and Weyers 1998: ch. 2; Thomasma et al. 1998: ch. 1; Rosenfeld 2004: 131–5; van Delden, Visser, and Borst-Eilers 2004; Griffiths, Weyers, and Adams 2008: ch. 3.

[73] Article 40 of the Dutch Criminal Code explicitly allows for this defence: 'A person who commits an offence as a result of a force he could not be expected to resist [*overmacht*] is not criminally liable.' For more on the Dutch defence of necessity see Lewis 2007: 76–83, 124–36.

ability to make decisions for herself.[74] After discussing the matter with a colleague and with Ms B's son, Dr Schoonheim decided to administer euthanasia. Like Dr Postma, he then notified the authorities and, like her, he was charged. At his trial in April 1983 Dr Schoonheim's defence of necessity was rejected by the court, a decision upheld by the Court of Appeals. However, when it heard the case in November 1984 the Supreme Court concluded that the necessity defence had not been adequately considered by the lower courts. Among other things, it directed that reference be made to ' "responsible medical opinion" tempered by the "norms of medical ethics" ' in determining when a physician's actions could be justified by appeal to necessity.[75] The case was sent back to the Court of Appeals which asked the RDMA whether current ethical norms could justify euthanasia in cases of conflict of duty. When the RDMA replied in the affirmative the Court acquitted Dr Schoonheim.

The *Schoonheim* case established that physicians could appeal to necessity in order to justify euthanasia. However, it did not set out clear guidelines for determining when the defence of necessity would apply. In order to fill this gap, in 1984 the RDMA released a report on the 'requirements of careful practice' for all cases of 'conduct that is intended to terminate another person's life at his or her explicit request'—thus covering both euthanasia and assisted suicide.[76] Besides stipulating that these acts could be carried out only by a physician, the RDMA laid out five conditions: (1) the patient's request must be competent, voluntary, explicit, and persistent, (2) it must be based on full information, (3) the patient must be in a situation of intolerable and hopeless suffering, (4) there must be no acceptable alternative means of alleviating this suffering, and (5) the physician involved must consult at least one colleague whose judgement can be expected to be independent.[77] These conditions quickly became the unofficial guidelines for prosecutors in deciding whether to lay charges, since they furnished a basis for estimating the likelihood of conviction. In Dutch criminal law prosecutorial decision-making is centralized in the national Board of Procurators General. Once the conditions articulated by the RDMA were adopted by the Board then physicians who adhered to them could have a reasonable expectation of escaping prosecution. In this way, though euthanasia and assisted suicide both remained *de jure* prohibited under the Dutch Criminal Code, they were *de facto* permitted as long as the RDMA guidelines were observed.

The guidelines gained judicial recognition in the June 1985 case of Dr Pieter Admiraal, an anaesthesiologist who in November 1983 had euthanized Karin L, a thirty-four-year-old patient suffering from multiple sclerosis who was completely paralysed save for the movement of her left hand. Once the trial court had satisfied itself that Dr Admiraal had met the requirements of careful practice it acquitted him. At about the same time the State Commission on Euthanasia (established in 1982) published an

[74] Griffiths, Bood, and Weyers 1998: 323–4.
[75] Smies 2003–4: 15.
[76] Griffiths, Bood, and Weyers 1998: 65.
[77] Thomasma et al. 1998: 9.

advisory report in which it recommended amending the Criminal Code to formally legalize euthanasia in cases where the RDMA's requirements of careful practice were met. It also recommended that requests for euthanasia made in advance directives be honoured and that all cases of assisted death be reported as such; in this vein it advised prosecuting doctors who instead file a natural death certificate. The reporting procedure for euthanasia or assisted suicide was clarified by the Minister of Justice in 1990: physicians must not file a natural death certificate but instead must inform the local pathologist and complete a checklist of the requirements of careful practice. The pathologist then contacts the public prosecutor who makes the initial determination whether a criminal charge is warranted. This determination is then subject to review all the way up to the Board of Procurators General and even the Minister of Justice. In 1993 this notification procedure was formalized in legislation that amended the Law on the Disposal of Corpses. This amendment in no way changed the legal status of euthanasia or assisted suicide, both of which remained unlawful under the Criminal Code. Physicians, however, now had further assurance that they would not be subject to prosecution as long as they adhered to the RDMA guidelines.

The most influential intervention in the euthanasia debate by a government-appointed body was that of the Remmelink Commission, which was constituted in January 1990 and reported in September 1991.[78] The Commission's mandate was not to make recommendations concerning the legal status of assisted death. Instead, it was to carry out an empirical study of the incidence of both voluntary euthanasia and assisted suicide, along with other end-of-life measures that also had the effect of hastening death (nonvoluntary euthanasia, withdrawal of life-sustaining treatment, administration of potentially lethal doses of analgesics, etc.). The format of the Commission's research consisted of interviewing a sample of 400 physicians, asking these physicians to complete a questionnaire for each of their patients that would die in the next six months, and analysing 8,500 death certificates completed in the preceding six months. Some of the results of this empirical study will be analysed in the next chapter (§7.4). Although the Commission's findings remain controversial, at least outside the Netherlands, their effect at the time was largely to reassure both the public and the government that euthanasia and assisted suicide were being practised both sparingly and responsibly. In response, the government effectively recognized that euthanasia had a legitimate place alongside palliative care in end-of-life treatment.

By the early 1990s most of the essential elements of the Dutch assisted death policy were in place, though largely in the shape of guidelines for prosecution under the existing Criminal Code statutes. One of those elements was that, though patients need not be diagnosed with a terminal condition, they must be experiencing suffering variously characterized as 'unacceptable', 'intolerable', or 'hopeless and unbearable'. It was clear that these formulae were meant to apply to physical suffering but less clear

---

[78] Van der Maas, van Delden, and Pijnenborg 1992. A brief summary of the Commission's findings appeared in van der Maas et al. 1991.

that they might also encompass psychological or emotional suffering with no organic basis. This aspect of the guidelines was addressed in the case of Dr Boudewijn Chabot, a psychiatrist who in September 1991 supplied his fifty-year-old patient, Hilly Bosscher, with lethal medication at her request. Ms Bosscher had endured extreme depression for a number of years after the failure of her marriage and the deaths of her two sons (both at age twenty) but she was by all accounts physically healthy. She had rejected all offers of palliative care and was steadfast in her desire to die. At his 1993 trial for assisting a suicide Dr Chabot invoked the defence of necessity, a defence that the court accepted, noting explicitly that it was equally available in cases where the patient's suffering is psychological rather than physical. When this verdict was appealed in 1994 the Supreme Court affirmed that necessity can apply to cases of non-somatic suffering.[79] In the light of the *Chabot* decision the Minister of Justice announced that henceforth physical suffering would no longer be required for immunity from prosecution and charges were dropped against eleven physicians who had assisted the deaths of psychically ill patients.[80]

Later in the decade the case of Dr Philip Sutorius threatened to push the envelope even further by eliminating the suffering requirement entirely. In April 1998 Dr Sutorius assisted the suicide of Edward Brongersma, an eighty-six-year-old former senator. Senator Brongersma suffered from no physical or mental illness; his reasons for wanting to die were concern about further physical decline, a feeling that his existence was hopeless, and a general 'tiredness of life'.[81] Dr Sutorius's acquittal at his 2000 trial was appealed by the Minister of Justice and subsequently overturned in 2001 by the Court of Appeals, which held that the patient's suffering must be of a medical (physical or psychological) and not merely an 'existential' nature. This ruling was affirmed by the Supreme Court in 2002.

Throughout the 1980s and 1990s various attempts were made to amend the Dutch Criminal Code so as to bring its provisions concerning assisted death into line with the *de facto* policy governing prosecution. These efforts finally yielded results when the Termination of Life on Request and Assisted Suicide (Review Procedures) Act passed both Houses in the Dutch Parliament and came into effect in April 2002. The legislation introduced exceptions to the Criminal Code articles governing euthanasia and assisted suicide, stipulating that these acts would not be punishable when both the requirements of due care and the notification procedure have been observed. The due care criteria laid out in the act stipulate that the attending physician must (*a*) be satisfied that the patient has made a voluntary, explicit, and carefully considered request, (*b*) be satisfied that the patient's suffering is unbearable, and that there is no prospect of

[79] However, the Court rejected Dr Chabot's appeal to necessity, on the ground that no independent medical expert had personally examined Ms Bosscher, and convicted him of assisting her suicide. No punishment was imposed (Griffiths, Bood, and Weyers 1998: 333–8).

[80] However, to this day there seem to be relatively few cases in the Netherlands of euthanasia for patients with psychiatric illnesses ('Euthanasia still a taboo for mental patients—even in the Netherlands', *NRC Handelsblad*, 25 November 2009).

[81] Smies 2003–4: 24; Lewis 2007: 99–101.

improvement, (*c*) have informed the patient about his/her situation and prospects, (*d*) have come to the conclusion, together with the patient, that there is no reasonable alternative in the light of the patient's condition, (*e*) have consulted at least one other, independent, physician, who must have seen the patient and given a written opinion on the due care criteria in (*a*)–(*d*), and (*f*) exercise due medical care and attention in terminating the patient's life or providing assistance with the patient's suicide. The legislation also made provision for assisted death in the case of currently incompetent (but formerly competent) patients who had included such a request in their advance directive. Finally, the due care criteria were also stipulated to apply to 'mature minors' between the ages of twelve and eighteen as long as they were 'deemed to be capable of making a reasonable appraisal of their own interests' and their parents or guardians had either been consulted (ages sixteen to eighteen) or had consented (ages twelve to sixteen).

In addition to formally legalizing euthanasia and assisted suicide (subject to the requirements of due care) the legislation also laid out a new notification procedure by establishing regional review committees. As before, in a case of assisted death the physician is not permitted to issue a natural death certificate. Instead, the physician must notify the municipal pathologist of the cause of death and complete a model form detailing whether and how the requirements of due care have been met. The pathologist then completes a form notifying the regional review committee and forwards the physician's report. The committee makes a determination of whether the due care criteria have been satisfied. If so, then no further action is taken, but if not, then the committee must inform the Board of Procurators General, which makes the decision whether to initiate a prosecution. The regional review committees are intended to serve as a buffer between physicians and justice officials, so that only in exceptional cases need prosecutors be involved in cases of assisted death. There are currently five such committees, whose jurisdiction is divided geographically, each of which is mandated to make an annual report to the government concerning its case load for the year.

It is important to understand that the Dutch euthanasia law regulates only voluntary euthanasia and assisted suicide. It does not apply to, and therefore does not regulate, any other medical means of hastening death, whether the withholding or withdrawal of treatment or the administration of potentially life-shortening analgesics or sedatives (the so-called double effect cases). Perhaps more significantly, the law also does not apply to nonvoluntary euthanasia—that is, the intentional termination of life of a patient who is not competent to make a request.[82] Over the years some prominent cases in this category have also come before the Dutch courts.

---

[82] As noted above, the law does recognize requests for euthanasia in advance directives, as long as the person was competent at the time of drawing up the directive. Since Dutch law defines euthanasia as the intentional termination of life by a physician of a competent adult at that person's explicit request, the notion of nonvoluntary euthanasia is actually an oxymoron for the Dutch. However, for reasons of terminological uniformity I shall continue to distinguish between voluntary and nonvoluntary euthanasia.

The earliest case of an incompetent patient, however, concerned not euthanasia but the withdrawal of medical treatment. In June 1987 Gerard Stinissen initiated a civil action requesting termination of the tube feeding of his wife Ineke, who had been in a permanent vegetative state since 1974. He had requested that the nursing home cease artificial feeding, but to no avail. Although both the District Court and the Court of Appeals acknowledged that tube feeding is medical treatment, both took the view that judgements concerning such treatment should be made by doctors, not courts, and refused to intervene. Nonetheless, after the Court of Appeals' decision Ms Stinissen's doctor decided to stop the artificial feeding, and she died in January 1990.

The first nonvoluntary euthanasia case involved Dr Henk Prins, a gynaecologist who in March 1993 ended the life of four-day-old baby Rianne, born with spina bifida and hydrocephalus, resulting in severe brain damage. Dr Prins believed that surgery on the baby would be futile and that she would suffer unbearably. After consulting with a number of colleagues, all of whom agreed with his prognosis, and with the concurrence of the parents, he administered a lethal injection. The District Court accepted his defence of necessity on the ground that (a) the baby's suffering had been hopeless and unbearable and there had not been another medically responsible way to alleviate it, (b) both the decision-making leading up to the termination of life and the way in which it was carried out had satisfied the requirements of careful practice, (c) his behaviour had been consistent with scientifically sound medical judgement and the norms of medical ethics, and (d) termination of life had taken place at the express and repeated request of the parents as legal representatives of the baby.[83] His acquittal was upheld by the Court of Appeals. Similarly, in April 1994, with the agreement of the parents, Dr Gerard Kadijk terminated the life of a twenty-four-day-old infant with trisomy thirteen (a serious chromosomal anomaly incompatible with survival). The baby appeared to be in severe pain after brain tissue had protruded from her skull and death was expected within six months. Like Dr Prins, Dr Kadijk pleaded necessity at trial, was acquitted, and had his acquittal upheld by the Court of Appeals.[84]

The trials of Drs Prins and Kadijk effectively established a number of legal principles concerning nonvoluntary euthanasia: (a) despite the requirement of an explicit patient request in the prosecutorial guidelines for euthanasia, such a request is not necessary in order to invoke the defence of necessity, (b) the crucial factor triggering such a defence is the presence of unbearable suffering for which no alternative treatment is available, (c) in cases of such suffering it is not worse, and arguably is better, to actively terminate life rather than to allow the patient to die. However, the case law by itself did not provide doctors with sufficient guidance in order to determine when they might be prosecuted, and so once again the need for generally accepted guidelines presented itself.

---

[83] Smies 2003–4: 22; Lewis 2007: 129–30; Griffiths, Weyers, and Adams 2008: 227.
[84] Griffiths, Bood, and Weyers 1998: 344–51; Lewis 2007: 130; Griffiths, Weyers, and Adams 2008: 227.

Where infants were concerned this need was met by the Groningen Protocol, developed in 2002 by doctors at the University Medical Centre in Groningen, with the assistance of a local prosecutor, and published nationwide in 2005.[85] The criteria for euthanasia embodied in the Protocol include (*a*) hopeless and unbearable suffering on the part of the infant, coupled with prognosis of a very poor quality of life, (*b*) confirmation of the foregoing by at least one independent physician, (*c*) informed consent by both parents, and (*d*) performance of the procedure in accordance with the accepted medical standard. The Protocol was subsequently adopted by the Dutch Paediatrics Association for national use.[86] Under its terms physicians are required to record the death as an unnatural one and submit a full report of each case to a national Committee of Experts, which will then decide whether the criteria have been met and make 'recommendations' to the prosecutorial authorities.[87] Following the Protocol does not guarantee that the physician will not be prosecuted; however, it was developed on the basis of a survey of twenty-two cases reported to prosecutors over the preceding seven years, in none of which was a prosecution initiated. Needless to say, Dutch criminal law governing nonvoluntary euthanasia has not been changed; the Protocol relies entirely on the by now familiar device of guidelines for prosecutorial discretion. In this respect nonvoluntary euthanasia in the Netherlands is currently in much the same situation as voluntary euthanasia was before the law reform of 2002.

With the enactment of the Law on Euthanasia in September 2002 Belgium became the second of the Benelux countries to legalize euthanasia.[88] The Belgian legislation was clearly influenced by, and to some extent modelled upon, the Dutch law that came into effect in the same year. However, the process leading to its adoption was very different and the law itself departed from its Dutch counterpart in several significant respects. As we have seen, the Dutch law essentially codified pre-existing practice that had developed gradually over a period of three decades, shaped by case law, medical opinion, and government reports. Virtually none of those preconditions were in place in Belgium. There was little debate about euthanasia in that country prior to 1995 and no case law to fall back on since there had been virtually no prosecutions for mercy-killing.[89] Furthermore, no medical association in the country had taken the position that euthanasia could be accepted medical treatment or meet

---

[85]   Verhagen and Sauer 2005; Griffiths, Weyers, and Adams 2008: 231 ff.

[86]   Lewis 2007: 130.

[87]   Griffiths, Weyers, and Adams 2008: 234 ff.

[88]   An English translation of the legislation can be found in *Ethical Perspectives*, 9/2–3 (2002), 182 ff. For an analysis of the legislation and an account of the process leading to its adoption see Lewis 2007: 153–7; Griffiths, Weyers, and Adams 2008: chs. 8 and 9.

[89]   By contrast with the Dutch Criminal Code, the Belgian Penal Code does not define termination of life on request as a distinct criminal offence. Prosecutions would therefore invoke either article 393 (manslaughter), article 394 (murder), or article 397 (poisoning) (Broeckaert 2001: 95; Lewis 2009: 125). The relative absence of prosecutions, as compared to the Dutch experience, is quite remarkable since there seems no doubt that euthanasia was being practised in Belgium; see e.g. the survey results reported in Deliens et al. 2000.

the 'requirements of careful practice'. If the Dutch process leading to formal decriminalization was a bottom-up one, the corresponding Belgian process was very much
top-down.

During the 1980s and 1990s several euthanasia bills had been submitted to the
Belgian Parliament with no success.[90] The issue began to gain traction in 1996 when
the Presidents of the Senate and the House of Representatives made a joint request to
the newly established Belgian Advisory Committee on Bioethics for advice on
whether euthanasia should be legalized. The Committee responded in 1997 with its
Advice No. 1 Concerning the Desirability of a Legal Recognition of Euthanasia.[91] The terms
of reference for the Committee stipulated that its reports must reflect the diversity of
public opinion on the topic in question. Instead of formulating a recommendation
concerning euthanasia, therefore, the Committee outlined four possible ways of
proceeding, ranging from outright decriminalization to outright prohibition, with
the Dutch policy as one intermediary option. As we will see, the legislation eventually
adopted in 2002 essentially took up this last option (with important modifications).
Meanwhile, in 1999 the Committee produced its second report on end-of-life issues:
Advice No. 9 Concerning Termination of Life of Incompetent Patients.[92] The second report
was necessary since for its first report the Committee had adopted the Dutch definition
of euthanasia as 'the intentional termination of life on request'; questions of (what we
would call) nonvoluntary euthanasia of incompetent patients (such as infants) therefore
required separate treatment. True to its mandate, the Committee once again limited
itself to outlining different possible legal regimes ranging this time from partial
decriminalization to outright prohibition.

The Law on Euthanasia also adopts the Dutch definition; it therefore does not deal
with nonvoluntary euthanasia and no official action has been taken in Belgium to date
on that front.[93] In a number of respects the law mirrors the Dutch legislation. It sets
out the conditions under which euthanasia administered by a physician will not
constitute a criminal offence,[94] including: (*a*) a legally competent patient must make
a voluntary, well-considered, and durable request, (*b*) the patient must be in a
medically futile condition of constant and unbearable physical or mental suffering
that cannot be alleviated in any other way, (*c*) the patient must be fully informed about
his/her diagnosis, prognosis, and alternative treatment options, and (*d*) a second,
independent physician must be consulted and that physician must also examine the
patient. As in the Netherlands, the Belgian law therefore focuses on suffering and does

---

[90] Broeckaert 2001: 95.

[91] For an English translation see Nys 1997.

[92] For a critical review of this report see Strubbe 2000.

[93] However, there is evidence that the nonvoluntary euthanasia of infants has nonetheless been practised
in Belgium (Provoost et al. 2005; Provoost et al. 2006; Vrakking et al. 2007).

[94] Oddly enough, the Act does not specify which offence is not committed if the conditions are met
(murder? manslaughter? poisoning?) unlike the Dutch law which formally amends articles 293 and 294 of the
Criminal Code. The Act on Euthanasia leaves the Belgian Penal Code unchanged.

not require the patient to be in a terminal condition.[95] It also explicitly allows for 'euthanasia directives'—advance directives in which euthanasia is requested under certain specified circumstances—but they can be triggered only by the complete unconsciousness of the patient and not by other conditions, such as dementia.[96] Finally, the law stipulates a notification procedure with various documents to be completed by the physician and forwarded to a Federal Control and Evaluation Commission. The task of the Commission is to satisfy itself that each case has conformed to the conditions of the legislation; if it is not satisfied then it is to turn the case over to the public prosecutor. It is also mandated to publish biannual statistical reports on the operation of the legislation.[97]

Despite these similarities, however, the Belgian law also contains some noteworthy departures from its Dutch counterpart. The most striking is the absence of any mention of assisted suicide. This omission may be due to the fact that, unlike the Dutch Criminal Code, the Belgian Penal Code does not explicitly prohibit assisting a suicide.[98] Whatever the reason, the law's silence concerning assisted suicide struck many commentators as anomalous, since if euthanasia is accepted as lawful (under appropriate conditions) how could assisted suicide not be accepted as well? The anomaly was addressed in 2004 by the Federal Control and Evaluation Commission, which stated that it would consider assisted suicide to fall within the definition of euthanasia. The Belgian law also requires that patients requesting euthanasia be adults or 'emancipated minors'—basically, minors who are independent of their parents (e.g. due to marriage). It therefore does not apply to other 'mature minors' (between the ages of twelve and eighteen).[99] It additionally requires that requests for euthanasia be in written form (the Dutch policy states that, while a written request is preferable, it is not mandatory). Finally, the law stipulates that the patient's 'unbearable physical or mental suffering' must result from 'a serious and incurable disorder caused by illness or accident'. It is therefore unlikely to excuse euthanasia for patients, like Hilly Bosscher, whose suffering was due to external circumstances. In all these respects the current Belgian policy on assisted death is more restrictive than the Dutch.

In Luxembourg a bill to legalize both euthanasia and assisted suicide passed into law in March 2009, completing the Benelux sweep. The passage of the bill occasioned a

---

[95] However, if the patient's condition is not terminal then the attending physician must consult yet another physician 'who is a psychiatrist or specialist in the disorder in question'.

[96] Lewis 2009: 127.

[97] The FCEC has reported that in the first five years of legal euthanasia in Belgium the number of cases rose from 235 in 2003 to 495 in 2007 (Lewis 2009). However, an independent survey found a higher number of cases for 2007 (Bilsen et al. 2009).

[98] Nys 2003: 241–2.

[99] There have been recent efforts in the Belgian Parliament to extend the option of euthanasia to 'mature minors', thus far without success ('Teens need right to "medically assisted suicide"', *Daily Telegraph*, 26 March 2008). Despite the absence of anything in Belgium corresponding to the Groningen Protocol, euthanasia of severely handicapped neonates and infants is also practised (Provoost et al. 2005; Provoost et al. 2006; Vrakking et al. 2007).

minor constitutional crisis, since the Grand Duke Henri, whose assent was necessary in order for any bill to become law, indicated in December that he would refuse assent to the bill. As a result, the legislature voted to limit his constitutional power to promulgating, rather than approving, legislation. Most of the provisions of the Luxembourg legislation (both substantive and procedural) closely follow the Belgian law, except for the fact that assisted suicide is explicitly covered as well as euthanasia. The notification procedure—to a National Control and Evaluation Commission—is also essentially identical. However there is at least one other significant difference between the two policies: besides adults and 'emancipated minors', under the Luxembourg law mature minors between the ages of sixteen and eighteen may also request assisted death with the permission of their parents or guardians. Both this provision and the inclusion of assisted suicide move the legislation a little closer to the Dutch model.

Whatever their differences, the commonalities among the three Benelux countries are strong: each has special-purpose legislation designed to both legalize and regulate assisted death. They remain the only European jurisdictions to allow for legal euthanasia; however, they are not alone in making room for legal assisted suicide. In Switzerland voluntary euthanasia remains a criminal offence, though with a reduced penalty.[100] Assisting a suicide has also been a crime since 1942, but with a significant loophole. Article 115 of the Swiss Penal Code reads as follows: 'Any person who, yielding to selfish motives, incites or assists an individual to commit suicide shall, in the case where suicide is achieved or attempted, be punished by up to five years' confinement or imprisonment.' The requirement of a selfish motive here is crucial, since it logically implies that in the absence of such a motive assisting a suicide is not an offence. What this requirement amounts to in practice has been glossed by the Swiss National Advisory Commission for Biomedical Ethics in the following way: 'The reasons are deemed to be selfish if the offender is *pursuing personal advantage.* Such gains may be of a material nature . . . but also non-material or emotional (e.g., gratification of hatred, a desire for revenge, or spite).'[101] The further condition that must be satisfied in an assisted suicide concerns the mental capacity of the 'victim'. Article 16 of the Swiss Civil Code states that 'mental capacity is possessed by anyone who does not lack the ability to act rationally on account of minority or as a result of mental illness, mental deficiency, inebriation, or similar conditions'.[102] Assisting the suicide of a person deemed to lack mental capacity may be punishable as a homicide.

Nothing in article 115 requires that the person assisting a suicide be a physician and the most distinctive feature of the Swiss situation is the role played by the various not

---

[100] Under article 111 of the Swiss Penal Code the minimum penalty for the intentional killing of another person is five years' imprisonment. However, under article 114 the minimum penalty for killing another person 'for decent reasons, especially compassion' and 'on the basis of his or her serious and insistent request' is three days' imprisonment (with a maximum of three years).

[101] Swiss National Advisory Commission for Biomedical Ethics (NEK-CNE) 2005: 7 (emphasis in original).

[102] Ibid. 56.

for profit right-to-die organizations active in the country.[103] The largest of these groups is Exit Deutsche Schweiz, currently numbering about 50,000 members. Since 1990 it has been providing active assistance with suicides for members afflicted with a disease with 'poor prognosis, unbearable suffering, or unreasonable disability'.[104] Members who want an assisted suicide must approach Exit of their own free will and the organization will provide the service only in those cases in which its criteria are met. Those criteria require that the applicant be adult, competent, and be suffering from 'a fatal illness, a severe disability deemed unacceptable or unbearable pain for which there is no prospect of relief'.[105] In order to avoid all suspicion of material gain from the suicide, Exit charges only a nominal annual membership fee and then offers all its services to members at no additional charge. All applicants must be examined by a doctor who, if satisfied that the criteria have been met, provides a prescription for a lethal dose of a barbiturate. Most Exit-assisted suicides take place in the patient's home, although a small number occur in nursing homes or in a room provided by the organization. Since 2006 some Swiss hospitals have allowed Exit-assisted suicides to be carried out on their premises, although no hospital staff themselves are allowed to participate. After each death the Exit volunteer who has attended it notifies the police who, along with the medical examiner, conduct an investigation. If they are satisfied that there has been no violation of article 115 then no charges are laid. There is no central notification system in Switzerland to which cases of assisted suicide must be reported.

Essentially the same procedures are followed by Dignitas, which has facilitated over 1,000 assisted suicides since 1998.[106] The major difference between the two organizations is that Dignitas offers its services to non-residents; its membership base of about 6,000 is drawn from fifty-two different countries around the world. The majority of persons who carry out Dignitas-assisted suicides are foreigners, with the largest numbers coming from Germany and Britain. None of the Benelux countries offer assisted death to non-residents, since in all three countries patients are expected to have a long-term relationship with their physician. This makes Switzerland the only country in the world to allow 'suicide tourism', a practice that has led to considerable domestic criticism of Dignitas's activities. Initiatives to change the law so as to prohibit this traffic have been suggested but so far none has succeeded.[107]

---

[103] Besides Exit Deutsche Schweiz and Dignitas (the two organizations discussed in the text) there are three others who offer assisted suicides: Exit ADMD Suisse Romande, Ex-International, and SuizidHilfe (Baezner-Sailer 2008).

[104] Bosshard and Ziegler 2007: 529.

[105] Baezner-Sailer 2008: 142.

[106] However, Dignitas has recently experimented with a different suicide method (oxygen deprivation with helium) which bypasses the need for a doctor's prescription, thereby effectively demedicalizing assisted suicide (Ogden, Hamilton, and Whitcher 2010).

[107] The latest proposal is that a 'death tax'—a fine of 50,000 Swiss francs—be levied against Dignitas for any suicide assisted for a person who has not been resident in Zurich for at least a year. It is to be put to a referendum later this year (2010).

Because of the role played by the private right-to-die organizations, assisted suicide in Switzerland is much less closely regulated than it is in the Benelux countries. Nonetheless, 'duty-of-care criteria' for these cases have been developed by both the Swiss Academy of Medical Sciences and the National Advisory Commission for Biomedical Ethics.[108] Touching as they do on such familiar themes as patient decisional capacity, a voluntary and enduring request, the presence of 'severe illness-related suffering', an independent second opinion, etc., these criteria are very similar to those which evolved over time in the Netherlands and were subsequently written into law in all three Benelux countries. Although they have no legal force in Switzerland, they do serve the purpose of guiding police and medical examiners in deciding whether to pursue a prosecution for a suicide assisted by one of the organizations.

The issue of patient decisional capacity was tested in the Swiss Federal Tribunal in a case decided in November 2006. The complainant, known only as X.Y., was a fifty-three-year-old man with a severe bipolar affective disorder who had requested assistance with suicide from Dignitas. The organization was prepared to provide its usual services, but the physician consulted refused to provide a prescription for sodium pentobarbital. X.Y. then petitioned the court that Dignitas be allowed access to the medication without a prescription. When this request was refused in the lower courts, he appealed to the Federal Tribunal. The Tribunal upheld the lower courts' decision that sodium pentobarbital should be dispensed only by prescription, but also addressed the question of whether a person suffering from a severe mental illness could qualify for an assisted suicide:

It cannot be denied that an incurable, long-lasting, severe mental impairment similar to a somatic one can create suffering out of which a patient would find his/her life in the long run not worth living anymore. . . . However, utmost restraint needs to be exercised. It is imperative to distinguish between a desire to die that is an expression of a treatable mental disorder requiring treatment and one that is based on a self-determined, carefully considered, and lasting decision of a lucid person ('balance suicide') that may need to be respected.[109]

In this way the Tribunal established that suffering due to a psychiatric disorder could be an acceptable ground for assisted suicide in Switzerland.

Every regulatory regime we have thus far canvassed has been in Europe. The only North American jurisdictions to enact legislation legalizing any form of assisted death are the states of Oregon and Washington in the north-west United States. In November 1994 voters in Oregon passed Ballot Measure 16—the Oregon Death With Dignity Act (ODDA)—by a margin of 51 to 49 per cent.[110] The effect of the Act was

---

[108] Swiss Academy of Medical Sciences (SAMS) 2004; Swiss National Advisory Commission for Biomedical Ethics (NEK-CNE) 2006.

[109] X.Y. (2006), 6.3.5.1 (trans. Lara Pehar).

[110] For accounts of the events leading to the adoption of the ODDA, see Cohen-Almagor 2001: 158–65; Ganzini 2004; Tucker 2004: 267–8; Lewis 2007: 150–2.

to legalize assisted suicide—but not euthanasia—under carefully controlled conditions. A group of doctors, patients, and nursing homes in Oregon immediately filed a class action complaint against the state. In December 1994 the Oregon Federal District Court issued a preliminary injunction against the Act and in August 1995 made the injunction permanent.[111] In February 1997 the Ninth Circuit Court reversed this injunction on the ground that the complainants did not have standing, since they faced no infringement under the Act of life or liberty.[112] When the US Supreme Court refused to review this decision, the state legislature put Measure 51, which would repeal the ODDA, on the ballot for the November 1997 election. The citizens of Oregon reaffirmed the Act, this time by a margin of 60 to 40 per cent.

The ODDA has been in force in Oregon since 1997 and during that time has survived one further legal challenge. In November 2001 US Attorney-General John Ashcroft issued an interpretative rule to the federal Drug Enforcement Administration (DEA) stating that physician-assisted suicide is not a legitimate purpose for prescribing medication regulated by the Controlled Substances Act. Under this rule physicians in Oregon who prescribe for this purpose could have their DEA registrations suspended, regardless of the ODDA, so that they would no longer be able to prescribe controlled substances. In April 2002 a US District Court issued a permanent injunction against the Ashcroft rule.[113] This injunction was upheld by the Ninth Circuit Court in May 2004 and then by the US Supreme Court in January 2006.[114] When this decision by the Supreme Court is combined with its 1997 decisions in Glucksberg and Quill the net result is that states are constitutionally permitted to legalize assisted suicide but not constitutionally required to do so.

Many of the provisions in the ODDA will by now be familiar: patient decisional capacity, a voluntary, informed, and repeated request, consultation with a second physician, etc. All cases falling under the Act must be documented and reported to the Oregon Department of Human Services, which is required to publish annual statistical overviews of reported cases. However, in certain important respects the Oregon policy stakes out its own distinctive ground. Unlike all three Benelux countries it permits only physician-assisted suicide, not euthanasia. But unlike Switzerland it allows no official role for private right-to-die organizations in the process; assisted suicide is to be both provided and reported by physicians. The ODDA applies only to adults (eighteen years of age or older), making no provision for 'mature' or 'emancipated' minors. It also formally requires patients to be residents of the state. More significantly, the Act requires patients to have been diagnosed with a terminal disease, defined as 'an incurable and irreversible disease that has been medically confirmed and will, within reasonable medical judgment, produce death within six months'. There is no requirement of suffering, 'unbearable' or otherwise. The Oregon policy therefore inverts the eligibility criteria in the European jurisdictions, all of which require suffering and none

[111] Lee (1995).   [112] Lee (1997).
[113] Oregon (2002).   [114] Oregon (2004); Gonzales (2006).

of which requires a terminal condition. In this respect it is simultaneously more permissive and more restrictive than these other policies.[115]

In November 2008, when voters approved Ballot Initiative I-1000 by a wide margin of 58 to 42 per cent, Washington became the second state in the union to legalize physician-assisted suicide. The legislation came into effect in March 2009 and the first assisted suicide under the terms of the law took place in May of the same year.[116] With only one or two relatively minor variations, the Washington Death With Dignity Act (WDDA) is a clause-by-clause copy of its Oregon counterpart. Like the ODDA, the Washington legislation does not refer to the practice it authorizes as 'assisted suicide', but rather as 'death with dignity' or 'self-administering medication to end one's life in a humane and dignified manner'. Both statutes contain clauses stating that the practice authorized by their provisions does not constitute suicide or assisted suicide, and the WDDA explicitly prohibits the mandated annual reports by the Department of Health from referring to this practice in this way; it further requires that the cause of death be reported as the patient's 'underlying terminal disease'. The terminological issue featured prominently in pre-election discussions of Initiative I-1000, with opponents of the measure insisting that it would legalize assisted suicide while proponents preferred the blander language of death with dignity. The issue is driven primarily by the social stigma attached to suicide. The Annual Reports issued by the Department of Human Services for the first eight years of the Oregon policy used the language of physician-assisted suicide. This practice was abandoned in 2006, largely at the behest of families and right-to-die organizations.[117]

From time to time initiatives to legalize assisted suicide have been undertaken in various other state legislatures, always without success. However, in December 2008 Montana became the only American jurisdiction to achieve this result by judicial, rather than legislative, means. Judge McCarter of the First Judicial District Court ruled that the state's prohibition of physician-assisted suicide violated rights to individual privacy and dignity guaranteed by the state constitution. In the following month Judge McCarter denied a request by the Montana Attorney-General's office that her ruling be stayed. Upon appeal by the Attorney-General, in December 2009 a divided Montana Supreme Court overruled Judge McCarter's constitutional decision but also found that nothing in state law prohibited assisting a suicide.[118] It is, of course, open to the Montana state legislature to close that legal loophole. Until it chooses to do so, Montana arguably has the most liberal assisted suicide policy in the country,

---

[115] After more than a decade the number of patients opting for assisted suicide under the terms of the ODDA remains small: a total of 460 for the twelve-year period 1998–2009 (an average of less than forty per year).

[116] Altogether, thirty-six assisted suicides were carried out under the terms of the WDDA in its first (partial) year of operation (Washington State Department of Health 2009 Death with Dignity Act Report). It is too early to tell whether the assisted suicide rate in Washington will differ from that in Oregon.

[117] However, by any reasonable definition what the Oregon and Washington laws both authorize is physician-assisted suicide, and I shall continue to refer to it as such.

[118] *Baxter* (2009).

since no legislative guidelines have yet been enacted to regulate it.[119] Judge McCarter's ruling specified only three requirements: that the patient must be mentally competent and terminally ill and that the physician's involvement in the treatment must be limited to prescribing the lethal medication.

Montana was not, however, the first jurisdiction to legalize any form of assisted death by judicial fiat. That distinction belongs to Colombia, whose Constitutional Court struck down the prohibition of euthanasia in May 1997.[120] Ironically, the case had been brought to the Court by euthanasia opponents who wished to strengthen the existing law regarding 'mercy killing'; instead, to their dismay, it was dismantled by a 6–3 majority on the ground that it violated constitutional guarantees of autonomy and dignity. The effect of the decision was to decriminalize voluntary euthanasia when practised by physicians.[121] The Court suggested the sorts of guidelines that would need to be put in place to regulate the practice, but left their implementation to Congress. However, to date the legislators have failed to rise to this challenge.[122] As a result voluntary euthanasia remains in a kind of legal limbo in Colombia: decriminalized, and also practised, but entirely unregulated.[123]

6.3 Last Words

This chapter has surveyed the legal status of assisted death in three prohibitionist and eight regulatory jurisdictions.[124] Each of these two camps leaves us with important questions to pursue. For the former the main issue is the rationale and justification for the 'bright line' they attempt to maintain between assisted death and lawful end-of-life measures that may also have the effect of hastening death. How can this line be drawn in a non-arbitrary manner? Why draw it just there (between, say, terminal sedation and euthanasia)? If, as argued earlier, the line lacks ethical significance, why is it important to hold it as a matter of law and public policy? For the regulatory regimes, which do not attempt to hold this line, the questions are different. Which forms of assisted death are to be permitted? Assisted suicide? Voluntary euthanasia? Nonvoluntary

---

[119] By the time of writing at least one physician-assisted suicide had been carried out in Montana ('At least 1 assisted suicide in Montana', Associated Press, 10 April 2010).

[120] Michlowski 2009.

[121] Interestingly, the decision left the criminal prohibition of assisting a suicide in place.

[122] The only bill designed to put a regulatory mechanism in place was introduced in August 2006 but then withdrawn in November 2007, when it became clear that it would be rejected (Michlowski 2009: 210 ff.).

[123] Ceaser 2008.

[124] Sharp-eyed readers will have noticed that, strictly speaking, Montana and Colombia are not regulatory jurisdictions, since they have not yet enacted formal guidelines and conditions to govern the provision of assisted suicide or euthanasia. However, in both cases the courts that legalized the practice(s) in question recommended appropriate guidelines. If these measures remain legal in these jurisdictions then regulations will eventually have to be imposed.

euthanasia? If lines are to be drawn here as well, what is their normative basis? Under what conditions is assisted death to be allowed? Why just those? How effective are these conditions at preventing abuses? How do we keep ourselves from sliding down the slippery slope to unacceptable practices (whatever these may be)? Finally, how portable are these policies? If they work well in one jurisdiction can they be expected to work equally well in another?

These questions will be addressed in the next chapter.

7

From Prohibition to Regulation

We have now reached the heart of the matter: the choice of a legal policy governing assisted suicide and euthanasia. As outlined in the previous chapter, there are, broadly speaking, two options: prohibiting both or legalizing at least one under a regulatory regime. This chapter will defend the latter option for the three common law jurisdictions under discussion. The results of the ethical discussion in Part I clear away one possible objection to a regulatory policy—namely, that the practices in question are morally impermissible—but they do not by themselves make the case for such a policy. The most common and influential objections to a legal regime for assisted death turn on issues that are germane for justifying a social policy but not for justifying the particular practices themselves. Only when they have been dealt with will the case for legalization be complete.

Before we get to the main business of the chapter, a terminological note is in order. Throughout the discussion I have consistently spoken about legalizing assisted death, rather than decriminalizing it. The contrast between legalization and decriminalization is frequently invoked for a number of practices that the state likes to control, including (besides assisted death) prostitution, drug use, and abortion. Despite the popularity of the distinction, however, there appears to be no common understanding of exactly what it means. So the best thing I can do is to state as clearly as possible what I mean by it.[1] By decriminalizing a practice I mean repealing any and all criminal statutes governing that practice. Decriminalization is consistent with regulating (or even prohibiting) the practice by other, non-criminal, legal means. This is the sense in which abortion has been decriminalized in Canada: the previous criminal statute regulating the practice was struck down by the Supreme Court in its 1988 *Morgentaler* decision and was never replaced either in whole or in part. There is, therefore, no criminal regulation of abortion in Canada today; nonetheless, the practice is still regulated in other ways (through provincial licensing laws, certification requirements

---

[1] Lance Stell (1998: 245–7) draws a distinction that is similar, though not quite identical, to mine. However, he then argues in favour of decriminalization rather than legalization with a regulatory regime.

for medical practitioners, hospital regulations concerning late-term abortions, require-ments of competent medical practice, etc.). In most other countries there is still criminal legislation governing abortion, though it may be just as liberal in its effect as the current regime in Canada; in those cases abortion has not been decriminalized, though it has been legalized. By legalizing a practice I mean making some legal provision for it—i.e. not completely prohibiting it. Legalization is consistent with imposing no restrictions on it whatever—leaving it completely unregulated—or with permitting it subject to a regulatory regime. Abortion was legalized, but not decrim-inalized, in Canada in 1969 when the previous criminal statute was amended to stipulate conditions under which performing an abortion would not be an offence.

It should be obvious that decriminalization and legalization are not mutually exclusive; a practice can be legalized by decriminalizing it. But neither are they mutually entailing. A practice that has been decriminalized may not be legalized, since it may be completely prohibited by other (legal) means. And a practice that has been legalized may not be decriminalized since, like abortion in Canada from 1969 to 1988, the legal provision for it may remain in a body of criminal law. Decriminaliza-tion and legalization are just partial descriptions of two different legal regimes for a practice, each of them compatible with both regulation and deregulation.

If we apply this distinction to the case of assisted death, then there are at the time of writing two jurisdictions in which either euthanasia or assisted suicide has been decriminalized: Colombia and Montana. In the former the previous (criminal) law governing euthanasia was struck down by the courts and has not been replaced (nor have any regulations been imposed). In the latter the courts found that the existing (criminal) law did not prohibit assisted suicide (which so far also remains unregulated). In the three Benelux countries euthanasia has been legalized, but not decriminalized.[2] In Switzerland, assisted suicide is legal (under certain conditions) but has not been decriminalized. In Oregon and Washington euthanasia remains a criminal offence while assisted suicide has been legalized, but not decriminalized.

The policy for which I shall be arguing is one of legalization (and regulation), not decriminalization. What I will be urging is not that all criminal legislation governing euthanasia and assisted suicide be repealed, but that it be amended to permit these practices under stipulated conditions.

7.1 The Case for Law Reform

Making the positive case for a regulatory policy is the easy part; answering all the objections to it is more difficult. The positive case is easy because it appeals to the same two values that pervaded our earlier ethical discussion: well-being and autonomy. But

---

[2] In the Netherlands and Luxembourg physician-assisted suicide was also legalized, but not decriminal-ized. The legal situation regarding assisted suicide in Belgium is more complicated (see §6.2, above).

because we are now talking about issues of public policy, I will put the appeal to these values in rather different language by invoking two civic virtues we expect of citizens in any decent society: compassion and respect.[3] I take compassion to include both sympathy for those who find themselves in dire circumstances and a disposition to do what we can to help them. Compassion is owed to those whose lives have been blighted by natural disaster, war, poverty, bigotry, abuse, or personal violence. It is also owed to those in the dying process, if that process is accompanied by serious suffering.

It is for these people that hospice palliative care was developed, as a means of making the end of life as comfortable as possible. We have already canvassed some of the resources that can be marshalled to deal with suffering, whether it is physical or psychosocial. But experience shows that even the best palliative care may be unable to alleviate all sources of suffering.[4] The most dramatic form of suffering, and the one for whose management palliative medicine has the most effective means at its disposal, is physical pain. Modern pharmacology can provide adequate pain relief for most patients in the end stages of debilitating illnesses such as cancer. Most patients, but not all.[5] Other symptoms—nausea, vomiting, dizziness, agitation, delirium, shortness of breath, severe itching, pressure sores, offensive odours from wounds, and the like—are typically harder to alleviate than pain. Furthermore, for many people these strictly physical symptoms, distressing though they might be, are not their only — or even their most important—concern in the dying process. Patients who have sought an assisted suicide in Oregon, where it is legally available, tend to cite other motivating factors as more significant, including loss of independence or control, indignity, loss of a sense of self, and diminished ability to engage in the activities that made their lives meaningful.[6] Most of these patients are already in a hospice when they request an assisted suicide and their strictly physical symptoms are under adequate control. Their suffering is instead psychosocial, consisting in the conviction that their illness has robbed their life of all point or meaning. For this form of suffering palliative medicine may have little to offer.[7] In short, just as we have the concept of medical futility for cases in which any further treatment of the patient's disease condition would be useless, so we must also face the fact of palliative futility, when none of the standard palliative measures can restore to the patient a life worth living.

---

[3] By calling these virtues civic I mean to signal that we owe them to our fellow citizens. However, I am not denying that they are also owed to people in other countries.

[4] Angell 2004; Cassell 2004; Quill and Battin 2004a.

[5] Twycross 1994: 2; Chater et al. 1998; Quill 1998. For the unfortunate minority, sedation to unconsciousness may remain an effective pharmacological option for pain control but may be seen by the patient as in no way preferable to assisted death.

[6] See e.g. Ganzini 2004; Pearlman and Starks 2004; Rosenfeld 2004: chs. 5 and 6. A study of requests for euthanasia over a twenty-five year period in the Netherlands found that pain had declined dramatically as a motivating reason, paralleled by an increase in the importance of such factors as hopelessness and deteriorating health (Marquet et al. 2003).

[7] There is, of course, more to good quality palliative care than the administration of drugs. But even such non-pharmacological resources as counselling or companionship may fail to restore meaning to life.

Under those circumstances patients have various means of hastening their death. They can, of course, refuse all further treatment of their disease condition. If they are in palliative care then they will already have done this, but they can still refuse food and fluids and elect to die of dehydration. If they are suffering intractable physical symptoms then they can request terminal sedation. For many patients one or another of these measures may suffice for them in the dying process. But the experience of jurisdictions in which assisted death is legal shows that some patients–not many–will prefer it to these other options. Indeed, even where it is not legal many patients at the end of life express a strong interest in assisted death.[8]

We may think of the big picture in the following way. In developed societies a majority of people die in healthcare institutions rather than at home. For a majority of these people some end-of-life treatment decisions are made. A minority of this majority, mainly those with advanced cancers, will decide to forgo any further treatment of their disease condition and enter palliative care. A minority of that minority will continue to find their symptoms (whether physical or psychosocial) sufficiently distressing that they wish to hasten their death (Anita and Bill are members of this minority). Some members of this group will want to hasten their death by means of assisted suicide or euthanasia (rather than, say, refusal of food and fluids). Their numbers will not be great, but their suffering will. It is the mark of a compassionate society that it responds most to those whose need is greatest. What I have been calling the Conventional View permits patients access to all palliative measures with the exception of assisted death. In drawing this ethical and legal bright line the Conventional View denies some patients—including many whose present condition and future prospects are the grimmest—access to what they themselves believe to be the best remedy for their suffering. In doing this it fails the test of compassion.

It fails the test of respect as well. The basis of respect for others is a willingness to acknowledge their right to make their own decisions about their lives in accordance with their own value system. In other words, respect is directed at autonomy or self-determination, just as compassion is directed at suffering or hardship. A society that practises the civic virtue of respect makes allowance for diversity and difference (for J. S. Mill's 'experiments in living') and understands that the customs and lifestyles of others may be just as meaningful for them as ours are for us, though they may seem strange or even incomprehensible. If respect requires allowing others to live their lives according to their own lights, then it must also allow them to manage their dying process in the same way. In medical contexts respect foregrounds choice, consent, request, refusal. It allows patients to choose for themselves which of the array of end-of-life measures will best enable them to manage the dying process on their own terms. No one size here fits all; people just differ in the importance they attach to certain life conditions (independence, say, or control) and in what they take to be their cultural or spiritual commitments. For the minority who will choose assisted death

[8] See e.g. Ganzini et al. 1998; Emanuel, Fairclough, and Emanuel 2000.

when presented with the option their choice is an affirmation of their values, their priorities, their self-determination. In denying them this option the Conventional View disrespects them.

7.2 A Model Policy

Compassion and respect call for a legal regime for assisted death. But which regime? What should such a policy look like? Not being a lawyer, I am not competent to draft legislation that would enable a jurisdiction to navigate the route from prohibition to regulation. Instead, my strategy in this section will be to outline what I believe to be the ideal type of a policy: the terms and conditions that best embody the demands of compassion and respect. Not surprisingly, it is also the policy that best incorporates the results of our earlier ethical discussions of assisted suicide, voluntary euthanasia, and nonvoluntary euthanasia.

In calling it an ideal type I mean to signal that it represents the optimal end state of the law reform process in the prohibitionist jurisdictions. However, it is emphatically not being advanced as (necessarily) the optimal starting point for that process. Where to start is a matter of legal and political strategy, not legal and political philosophy. The Model Policy outlined here will almost certainly need to be modified to fit the realities of a particular jurisdiction, especially a sober analysis of what is achievable given current legal, social, and political circumstances. I will return to these strategic matters in the next chapter (§8.2). Here I prescind from them in order to sketch the best case: the policy any retreat from which will come at some significant ethical cost.[9]

Patients

Patients eligible for assisted death will fall into two categories: competent and non-competent. For the former the standard of decisional capacity is the one embedded in the Doctrine of Informed Consent: the patient must have the ability to make reasoned decisions *about this kind of treatment*—i.e. treatment that will hasten death. That capacity will include the patient's ability to understand her current diagnosis and prognosis, the available options for treating her condition (if any), the risks and benefits of each of these, the other available options for palliative treatment, and the implications of choosing assisted death. Because of the finality of this choice, there is a case here for setting a high standard of decisional capacity. However, there is no reason for it to be higher than the standard for other comparable end-of-life decisions, such as refusing life-sustaining treatment or requesting terminal sedation. The stakes are just as high for these conventionally accepted measures. For adults (eighteen years of age or over),

---

[9] In formulating this policy I have drawn on the legislation currently in force in the various regulatory regimes as well as proposals in the following sources: Benrubi 1992; Quill, Cassel, and Meier 1992; Miller et al. 1994; Baron et al. 1996; Downie and Bern 2009. However, the policy I am proposing is not identical in all respects to any of these.

decisional capacity should be the default presumption, which can be overturned only by evidence of impaired cognitive functioning.[10] If some such impairment is suspected, whether due to depression or some other cause, then a qualified neutral party should assess the patient's decisional capacity.

However, there is no justification for restricting decisional capacity in this context to adults; some provision must also be made for decision-making by 'mature minors' (between the ages of twelve and eighteen).[11] In this case, it may be best to reverse the presumption of capacity, so that adolescents will need to demonstrate that they have the maturity to handle a decision of this magnitude. If so, then the decision should be left in their hands, though (especially in the case of younger adolescents) consultation with parents or legal guardians may be mandated; the rule of thumb should be that if a minor is deemed to be competent to refuse life-sustaining treatment then she is also competent to request life-shortening treatment.[12] If not, then the decision must be made by the minor's legal representatives, based both on the patient's wishes and on her best interest.

There is also no justification for restricting euthanasia to competent patients. Among those who lack contemporaneous decisional capacity (e.g. through dementia or permanent unconsciousness) some will have been able to register their wishes in advance, whether in a written instrument or by more informal means. A legal policy should allow for 'euthanasia directives', which should be accorded the same weight as advance refusals of life-sustaining treatment. In cases where the patient's prior wishes are in doubt, the treatment decision should be based on the patient's best interest. The best-interest standard will be the only one applicable to patients, such as infants, who have never had decisional capacity. Again the rule of thumb must be that if withholding or withdrawing life-sustaining treatment is justified in these cases then so is euthanasia.

Finally, if a jurisdiction wishes to prevent 'assisted death tourism' then it is entitled to restrict access to the service to those who satisfy a residency requirement.

---

[10] For a survey of empirical studies of decisional capacity in end-of-life decision-making, see Rosenfeld 2004: ch. 7.

[11] As noted earlier (§6.2), this is one of the issues on which the euthanasia policy in place in the Netherlands and Luxembourg differs from that in Belgium: in the former jurisdictions 'mature minors' may request euthanasia, while in the latter (except for those who are 'emancipated'—i.e. living independently) they may not. The assisted suicide policies in Oregon and Washington apply only to patients who have attained the age of majority.

[12] In 2008 the Bioethics Committee of the Canadian Paediatric Society issued a position statement calling for greater participation by minors in decisions concerning the withholding or withdrawal of life-sustaining treatment (Bioethics Committee 2008). Presumably the same arguments would apply to requests for assisted death (should it become legal). In its decision in A.C. (2009) the Supreme Court of Canada ruled that when adolescents below the age of 16 refuse life-sustaining treatment they must be given the opportunity to demonstrate that they have 'mature medical decisional capacity'; should they succeed in doing so, then their wishes must be given significant weight in applying a 'best-interest' standard. Again, presumably the same would apply were a minor to request life-shortening treatment. Cf. Downie and Bern 2009: 49.

Grounds

A compassionate policy must be responsive above all to suffering. In order to qualify for assisted death, therefore, a patient must be afflicted by a kind and degree of suffering that surpasses her limits of toleration. Where those limits lie must be ultimately up to the patient to determine; this will be a personal and individual decision. The suffering in question may, but need not, result from such physical symptoms as pain, nausea, dizziness, shortness of breath, etc. It may also be psycho-social, including such familiar forms of distress as loss of dignity, loss of independence, loss of the ability to do what makes life worth living, etc. The common denominator for all these forms of suffering is that they must be the product of some diagnosable medical condition (such as an illness or disability). It is not enough to be simply 'tired of life'; assisted death is a form of medical treatment and, as such, should be reserved for the relief of suffering due to a medical condition. Those who are simply fed up with living may seek such relief as they can find on their own, but they have no right to request the assistance of a medical practitioner. A practitioner, therefore, has the right to exercise professional judgement in determining whether a patient's request con-forms to the stated criteria; there is no obligation to respond affirmatively to requests deemed to be groundless or frivolous.[13]

While assisted death is a legitimate end-of-life option, because of its finality it should be considered a palliative last resort. A policy cannot require that a patient's suffering be intractable—that is, untreatable by any other palliative measure—since the patient has the right to refuse these other measures. But it can, and should, require that the underlying illness or disability be incurable, that the suffering be permanent (thus in need of relief by some palliative means), and that the patient be fully briefed on other ways of dealing with her symptoms and urged to try them before requesting assisted death.

The suffering requirement may seem to rule out euthanasia for some non-competent patients: for instance, those who are permanently unconscious and therefore (we assume) incapable of experiencing any form of distress. But a person in this condition can declare in advance that she regards continued life in this condition as intolerable; in that case, she can still be considered to be suffering from her condition.[14]

Finally, no mention has been made here of the requirement that the patient be in a terminal condition. In the broadest sense, virtually all patients who satisfy the suffering requirement will be afflicted with some condition that will (sooner or later) be fatal. In this sense, therefore, a requirement of a terminal diagnosis would be redundant. If the requirement is drawn more narrowly, however, by stipulating (as Oregon and Washington do) that the patient must be within six months of death from her illness,

---

[13] In the Netherlands approximately two-thirds of requests for euthanasia or assisted suicide are refused by physicians.

[14] Recall that suffering was characterized earlier (§4.2) as 'any experience or condition of life to which we are averse'; it therefore need not be a condition which the patient is currently capable of experiencing.

then it is unjustifiable. Being terminal in this sense is neither necessary nor sufficient to qualify for assisted death: not necessary because it is cruel to deny this option to a patient who is experiencing intolerable suffering but still has a life horizon beyond six months, and not sufficient because being terminal but not suffering provides no grounds for hastening death. A compassionate policy must therefore require only suffering, not an arbitrary length of remaining life. In any case, prognoses of specific lengths of time remaining to patients are seldom more than informed guesswork; you only know for sure that someone had less than six months to live after she has died.[15]

Request

Assisted death is a treatment request, not a treatment refusal. A patient can refuse life-sustaining treatment simply by saying 'no' to it. As mentioned earlier, because of the (potential) finality of such a refusal, there is a case for requiring that it be written rather than oral, and perhaps also that it be stable over a short period of time. It is standard for regulatory policies concerning assisted death to require that requests be in writing and that they be properly witnessed. The patient's written request then becomes part of the documentary record of the treatment. In the event that a patient is physically incapable of signing a written document, some other legally recognized means of registering the request must be provided. A requirement that the request be repeated at least once over a period of, say, a few days may also be appropriate in order to determine that this decision represents the patient's settled frame of mind. However, this requirement must be waivable in cases in which the patient's suffering would make it an act of cruelty to enforce a delay. A request must be revocable by the patient at any time.

Whatever form the patient's request takes, it must be both voluntary and informed. In order to be voluntary it must be free of undue influence, whether by family, friends, or healthcare providers. Influence will be 'undue' when it rises to the level of fraud, deceit, duress, or coercion. A patient's decision should be deemed to be voluntary unless there is some reason to think that it is not, in which case the patient should be offered counselling or access to a trusted adviser. In order for the request to be informed the patient must be provided with adequate information concerning her diagnosis and prognosis, the treatment options (both therapeutic and palliative) that are available, the probable outcome of each of these options, and the risks attached to each option. In short, she must be given all the information which a reasonable person in her circumstances would require in order to make a reasoned decision to hasten death (whether by assisted death or any other end-of-life measure). In order to ensure that the patient is adequately informed about other palliative treatment options, it would be sound practice to require a consultation with a palliative care team (the 'palliative filter').

---

[15] In Oregon, which requires the six-month horizon, some patients who have elected assisted suicide have lived well beyond that deadline before using the prescribed medication.

In the case of a non-competent patient the request for assisted death must be made by a substitute decision-maker. The standard for such decision-making will be either substituted judgement (if the patient's wishes are known) or best interest (if they are not). An advance directive requesting assisted death, executed by the patient while competent, should be considered conclusive for the purpose of the substituted judgement standard, unless there is reliable evidence that the patient subsequently changed her mind. Whichever standard is appropriate in a particular case, the substitute decision-maker must be provided with all the information whose disclosure to the patient would be obligatory, were she decisionally capable. An informed request by a substitute decision-maker should be considered conclusive unless there is some reason to suspect an ulterior motive, such as personal gain. In that case, the request should be referred to a neutral body, such as an ethics committee, in order to ensure that it conforms to either of the foregoing standards.

Providers

Assisted death is a form of medical treatment and should be offered only by qualified medical practitioners. In this respect, therefore, a regulatory policy should follow the model provided by the Benelux countries and by Oregon and Washington, not that of Switzerland where assisted death is offered by private not for profit organizations. For the purpose of the policy, therefore, the forms of assisted death to be legalized and regulated are *physician*-assisted suicide and *physician*-administered euthanasia. The policy takes no stand, either way, on whether forms of assistance with suicide offered by friends, family members, or non-medical organizations should be legal.

Assisted death is a controversial matter. Some physicians will have no religious or ethical objection to providing this service for their patients, while for others it will violate the dictates of their conscience. A policy must include a 'conscience clause' that enables providers to decline to offer the service on grounds of personal conviction. However, it must also require that they not abandon patients who indicate a desire to request an assisted death; in such a circumstance they must at a minimum inform their patients where they might find a provider willing to help them. Likewise, no health-care institution should be required to offer assisted death if doing so would be prohibited by its mission statement; in that case, however, it must ensure that patients have adequate notice of its policy before entering hospice palliative care.

Procedure

Some aspects of the required procedure have already been mentioned, including the form of the patient request and the healthcare provider's obligation of disclosure. Additionally, again because of the finality of assisted death, it would be sound practice for a policy to require an independent medical opinion on the patient's diagnosis and prognosis. In cases in which there is reason to doubt the patient's decisional capacity, expert opinion on that question should be sought as well. It would also be sound practice to require the attending physician to be present for an assisted suicide to deal with any possible complications (this is not currently the case in Oregon). Any case of assisted death must be fully documented at every stage and should be reported to the appropriate health authority; cause of death must be reported as 'assisted suicide' or 'euthanasia', not death by natural causes. The body that receives these reports should review them and flag any anomalies; suspicious cases should be reported to the appropriate officials in the criminal justice system for possible investigation. The health authority should publish regular, preferably annual, statistical reports on the operation of the policy within its jurisdiction, providing such information as is necessary for effective oversight.

Treatment

A policy must make both forms of assisted death available to patients who request them. A policy that provides only for assisted suicide but not for euthanasia will be discriminatory, since it will make assisted death unavailable to any patient whose condition prevents her from self-administering an oral dose of lethal medication.

7.3 The Slippery Slope

A strong case can be made for the legal regime outlined in the previous section, based on the civic virtues of compassion and respect. However, this is far from the end of the matter. While some opponents of legalization object to it on ethical grounds—usually by invoking some version of the sanctity of life—the most important and influential objections are, at least on the face of them, not ethical but practical. All these objections take the same basic form: they concede that legalizing assisted death would benefit some dying patients, but they contend that it would come at too high a cost to others. This line of response to the case for law reform raises issues of public risk that were not on the table in our ethical discussion. Responding to it is the business of the next three sections.

It is only fair to warn the reader that the pages to follow contain a great many references to the empirical literature concerning assisted death. While this may sometimes make for less than scintillating reading, it is to my mind unavoidable. The case for (or against) a regulatory policy for assisted death rests firmly on matters of fact. The opponents of such a policy often make confident claims about the facts— usually to the effect that legalizing assisted death would put vulnerable sectors of the population at risk—with little or no supporting evidence. It is my firm belief that public policy—on any issue, but certainly on this one—must be evidence-based. Assisted suicide has been legal in Oregon for more than a decade and both forms of assisted death have been legal in the Netherlands for more than two decades. These two jurisdictions provide us with a wealth of information about how their respective policies have worked out. There is just no excuse for not consulting and utilizing this information. Since I don't expect you to accept any factual claims I will make just on my say-so, I have tried to back them all up with the relevant evidence. To paraphrase the *X-Files*: the facts are out there; all we need to do is look for them.

In a often-cited article published more than fifty years ago Yale Kamisar established the gold standard for objections to legalized assisted death. Kamisar observed, correctly, that proponents of legalization often assumed that arguments on the other side of the question are necessarily religious in character. To counteract this assumption he set out to formulate what he considered to be the main non-religious objections. After acknowledging that an ethical case could be made for voluntary euthanasia, at least in some circumstances, he summarized those objections in the following way: 'I see the issue, then, as the need for voluntary euthanasia versus (1) the incidence of mistake and abuse; and (2) the danger that legal machinery initially designed to kill those who are a nuisance to themselves may someday engulf those who are a nuisance to others.'[16] These two objections to legalization remain the most frequently heard at the present day.

It is important to distinguish them, as Kamisar did, for they are quite different. The difference can be best illustrated if we take the Model Policy outlined in the previous section as our baseline. Kamisar's first objection rests on the claim that the various conditions and safeguards built into this policy will inevitably be violated, either unintentionally (mistake) or intentionally (abuse), so that cases of assisted death will occur which are not authorized by the terms of the policy. Call this the *argument from mistake and abuse*. His second objection rests on the claim that those conditions and safeguards will inevitably be expanded, so that cases of assisted death that are not authorized by the terms of the Model Policy will come in time to be authorized by an Expanded Policy. Call this the *slippery slope argument*. The common feature of the two arguments is the claim that, while the cases of assisted death permitted by the terms of the policy as written may be ethically justified, implementing the policy will inevitably lead to cases which are unjustified. The arguments differ in the way in which they envisage this slippage from the justified to the unjustified occurring: the former argument claims that it will occur even if the terms of the policy remain unchanged, while the latter argument attributes it to a change in those terms. (While the arguments are different, they are obviously quite compatible with one another; Kamisar employs both, as do many other critics.)

Of the two arguments, the latter is the easier to deal with. It will be the subject of this section, with the issues around mistake and abuse addressed in the next. As we are envisaging it, the slippery slope argument consists of two claims, both of which must be true for the argument to have any force:

The empirical claim. If the Model Policy is implemented then (certainly, inevitably, or at least highly probably) it will mutate into the Expanded Policy.

---

[16] Kamisar 1958: 976. Kamisar, by the way, did cite such evidence as was available to him at the time.

The normative claim. At least some cases of assisted death permitted by the Expanded
Policy (but not by the Model Policy) will be patently ethically unacceptable.

The problem for the argument is that it is difficult to find (or imagine) an Expanded
Policy such that both claims are true. It is easy to make the normative claim true, by
invoking what Kamisar calls the 'parade of horrors': the Nazi death camps or the
'euthanasia programme' aimed at eliminating the 'mentally deficient' and otherwise
'unfit'.[17] But these examples of what might lie at the bottom of the slope spectacularly
fail to satisfy the empirical claim. No sane person thinks that the Dutch euthanasia
policy or the Oregon assisted suicide policy is going to lead to genocide, or that this
would be the outcome if the Model Policy were implemented in any of the common
law jurisdictions.

In a more recent article Kamisar has suggested that it will be impossible to hold the
line between assisted suicide and voluntary euthanasia and between euthanasia for
terminal and non-terminal cases.[18] Others have made the same suggestion for the line
between voluntary and nonvoluntary euthanasia.[19] These empirical claims are much
more plausible (none of these lines have been held in the Netherlands). However, as
we have learned in the earlier chapters of this book, all these practices are ethically
justifiable (under appropriate conditions), in which case the normative claim is false. In
any case, a slippery slope argument that rests on locating nonvoluntary euthanasia or
euthanasia for non-terminal patients at the bottom of the slope cannot be effective
against the Model Policy, since its terms already permit these practices. The irony here
is that, because the Model Policy is already so liberal, it is rather insulated against
slippery slope arguments, since it is difficult to think of practices that lie outside its
terms but would fit within the terms of a likely (or inevitable) successor.[20]

Difficult, but perhaps not impossible. The policy in place in Oregon, which is
narrower than the Model Policy in a number of important respects, seems quite stable
and unlikely to expand. On the other hand, the policy now in place in the Netherlands
evolved over a period of nearly thirty years, during which its guidelines were
expanded by a series of court decisions. The Dutch experience suggests that if the
Model Policy were once implemented its terms might be vulnerable to expansion in
one or more of the following ways:

Terminal illness. Since the Model Policy insists on intolerable suffering as a qualifying
condition for assisted death, patients with terminal illnesses who are not suffering are
not eligible. This restriction could be weakened to the disjunctive condition that *either*
intolerable suffering *or* a terminal condition would suffice. I don't regard this development as very likely (it is noteworthy that it has not occurred in the Netherlands,
whose policy from the beginning has been focused on suffering), but I cannot claim

---

[17] Kamisar 1958: 1030 ff.   [18] Kamisar 1995.   [19] e.g. Arras 1998: 283–4.
[20] To paraphrase 'Everything's up to date in Kansas City' from *Oklahoma*, 'it's gone about as fer as
it can go'.

that it is impossible. So the empirical claim is *sort of* satisfied. But the normative claim is not. While my own view is that intolerable suffering is necessary, others have disagreed and it seems to me that the point is arguable either way.[21] Making assisted death available to patients just on the ground of a terminal prognosis (as is done in Oregon) certainly does not qualify as 'patently unacceptable'.

'Existential' suffering. Since the Model Policy insists that suffering must be the result of a diagnosable illness or disability, senior citizens who are otherwise healthy but feel that their life has lost meaning are not eligible. This restriction could be weakened to permit assisted death in these cases. There is certainly a possible scenario—perhaps a legal challenge to the arbitrariness of excluding certain forms of suffering—which could lead to this result (though the Dutch have so far resisted it). But again this would not satisfy the normative claim. The option of providing the medical service of an assisted death to, say, octogenarians who are just 'tired of life' seems to me debatable, not patently unacceptable.[22]

Non-medical providers. Since the Model Policy permits assisted death to be provided only by qualified medical practitioners, it does not apply to family members or non-governmental organizations that might provide this service. In principle at least, this restriction could also be weakened, but that seems to me very unlikely since medical expertise can be defended here as necessary to protect patient safety. Once again it is noteworthy that the Dutch have not gone this route; from the beginning assisted death has been a medical matter for them.

I am hard pressed, therefore, to think of any expansion of the Model Policy that would be empirically likely (let alone certain) and that would result in permitting patently unacceptable cases of assisted death. (Think about it—if the expansion would have that result, what exactly would be the social, political, or legal forces behind it?) I conclude that the policy is not readily susceptible to slippery slope objections. Before leaving the topic, however, it is worth pointing out that if you want to run a slippery slope argument for end-of-life measures then the practice at the top of the slope is not assisted suicide or euthanasia but treatment refusal.[23] What is ethically problematic about all the end-of-life measures we have surveyed is their capacity to hasten death.[24] Once we have accepted any of them—even treatment refusal—then we have accepted that hastening death is ethically permissible and we are on the top of the slope. From that vantage point the administration of high-dose opioids, terminal sedation, assisted

---

[21] Cf. Ackerman 1998.

[22] The requirement of illness or injury as the source of suffering is rejected by Varelius 2007 and Cassell and Rich 2010. A Dutch group has recently been lobbying for assisted death to be made available to anyone over the age of seventy who feels 'tired of life' (Folkert Jensma, 'A citizen's group wants to legalize assisted suicide for people over 70', *NRC Handelsbad*, 8 February 2010). By May 2010 a petition asking the Dutch parliament to debate this issue had gathered more than 117,000 signatures.

[23] Cf. Levy 2008.

[24] I continue to assume here that the administration of high doses of opioids or sedatives can hasten death; see §3.1.

suicide, voluntary euthanasia, and nonvoluntary euthanasia are just further points on the slope.[25] If you want to stay off the slope entirely then you must reject most of the conventional end-of-life treatment measures.

7.4 Protecting the Vulnerable

Of all the practical arguments against the legalization of assisted death, concerns about mistake or abuse stand out as the most common and the most influential. When courts have refused to overrule laws governing assisted death, they have done so primarily on the ground that a blanket prohibition is necessary in order to protect vulnerable sectors of the population. Thus the appeal by Justice Sopinka of the Canadian Supreme Court to 'a substantial consensus among western countries, medical organizations and our own Law Reform Commission that in order to effectively protect life and those who are vulnerable in society, a prohibition without exception on the giving of assistance to commit suicide is the best approach'.[26] Likewise Chief Justice Rehnquist for the US Supreme Court: 'the State has an interest in protecting vulnerable groups—including the poor, the elderly, and disabled persons—from abuse, neglect, and mistakes'.[27] And finally the European Court of Human Rights: 'States are entitled to regulate through the operation of the general criminal law activities which are detrimental to the life and safety of other individuals. . . . The law in issue in this case . . . was designed to safeguard life by protecting the weak and vulnerable and especially those who are not in a condition to take informed decisions against acts intended to end life or to assist in ending life.'[28]

The same theme runs through a series of official reports over the past three decades dealing with the issue of legalization. In 1983 the Law Reform Commission of Canada (referred to, above, by Sopinka) recommended against legalization of assisted death in part on the ground that 'it would be open to serious abuses'.[29] Eleven years later the New York State Task Force on Life and the Law made the same point: 'Legalizing assisted suicide and euthanasia would pose profound risks to many individuals who are ill and vulnerable.'[30] In the following year a majority on a committee of the Canadian Senate also argued against legalization on the ground that it 'could result in abuses, especially with respect to the most vulnerable members of society'.[31] More recently, the same concerns were expressed by many witnesses before the House

---

[25] I have argued in the earlier chapters that none of the following distinctions is capable of preventing a slide down the slope: intending/foreseeing, doing/allowing, voluntary/nonvoluntary.

[26] *Rodriguez* (1993*b*), 613.

[27] *Glucksberg* (1997), 2273.

[28] *Pretty* (2002), para. 74.

[29] Law Reform Commission of Canada 1983: 18.

[30] New York State Task Force on Life and the Law 1994: 120.

[31] Special Senate Committee on Euthanasia and Assisted Suicide 1995: 71.

of Lords committee established to examine Lord Joffe's Assisted Dying for the Terminally Ill Bill.[32]

The issue of protecting the vulnerable has also been uppermost in the minds of critics of legalization from Kamisar onward. The first step in dealing with it is to distinguish the two aspects of the issue—mistake and abuse—that Kamisar noted. To put the matter simply: mistakes are unintentional and (we may assume) innocent, abuses are intentional and culpable. Presumably the kinds of mistakes that are in question here are ones made by doctors in their diagnoses and/or prognoses. It is best just to concede up front that there will be such mistakes: patients will sometimes be misdiagnosed and predictions about the subsequent course of their illness will sometimes be off the mark. The literature is replete with first-person accounts by patients who say something like the following: 'My doctor gave me six months to live but here I am five years later. I'm sure glad I didn't have the option of an assisted death.' Mistakes will be made because doctors are human and because medicine is both art and (inexact) science. There is no reason to expect more mistakes in end-of-life scenarios than in other contexts; in fact, there is reason to expect fewer since when the stakes are highest doctors are likely to be particularly careful in diagnosis and prognosis. In the light of the heightened stakes assisted death policies standardly require a second opinion, as does the Model Policy proposed earlier in this chapter. But even with the best safeguards mistakes will still happen. And they matter more in this context for the reason noted by Kamisar: 'Under any euthanasia program the consequences of mistake, of course, are always fatal.'[33] Kamisar argues that 'the incidence of mistake of one kind or another is likely to be quite considerable' and then concludes: 'If this indeed be the case, unless the need for the authorized conduct [i.e. euthanasia] is compelling enough to override it, I take it the risk of mistake *is* a conclusive reason against such authorization.'[34]

There are two issues here: the need for assisted death balanced against the incidence of mistake. On the latter, Kamisar's own discussion fails to make the case that it 'is likely to be quite considerable'. We know from the experience of the regulatory jurisdictions that over eighty per cent of patients who opt for assisted death have been diagnosed with end-stage cancer. Kamisar himself acknowledges that 'the percentage of correct diagnosis is particularly high in cancer'[35] and ends his discussion by conceding that 'the incidence of error may be small in euthanasia'.[36] His case against legalization really rests on the contention that the need for assisted death is not 'compelling' enough to outweigh even a small likelihood of mistake. I have already

---

[32] Select Committee on the Assisted Dying for the Terminally Ill Bill 2005: 50–2. Without explicitly endorsing these concerns, the Committee did recommend a number of changes in Lord Joffe's bill designed to reduce the likelihood of abuse.

[33] Kamisar 1958: 976.

[34] Ibid. (emphasis in original).

[35] Ibid. 996. Most of the remaining cases involve neurodegenerative diseases such as amyotrophic lateral sclerosis and multiple sclerosis, where the rate of diagnostic error is also quite low.

[36] Ibid. 1012.

argued that the need is great on the part of the minority of dying patients whose suffering cannot be adequately controlled by other palliative measures and I will not repeat that argument here.[37] An acceptable policy must include safeguards designed to reduce the probability of medical error to a minimum. But it cannot be reduced to zero and it would be cruel to deny the relief of an assisted death to those in need of it by insisting on medical infallibility.

In any case, the problem of mistake is no longer the one that chiefly bothers critics of legalization. John Keown, for instance, who has latterly become the most prominent of these critics, barely mentions it and then only in the context of misdiagnosis of permanent vegetative state.[38] His primary concern, and that of the others, is not mistake but abuse. Let us be clear again about the difference. A regulatory regime for assisted death is abused when its terms are intentionally (or at the very least negligently) ignored or evaded or compromised so as to yield results that those very terms do not permit. In short, mistakes can be innocent but abuses are culpable. So the key questions about the Model Policy are: in what ways might it be abused? And how likely are these abuses?

The concern about abuse often takes the form of pointing to a sector of the population who might be particularly vulnerable to abuse; this is the theme that runs through the various court decisions and government commissions cited earlier in this section. Usually that population is identified on the basis of one (or more) of the following features:

Gender

At least on the face of it, there are significant parallels between the legalization of assisted death and the legalization of contraception and abortion: in both cases one of the primary arguments motivating the 'pro-choice' movement appeals to self-determination or control over our lives—'our bodies, ourselves'.[39] Since feminists support women's choice when it comes to contraception and abortion, we might expect them to support the availability of safe, legal assisted death as well. Many doubtless do, but not all. Some worry that requests for assisted death by women might not be genuinely autonomous, or that women might be particularly susceptible to 'the ideal of feminine self-sacrifice'.[40]

Our best evidence concerning gender patterns in assisted death comes, unsurprisingly, from the legal regimes in place in the Netherlands and Oregon. Empirical

---

[37] But see the further discussion in the next section, in the context of the integration of assisted death into hospice palliative care.

[38] Keown 2002: 226–7. As noted earlier (§5.1), there is a known problem of misdiagnosis of 'disorders of consciousness', including PVS. However, this problem is just as acute for the (currently legal) practice of 'allowing to die' by withdrawing food and fluids as it would be for a policy of (nonvoluntary) euthanasia in such cases. In any case, even if the Model Policy were fully implemented, very few cases of euthanasia would fall into this category.

[39] D. S. Davis 1998.

[40] Wolf 1996; George 2007 (the phrase is George's). See also Tomsons and Sherwin 2010.

studies of the former have been conducted about every five years since 1990, beginning with the Remmelink Report,[41] and the Oregon Public Health Division publishes annual statistical reports concerning the latter. One way to determine whether women have been selectively victimized by these regimes is to compare the gender breakdown of patients who have opted for assisted death with that of the general population. As Katrina George puts it: 'a significantly higher incidence of voluntary euthanasia and physician-assisted suicide among women than men would suggest that women are susceptible to these practices'.[42] However, as George herself shows, the available data do not reveal a 'significantly higher incidence' or, indeed, a higher incidence at all. When the data from the Dutch studies are aggregated 51 per cent of the total deaths were men, 49 per cent were women.[43] The figures for Oregon (1998–2009) are 53 per cent men, 47 per cent women.[44]

It seems clear, then, that women in these jurisdictions are not electing assisted death in numbers that are out of line with their proportion of the general population.[45] Perhaps, however, women's reasons for wanting an assisted death are different from men's, reflecting the 'ideal of feminine self-sacrifice'. This might be the case, for instance, if women cited not wanting to be a burden to their family as a reason more frequently than men. Though studies have been done of patients' reasons for requesting assisted death, none to my knowledge have broken the results down by gender. What we do know is that among Oregon patients fear of burdening their family ranks fairly low on the list of stated reasons, well below loss of independence, wanting to control the time and manner of death, and the prospect of worsening pain or quality of life.[46] It remains possible, of course, that these overall results conceal a marked gender difference, but so far we have no evidence to support this hypothesis.

We are left, then, with concerns about the autonomy of women's choices for assisted death. I know of no hard data that support these concerns, and in the absence of data it seems to me that feminists should deploy them with caution. They are an ironic echo of the similar claim made by pro-life groups in the abortion debate, to the effect that women do not make free and autonomous choices to have abortions; instead, they are pressured into doing so by their husbands and boyfriends. Until we have some empirical evidence of such pressures to choose assisted death, our default assumption must be that women are as capable of making informed, autonomous decisions in end-of-life matters as are men. It is certainly worth noting that the three

---

[41] van der Maas, van Delden, and Pijnenborg 1992; van der Maas 1996; Onwuteaka-Philipsen et al. 2003; van der Heide et al. 2007.

[42] George 2007: 3.

[43] Ibid. 4. George's calculation includes only the first three studies (for 1990, 1995, and 2001). However, including the data for 2005 yields the same result.

[44] Ibid. 5.

[45] Battin et al. 2007: 594. However, it appears that more than 60 per cent of those who had suicides assisted by the two largest Swiss organizations during the period 2001–4 were women (Fischer et al. 2008).

[46] Ganzini, Goy, and Dobscha 2009; see also Oregon Public Health Division, 2009 Summary of Oregon's Death with Dignity Act, Table 1.

people (Sue Rodriguez, Dianne Pretty, Debbie Purdy) who have led the fight for law reform recently in Canada and the United Kingdom have all been women.

Age

Might the vulnerable population be the elderly? Not according to the available data. The relevant comparison for any given age group is between its rate of assisted death and its overall death rate. In Oregon (1998–2006) 10 per cent of all patients who died by assisted suicide were age eighty-five or older, whereas 21 per cent of all Oregon deaths were in this age group. The median age was seventy and about one-third were under the age of sixty-five. In the Netherlands the rate of assisted death (as a percentage of all deaths in the age group) was lowest for patients over eighty and four times higher for those below sixty-five.[47]

Even so, one might worry that the elderly could be particularly susceptible to coercion, subtle or otherwise, on the part of caregivers.[48] However, it would stereotype the elderly to assume, in the absence of evidence in a particular case, that they are less able to make autonomous decisions about their end-of-life care than their younger fellows.[49] The coercion worry might require heightened vigilance about the voluntariness of end-of-life decisions by the elderly, but presumably that would apply to all such decisions and not just the choice of assisted death.

Poverty

The poor might be disproportionately represented among patients who opt for assisted death, either because they cannot afford high quality palliative care or because they are subtly steered in that direction by physicians who prefer to treat their more affluent fellow patients. However, such data as we have do not support these hypotheses. Neither the Dutch nor the Oregon data directly report income levels for patients who die under the auspices of their policies. However, indirect measures in the Netherlands suggest that the rate of assisted death is somewhat higher for those who are better off.[50] Of course, economic status is doubtless less of an issue in the Netherlands, with its universal healthcare coverage.[51] So what about Oregon? For the period 1998–2009 only 1.3 per cent of patients who died under the Oregon Death with Dignity Act were uninsured and over 85 per cent were already enrolled in hospice.[52] Furthermore, they tended to be more highly educated than the state population as a whole.[53] Of course, these results might be peculiar to Oregon, a relatively prosperous state with an

---

[47] Battin et al. 2007: 594. This may reflect the fact that more than 80 per cent of patients who elect assisted death have end-stage cancer, which tends to kill before old age.

[48] This was one of the concerns that led the American Geriatric Society to oppose legalization of assisted death. However, other advocacy groups for the elderly, such as AARP, have taken a position of neutrality on the issue (Francis 1998: 76).

[49] Ibid.

[50] Battin et al. 2007: 594.

[51] Kimsma and van Leeuwen 2004: 222.

[52] Ganzini and Dahl 2008: 69.

[53] Ibid. However, this disparity might in part reflect the fact that patients with more education found it easier to navigate the request procedure of the ODDA (Tolle et al. 2004).

overwhelmingly white population.[54] Elsewhere in the country there may be more reason for concern about the quality of end-of-life care available to the poor (though this concern may also begin to diminish as the benefits of President Obama's health-care reform begin to kick in). Ironically, the chief reason for concern about the poor might end up being exactly the opposite of the one usually voiced: if they are underrepresented among patients who opt for assisted death (as it appears they are) then perhaps they do not yet have adequate access to this service.

Race/ethnicity

The Dutch data do not include information about the race or ethnicity of patients who die by euthanasia or assisted suicide, but no suggestion has been made that the numbers are proportionally higher among the country's visible minority.[55] In the United States race correlates highly with poverty, and there is evidence that African Americans on the whole receive less adequate medical treatment than whites.[56] The Oregon data, however, do not support the conclusion that assisted suicide is skewed towards racial or ethnic minorities. In the 1998–2009 period nearly 98 per cent of all patients dying by assisted suicide were white; of the remainder most were Asian and exactly one was black. Of course, as noted above, Oregon does not have a large black population; it may not be safe, therefore, to extrapolate its experience to other states.

Disability

Some of the fiercest opposition to law reform in the three common law jurisdictions has come from disability rights advocates. In the United States the national organiza-tion Not Dead Yet (named ironically after a Monty Python skit) has intervened to argue against legal assisted suicide in a number of prominent court cases as well as opposing the ballot initiatives in Oregon (1997) and Washington (2008).[57] However, not all disability rights groups have been oppositional on this issue; in the United States AUTONOMY, Inc. has supported the legalization of assisted suicide and the organ-ization then known as COPOH (the Coalition of Provincial Organizations of the Handicapped) intervened on behalf of Sue Rodriguez during her journey through the Canadian judicial system.[58] Opposition is also far from uniform among members of the disability community; in fact, some studies have shown that support among persons with disabilities for legalizing assisted suicide runs at roughly the same level as it does for the general population.[59] It is also noteworthy that all the recent challenges to the assisted suicide laws in Canada and the United Kingdom were

[54] As Linda Ganzini and Edgar Dahl (2008: 75) have put the matter: 'It might very well be that it is not so much the legal safeguards, but the social safety net that prevents abuses in end-of-life care from happening.'
[55] On the contrary: see Kimsma and van Leeuwen 2004: 222.
[56] See the studies summarized in Gorsuch 2006: 126.
[57] Coleman 2010. Not Dead Yet filed *amicus* briefs in *Glucksberg* (1997), *Quill* (1997), and *Baxter* (2009).
[58] For AUTONOMY, Inc. see Batavia 2004. For COPOH see Bickenbach 1998.
[59] On the diversity of opinion within the disability community, see Fadem et al. 2003; Drum et al. 2010; Krahn 2010.

launched by women with disabilities: Sue Rodriguez (amyotrophic lateral sclerois), Dianne Pretty (motor neurone disease), and Debbie Purdy (multiple sclerosis).

Opponents of legalization have cited societal discrimination against persons with disabilities, and the lack of acceptable alternatives available to them, as reasons for doubting whether a request for assisted death by a disabled person could ever be genuinely autonomous.[60] They are also concerned that both cost-cutting considerations and devaluation of the lives of disabled persons by physicians will lead to pressures to opt for assisted death.[61] Commentators on the other side of the debate tend to acknowledge the legitimacy of these concerns but respond by arguing that characterizing persons with disabilities as incapable of autonomous decision-making simply perpetuates a negative stereotype about them and denying them access to assisted death on that ground constitutes an objectionable form of paternalism.[62]

Attempting to determine whether the legal regimes have discriminated on the basis of disability is a tricky matter. For one thing, we need to settle on an acceptable definition of disability. Anita Silvers defines it as 'the substantial limitation of one or more major life activities due to a physical or mental impairment' and on that basis distinguishes between disability and illness.[63] But it would seem apparent that anyone experiencing end-of-life suffering sufficiently serious to motivate a request for assisted death would almost certainly qualify as disabled on this definition; after all, even extreme pain alone will substantially limit major life activities. Virtually everyone who has sought an assisted death in the Netherlands or Oregon would then be classified as disabled. The alternative is to confine disability to something like 'preexisting impairments or chronic conditions present prior to a terminal illness'.[64] But in that case it becomes impossible to determine how many persons who have died under the Netherlands and Oregon policies were disabled. The Dutch data do not classify patients on the basis of their underlying condition. In Oregon for the period 1998–2009 7.6 per cent of patients who have died under the Oregon Death with Dignity Act had amyotrophic lateral sclerosis. A higher proportion of ALS sufferers sought assisted suicide during this period than did cancer patients.[65] However, what exactly this means is anyone's guess. Is ALS (or MS or motor neurone disease) a disability? It is certainly common to think so, but all these conditions are themselves fatal; they are therefore not 'preexisting impairments or chronic conditions present prior to a terminal illness'.[66] So it is not clear whether the Oregon data concerning ALS have any bearing on the disability issue. Furthermore, if they do it is also unclear what conclusion we should draw from the data. Unlike cancer, ALS tends to kill slowly,

---

[60] Bickenbach 1998. Bickenbach argues that Sue Rodriguez is an exception to this general rule.

[61] Coleman 2010; Golden and Zoanni 2010.

[62] Silvers 1998; Batavia 2004.

[63] Silvers 1998: 137, 146.

[64] Drum et al. 2010: 3. The reference to terminal illness is meant to fit within the Oregon criteria for assisted suicide.

[65] Ibid. 5. This has been true as well in the Netherlands (Rosenfeld 2004: 141).

[66] Oddly, despite their use of this definition, Drum, White, Taitano, et al. 2010 treat ALS as though it were a disability.

providing the patient with ample time to make a request for assisted suicide and act on it; that fact by itself may explain why a higher proportion of ALS patients than cancer patients choose to go this route.

One study of this issue using data from both the Netherlands and Oregon concluded that 'there is thus no evidence that physician-assisted dying poses heightened risk to people with disabilities who are not also seriously ill'.[67] The more cautious conclusion, concerning Oregon alone, is that 'the issue whether [the ODDA] disproportionately affects people with disabilities is still unresolved'.[68] There is indeed no evidence of abuse on this ground, but this result is largely due to the lack of meaningful data together with the ambiguities concerning the definition of disability.

Thus far we have looked at one version of the argument from abuse, which consists of pointing to heightened risks for one or another specially vulnerable group. But it frequently takes another form, which consists of arguing that, however carefully they may be formulated and monitored, the conditions and safeguards of any policy of assisted death will inevitably be violated, to the detriment of patients. This issue of (non-)compliance has tended to dominate the debate between proponents and opponents of legalization. The contested ground, the field of battle, between the two sides has been the empirical data on the operation of the assisted death policies in the Netherlands and Oregon. The two sides derive their data from the same sources: the studies done of the Dutch policy for four selected years (1990, 1995, 2001, 2005) and the annual statistical reports that have been issued by the Oregon Public Health Division since 1998. Given the common sources, it is quite remarkable how the data have been used to support two diametrically opposed conclusions: that the policies are working just fine and that they are fatally flawed.[69]

My interest lies not in combing through these data yet again but in determining what could, in principle, be concluded from them concerning the incidence of abuse in either of these jurisdictions. Recall that an abuse, as opposed to a mistake, is an intentional (or at least negligent) breach of the conditions of a policy which results in an assisted death which is not sanctioned by those very conditions. In order to demonstrate abuse it is not enough to demonstrate non-compliance; it is also necessary to show that the safeguards in the policy were circumvented in a manner that resulted in harm to the patient.[70] Not all instances of non-compliance, therefore, are also abuses. Perhaps the only thing that the critics and defenders of the Dutch policy have

---

[67] Battin et al. 2007: 594–5.   [68] Drum et al. 2010: 12.

[69] There have been many voices on both sides of this debate, but here are the main ones. First, the Netherlands. Critics: Keown 2002: chs. 8–13; Cohen-Almagor 2004; Gorsuch 2006: ch. 7, §7.1. Defenders: Battin 1994: ch. 6; Thomasma et al. 1998; Griffiths, Bood, and Weyers 1998; van Delden, Visser, and Borst-Eilers 2004; Griffiths, Weyers, and Adams 2008: pt. I. Now Oregon. Critics: Foley and Hendin 2002; Keown 2002: ch. 15; Gorsuch 2006: ch. 7, §7.2; Hendin and Foley 2008. Defenders: Ganzini 2004; Goodwin 2004; Combs Lee 2004; Quill 2007.

[70] The critics have attempted to identify some such cases under the Oregon policy (Keown 2002: 174–6; Foley and Hendin 2002: 146–50, 156–8; Gorsuch 2006: 123–5; Hendin and Foley 2008). However, the facts of these cases remain in dispute (Reagan 1999; Goodwin 2004).

agreed on is that the reporting rate has been too low, especially in the early years. Since the 1980s Dutch physicians who perform euthanasia or assist a suicide have been required to file a report of the case in which they complete a checklist of the applicable guidelines. The 1990 study (the Remmelink Report) found that only 18 per cent of all cases were being reported. This figure subsequently rose to 41 per cent in 1995, 54 per cent in 2001, and 80 per cent in 2005.[71] If some cases of euthanasia continue to be unreported this does not by itself show that any such case involved an abuse—that the request was not genuinely voluntary or adequately informed, or that the patient's suffering was not permanent and unbearable, or . . . That verdict could be rendered only by an inquiry into the case.

Furthermore, it is neither reasonable nor fair to demand perfect compliance with a policy of assisted death. Some degree of non-compliance with the terms of a policy—any policy—is inevitable; that much is guaranteed by human nature. Shortcuts will be taken, safeguards will be ignored, corners will be cut. Assisted death within the terms of a regulatory policy represents an exception to the general prohibition of homicide (or assisting a suicide). There are other such exceptions, each regulated by specified rules or conditions. Killing in self-defence is one of them. Allowing people to use deadly force to defend themselves can be justified by reference to rights to life and bodily security, but in order to prevent abuses the exception must be limited; thus the need for conditions such as reasonable apprehension of serious harm, no realistic alternative, and proportionality. Compliance with these conditions will not be perfect, with the result that some unjustified homicides will go unpunished. But no one suggests that imperfect compliance is a sufficient reason to eliminate self-defence as a justification for homicide or that the conditions need to be redrafted in a way that makes them airtight. The same holds for the rules of war, which define the justifying conditions for another kind of killing which is an exception to the prohibition of homicide; their violation will also lead to the deaths of innocent persons. We have no alternative, however, to maintaining them as a regulatory framework for the conduct of military operations; we can neither prohibit killing in war (since that would eliminate the right of collective self-defence) nor can we formulate the rules in some way that will ensure perfect compliance.

Turning back now to assisted death, drawing up the appropriate regulatory framework is a balancing exercise. If we prohibit physician-assisted suicide and euthanasia entirely then we will force some dying patients to endure needless suffering.[72] Similarly, if we permit the practices but insist on airtight conditions then the

---

[71]   The low figures in the earlier years seem to be due in part to uncertainty on the part of physicians about the possibility of self-incrimination. Since the passage of the 2002 euthanasia law, this appears to be less of an issue. Instead, most unreported cases seem to involve the administration of high-dose opioids (rather than the drugs recommended for euthanasia) with resulting uncertainty in the physician's mind about whether this constituted euthanasia; see van der Heide et al. 2007: 1964; Griffiths, Weyers, and Adams 2008: 199–204; Rurup et al. 2008; Buiting et al. 2010. When the opioid cases are subtracted, the reporting rate for 2005 rises to 99 per cent. There is no similar check on the reporting rate in Oregon.

[72]   In any case, there will be some degree of non-compliance with the prohibition, since assisted death is practised clandestinely in all the common law jurisdictions.

regulatory regime itself will stand in the way of effective relief for many of these patients. On the other hand, if we permit the practices with no safeguards then we will be exposing some patients to avoidable risks. So we have to aim somewhere in the middle, at a reasonable set of safeguards to prevent most abuses, knowing full well that imperfect compliance will result in some abuses. There are costs to both permitting assisted death and limiting it: the permission risks harm to third parties (through abuse) and the limitation risks harm to the intended beneficiaries of the policy (by limiting access). As we raise the bar of regulation we decrease the risk to third parties and increase it for patients; as we lower the bar the reverse will be true. The best regulatory regime is the one with the optimal balance of these costs. No regime can eliminate all of them.

The data from the Netherlands and Oregon give us some basis for estimating the costs on one side of the balance sheet. In 2005 there were 2,410 deaths from euthanasia and assisted suicide in the Netherlands, which constituted 1.9 per cent of all deaths during that year.[73] If we extrapolate those figures to the three common law countries then the expected number of deaths in Canada under a similar policy would have been approximately 4,770, in the United Kingdom 12,000, and in the United States 47,000.[74] This gives us a rough idea of the number of patients who would elect assisted death every year in these countries if it was legally available under the terms of the Dutch policy, thus the number whose suffering would remain unrelieved if assisted death were not available.[75] It is entirely reasonable to erect safeguards that make it more difficult for patients to obtain an assisted death, in order to protect vulnerable third parties. But making those safeguards too strict would come at an unacceptable cost to a significant minority of the population in particularly dire circumstances.

Before concluding this discussion it would be remiss of me not to say something about the so-called 'Remmelink 1000'. In its 1990 study the Remmelink Commission sorted end-of-life measures into four categories: (1) euthanasia or assisted suicide with an explicit request by the patient, (2) the withholding or withdrawing of life-prolonging treatment, (3) the administration of high doses of opioids to alleviate pain or other intractable physical symptoms, and (4) the intentional termination of life without an explicit request by the patient.[76] The study found roughly 1,000 cases falling into the

---

[73] The most recent (2009) figures for the Netherlands are somewhat higher: 2,636 deaths constituting 2 per cent of all deaths for the year. Following a few years of decline, the number of assisted deaths in the Netherlands appears to be rising. However, the increase may be due more to improved reporting of cases since the 2002 law came into effect than to a rise in the number of requests made to physicians. Furthermore, putting these figures in historical context the 2009 total is still roughly equal to the figure of 2,700 assisted deaths reported for 1990 by the Remmelink Commission.

[74] These extrapolations are based on overall death rates for these three countries. Under the much more restrictive Oregon policy the comparable figures would be approximately 500 deaths in Canada, 925 for the UK, and 4,620 for the US.

[75] Of course, many of these patients would have other means available to them of relieving their suffering, up to and including terminal sedation. But the Dutch patients also had these alternatives and chose assisted death, presumably because in their judgement it offered the most effective means of relief. I am assuming that the same would be true of Canadian, British, or American patients.

[76] In the 2005 study 'continuous deep sedation' was added as a fifth category.

fourth category (approximately 0.8 per cent of all deaths that year). In the subsequent Dutch studies the number (and percentage) of cases in this category has declined somewhat, but in the most recent (2005) study they still constituted 0.4 per cent of all deaths. Critics have frequently used these cases as proof that the guidelines and safeguards in the Dutch policy are ineffective.[77]

We are already familiar with the end-of-life measures that define the first three categories. By contrast the cases that fall into the fourth category are somewhat of a mixed bag. They all share the feature that in them a lethal dose of medication was administered to the patient with the intention of hastening death; this is what distinguishes them from categories (2) and (3). What distinguishes them from category (1) is the absence of an explicit request by the patient. To understand this better we need to know that, under the terms of the Dutch policy, a patient's request for euthanasia or assisted suicide must be 'express and earnest', where this is operationalized to mean that 'the request must be well-considered: informed, made after due deliberation and based on an enduring desire for the end of life (evidenced for instance by its having repeatedly been made over some period of time)'.[78] Most of the cases in the 'Remmelink 1000' lacked a request that met this standard, for one of two reasons: either there was no patient request at all or the request failed to qualify as 'express and earnest'.[79] The cases in the former group were all instances of nonvoluntary euthanasia involving infants, patients in a permanent vegetative state, and cancer patients who were near death and suffering but unable to make a request. In many of these cases substitute decision-makers (usually family members) were consulted. For the cases in the latter group some consultation with the patient was possible but the standard of an 'express and earnest' request was not met; in at least some of these cases there was prior discussion about euthanasia with the patient. The drug administered in most of these cases (in both groups) was an opiate (rather than a barbiturate, which is the norm for euthanasia); this suggests that many of the cases were on the borderline of category (3). Most patients involved were already near death; in 80 per cent of cases life was estimated to have been shortened by less than a week.[80]

There is obviously much room for disagreement over the significance of these cases. I will confine myself to just two observations. First, from the fact that none of the cases fell within the conditions of the Dutch policy we cannot conclude that all of them (or indeed any of them) were ethically unjustified. I have already argued (§§5.1 and 5.2) that nonvoluntary euthanasia can be justified (under appropriate conditions). Furthermore, many of these cases appear to have been responses by doctors to exigent circumstances of patients in extreme distress in the final stages of the dying process;

---

[77] Keown 2002: ch. 10; Gorsuch 2006: ch. 7.

[78] Griffiths, Weyers, and Adams 2008: 79.

[79] For information on these cases see van der Maas et al. 1991: 672; van der Maas 1996: 1701–2; van der Heide et al. 2007: 1960; Griffiths, Weyers, and Adams 2008: 180–2.

[80] For a recent profile of the cases falling into this category in Belgium, see Chambaere et al. 2010: 896–7.

who would argue that they must be left to suffer because they were incapable of an explicit request?

The second observation is that the incidence of these cases may have little, if anything, to do with the Dutch euthanasia policy. Attributing it to the existence of the policy would require providing evidence to support at least one of the following claims: *either* more cases of this sort occurred after the development of the policy than before *or* more occur in the Netherlands (presumably as a result of the policy) than elsewhere. However, there is no evidence to support the first claim, since no study with the Remmelink methodology was carried out in the Netherlands before 1990 (by which time the Dutch guidelines were already well established). We simply do not know what effect (if any) the development of these guidelines had on cases of assisted death in this category.[81] We are in a slightly better evidential situation with respect to the second claim, since some studies utilizing a version of the Remmelink methodology have been done in other jurisdictions.[82] These studies have found an incidence of 'termination of life without explicit request' in Australia, the United Kingdom, and five other European countries that is similar to that of the Netherlands.[83] However, none of them was as thorough as the four Dutch studies carried out since 1990, and comparative conclusions are therefore rather hazardous.[84] It would be foolhardy to draw the conclusion that the incidence of these cases is no higher in the Netherlands than in prohibitionist jurisdictions, but it would be equally foolhardy to draw the opposite conclusion. What we know with certainty is that assisted death is practised in those jurisdictions, despite its illegality, and that some of those cases will be similar to the 'Remmelink 1000'. What we don't know with certainty is whether the advent of legal euthanasia in the Netherlands has led to more such cases than occurred previously or more than occur in other places. But in that case the confirmed incidence of these cases in the Netherlands cannot be imputed to the country's euthanasia policy.

7.5 Q & A

The two preceding sections have dealt with the most common and influential practical objections to the legalization of assisted death. But there have been many others, and they too deserve a hearing. They are voiced here as questions by a sceptical, but not hostile, interlocutor.

---

[81] van Delden, Visser, and Borst-Eilers 2004: 208. However, we do know that the incidence of these cases declined after passage of the Dutch euthanasia law in 2002 (van der Heide et al. 2007). We have slightly better information about Belgium, since surveys utilizing the same methodology were done both before and after the 2002 enactment of the euthanasia law. These show that the rate of 'ending of life without patient's explicit request' actually fell between 1998 and 2007 (Bilsen et al. 2009). However, the rate remains higher in Belgium than in the Netherlands (Chambaere et al. 2010).

[82] Kuhse et al. 1997; Deliens et al. 2000; van der Heide et al. 2003; Seale 2006.

[83] They also found an incidence of voluntary euthanasia (within the Dutch definition) in all these countries, though in most cases at a lower rate than in the Netherlands.

[84] Neil Gorsuch (2006: 134–7) criticizes the Australian study.

You make a decent case in favour of legalization, but how do you know that the public is ready for this? In the three common law countries on which we have been focusing, the idea of legalizing either euthanasia or assisted suicide has been on the public agenda, with varying degrees of prominence, since at least the 1970s. For any informed member of the public, therefore, it is not exactly a novel idea. In recognition of this fact the topic has been a regular item for decades in public opinion surveys. The most recent polls as of this writing (2010) show strong majorities in both Canada and the United Kingdom in favour of legalizing euthanasia, while Americans remain more divided on the issue.[85] However, these poll results need to be interpreted with some care, since responses are known to be sensitive to the phrasing of the question.[86] In these particular polls respondents were simply asked whether they support or oppose legalizing euthanasia in their particular country. Simple, comprehensible, straightforward, to the point, one might think. However, in leaving 'euthanasia' undefined the survey was vulnerable to ambiguity between 'active' measures (administering a lethal injection) and 'passive' ones (withholding or withdrawing life-sustaining treatment). Not everyone confines euthanasia to the 'active' side, as I have done; others are quite happy to speak, as well, of 'passive euthanasia'. But in that case, it is impossible to tell how many respondents interpreted the question as asking about the former and how many had in mind the latter.

A recent study has shown that support for euthanasia is higher among respondents who do not distinguish between euthanasia proper and withholding/withdrawing treatment than among those who do.[87] This result suggests that more meaningful data might be obtained by using questions that disambiguate euthanasia by stipulating its 'active' meaning. Various Gallup polls in Canada and the United States have tried this strategy. In 2002 a Canadian survey used the following question: 'When a person has an incurable disease that is immediately life-threatening and causes that person to experience great suffering, do you or do you not think that a competent doctor should be allowed by law to end the patient's life through mercy killing if the patient has made a formal request in writing?'[88] That is certainly more specific, though a little wordy. But it has its own problems: specifying that the disease is 'incurable' and 'immediately life-threatening' and that it causes 'great suffering' is open to criticism on the ground that it appeals too much to the respondent's empathy; likewise, stipulating that the doctor is 'competent' may also bias responses toward the favourable. (On the other hand, calling the act 'mercy killing' could have the opposite effect.) More recently, Gallup has used a rather simpler question to sample opinion in the United States: 'When a person has a disease that cannot be cured, do you think that doctors should be

---

[85] Canada: 67% of respondents strongly or moderately support legalization with 23% opposed. United Kingdom: 71% support, 18% opposed. United States: 42% support, 36% opposed. *Source*: Angus Reid (10 February 2010).

[86] Hagelin et al. 2004; Marcoux, Mishara, and Durand 2007.

[87] Marcoux, Mishara, and Durand 2007: 237.

[88] Ibid. 2007: 236. Result: 81% yes, 14% no.

allowed by law to end the patient's life by some painless means if the patient and his or her family request it?'[89] Now there is no mention of suffering or of a threat to life, nor of the doctor's competence, but also no mention of mercy killing. Instead, we have only the vague 'end the patient's life by some painless means', which the respondent is free to interpret as anything from ramping up pain medication to terminal sedation to a lethal injection.

While it is worth noting the context-dependence of these poll results, it is also easy to make too much of it. The fact is that every question on euthanasia, no matter how it is phrased, has yielded a pro-legalization majority in each of the three countries. Furthermore, when the question very carefully distinguishes between administering a lethal injection and withdrawing life support, a solid majority of Canadians still find the former acceptable.[90] It is very likely that the strong majority in the UK is equally robust.[91] Leaving aside issues about the wording of the question, these survey results are also quite stable over time. Similar results were obtained in the UK in 1994,[92] and in the US in 1996.[93] This stability suggests that the current level of support is not a function of any recent high-profile cases of euthanasia in these countries.[94]

While survey results for assisted suicide are less plagued by ambiguities of definition, they do present their own problems. Perhaps inspired by recent developments in the United Kingdom (§6.1), many polls have asked respondents whether family members should be prosecuted for assisting terminally ill relatives to die.[95] However interesting the results might be, they tell us little about attitudes toward legalizing *physician-assisted suicide*. Some polls, however, do put the 'right' question and find majority support for legalization. A May 2007 Gallup survey in the US asked respondents 'When a person has a disease that cannot be cured and is living in severe pain, do you think doctors should or should not be allowed by law to assist the patient to commit suicide if the patient requests it?'[96] More recently a YouGov poll in the UK asked 'Do

[89] *Source*: Gallup News Service, 31 May 2007. Result: 71% yes, 27% no.

[90] Marcoux, Mishara, and Durand 2007: 236. Result: 69% pro for the former, 86% for the latter.

[91] On the other hand, the Gallup results which, using the question cited in the text, consistently show support for legalizing euthanasia at around 75 per cent among Americans, are out of line with other polls, which tend to locate support in the 45–55 per cent range.

[92] O'Neill et al. 2002. The question in this survey was 'Suppose a person had a painful incurable disease. Do you think that doctors should be allowed by law to end the patient's life, if the patient requests it?' For some reason, the authors of this article interpreted the survey results as pertaining to physician-assisted suicide, but the more natural construal of the question would suggest euthanasia.

[93] DeCesare 2000. This study also shows support for legalization rising in the US from 1977 to 1996.

[94] Furthermore, experience in the Netherlands shows that once a euthanasia policy is in place public support for it tends to grow (Rosenfeld 2004: 135–6).

[95] Results: Canada: 25% yes, 41% no; UK: 14% yes, 61% no; US: 37% yes, 34% no. *Source*: Angus Reid (10 February 2010). The British figures almost certainly reflect the recent controversy over possible prosecution of family members who accompany loved ones to Switzerland for an assisted suicide.

[96] *Source*: Gallup News Service (31 May 2007). Result: 56% yes, 38% no. Gallup has done annual polls using this question since 1996, with support for legalization ranging from a low of 52% to a high of 68%. Gallup's poll questions produce the anomalous result that more Americans favour legalizing euthanasia than assisted suicide. But this is due, in my opinion, to the ambiguous expression 'end the patient's life by some painless means' which is used in the 'euthanasia' survey. For survey results for some US states see Stutsman 2004: 247–8.

you think the law should be changed to allow people in the latter stages of terminal illnesses such as cancer (for example, people diagnosed as having six months to live) to receive a prescription from their doctor to end their suffering, subject to a range of safeguards?' This question, clearly modelled on the Oregon policy, yielded a strong majority in favour of law reform.[97] This level of support in Britain for legalizing assisted suicide is consistent with the similar result for legalizing euthanasia and is, moreover, stable over time.[98] In all three countries I would expect stronger support for legalizing assisted suicide than for euthanasia. In Canada and the United Kingdom a strong majority appears to favour legalizing either, while in the United States a stable majority can be found only for assisted suicide.[99]

The liabilities in some of the polling instruments notwithstanding, I regard these results (for both euthanasia and assisted suicide) as pretty reliable.[100] Furthermore, they have been put to the test three times in the United States, in referenda in Oregon and Washington, each of which returned a majority in favour of legalizing assisted suicide (see §6.2, above). These referendum results also serve to show that opinions do not waver when the context of decision is real rather than merely hypothetical and when people have been exposed to arguments on both sides of the question. Furthermore, the attitudes of the general public appear to be mirrored in the population most likely to avail themselves of assisted death. Surveys of patients with terminal illnesses have found a strong majority in favour of legalizing either euthanasia or assisted suicide, as well as a significant minority who report that they would seriously consider making a request for assisted death.[101]

OK, that's all very well, but what about health care providers? Are they ready for it? That's a fair question, since no legal regime for assisted death would be viable if physicians were uniformly opposed to it and unwilling to participate in it. We know already (§1.4) that the major medical associations in the three common law countries all oppose legalization since they all endorse the Conventional View, which isolates assisted death as unacceptable medical practice. The position of the American Medical

---

[97] *Source: Sunday Telegraph*, 21 February 2010. Result: 75% yes, 14% no. In a February 2010 ICM survey in the UK 76 per cent of respondents agreed that 'a mentally competent adult should be legally allowed to receive a doctor's assistance to die if they are suffering unbearably from a terminal illness from which they are expected to die in six months'. *Source*: ibid.

[98] The same YouGov question yielded 76% in favour, 13% opposed in May 2006.

[99] It is noteworthy that ballot initiatives to legalize both euthanasia and assisted suicide failed in the states of Washington (1991) and California (1992), though in each case with 46 per cent in favour, while initiatives to legalize assisted suicide alone passed in Oregon (1994 and 1997) and Washington (2008). For recent poll results specifically for the Oregon legislation see Ganzini and Dahl 2008: 74–5. The legislation continues to enjoy strong popular and political support in Oregon itself (Stutsman 2004: 245–6).

[100] For more public opinion results in the United States see Stutsman 2004, 245–9.

[101] Emanuel et al. 1996; Wilson et al. 2000; Emanuel, Fairclough, and Emanuel 2000; Wilson et al. 2007; Eliott and Olver 2008. A survey of patients with amyotrophic lateral sclerosis (ALS) found that a majority would consider assisted suicide (Ganzini et al. 1998). For an analysis of the methodology of this type of study see Rosenfeld 2004: ch. 4.

Association is typical: 'Euthanasia is fundamentally incompatible with the physician's role as healer, would be difficult or impossible to control, and would pose serious societal risks.'[102] However, the opposition to legalization by medical bodies is not universal in these countries. During the period prior to the vote in 1994 on Ballot Measure 16—the Oregon Death with Dignity Act—the Oregon Medical Association adopted a neutral position on the issue.[103] (By contrast, the Washington State Medical Association opposed Ballot Initiative I-1000 in 2008, despite the fact that a majority of its membership supported the measure.)[104]

For the most part, colleges of physicians have also taken adverse positions. However, here too there are exceptions. In the UK when the Select Committee of the House of Lords was examining the Assisted Dying for the Terminally Ill Bill, the Royal College of Physicians of London submitted written evidence in which it took a neutral stance on the bill, in recognition of the fact that opinion was divided among its members. Instead, it suggested a number of issues that needed to be taken into account in any change in the law.[105] In October 2009 the Quebec College of Physicians took a further step, calling for changes in the Canadian Criminal Code to facilitate a wider variety of treatment options in end-of-life care, including euthanasia.[106]

In any case, the opposition to assisted death by the major medical associations does not reflect a similar unanimity among their members. Polls of doctors in the UK have tended to show that a significant minority (usually around a quarter) of respondents favour legalizing either euthanasia or assisted suicide.[107] In a literature review of thirty-nine studies of attitudes of American physicians done between 1991 and 2000 the

---

[102] AMA Policy Statement E-2.21 (issued June 1994, updated June 1996). Policy Statement E-2.211 uses exactly the same wording for physician-assisted suicide. Cf. the Canadian Medical Association policy statement Euthanasia and Assisted Suicide (Update 2007): 'Canadian physicians should not participate in euthanasia or assisted suicide.' For a brief while in 2005 the British Medical Association adopted a stance of neutrality on a change in the law, but in 2006 reverted to its position of opposition in which it 'insists that physician-assisted suicide [and euthanasia] should not be made legal in the U.K.' (*End-of Life Decisions: Views of the BMA*, July 2006).

[103] In 1997 the OMA switched its position to support the repeal of the ODDA. After the legislation was reaffirmed it resumed its earlier position of neutrality.

[104] A survey commissioned by the WSMA prior to the vote found that 50 per cent of respondents would support it while 42 per cent were opposed ('Doctors divided on assisted suicide', *Seattle Times*, 22 September 2008).

[105] Select Committee on the Assisted Dying for the Terminally Ill Bill 2005.

[106] Collège des Médecins du Quebec 2009. In Canada the self-regulating bodies for the profession are a provincial matter. In response to the College's statement the Quebec government established a non-partisan *ad hoc* commission to sample public opinion and solicit expert input on euthanasia. In a 2009 Angus Reid poll in Quebec 77 per cent of respondents favoured legalizing euthanasia (with 78 per cent in favour for physician-assisted suicide); this is the highest level of support in Canada.

[107] Clark et al. 2001; Dickinson et al. 2002; Pasterfield et al. 2006; Kitching, Stevens, and Forman 2008; Seale 2009b. A 2009 poll of general practitioners in the UK found that 38 per cent favoured legalizing assisted suicide ('Two-fifths of GPs want assisted suicide legalised', healthcarerepublic.com, 5 February 2009). The same percentage said that they would be prepared to assist a patient's suicide if allowed by law. In a 2007 survey of GPs 30 per cent favoured a change in the law and 42 per cent would be prepared to assist a suicide (*Daily Telegraph*, 19 May 2007). In 2006 the Royal College of Physicians surveyed its Fellows and Members, with 26 per cent indicating that they favoured a change in the law to permit either euthanasia or assisted suicide ('RCP cannot support legal change on assisted dying–survey results', RCP News, 9 May 2006).

proportion who supported legalizing euthanasia varied from a quarter to more than a half, with a slightly wider range for assisted suicide.[108] A 1996 survey of Canadian physicians found that a quarter of respondents would be willing to practise either euthanasia or assisted suicide if these measures were legalized.[109] More recently, a poll of medical specialists in Quebec revealed that three-quarters of respondents supported legalizing euthanasia.[110]

There have been enough studies in all three countries to support the generalization that while doctors tend (with a few exceptions) to be less supportive of a change in the law than the general public, they are far from uniformly opposed.[111] Indeed, many studies show not only a significant minority in favour of legalization but, more importantly, a similar minority prepared to practise within the terms of the law should it be changed. We should keep in mind that in jurisdictions such as Oregon or the Netherlands the number of patients who request assisted death is quite small and the number who follow through with it is even smaller. It may be, therefore, that only a minority of physicians will be called upon to provide the service. To put it in crude economic terms, as long as the supply is adequate to meet the demand then a legal regime for assisted death can be workable.[112] In fact, it seems that a minority is already willing to provide the service, in advance of any change in the law. A 1994 survey of UK physicians found that a third of respondents had been asked by patients to take active steps to hasten death and more than ten per cent had complied with such a request.[113] These results are consistent with a number of surveys of American physicians done during the 1990s.[114] More dramatically, a 1997 survey of physicians treating HIV patients in the San Francisco Bay area found that more than half of respondents had at least once assisted the suicide of a patient.[115]

---

[108] Dickinson et al. 2005. The range of support for euthanasia was 23–63 per cent, for assisted suicide 14–66 per cent. A majority of physicians in Oregon supported the legalization of assisted suicide before the Oregon Death with Dignity Act came into effect (Lee et al. 1996).

[109] 'Doctors divided on euthanasia acceptance (National Survey)', *Medical Post*, 8 October 1996.

[110] *Source*: IPSOS DESCARIE, 13 October 2009.

[111] The gap between medical and public support for legalization might be partly explained by the fact that doctors are generally more knowledgeable about the definition of euthanasia and the difference between it and withdrawal of life support; their responses may, therefore, be more selective on this issue. However, this would not explain the similar gap on assisted suicide, about which there is less public confusion. I speculate that the gap has more to do with the fact that physicians would be the ones called on to provide assisted deaths, should the law be changed.

[112] The history of abortion teaches us that it may be one thing to change the law and quite another to ensure that the service is equally available to all who want it. Under a policy of legal assisted death there will inevitably be patients who meet the criteria but are unable to find a willing physician. This has been a problem during the first year of the policy in Washington ('Why some couldn't die on their own terms', *Seattle Times*, 7 March 2010). Right-to-die societies, such as Compassion and Choices in Washington, may be able to help match patients and physicians, and the willingness (or otherwise) of individual doctors to provide the service may become better known over time.

[113] Ward and Tate 1994. In this survey 48 per cent of respondents said that the law on euthanasia in the UK should be similar to the legal regime in place at that time in the Netherlands. A more recent survey in the UK (Seale 2006) found a much lower percentage (1.4 per cent) of physicians who had engaged in euthanasia.

[114] Fried et al. 1993; Shapiro et al. 1994; Doukas et al. 1995; Back et al. 1996; Lee et al. 1996; Emanuel et al. 1996; Meier et al. 1998; Emanuel et al. 2000.

[115] Slome et al. 1997. The exact figure was 53 per cent.

Finally, we should acknowledge that doctors are not the only healthcare providers attending patients at the end of life. In determining whether a legal regime of assisted death would be viable, the attitudes of nurses are at least as important as those of physicians.[116] However, we have much less information in this case. In its submission to the Select Committee of the House of Lords on the Assisted Dying for the Terminally Ill Bill the Royal College of Nursing took a position firmly against the legalization of euthanasia. However, as with the comparable medical bodies, there is no reason to assume that this position represents the views of all, or even most, practising nurses. In 2003 the *Nursing Times* conducted a survey of UK nurses in which two-thirds of respondents indicated that euthanasia should be legalized and one-third thought that nurses should be allowed to assist in the suicides of their patients.[117] A more recent (2009) survey yielded the result that two-thirds of respondents favoured legalization of assisted suicide, though slightly fewer than half said that they would be willing themselves to help terminally ill patients end their lives if the law allowed it.[118]

But isn't helping patients to die contrary to a doctor's professional duty? I've already argued (§§4.1–2) that, under appropriate circumstances, neither assisting a suicide nor administering euthanasia is an instance of wrongful killing, since these acts do not share the wrong-making features of unjustified homicides. That means that they do not violate any general duty—any duty incumbent on everyone—not to kill (or assist a killing). But it remains possible that they might violate a duty that is specific to doctors by virtue of their role or profession. The idea of role-specific duties is itself perfectly legitimate: teachers have specific duties to their students, plumbers to their customers, politicians to their electorate. So doctors doubtless have role-specific duties as well. Could these duties include the duty not to kill? Some have argued that they do.[119] This claim often fails to rise above the level of a trite slogan ('Doctors should cure, not kill') or a reference to the Hippocratic Oath ('I will not give anyone a deadly drug if asked for it'). At other times it merely invokes the authority of a long tradition in which physicians have allegedly refrained from helping their patients to die.[120]

But let us assume that the claim can take a more serious and substantive form than that. If so, then it invites us to ask what the role-specific duties of a doctor are. Doubtless there are many such duties, owed to different parties (their patients, the healthcare institutions for which they work, their profession, their society, etc.) and

---

[116] Where assisted death is legal, nurses are often involved in the decision-making process and even the actual practice; see Inghelbrecht et al. 2010 for the experience in Belgium.

[117] Hemmings 2003. This survey has, however, been criticized on the ground that neither the questions used nor the complete results were reported (Holt 2008).

[118] *Source: Independent Nurse*, 20 April 2009. A 2001 survey found that a majority of hospice nurses in Oregon support the Oregon Death with Dignity Act (Ganzini 2004: table 11.2).

[119] Gaylin et al. 1988; Kass 1989; Pellegrino 1992; Baumrin 1998.

[120] e.g. Baumrin 1998.

with different contents (honesty, confidentiality, trust, competence, etc.). But presumably the relevant item for present purposes is the duty of care they owe to their patients. At the most abstract level, it seems plausible to think that this duty takes two main forms: the duty to do what is best for the patient and the duty to respect the patient's autonomy. It should be obvious that there is nothing in either duty that precludes acting on a request by a competent patient for assisted death when that is the best means of preventing further intolerable suffering. On the contrary, granting a competent request under these circumstances seems required by the duty to respect the patient's autonomy, and I need not repeat here the earlier argument (§1.1) that an assisted death can be in the patient's best interest.[121]

We reach the same result if we invoke the familiar 'Georgetown principles' for biomedical ethics.[122] The two aspects of the duty of care distinguished above invoke the principles of beneficence and autonomy, both of which are capable of supporting assisted death. The principle of non-maleficence requires physicians not to harm their patients or make their condition worse. When a patient is experiencing intolerable suffering that cannot be effectively relieved by any other end-of-life measure (short of terminal sedation) then the refusal of assisted death prolongs that suffering; since this has the result of making the patient's dying process worse than it needs to be, it arguably violates the non-maleficence principle. Indeed, it can be plausibly argued that doctors have an especially stringent role-specific duty of care, owed to their patients, not to allow them to suffer if they have the means to prevent that suffering.[123] Far from precluding offering patients an assisted death, the most widely accepted ethical principles governing the physician–patient relationship would seem (at least sometimes) to require it.

Perhaps, however, we are looking in the wrong place for the role-specific duties incumbent on doctors. They are, after all, professionals who are bound by the code of ethics of their profession; perhaps it is that code that prohibits assisting a patient's death. The Canadian Medical Association, for instance, takes the view that 'Canadian physicians should not participate in euthanasia or assisted suicide'.[124] It also has a Code of Ethics, so perhaps it is the principles embodied therein that explain why offering assisted death is unethical. The CMA's Code contains no fewer than fifty-four distinct principles.[125] None of them explicitly mentions assisted death and the vast majority of

---

[121] Leon Kass (1989: 29–30) has argued that medicine has a much narrower and more specific goal than the patient's good, namely 'the naturally given end of health'. Since assisting the death of a patient is hardly conducive to restoring the patient's health, it is easy to see how this construal of the doctor's duty might preclude killing (as Kass urges that it does). However, if the medical arts are to be devoted only to maintaining or restoring health, it becomes difficult to find a rationale for any purely palliative measures.

[122] Beauchamp and Childress 2009.

[123] 'A doctor's commitment to acting for patients' good creates a clear obligation to help a patient avoid an agonizing, protracted death. Allowing a patient to suffer when the suffering could be ended is an obvious violation of the duty of beneficence' (Rhodes 1998: 171).

[124] CMA, Euthanasia and Assisted Suicide (Update 2007), p. 2.

[125] CMA, Code of Ethics (Update 2004).

them, while laudable as norms governing the physician–patient relationship, are not specifically germane to this practice. But some would appear to be applicable:

1. Consider first the well-being of the patient.
3. Provide for appropriate care for your patient, even when cure is no longer possible, including physical comfort and spiritual and psychosocial support.
12. Inform your patient when your personal values would influence the recommendation or practice of any medical procedure that the patient needs or wants.
14. Take all reasonable steps to prevent harm to patients; should harm occur, disclose it to the patient.
19. Having accepted professional responsibility for a patient, continue to provide services until they are no longer required or wanted...
27. Ascertain wherever possible and recognize your patient's wishes about the initiation, continuation or cessation of life-sustaining treatment.

I can find nothing in any of these principles that would preclude a physician from acting on a competent patient's request for assisted death when the patient is experiencing intense suffering during the dying process. On the contrary, principles 1, 3, and 14 would seem to require it (as long as it is not unlawful), while principle 19 would seem to prohibit abandoning a patient and principle 12 would seem to require notifying the patient when providing this service would violate the physician's conscience. Principle 27 requires respect for the patient's own choices about end-of-life care, though only as far as life-sustaining treatment is concerned. It is left entirely unclear why the same respect should not be offered in the case of life-shortening treatment.

All right, but wouldn't helping patients to die undermine the physician–patient relationship? So it has seemed to some of the critics, Leon Kass for example: 'The patient's trust in the doctor's wholehearted devotion to the patient's best interests will be hard to sustain once doctors are licensed to kill.'[126] Kass's worry is that, if euthanasia were legalized, patients will never be certain that their doctors won't choose just to kill them off, especially if they are old and poor, rather than go to the trouble of treating them. I'm not a doctor, but if I were I think that I would be pretty insulted by this suggestion. The doctors I know, including the ones who are treating patients well advanced in the dying process, are dedicated to doing the best they can for those under their care. I don't believe that would change one bit were they able to offer their patients the option of euthanasia or assisted suicide, in addition to all of the conventional forms of

---

[126] Kass 1989: 35. Cf. Pellegrino 1996: 163: 'How is the patient to know when his doctor is persuading or even subtly coercing him to choose death? The doctor's motives may be unconsciously to advance her own beliefs that euthanasia is a social good to relieve herself of the frustrating difficulties of caring for the patient, of her distress with the quality of life the patient is forced to lead, or promote her desire to conserve society's resources, etc. How will the patient ever be sure of the true motive for his doctor's recommendation?'

palliative care. There is no evidence that patients in the Netherlands or Oregon trust their doctors less than those in prohibitionist jurisdictions, or less than they did before assisted death was legalized. Speaking just for myself, what would lead me to trust my doctor less is the suspicion that he is suppressing some form of treatment that would ease my suffering due to his own personal qualms.

But Kass is also worried about the effects of legalization on the physicians themselves: 'The psychological burden of the licence to kill (not to speak of the brutalization of the physician-killers) could very well be an intolerably high price to pay for physician-assisted euthanasia, especially if it also leads to greater remoteness, aloofness, and indifference as defenses against the guilt associated with harming those we care for.'[127] But are doctors in the Netherlands or Oregon who have assisted the deaths of their patients more psychologically burdened and brutalized than doctors elsewhere, and do they now treat their patients with greater remoteness, aloofness, and indifference? Kass has provided no evidence to think so.[128]

More specifically, isn't helping patients to die inconsistent with the goals of palliative care? It is not at all clear (to me at least) why palliative care and assisted death are sometimes thought to be antithetical.[129] Recall the World Health Organization characterization of palliative care (cited in §3.1) as 'an approach that improves the quality of life of patients and their families facing the problem associated with life-threatening illness, through the prevention and relief of suffering by means of early identification and impeccable assessment and treatment of pain and other problems, physical, psychosocial and spiritual'. This definition appears to leave room for a wide array of measures, all of which are aimed at 'the prevention and relief of suffering' and the 'treatment of pain and other problems, physical, psychosocial, and spiritual'. Both assisted suicide and euthanasia would seem to fit comfortably within that mandate. Experience in the jurisdictions where these measures are legal has shown that only a small minority of patients will opt for assisted death when offered the full spectrum of palliative measures. But for that minority, it is important that this option be available, since they have come to the conclusion that nothing else on offer is sufficing to reduce their suffering to a tolerable level. In Oregon more than 85 per cent of patients who have opted for assisted suicide have been in a hospice; for them the choice between other palliative measures and assisted death was not 'either/or' but 'both/and'.[130] In fact it seems fair to say that we can't know how well the conventional palliative measures are serving the needs of dying patients until we make the option of assisted

---

[127] Kass 1989: 35–6.

[128] The effects on Dutch physicians of participating in assisted death have been studied in Haverkate et al. 2001; Obstein, Kimsma, and Chambers 2004; Shalowitz and Emanuel 2004. First-person accounts by Dutch physicians can be found in Keizer 1997; Thomasma et al. 1998: pt. II sect. 1; Kimsma and van Leeuwen 2004: 230 ff.; Admiraal 2008.

[129] e.g. in Pereira et al. 2008. For the opposing view see Gill 2009.

[130] The complex, diverse, and often ambiguous relationships between Oregon hospice programmes and the Death with Dignity Act are nicely explored in Ganzini 2010 and Campbell and Cox 2010.

death legally available to them. I see no reason why assisted death should not be thought of as a measure of last resort within palliative care, not as an alternative to it. In Belgium we have an example in which the development of palliative care and the movement to legalize euthanasia grew up side by side, with little antagonism, and in which this model of 'integral palliative care' has worked to mutual benefit.[131]

Some polls of physicians have found opposition to legalization to be strongest among palliative care specialists.[132] However, there is some evidence of movement on this issue. In 2006 a working group on physician-assisted death set up by the Canadian Hospice Palliative Care Association released an Issues Paper for discussion within the Association; no final position on the legalization issue has been taken as of this writing. In the following year the American Academy of Hospice and Palliative Medicine, reflecting the existence of 'deep disagreement' on the issue, adopted a position of 'studied neutrality' on legalization.[133] It is not surprising, I think, that healthcare providers who work with dying patients—and the organizations that represent them—should feel especially conflicted over this issue. For one thing, should any form of assisted death become legally available they will find themselves on the front lines having to make some very difficult personal and professional decisions. In addition, any demand for assisted death on the part of dying patients—especially those already in a hospice—could seem like a rejection and indictment of the services provided by those who are dedicated to caring for them ('I've done my best for him, but he still insists he wants to die'). On the other hand, most palliative care physicians recognize that a minority of dying patients will experience refractory symptoms, including pain, which are not responsive to the strongest pharmacological agents (short of terminal sedation).[134] Furthermore, where assisted death is legal the reasons most frequently given by patients for seeking it do not cite strictly physiological symptoms, such as pain or nausea or shortness of breath, but rather those 'psychosocial and spiritual' problems noted by the WHO, including a sense of meaninglessness or hopelessness, loss of independence, isolation, indignity, and inability to engage in the activities that make life worth living. While good hospice care can go some way towards alleviating these concerns, they are the forms of suffering least susceptible to a medical remedy. Patients who find them intolerable are bearing witness not to the failure of even the best conventional palliative care but to its limits.

---

[131] Bernheim et al. 2008.

[132] e.g. the 2006 Royal College of Physicians survey, where 95 per cent of specialists in palliative medicine were opposed ('RCP cannot support legal change on assisted dying—survey results', RCP News, 9 May 2006).

[133] Position Statement on Physician-Assisted Death, adopted 14 February 2007. The Oregon Hospice Association opposed the Oregon Death with Dignity Act before it was adopted in 1994 and supported its repeal in 1997; now that the ODDA is in effect the OHA has no position on it, except that no Oregon hospice should turn away a patient on the ground that he is considering exercising his rights under the law (personal communication from Ann Jackson, CEO of the OHA, 18 January 2007).

[134] Twycross 1994: 2; Chater et al. 1998; Quill 1998. A symptom is considered refractory 'if all other possible treatments have failed, or . . . no methods are available for alleviation within the time frame and risk/benefit ratio that the patient can tolerate' (Cherny and Portenoy 1994: 31).

That's all very well, but aren't you worried that legalizing assisted death would erode the delivery of other forms of palliative care? This has not been the experience in the jurisdictions that have legalized assisted death. In Oregon both the rate of use of hospice facilities and the quality of hospice care appear to have risen since the passage of the Oregon Death with Dignity Act in 1994.[135] Furthermore, in Oregon the percentage of patients electing assisted suicide who were already enrolled in a hospice has increased in recent years. As mentioned earlier, Belgium provides us with an example of a jurisdiction in which the provision of other end-of-life measures and euthanasia have developed together in the model of 'integral palliative care'.[136] The fact that legalization of assisted death and improved delivery of palliative care have gone hand in hand in these jurisdictions should not surprise us: if patients have the option of an assisted death then doctors have a strong motive for ensuring that it is chosen truly as a last resort and not for lack of adequate end-of-life care.

The Netherlands is sometimes cited as just the opposite: a jurisdiction in which the legalization of euthanasia has come at the expense of the development of good quality palliative care.[137] But this conclusion appears to be largely based on a misunderstanding about the delivery of palliative care in that country.[138] As compared to other jurisdictions, such as the UK, the Netherlands has traditionally had relatively few institutions—hospices—dedicated solely to the provision of palliative care. Instead, these services were for the most part provided in nursing homes, hospital units, or at home by family physicians. This situation has latterly begun to change, so that as of 2006 there were two hundred specialized institutions for hospice palliative care in the country. Most palliative care, however, is still provided at home by family physicians. There is no evidence to suggest that the quality of that care is inferior to what is available in other countries; indeed, a recent 'Quality of Death' index devised by the Economist Intelligence Unit ranked the Netherlands seventh out of forty countries evaluated (ahead of both Canada and the United States).[139] Furthermore, palliative care in the Netherlands is fully covered by private or public health insurance.

Shouldn't we wait until we can guarantee every dying patient high-quality palliative care before making assisted death available? The provision of hospice and palliative care has expanded dramatically over the past two or three decades, but we doubtless still have a considerable distance to go before every patient who needs it has access to it. I've argued that assisted death should be considered a legitimate last-resort option within palliative care, not as an alternative to it. In that case the provision of 'high-quality palliative care' should include making assisted death available to those for whom the

---

[135] Ganzini et al. 2001; Goy et al. 2003; Ganzini and Dahl 2008: 69; Gill 2009: 38–9.

[136] Bernheim et al. 2008.

[137] e.g. by Keown 2002: 111; Cohen-Almagor 2004: 126.

[138] Van Delden, Visser, and Borst-Eilers 2004: 213–14; Griffiths, Weyers, and Adams 2008: 18.

[139] 'The UK has the highest quality of death', Economist Intelligence Unit, 14 July 2010. Belgium ranked fifth in the same index.

more conventional measures do not suffice. We should not think that we must choose between two policy aims: expand access to the conventionally accepted end-of-life measures or legalize assisted death. We can, and should, do both—as was done in Belgium when the Law on Palliative Care, guaranteeing patients the right to obtain information on palliative care options from their physicians, was passed in the same month (June 2002) as the Law on Euthanasia.[140] We should also keep in mind that even the best end-of-life care will not eliminate the demand for assisted death.[141]

Of course, the goal of ensuring the best palliative care for everyone will not be achieved overnight, especially in a period of continually expanding healthcare costs. But meanwhile we can't say to someone whose end-of-life suffering is so intense that they want the relief of an assisted death: 'Yes, we understand that this is hard for you but, you see, not everyone yet has access to the same quality of palliative care that you have enjoyed. We realize that it has not worked for you and nothing will work but an assisted death. But you will just have to wait until we've been able to expand our palliative services to everyone who needs them.' That would be unspeakably cruel.

Why do patients need doctors to help them die? Can't they just do it themselves? Let's put this question to Anita who, you will recall, is enduring the end stage of cancer and wants to cut short any further suffering. You are right that she could achieve this aim by jumping off a bridge, or throwing herself under a subway train, or hanging herself, or shooting herself in the head. (Note that Bill, who is bedridden with ALS, does not have most of these options, which is why persons with disabilities will have a special need for assistance.[142]) But ask yourself: would Anita regard any of these scenarios as a good way to die? Would you regard them as a good way to die (for yourself)? And then ask yourself: what would the impact of any of them be on Anita's family? Why would she choose to end her life with an act of violence, if other options were available? Wouldn't a peaceful and gentle end, with her family gathered round, be better for all of them?[143]

---

[140] Griffiths, Weyers, and Adams 2008: 269; Lewis 2009: 134.

[141] Gill 2009: 28–9.

[142] On the other hand, a recent study found that the risk of suicide for ALS patients in Sweden (where assisted suicide is illegal) is six times higher than for the general population (Fang et al. 2008). The risk is highest in the earlier stage of the illness, which suggests that the unavailability of assisted suicide is forcing patients to end their lives earlier than they might otherwise choose.

[143] Marcia Angell tells the story of her father, who shot himself at age eighty-one in the end stages of prostate cancer (Angell 2004). She concludes: 'If physician-assisted suicide had been available to my father, as it is to the people of Oregon, I have no doubt that he would have chosen a less violent and lonely death.' See also Batavia 2004: 67–8. By contrast, Ben Fogelson has published a first-person account of how he helped his mother to die under the terms of the Oregon policy ('Taking mom home: a Eugene man's journey with his mother to the end', *Eugene Weekly*, 5 August 2010). I know of no empirical research that compares the impact on surviving family members of medically assisted suicide versus suicide by other means. However, a Dutch study did show that the bereaved family and friends of cancer patients who died by euthanasia had less traumatic grief symptoms and less post-traumatic stress reactions than the family and friends of patients who died of their illness (Swarte et al. 2003).

Of course, Anita could try to manage this peaceful and gentle end on her own, by stockpiling a supply of opiates or barbiturates until she thought she had enough to do the job. Her death would still be a lonely affair, since anyone who remained with her would risk a charge of assisting her suicide. Furthermore, it is easy to make mistakes, so that instead of dead she could end up brain-damaged or in an emergency room having her stomach pumped. Anita almost certainly lacks what doctors have—namely, the expertise to bring about her death efficiently and safely (that is, without unwanted side effects). Like every other end-of-life measure, this one is best managed by those who know how to do it (and have legal access to the best pharmacological means).[144] Anyway, would Anita's physician not feel that he had abandoned his patient if he had gone through every other palliative measure with her and then left her to take the last step on her own?

Why do patients need assisted death, when they can die by refusing food and water? By contrast with the last question, this one at least compares medically assisted death with another end-of-life option that can be carried out in a healthcare institution (very commonly a hospice) and under medical supervision. We have already seen (§2.2) that competent patients have the moral and legal right to refuse any form of life-sustaining treatment, including nutrition and hydration. Some have argued that the availability of this option to patients who wish to die renders legalization of assisted death unnecessary.[145] Certainly it has some advantages. Many patients who are well advanced in the dying process lose their appetites spontaneously. Furthermore, if a patient makes a conscious decision to refuse food and fluids, carrying out this decision does not require the cooperation of any physician (on the contrary: attending physicians are required not to intervene). Finally, in prohibitionist jurisdictions it has the considerable advantage of being legal. However, it also has serious drawbacks.[146] First, it is slow: depending on the condition of the patient, it will take anywhere from a few days to a couple of weeks for death to occur if no fluids are taken, longer if some are. Second, it is difficult or impossible to control the timing of death. This can be an important matter if a patient wishes to be able to say a final goodbye to his family or to have them gathered around at the end. Third, especially in the early stages the process may be attended by some discomfort (though nothing that cannot be alleviated in a medical setting).[147] Fourth, it is not easy: it may require some degree of willpower to persist with it, at least until the body begins to shut down.[148] Finally, some patients (and their families) may find the idea

---

[144] There are complications even in some cases of physician-assisted suicide (Groenewoud et al. 2000; Ganzini and Dahl 2008: 74).

[145] Printz 1992; Bernat, Gert, and Mogielnicki 1993.

[146] Quill, Lo, and Brock 1997; Miller and Meier 1998: 561; Batavia 2004: 68–9; Brock 2004: 132. David Orentlicher (1998: 306) makes similar points about terminal sedation.

[147] Nurses who had attended both patients who died by refusing food and fluids and patients who elected physician-assisted suicide rated the overall quality of the deaths the same for the two groups. (Ganzini et al. 2003: 363).

[148] In a study of 126 patients who decided to refuse food and fluids in order to die, sixteen (13 per cent) did not carry it through to the end (Ganzini et al. 2003: 361).

of death by dehydration repugnant. The virtues of assisted death are that the process can be quick, painless, easy, and scheduled when the patient wants it. When both options are legally available, some patients will still choose to die by stopping food and water, as is their right. But others will prefer assisted death; having the former available does not eliminate demand for the latter.[149]

7.6 Last Words

This chapter has articulated a Model Policy for assisted death which is responsive to the civic virtues of compassion and respect. But most of it has been devoted to defending that policy against an array of practical objections. I will not revisit these objections, and the responses to them, in this concluding section. Instead, I want to return to a theme briefly mentioned at the end of §7.3. It will be obvious by now that assisted death policies, both actual and proposed, have attracted a quite remarkable amount of critical attention. Perhaps that is as it should be. But what seems to me equally remarkable is the lack of attention to existing policies concerning the conventionally accepted end-of-life measures. I find this surprising for three reasons. First, the salient feature shared by all the end-of-life measures is their capacity for hastening death. Just to take the most obvious instance, in most cases death is hastened just as certainly (though not as quickly) by the cessation of all life-sustaining treatment as it is by assisted suicide or euthanasia. Terminal sedation, at least when coupled with with-drawal of food and fluids, is also an effective means of hastening death. If the hastening of death is the ethically salient issue—as it seems it should be—then surely we should be just as concerned about slippery slopes, mistakes, and abuses where these measures are concerned as we are when dealing with assisted death. Despite this fact, and despite the elaborate regulatory regimes that have been implemented or proposed for assisted death, these other measures remain entirely unregulated by law *and none of the critics seems even to notice, let alone care.*

The second reason that I find this selective critical attention surprising has to do with sheer numbers. To keep matters simple, let's just look at the most recent study of the Dutch policy, reporting results for 2005.[150] That study found that euthanasia and assisted suicide accounted for 1.7 per cent of all deaths that year in the Netherlands. It also found that 'withholding or withdrawing of life-prolonging treatment' accounted for 15.6 per cent of all deaths and 'continuous deep sedation' accounted for a further 8.2 per cent.[151]

---

[149] Ibid. In Oregon hospices three times as many patients choose to die by refusing food and fluids as by assisted suicide; most of the former group are women (telephone interview with Ann Jackson, CEO of the Oregon Hospice Association, 16 February 2007).

[150] van der Heide et al. 2007.

[151] There has been a significant increase in the use of terminal sedation in the Netherlands since 2001, during the same period that the incidence of euthanasia and assisted suicide declined (Rietjens et al. 2008). It is difficult to avoid the conclusion that some Dutch physicians have begun preferring the former (unregu-lated) measure to the latter (regulated) one. The same worrisome increase in the incidence of terminal sedation has been observed in Belgium (Bilsen et al. 2009).

Just think about those figures for a minute. If they are all accurate, then during that year Dutch patients died nine times more often by so-called 'passive' means, and nearly five times more often by terminal sedation, than they did by both means of assisted death combined. If our aim is to prevent needless deaths—as it appears it should be—then should we not be just as concerned to avoid abuses in these other cases? Indeed, because they are so much more common, should we not be *more* concerned?

The third reason is that the opportunity for and likelihood of abuse seem just as great in these other cases.[152] If patients who are old or poor or disabled are vulnerable to pressure by family or physician to request assisted death, then surely they are just as vulnerable to pressure from the same sources to refuse treatment or request terminal sedation. If they need protection against the former pressures then surely they also need protection against the latter.

For all these reasons I find it quite remarkable that everyone is so obsessed with ensuring adequate regulation of assisted death and no one is suggesting heightened regulation of the conventional end-of-life measures.[153] But I do have an explanation of this phenomenon: it is due to the acceptance by the critics of the Conventional View, which draws an ethical bright line between assisted death and the other measures. We have seen already that this line cannot be justified, but the critics nonetheless assume it by endorsing either the sanctity of life, the Doctrine of Double Effect, or the Doctrine of Doing and Allowing.[154] From the perspective of the Conventional View it is, of course, assisted death that stands in need of both special justification and special regulation. If that view is rejected—as it should be—then this disparity of attention and scrutiny cannot be sustained. Patients in the dying process would be better served by more attention to the commoner risks and less attention to the rarer ones.

---

[152] Orentlicher 1998: 306–7.

[153] Almost no one. Jocelyn Downie (2004: ch. 9) is a notable exception; Downie, of course, supports legalizing assisted death (with regulatory safeguards). See also Stell 1998: 146–7; Battin 2005: 58–9; Dworkin 2008. It is doubtless unrealistic to think of raising regulation of the conventional end-of-life measures to the level appropriate for assisted death, but surely a higher level of scrutiny is possible. If the critics of assisted death are to be believed, it should be a matter of some urgency.

[154] John Keown (2002: chs. 2 and 4) and Neil Gorsuch (2006: chs. 4 and 9) both endorse the first two.

8

Epilogue

The essential work of this book, both ethical and legal, is now complete. Because it has been a lengthy, and sometimes winding, discussion, the first section of this chapter offers a brief overview of its main argumentative lines. The next section then addresses the practical question of where those seeking law reform might go from here.

8.1 A Summary of the Argument

The discussion has focused on four end-of-life measures: withholding/withdrawing life-sustaining treatment, administering analgesics in high doses to control intractable symptoms, deep continuous sedation to the point of death, and assisted death (euthanasia and assisted suicide). These four have been selected because each of them, while offering the promise of relief of suffering during the dying process, also has at least the potential of hastening death.[1] According to (what I have been calling) the Conventional View, the first three measures are ethically permissible (under appropriate conditions) and should be legally permitted, while the fourth is impermissible and should be prohibited. The argument of this book has been directed against this view, in both its ethical and legal aspects.

The ethical argument has employed two strategies, one constructive and one defensive. The former consisted of identifying the best justification for the conventionally accepted measures, beginning with the least controversial (withholding/withdrawing treatment) and culminating with the most controversial (terminal sedation). In the case of decisionally capable patients, where these measures are voluntary, their best justification will point to the way in which they serve two basic values: patient well-being and patient self-determination (or autonomy). It is always a good defence of a treatment (or nontreatment) regime that (*a*) it is in the patient's best interest, and

---

[1] The question of whether pain management techniques and terminal sedation do in fact hasten death was addressed in §3.1, above.

(*b*) it has been subject to the patient's informed consent (or refusal). Cases of decision-ally incapable patients are more complicated, since the normal appeal to patient autonomy will there be unavailable. However, where the patient was formerly competent it may still be possible to base a treatment decision on precedent autonomy or, alternatively, invoke sufficient evidence of prior wishes to utilize a substituted judgement standard. Only where the patient has never been competent do substitute decision-makers need to fall back on a best interest standard. However, this appeal to patient well-being alone is capable (under appropriate conditions) of justifying any of the conventionally accepted measures.

The next step in the constructive argument is then both simple and obvious: exactly the same justification is available for the measures of assisted death, up to and including nonvoluntary euthanasia. The ethical foundation of the conventionally accepted measures is therefore equally available for the conventionally rejected ones. At least as far as the basic justifying values for end-of-life measures are concerned, it is inconsistent to defend the former and condemn the latter.

The constructive argument results in a *pro tanto* case in favour of assisted death (when it is requested by a competent patient and/or serves the best interest of the patient). However, that case is defeasible, since there may be other ethically salient factors in play that enable a bright line to be drawn between assisted death and the other measures. The defensive argument then engages three of the most prominent attempts to justify such a line. The Doctrine of Double Effect relies on the ethical salience of the intending/foreseeing distinction. The DDE holds that it may some-times be permissible to bring death about as a foreseen but unintended result of one's action, though it would be impermissible to bring it about as an intended result. In this way it attempts to draw a bright line between assisted death (where death is intended) and the administration of high-dose analgesics and sedatives (where death may be foreseen but is unintended). The Doctrine of Doing and Allowing, on the other hand, invokes the ethical salience of the doing/allowing distinction. The DDA holds that it may sometimes be permissible to allow death to happen, though it would be imper-missible to make it happen. In this way it attempts to draw a bright line between assisted death (which causes death) and the withholding or withdrawal of treatment (which allows death to happen).

Both doctrines will condemn assisted death, though on quite different grounds (intention in the one case, causation in the other). However, both suffer from similar liabilities. First, ambiguities concerning intention and causation make it difficult for either doctrine to draw a sharp, as opposed to a fuzzy, line among end-of-life measures. Second, even under the most charitable assumptions about intention and causation, neither doctrine is able to draw the line just where the Conventional View requires it. The DDE will locate the administration of high-dose opioids and sedatives on the permissible side of the line, since (we are assuming) death is an unintended side effect of these forms of treatment. It will do the same for most cases of withholding or withdrawing treatment. But not all, since death is clearly the intended outcome in some cases of treatment refusal, such as the removal of a ventilator or a feeding tube. The DDA will locate most cases of withholding or withdrawing treatment on the permissible side of the line, but again not all, since it seems reasonable to regard the removal of a ventilator or feeding tube as causing death. Worse, the DDA will not exonerate high-dose pain management or terminal sedation, since (we are assuming) these measures are capable of causing death. Third, both doctrines must make the highly questionable assumption that, in the end-of-life scenarios with which we have been dealing, death is a harm to the patient. If that assumption is rejected, as it should be, then neither doctrine has any application to these scenarios. Finally, the ethical distinctions drawn by the DDE and the DDA have little intuitive plausibility in these scenarios. When all (other) salient factors are held equal—especially relief of patient suffering and respect for patient autonomy—neither the intending/foreseeing distinction nor the doing/allowing distinction seems to make any ethical difference.

For these reasons neither the DDE nor the DDA, taken by itself, can justify drawing an ethical bright line in just the place required by the Conventional View. When they are combined they yield the view that an end-of-life measure is impermissible when death is both intended and caused. The combined DDE/DDA, however, inherits most of the problems of its two components (see above) and it is still unable to locate the bright line where the Conventional View needs it, since in the aforementioned cases of treatment refusal (the removal of a ventilator or a feeding tube) death is both intended and caused. There appears to be no way, therefore, that these commonly invoked resources, either separately or in combination, can provide an ethical justification for the Conventional View.

There are two other resources commonly relied on by critics of assisted death. One is the claim that everyone has a right to life, interpreted as the right not to be killed. However, invoking this right to condemn euthanasia requires the implausible assumption that it cannot be waived by, or on behalf of, persons in circumstances in which death would be in their best interest. The other resource is the notion of the sanctity of human life. If it is to be more than a mere slogan, this notion needs an interpretation that will yield a convincing case against euthanasia. Under its usual interpretation the sanctity of life seems to appeal to the idea that intentional killing manifests disrespect for human life. Two versions of this idea were tested, one Thomistic and the other Kantian. The former takes basic human goods to be the appropriate objects of respect. However, it can deliver the desired result only by making two highly questionable assumptions: that these goods are incommensurable and that 'bare' life, in the absence of any other goods, itself has prudential value. The latter instead takes persons to be the appropriate objects of respect. However, its argument to this conclusion must invert the order of explanation between the value of persons and the prudential value of their lives. For these reasons neither of these sanctity-of-life views is able to explain how the intentional shortening of life can manifest disrespect—whether for persons or for the goods in their lives—when it is requested by a competent patient and/or serves the best interest of the patient. Neither view, therefore, can yield a convincing case against the permissibility of euthanasia.

Put negatively, the outcome of the ethical inquiry was a rejection of the Conventional View: there is no argument for the impermissibility of assisted death which will not also condemn other, conventionally accepted, end-of-life measures. Put more positively, there is a strong ethical case in favour of assisted death (under appropriate conditions) and no persuasive case against it. In short: *there is no good reason for thinking that assisted death is ethically unjustifiable.*

Turning now to the legal issues, the ethical permissibility of assisted death does not entail that it should be legally permitted, since there are important practical considerations concerning the consequences of legalization that also need to be taken into account. However, the ethical result does undermine one common argument against legalization: the argument that the law should not permit what is ethically impermissible.

The case in favour of legalization rests on two civic virtues: compassion for the suffering of dying patients and respect for their autonomy over their own dying process. These virtues then shape the terms of an ideal Model Policy for the common law jurisdictions, one that defines a regulatory regime for assisted suicide, voluntary euthanasia, and nonvoluntary euthanasia. The significant objections to such a policy are not ethical but practical. The most influential of these objections point to two alleged problems with the regulatory conditions and safeguards built into the policy: while they might initially permit only ethically justifiable practices they will inevitably be expanded to permit unjustifiable ones (the slippery slope argument) and, regardless of where the lines are drawn, they will inevitably be violated in ways that will put vulnerable populations at risk (the argument from mistake and abuse). However, the Model Policy is not vulnerable to a slippery slope argument, since it already includes most of the practices (including nonvoluntary euthanasia) that are usually thought to lie at the bottom of the slope. Nor is it more prone to problems of medical mistake (misdiagnosis or misprognosis) than the conventional end-of-life measures. As for abuse, there is no convincing evidence from the extant legal regimes in the Netherlands or Oregon that legalization will put vulnerable sectors of the population at risk. Furthermore, while it is reasonable to expect some degree of non-compliance with the terms of the policy, this is likely to be less of a problem for assisted death than for these other measures, which are currently entirely unregulated.

The two principal objections do not exhaust the practical obstacles that have been suggested for the path to law reform. However, there is no reason to think that any of these problems is insuperable. We already have the example of jurisdictions, such as the Netherlands and Oregon, that provide access to assisted death for patients who are suffering during the dying process while at the same time minimizing collateral risks to other members of society. Crafting a similar policy for any of the common law jurisdictions should not exceed the limits of our ingenuity. Compassion and respect for our fellow citizens demand no less from us.

8.2 The Way Forward

The previous chapter (§7.2) outlined a Model Policy that was defended as the best case, the ideal objective, for law reform concerning assisted death. However, two important questions remain unanswered. The first is whether, and if so how, that ideal needs to be modified in order to fit the local social/political/economic conditions in a particular jurisdiction. For one thing, the various common law jurisdictions have quite different systems for healthcare delivery and health insurance coverage. These differences may well make a difference, perhaps by making a policy that presupposes longstanding physician–patient relationships (such as that in the Netherlands) more or less appropriate, or by raising or lowering the concern that assisted death might be promoted as a cost-saving measure. In response to such considerations as these, one commentator who favours law reform has argued that the nature of healthcare delivery (and coverage) in the United States makes it advisable to aim at legalizing only assisted suicide and not euthanasia.[2]

Additionally, calculations need to be made of what is politically possible. For many people a legal regime for assisted suicide appears to be a more attractive option than one for euthanasia, despite the fact that there is no significant ethical difference between the two practices. It is noteworthy that ballot initiatives to legalize both assisted suicide and euthanasia failed in Washington (1991) and California (1992), while initiatives to legalize assisted suicide alone succeeded in Oregon (1994 and 1997) and Washington (2008). Likewise, in the United Kingdom the climate of opinion at the moment seems more favourable to the legalization of assisted suicide than euthanasia, which partially explains why Lord Joffe altered the bill he tabled in the House of Lords so as to delete all reference to the latter. These social/political realities might argue for focusing, at least initially, on securing a regulatory regime for assisted suicide (perhaps modelled on the Oregon policy), reserving until later the further task of broadening it to include euthanasia. I take no stand on these various issues of adaptation to local conditions, which need to be faced by law reform advocates. I would only point out that each retreat from the ideal model comes at an ethical cost, for it will deny access to assisted death to a group of patients whose need is no less urgent than those fortunate enough to be included.

The second question concerns not the objective of local law reform efforts but the means. Even if advocates agree on the policy whose implementation they wish to seek, they must still decide how best to bring it about. This question belongs properly to political strategy or tactics, or possibly political science, rather than political philosophy. Even if the same policy were (more or less) appropriate for all the various prohibitionist jurisdictions, the most effective strategy for putting it in place is bound to vary with local social, political, and legal conditions.[3] Broadly speaking, there appear to be four options available.

---

[2] Battin 2005: 63–6.   [3] This strategic issue is the subject of Lewis 2007.

The legislature. In a representative democracy policy decisions on important matters affecting the interests of the populace should ideally be made by elected legislators. Law reform by this route has a number of significant advantages. A legislative initiative will put the issue of assisted death up for debate in the public forum, where arguments on both sides of the question can be posed and assessed. Such an initiative can have the benefit of expert drafting and vetting by government lawyers, especially in the design of safeguards against abuse. A legislative committee examining a draft bill can arrange public consultations to facilitate input by interest and advocacy groups. Elected representatives will have ample opportunity to canvass the opinions of their constituents before deciding whether to support such a bill. Finally, and most importantly, a policy passed into law by this means will face no challenges to its legitimacy; opponents may seek to defeat or repeal it on some future occasion, but they cannot credibly claim that its enactment has thwarted or bypassed established democratic procedures.

However, the legislative route also faces some formidable obstacles. Like abortion, assisted death is a divisive and emotionally powerful issue, capable of galvanizing strong opinion on both sides. Unless under intense pressure for change, governments are normally reluctant to stir up opposition and risk a backlash of outrage on the part of influential interest groups. The politically astute strategy is to avoid dealing with these issues unless compelled to do so. At least in the parliamentary democracies governments do have some devices they can use to distance themselves from the controversy: rather than sponsor a government bill they can allow a private member's bill to come to a vote and they can allow a free vote with no party discipline. Even so, assisted death is likely to remain an issue that governments would rather avoid if at all possible.

Of the various regulatory regimes, the legislative route was the one followed in Belgium and Luxembourg. Since the mid-1990s bills to legalize assisted death (usually assisted suicide, often on the Oregon model) have been introduced in at least eighteen US state legislatures, thus far without success.[4] Public opinion on this issue remains more divided in the United States than in the other common law jurisdictions, and religiously based pro-life groups are much more vocal and influential. However, criminal law is under state jurisdiction and some states are much more liberal on this issue than others; the possibility of legislative success cannot therefore be entirely excluded. In the UK Lord Joffe has so far enjoyed no success with the bills he has introduced in the House of Lords, initially to legalize both forms of assisted death and latterly focusing solely on assisted suicide. Public opinion in the UK runs strongly in favour of law reform on assisted suicide, largely because of the number of Britons who have been seeking this service in Switzerland; it remains possible that legislators will eventually catch up. In Canada, despite the fact that public opinion is also strongly favourable, a government initiative on this issue is currently unthinkable and the private member's bill perennially introduced by Francine Lalonde (an MP from

---

[4] Rosenfeld 2004: 39. The closest call was in Hawaii in 2002; see Stutsman 2004: 253–4.

Quebec) is unlikely ever to attract majority support in the House of Commons, even in a free vote.[5] While it would be a mistake to rule out the possibility of legislative change in any of the prohibitionist jurisdictions, its prospects at the moment do not appear particularly bright.

The courts. Legal positivists are fond of reminding us that courts have the function of making law as well as applying it. There are two distinct ways in which they can shape policy concerning assisted death. In a constitutional democracy a top court may be empowered to strike down legislation that is found to violate constitutionally entrenched rights. This is what happened, rather unexpectedly, in Colombia in 1997, when the Constitutional Court declared the country's legal prohibition of euthanasia invalid.[6] However, similar challenges to the assisted suicide laws have failed in Canada (1993), the United States (1997), and the United Kingdom (2002).

The probability of success with any further challenge in these jurisdictions is therefore rather low, though the 1993 decision in the Canadian Supreme Court was very close and, with the subsequent experience of the Oregon policy to draw on, there is no guarantee that the Court would now reach the same conclusion were it to reconsider the matter.[7] The advantages of a successful constitutional challenge are obvious, since the goal of law reform can then be achieved without the need for all that messy political action; this was the result when the existing abortion laws were struck down in the United States in 1973 and in Canada in 1988. However, for that very reason court decisions of this sort will also elicit complaints of unwarranted 'judicial activism' and the bypassing of the democratic process. Furthermore, courts are better equipped to remove existing legislation than to craft its replacement. Few think that assisted death should be legally permitted with no oversight or regulation. Once the existing law has been invalidated, therefore, it becomes the task of the legislature to construct the appropriate regulatory regime. But legislators are not always willing or able to rise to this occasion (*vide* Colombia).

Sustaining a constitutional challenge is, however, only one way in which the courts can shape policy. The other is through the accumulation of case law as prosecutions for euthanasia or assisted suicide succeed or fail. It was via this route that euthanasia (and *a fortiori* assisted suicide) was gradually legalized in the Netherlands during a period of nearly thirty years before the process culminated with a formal change in the law in 2002. Early on the Dutch courts recognized necessity as an available defence against a charge of consensual homicide, and a sequence of acquittals (or convictions with token penalties) effectively determined the guidelines to be followed by prosecutors in deciding when to proceed with a charge. Though the politicians eventually came

---

[5] It was recently (21 April 2010) defeated in a free vote by a margin of 228–59.

[6] The 2009 decision by the Montana Supreme Court was rather different, since it found that nothing in state law prohibited assisted suicide.

[7] In the United States there is also the possibility of challenges to existing laws under the terms of state constitutions; see Tucker 2004: 270–1.

on board, it is fair to say that the Dutch assisted death policy was primarily the product of judicial, and not legislative, action.

It is doubtful that the same route could succeed in the common law jurisdictions. Few cases of euthanasia or assisted suicide involving physicians ever come to court, and when they do the charge is frequently reduced to a more minor offence (possibly in order to avoid a challenge to the law). Furthermore, the common law courts tend to interpret the necessity defence more narrowly than do their Dutch counterparts.[8] However, a related tactic might stand a better chance of success. During the 1970s and 1980s Dr Henry Morgentaler was prosecuted on four separate occasions for openly defying the then existing abortion law in Canada. At trial he attempted to invoke the defence of necessity. Though it was highly doubtful that this defence was legally available to him, the argument did succeed in convincing the jurors that Dr Morgentaler had acted in good faith and out of a genuine concern for his patients. All four juries refused to convict. As a result of these acquittals the abortion law became virtually unenforceable, at least in Quebec, until it was finally struck down on constitutional grounds in 1988. This kind of 'jury nullification' might well occur now if a physician were to be prosecuted for homicide or assisting a suicide, and if the jurors could be convinced that he had acted out of compassion for his patient.[9] A similar possibility in the United States is that a grand jury might refuse to prefer an indictment.[10]

The prosecutors. Legislators make criminal law and judges apply it, but only when cases are brought to them by public prosecutors. Because some degree of discretion must be employed to determine when a case is worth proceeding with, the prosecution service is another juncture in the system at which at least some instances of assisted death can be effectively legalized. The prosecution service played this role in the Netherlands from the 1970s to the formal legal amendment of 2002. Driven primarily by the court decisions in which the defence of necessity had been accepted, the Board of Procurators General worked out with the Royal Dutch Medical Association a set of guidelines whose observance would insulate physicians from legal action. Similar guidelines for the exercise of prosecutorial discretion were developed by the British Columbia Attorney-General following the assisted suicide of Sue Rodriguez in 1994. More recently, the Director of Public Prosecutions in the UK has published guidelines for cases of assisted suicide, though they are aimed primarily at determining when to proceed with a charge against family members or friends rather than physicians.

Like law reform by judicial fiat, prosecutorial discretion can determine a legal regime for assisted death without the need for formal legislative action. However,

---

[8] Lewis 2007: 83–94.   [9] Ibid. 96.

[10] Ibid. 97. This was the outcome in the well-known case of Dr Timothy Quill, who published an account of the assistance he provided for the suicide of one of his patients (Quill 1991). Although his actions were the subject of a criminal investigation, and Dr Quill and other witnesses testified before a grand jury, no indictment was forthcoming (Lewis 2007: 13–14).

for this very reason it also has several drawbacks.[11] Because the guidelines are likely to be vague and subject to interpretation, it can be very difficult for physicians (or laypersons) to determine when they will be safe from prosecution. The legal regime will also be unstable, since the guidelines could be revised, or withdrawn entirely, at any time. Finally, there are limits to the exercise of prosecutorial discretion, since if carried too far the guidelines will amount to a substantive change in the law, which is the exclusive prerogative of the legislature.

Since some steps have already been taken in this direction in the UK, at least for assisted suicide, they could in principle be expanded to govern the actions of physicians as well. However, in the Netherlands this step was taken with the cooperation of the Royal Dutch Medical Association, which early on took the view that voluntary euthanasia could be considered to be standard medical practice. Like its Canadian and American counterparts, the British Medical Association has so far shown little appetite for a similar stance. In Canada the administration of justice is a provincial matter; prosecutorial guidelines for the country as a whole could therefore be developed only by the agreement of provincial Attorneys-General and Ministers of Justice, a step that is unlikely unless driven by adverse decisions in criminal trials. Likewise, in the US this type of backdoor legalization could happen only on a state-by-state basis.

The people. If democracy is defined as the political system in which decision-making is ultimately exercised by the collective citizenry, then its purest expression is the referendum. It is by this means that the assisted suicide policies were installed in Oregon (1994 and 1997) and Washington (2008). Since these policies were put to a direct vote, there can be no doubt of their political legitimacy. Furthermore, referenda are by their nature responsive to public opinion on sensitive issues such as assisted death, overcoming the problem that the people may be more receptive to legalization than their elected representatives and sidestepping the necessity of persuading any political party to commit to the reform agenda. Having said that, a referendum is not an ideal mechanism for the adoption of bioethical policies which, due to their subject matter, are inevitably complex and nuanced.[12] The process provides no opportunity for careful clause-by-clause deliberation about the provisions to be built into the policy, since the electorate have only the option of taking or leaving the draft legislation on offer. Furthermore, public opinion on matters such as this can be quite volatile and subject to hijacking by interest groups with little reluctance to engage in inflammatory rhetoric.

Because referenda are rarely used in the parliamentary democracies to settle matters of domestic policy, this avenue is probably closed in Canada and the UK (a free vote in parliament is much more likely). But it remains open in the remaining twenty-two US states (besides Oregon and Washington), as well as the District of Columbia, where citizen-sponsored ballot initiatives are permitted; in those jurisdictions, despite its defects, the referendum route may represent the reformers' best hope, building on

---

[11] Lesser 2010: 333–4.   [12] Daar 1995.

the original success in Oregon and the subsequent exporting of the Oregon model next door to Washington.

8.3 Last Words

Since I am a philosopher, and not a political activist or strategist, I don't know which of the foregoing routes is likeliest to lead to law reform for assisted death. Just as policies themselves may need to be adapted to local conditions, so also may advocacy tactics. These matters can, and should, be left to advocacy groups who know their own jurisdiction and its possibilities. The aim of this book has not been to recommend strategy but to show that a strong ethical case can be made for assisted death, that there are no persuasive ethical objections against it, that its legalization is called for by the civic virtues of compassion and respect, and that fears that legalization will have negative spillover effects are unwarranted.

At the outset of this book I introduced two fictional patients, Anita and Bill, both of whom are either currently experiencing or anticipating what they regard as intolerable suffering during the dying process. Both want to avoid further suffering by accelerating that process. At that point I asked two questions: what options are available to them to enable them to minimize their suffering? What options should be available? We now have answers to these questions. If they live in a prohibitionist jurisdiction then they can hasten death by refusing food and fluids or, if the suffering becomes intense enough, combine that option with terminal sedation. I have argued that a society that practises the civic virtues of compassion and respect would expand their options to include assisted death. Speaking more personally, I want these options to be available to me, should I ever be so unfortunate as to be in need of them. Since I live in a prohibitionist jurisdiction, this will happen only if the question can be put to serious debate in the public and political forum. This book is meant as a contribution to that debate.

Cases Cited

A.C. (2009)	*A.C.* v. *Manitoba (Director of Child and Family Services)* (2009) 2 SCR 181
Baxter (2009)	*Baxter* v. *Montana* (2009) MT 449
Bland (1993)	*Airedale NHS Trust* v. *Bland* (1993) 1 All ER 821
Bouvia (1986)	*Bouvia* v. *Superior Court* (1986) 225 Cal. R.ptr. 297 (Cal. App. 2 Dist.)
Burke (2004)	*R (on the application of Burke)* v. *General Medical Council* (2004) EWHC 1879
Burke (2005)	*Burke, R (on the application of)* v. *General Medical Council* (2005) EWHC Civ 1003
Conroy (1985)	*In re Conroy* (1985) 98 NJ 321, 486 A.2d 1209
Cox (1992)	*R* v. *Cox* (18 September 1992 unreported), Crown Court at Winchester
Cruzan (1988)	*Cruzan* v. *Harmon* (1988) 760 SW.2d 408
Cruzan (1990)	*Cruzan* v. *Director, Missouri Department of Health* (1990) 497 US 261
de la Rocha (1993)	*R* v. *de la Rocha* (1993, 2 April) Ontario Court of Justice (unpublished)
Glucksberg (1997)	*Washington et al.* v. *Glucksberg et al.* (1997) 117 S.Ct. 2258
Gonzales (2006)	*Gonzales, Attorney General et al.* v. *Oregon et al.* (2006) 546 US
Latimer (1997*a*)	*R* v. *Latimer* (1997) 1 SCR 217
Latimer (1997*b*)	*R* v. *Latimer* (1997) 121 CCC (3d) 326
Latimer (1998)	*R* v. *Latimer* (1998) 131 CCC (3d) 191
Latimer (2001)	*R* v. *Latimer* (2001) 1 SCR 3
Lee (1995)	*Lee* v. *Oregon* (1995) 891 F. Supp. 1429 (D. Or.)
Lee (1997)	*Lee* v. *Oregon* (1997) 107 F.3d 1382 (9th Cir.)
Malette (1990)	*Malette* v. *Shulman* (1990) 72 OR (2d) 417 (CA)
Mataya (1992)	*R* v. *Mataya* (1992, 24 August) Ontario Court of Justice (unpublished)
Morgentaler (1988)	*R* v. *Morgentaler* (1988) 1 SCR 30
Morrison (1998*a*)	*R* v. *Morrison* (1998) NSJ No. 75, Case No. 720188
Morrison (1998*b*)	*R* v. *Morrison* (1998) NSJ No. 441, SH No. 147941
Ms B (2002)	*Ms B* v. *NHS Hospital Trust* (2002) EWHC 429 (Fam)
Nancy B (1992)	*Nancy B* v. *Hôtel-Dieu de Québec et al.* (1992) 86 DLR (4th) 385
Oakes (1986)	*R* v. *Oakes* (1986) 1 SCR 103

Oregon (2002)	*Oregon* v. *Ashcroft* (2002) 102 F. Supp. 2d 1077 (D. Or.)
Oregon (2004)	*Oregon* v. *Ashcroft* (2004) 368 F.3d 1118, CA 9 (Or.)
Perka (1984)	*Perka* v. *The Queen* (1984) 2 SCR 232
Pinzon-Reyes (1997*a*)	*Florida* v. *Pinzon Reyes* (26 June 1997), No. CF-96-0066A-XX, Florida Circuit Court, Highlands County
Pinzon-Reyes (1997*b*)	*Department of Health, Board of Medicine* v. *Ernesto Pinzon-Reyes* (20 October 1997), Case No. 97-0721
Pretty (2001)	*The Queen on the Application of Mrs Dianne Pretty (Appellant)* v. *Director of Public Prosecutions (Respondent) and Secretary of State for the Home Department (Interested Party)* (2001) UKHL 61
Pretty (2002)	*Pretty* v. *The United Kingdom*, No. 2346/02, ECHR 2002-III
Purdy (2009)	*R (on the application of Purdy)* v. *Director of Public Prosecutions* (2009) UKHL 45
Quill (1997)	*Vacco et al.* v. *Quill et al.* (1997) 117 S.Ct. 2293
Quinlan (1976)	*In re Quinlan* (1976) 355 A.2d 647 (NJ)
R.L. (1997)	*Child and Family Services of Manitoba* v. *R.L.* (1997) MJ No. 568
Rodriguez (1993a)	*Rodriguez* v. *British Columbia (Attorney General)* (1993) 76 BCLR (2d) 145
Rodriguez (1993b)	*Rodriguez* v. *British Columbia (Attorney General)* (1993) 3 SCR 519
Saikewicz (1977)	*Superintendent of Belchertown State School* v. *Saikewicz* (1977) 370 NE.2d 417 (Mass.)
Salgo (1957)	*Salgo* v. *Leland Stanford Jr Univ. Bd of Trustees* (1957) 317 P.2d 170 (Cal. Ct App.)
Sawatsky (1998)	*Sawatsky* v. *Riverview Health Centre Inc.* (1998) MJ No. 506 (QB)
Schloendorff (1914)	*Schloendorff* v. *Society of New York Hospital* (1914) 211 NY 125
Spring (1980)	*In re Spring* (1980) 405 NE.2d 115 (Mass.)
Wanglie (1991)	*In re Helga Wanglie* (1991), Fourth Judicial District (Dist. Ct. Probate Ct. Div.) PX-91-283, County of Hennepin, Minnesota
X.Y. (2006)	*X.Y.* v. *Health Directorate of the Canton of Zurich, Administrative Court of the Canton of Zurich, and Federal Department of Home Affairs* (2006, 3 November)

References

Ackerman, Felicia. 1998. 'Assisted Suicide, Terminal Illness, Severe Disability, and the Double Standard'. In Battin, Rhodes, and Silvers 1998.

Ad Hoc Committee of the Harvard Medical School. 1968. 'A Definition of Irreversible Coma'. *Journal of the American Medical Association* 205(6).

Admiraal, Peter. 2008. 'Physician-Assisted Suicide: A Doctor's Perspective'. In Birnbacher and Dahl 2008.

Allen, Woody. 1972. *Without Feathers*. New York: Random House.

Allmark, Peter, et al. 2010. 'Is the Doctrine of Double Effect Irrelevant in End-of-Life Decision Making?' *Nursing Philosophy* 11(3).

Angell, Marcia. 1991. 'The Case of Helga Wanglie: A New Kind of "Right to Die" Case'. *New England Journal of Medicine* 325(7).

—— 2004. 'The Quality of Mercy'. In Quill and Battin 2004b. Hopkins University Press.

Angus, Floyd, and Burakoff, Robert. 2003. 'The Percutaneous Endoscopic Gastrostomy Tube: Medical and Ethical Issues in Placement'. *American Journal of Gastroenterology* 98(2).

Arras, John D. 1998. 'Physician-Assisted Suicide: A Tragic View'. In Battin, Rhodes, and Silvers 1998.

Ashby, Michael. 1997. 'The Fallacies of Death Causation in Palliative Care'. *Medical Journal of Australia* 166(4).

Back, Anthony L., et al. 1996. 'Physician-Assisted Suicide and Euthanasia in Washington State'. *Journal of the American Medical Association* 275(12).

Baelz, P. R. 1980. 'Suicide: Some Theological Reflections'. In M. Pabst Battin and David J. Mayo (eds.), *Suicide: The Philosophical Issues*. New York: St Martin's Press.

Baezner-Sailer, Elke M. 2008. 'Physician-Assisted Suicide in Switzerland: A Personal Report'. In Birnbacher and Dahl 2008.

Baron, Charles H., et al. 1996. 'A Model State Act to Authorize and Regulate Physician-Assisted Suicide'. *Harvard Journal on Legislation* 33(1).

Batavia, Andrew I. 2004. 'Disability and Physician-Assisted Dying'. In Quill and Battin 2004b.

Battin, Margaret Pabst. 1994. *The Least Worst Death: Essays in Bioethics on the End of Life*. New York: Oxford University Press.

—— 2005. *Ending Life: Ethics and the Way We Die*. Oxford: Oxford University Press.

—— Rhodes, Rosamond, and Silvers, Anita (eds.) 1998. *Physician-Assisted Suicide: Expanding the Debate*. New York: Routledge.

—— et al. 2007. 'Legal Physician-Assisted Dying in Oregon and the Netherlands: Evidence Concerning the Impact on Patients in "Vulnerable" Groups'. *Journal of Medical Ethics* 33(10).

Baumrin, Bernard. 1998. 'Physician, Stay Thy Hand!' In Battin, Rhodes, and Silvers 1998.

Beauchamp, Tom L. 1993. 'Suicide'. In Tom Regan (ed.), *Matters of Life and Death: New Introductory Essays in Moral Philosophy*. 3rd edn. New York: Random House.

—— 1996a. 'Introduction'. In Beauchamp 1996b.

Beauchamp, Tom L. (ed.) 1996*b. Intending Death: The Ethics of Assisted Suicide and Euthanasia.* Upper Saddle River, NJ: Prentice-Hall.

—— and Childress, James F. 2009. *Principles of Biomedical Ethics.* 6th edn. New York: Oxford University Press.

Beaufort, Inez de. 2007. 'The View from Before'. *American Journal of Bioethics* 7(4).

Benjamin, Martin. 1976. 'Death, Where is Thy "Cause"?' *Hastings Centre Report* 6(3).

Bennett, Jonathan. 1995. *The Act Itself.* Oxford: Clarendon.

Benrubi, Guy I. 1992. 'Euthanasia—the Need for Procedural Safeguards'. *New England Journal of Medicine* 326(3).

Berg, Jessica W., et al. 2001. *Informed Consent: Legal Theory and Clinical Practice.* 2nd edn. Oxford: Oxford University Press.

Berger, Jeffrey T. 2005. 'Patients' Interests in Their Family Members' Well-Being: An Over-looked, Fundamental Consideration within Substituted Judgments'. *Journal of Clinical Ethics* 16(1).

Bernat, J. L., Gert, B., and Mogielnicki, R. P. 1993. 'Patient Refusal of Hydration and Nutrition—an Alternative to Physician-Assisted Suicide or Voluntary Active Euthanasia'. *Archives of Internal Medicine* 153(24).

Bernheim, Jan L., et al. 2008. 'Development of Palliative Care and Legalisation of Euthanasia: Antagonism or Synergy?' *British Medical Journal* 336(7649).

Bickenbach, Jerome E. 1998. 'Disability and Life-Ending Decisions'. In Battin, Rhodes, and Silvers 1998.

Billings, J. Andrew, and Block, Susan D. 1996. 'Slow Euthanasia'. *Journal of Palliative Care* 12(4).

Bilsen, Johan, et al. 2009. 'Medical End-of-Life Practices Under the Euthanasia Law in Belgium'. *New England Journal of Medicine* 361(11).

Bioethics Committee, Canadian Paediatric Society. 2008. 'Advance Care Planning for Paedi-atric Patients'. *Paediatrics and Child Health* 13(9).

Birnbacher, Dieter, and Dahl, Edgar (eds.) 2008. *Giving Death a Helping Hand: Physician-Assisted Suicide and Public Policy, an International Perspective.* New York: Springer.

Bosshard, Georg, and Ziegler, Stephen J. 2007. 'Role of Non-Governmental Organizations in Physician Assisted Suicide'. *British Medical Journal* 334.

Boyle, Joseph. 1980. 'Toward Understanding the Principle of Double Effect'. *Ethics* 90(4).

—— 1991. 'Who is Entitled to Double Effect?' *Journal of Medicine and Philosophy* 16.

—— 1995. 'A Case for Sometimes Tube-Feeding Patients in Persistent Vegetative State'. In Keown 1995.

—— 2004. 'Medical Ethics and Double Effect: The Case of Terminal Sedation'. *Theoretical Medicine and Bioethics* 25(1).

Bradley, Ben. 2004. 'When is Death Bad for the One Who Dies?' *Nous* 38(1).

—— 2007. 'How Bad is Death?' *Canadian Journal of Philosophy* 37(1).

—— 2008. 'The Worst Time to Die'. *Ethics* 118(2).

Brandt, Richard B. 1975. 'The Morality and Rationality of Suicide'. In Seymour Perlin (ed.), *A Handbook for the Study of Suicide,* New York: Oxford University Press.

Bratman, Michael E. 1987. *Intentions, Plans, and Practical Reason.* Cambridge, Mass.: Harvard University Press.

Brazier, M. 2004. 'Letting Charlotte Die'. *Journal of Medical Ethics* 30(6).

Brennan, Samantha. 1995. 'Thresholds for Rights'. *Southern Journal of Philosophy* 33(2).

British Medical Association. 2006. *End-of-Life Decisions: Views of the BMA*. London: BMA.

Brock, Dan W. 1991. 'Decisionmaking Competence and Risk'. *Bioethics* 5(2).

—— 1993. *Life and Death: Philosophical Essays in Biomedical Ethics*. Cambridge: Cambridge University Press.

—— 2004. 'Physician-Assisted Suicide as a Last-Resort Option at the End of Life'. In Quill and Battin 2004.

Brody, Baruch. 1995. 'Withdrawal of Treatment Versus Killing of Patients'. In Beauchamp 1996*b*.

Broeckaert, Bert. 2001. 'Belgium: Towards a Legal Recognition of Euthanasia'. *European Journal of Health Law* 8(2).

Broome, John. 2004. *Weighing Lives*. Oxford: Oxford University Press.

Brown, Bryson. 2010. 'Robert Latimer's Choice'. In Michael Stingl (ed.), *The Price of Compassion: Assisted Suicide and Euthanasia in Canada and the United States*. Peterborough: Broadview.

Buchanan, Allen, and Brock, Dan W. 1989. *Deciding for Others; The Ethics of Surrogate Decision Making*. Cambridge: Cambridge University Press.

Buiting, H. M., et al. 2010. 'Physicians' Labelling of End-of-Life Practices: A Hypothetical Case Study'. *Journal of Medical Ethics* 36(1).

Campbell, Courtney S., and Cox, Jessica C. 2010. 'Hospice and Physician-Assisted Death: Collaboration, Compliance, and Complicity'. *Hastings Center Report* 40(5).

Cantor, Norman L. 1993. *Advance Directives and the Pursuit of Death with Dignity*. Bloomington, Ind.: Indiana University Press.

Capron, Alexander Morgan. 1991. 'In Re Helga Wanglie'. *Hastings Center Report* 21(5).

Cassell, Eric J. 2004. 'When Suffering Patients Seek Death'. In Quill and Battin 2004.

—— and Rich, Ben A. 2010. 'Intractable End-of-Life Suffering and the Ethics of Palliative Sedation'. *Pain Medicine* 11(3).

Cavanaugh, T. A. 2006. *Double-Effect Reasoning: Doing Good and Avoiding Evil*. Oxford: Clarendon.

Ceaser, Mike. 2008. 'Euthanasia in Legal Limbo in Colombia'. *The Lancet* 371(9609).

Chambaere, Kenneth, et al. 2010. 'Physician-Assisted Deaths Under the Euthanasia Law in Belgium: A Population-Based Study'. *Canadian Medical Association Journal* 182(9).

Chang, Ruth. 1997. 'Introduction'. In Ruth Chang, (ed.), *Incommensurability, Incomparability, and Practical Reason*. Cambridge, Mass.: Harvard University Press.

Chater, Susan, et al. 1998. 'Sedation for Intractable Distress in the Dying: A Survey of Experts'. *Palliative Medicine* 12(4).

Chernevak, Frank A., McCullough, Laurence B., and Arabin, Birgit. 2006. 'Why the Groningen Protocol Should be Rejected'. *Hastings Center Report* 36(5).

Cherny, Nathan I., and Portenoy, Russell K. 1994. 'Sedation in the Management of Refractory Symptoms: Guidelines for Evaluation and Treatment'. *Journal of Palliative Care* 10(2).

Claessens, Patricia, et al. 2008. 'Palliative Sedation: A Review of the Research Literature'. *Journal of Pain and Symptom Management* 36(3).

Clark, David, et al. 2001. 'UK Geriatricians' Attitudes to Active Voluntary Euthanasia and Physician-Assisted Death'. *Age and Ageng* 30(5).

Cohen-Almagor, Raphael. 2001. *The Right to Die with Dignity: An Argument in Ethics, Medicine, and Law*. New Brunswick, NJ: Rutgers University Press.

Cohen-Almagor, Raphael 2004. *Euthanasia in the Netherlands: The Policy and Practice of Mercy Killing*. Dordrecht: Kluwer Academic.

Coleman, Diane. 2010. 'Assisted Suicide Laws Create Discriminatory Double Standard for Who Gets Suicide Prevention and Who Gets Suicide Assistance: Not Dead Yet Responds to Autonomy, Inc'. *Disability and Health Journal* 3(1).

Collège des Médecins du Quèbec. 2009. *Physicians, Appropriate Care and the Debate on Euthanasia: A Reflection*. Montreal: CMQ.

College of Physicians and Surgeons of Manitoba. 2007. 'Withholding and Withdrawing Life-Sustaining Treatment'. Statement no. 1602. Winnipeg: CPSM.

Combs Lee, Barbara. 2004. 'A Model That Integrates Assisted Dying with Excellent End-of-Life Care'. In Quill and Battin 2004.

Crown Prosecution Service. 2008. 'Decision on Prosecution—the Death by Suicide of Daniel James'.

Crown Prosecution Service. 2009. 'Interim Policy for Prosecutors in Respect of Cases of Assisted Suicide'. London: CPS.

—— 2010. 'Policy for Prosecutors in Respect of Cases of Encouraging or Assisting Suicide'. London: CPS.

Cuskelly, M., and Dadds, M. 1992. 'Behavioral Problems in Children with Down's Syndrome and their Siblings'. *Journal of Child Psychology and Psychiatry* 33(4).

—— and Gunn, P. 1993. 'Maternal Reports of Behavior of Siblings of Children with Down Syndrome'. *American Journal on Mental Retardation* 97(5).

D'Oronzio, Joseph C. 2002. 'The Suicide Note'. *Cambridge Quarterly of Healthcare Ethics* 11(4).

Daar, Judith F. 1995. 'Direct Democracy and Bioethical Choices: Voting Life and Death at the Ballot Box'. *University of Michigan Journal of Law Reform* 28(4).

Davis, Dena S. 1998. 'Why Suicide is Like Contraception: A Woman-Centered View'. In Battin, Rhodes, and Silvers 1998.

Davis, John K. 2002. 'The Concept of Precedent Autonomy'. *Bioethics* 16(2).

DeCesare, Michael A. 2000. 'Public Attitudes Toward Euthanasia and Suicide for Terminally Ill Persons: 1977 and 1996'. *Social Biology* 47(3/4).

De Graeff, Alexander, and Dean, Mervyn. 2007. 'Palliative Sedation Therapy in the Last Weeks of Life: A Literature Review and Recommendations for Standards'. *Journal of Palliative Medicine* 10(1).

DeGrazia, David. 2005. *Human Identity and Bioethics*. Cambridge: Cambridge University Press.

Delden, Johannes J. M. van. 2004. 'The Unfeasibility of Requests for Euthanasia in Advance Directives'. *Journal of Medical Ethics* 30(5).

—— Visser, Jaap J. F., and Borst-Eilers, Els. 2004. 'Thirty Years' Experience with Euthanasia in the Netherlands'. In Quill and Battin 2004*b*.

Deliens, L., et al. 2000. 'End-of-Life Decisions in Medical Practice in Flanders, Belgium: A Nationwide Survey'. *Lancet* 356(9244).

Dickinson, George E., et al. 2002. 'U.K. Physicians' Attitudes toward Active Voluntary Euthanasia and Physician-Assisted Suicide'. *Death Studies* 26(6).

—— 2005. 'US Physicians' Attitudes Concerning Euthanasia and Physician-Assisted Death: A Systematic Literature Review'. *Mortality* 10(1).

Donagan, Alan. 1977. *The Theory of Morality*. Chicago: University of Chicago Press.

——Kerridge, Ian, and Ankeny, Rachel. 2008. 'Managing Intentions: The End-of-Life Administration of Analgesics and Sedatives, and the Possibility of Slow Euthanasia'. *Bioethics* 22(7).

Doukas, D. J., et al. 1995. 'Attitudes and Behaviors on Physician-Assisted Death: A Study of Michigan Oncologists'. *Journal of Clinical Oncology* 13(5).

Downie, Jocelyn. 2004. *Dying Justice: A Case for Decriminalizing Euthanasia and Assisted Suicide in Canada*. Toronto: University of Toronto Press.

——and Anthony, Karen. 1998. 'The Push-Me/Pull-You of Euthanasia in Canada: A Chronology of the Nancy Morrison Case'. *Health Law Review* 7(2).

——and Bern, Simone. 2009. 'Rodriguez Redux'. *Health Law Journal* 16.

Dresser, Rebecca. 1986. 'Life, Death, and Incompetent Patients: Conceptual Infirmities and Hidden Values in the Law'. *Arizona Law Review* 28(3).

Dresser, Rebecca. 1989. 'Advance Directives, Self-Determination, and Personal Identity'. In Chris Hackler, Ray Moseley, and Dorothy E. Vawter (eds.), *Advance Directives in Medicine*. New York: Praeger.

——1994. 'Advance Directives: Implications for Policy'. *Hastings Center Report* 24(6).

——1995. 'Dworkin on Dementia: Elegant Theory, Questionable Policy'. *Hastings Center Report* 25(6).

——2003. 'Precommitment: A Misguided Strategy for Securing Death with Dignity'. *Texas Law Review* 81(7).

Drum, Charles E., et al. 2010. 'The Oregon Death with Dignity Act: Results of a Literature Review and Naturalistic Inquiry'. *Disability and Health Journal* 3(1).

Dussel, Veronica, et al. 2010. 'Considerations About Hastening Death Among Parents of Children Who Die of Cancer'. *Archives of Pediatric and Adolescent Medicine* 164(3).

Dworkin, Gerald. 2008. 'Should Physician-Assisted Suicide be Legalized?' In Birnbacher and Dahl 2008.

Dworkin, Ronald. 1993. *Life's Dominion: An Argument About Abortion, Euthanasia, and Individual Freedom*. New York: Random House.

Eliott, Jaklin A., and Olver, Ian N. 2008. 'Dying Cancer Patients Talk About Euthanasia'. *Social Science and Medicine* 67(4).

Elliston, Sarah. 2007. *The Best Interests of the Child in Healthcare*. Abingdon: Routledge-Cavendish.

Emanuel, Ezekiel J., et al. 1996. 'Euthanasia and Physician-Assisted Suicide: Attitudes and Experiences of Oncology Patients, Oncologists, and the Public'. *Lancet* 347(9018).

——et al. 2000. 'Attitudes and Practices of U.S. Oncologists Regarding Euthanasia and Physician-Assisted Suicide'. *Annals of Internal Medicine* 133(7).

——Fairclough, Diane L., and Emanuel, Linda L. 2000. 'Attitudes and Desires Related to Euthanasia and Physician-Assisted Suicide among Terminally Ill Patients and their Caregivers'. *Journal of the American Medical Association* 284(19).

Emanuel, Linda L. 1994. 'What Makes a Directive Valid?' *Hastings Center Report* 24(6).

——and Emanuel, Ezekiel J. 1989. 'The Medical Directive: A New Comprehensive Advance Care Document'. *Journal of the American Medical Association* 261(22).

Engelhardt, Tristram. 1975. 'Defining Death: A Philosophical Problem for Medicine and Law'. *Annual Review of Respiratory Disease* 112.

Epicurus. 1940. 'Letter to Menoeceus'. In *The Stoic and Epicurean Philosophers: The Complete Extant Writings of Epicurus, Epictetus, Lucretius, Marcus Aurelius*, ed. Whitney J. Oates. New York: Modern Library.

Fadem, Pamela, et al. 2003. 'Attitudes of People with Disabilities Toward Physician-Assisted Suicide Legislation: Broadening the Dialogue'. *Journal of Health Politics, Policy and Law* 28(6).

Faden, Ruth R., and Beauchamp, Tom L. 1986. *A History and Theory of Informed Consent*. New York: Oxford University Press.

Fang, Fang, et al. 2008. 'Suicide Among Patients with Amyotrophic Lateral Sclerosis'. *Brain* 131(10).

Feinberg, Joel. 1978. 'Voluntary Euthanasia and the Inalienable Right to Life'. *Philosophy & Public Affairs* 7(2).

Feldman, David B. 2006. 'Can Suicide be Ethical? A Utilitarian Perspective on the Appropriateness of Choosing to Die'. *Death Studies* 30(6).

Feldman, Fred. 1992. *Confrontations with the Reaper: A Philosophical Study of the Nature and Value of Death*. New York: Oxford University Press.

Finnis, John. 1980. *Natural Law and Natural Rights*. Oxford: Clarendon.

—— 1983. *Fundamentals of Ethics*. Washington: Georgetown University Press.

—— 1995. 'A Philosophical Case Against Euthanasia'. In Keown 1995.

—— Boyle, Joseph M., Jr., and Grisez, Germain. 1987. *Nuclear Deterrence, Morality and Realism*. Oxford: Clarendon.

Finucane, Thomas E., Christmas, Colleen, and Travis, Kathy. 1999. 'Tube Feeding in Patients with Advanced Dementia: A Review of the Evidence'. *Journal of the American Medical Association* 282(14).

Firlik, Andrew D. 1991. 'Margo's Logo'. *Journal of the American Medical Association* 265(2).

Fischer, S., et al. 2008. 'Suicide Assisted by Two Swiss Right-to-Die Organisations'. *Journal of Medical Ethics* 34(11).

Fohr, Susan Anderson. 1998. 'The Double Effect of Pain Medication: Separating Myth from Reality'. *Journal of Palliative Medicine* 1(4).

Foley, Kathleen, and Hendin, Herbert. 2002. 'The Oregon Experiment'. In Kathleen Foley and Herbert Hendin (eds.), *The Case Against Assisted Suicide: For the Right to End-of-Life Care*. Baltimore: Johns Hopkins University Press.

Folker, Anna P., et al. 1996. 'Experiences and Attitudes towards End-of-Life Decisions amongst Danish Physicians'. *Bioethics* 10(3).

Foot, Philippa. 1977. 'Euthanasia'. *Philosophy & Public Affairs* 6(2).

—— 1984. 'Killing and Letting Die'. In Jay L. Garfield and Patricia Hennessey (eds.), *Abortion and Legal Perspectives*. Amherst: University of Massachusetts Press.

Francis, Leslie Pickering. 1998. 'Assisted Suicide: Are the Elderly a Special Case?' In Battin, Rhodes, and Silvers 1998.

Frey, Raymond G. 1975. 'Some Aspects to the Doctrine of Double Effect'. *Canadian Journal of Philosophy* 5(2).

Fried, Terri R., et al. 1993. 'The Limits of Patient Autonomy: Physician Attitudes and Practices Regarding Life-Sustaining Treatments and Euthanasia'. *Archives of Internal Medicine* 153(6).

Ganzini, Linda. 2004. 'The Oregon Experience'. In Quill and Battin 2004.

——and Dahl, Edgar. 2008. 'Physician-Assisted Suicide in Oregon'. In Birnbacher and Dahl 2008.

——Goy, Elizabeth R., and Dobscha, Steven K. 2009. 'Oregonians' Reasons for Requesting Physician Aid in Dying'. *Archives of Internal Medicine* 169(5).

——2010. 'Strange Deathbedfellows'. *Hastings Center Report* 40(5).

——et al. 1998. 'Attitudes of Patients with Amyotrophic Lateral Sclerosis and their Care Givers toward Assisted Suicide'. *New England Journal of Medicine* 339(14).

——2001. 'Oregon Physicians' Attitudes about and Experiences with End-of-Life Care Since the Passage of the Oregon Death with Dignity Act'. *Journal of the American Medical Association* 285(18).

——2003. 'Nurses' Experiences with Hospice Patients Who Refuse Food and Fluids to Hasten Death'. *New England Journal of Medicine* 349(4).

Gastmans, Chris, and Lepelere, Jan de. 2010. 'Living to the Bitter End? A Personalist Approach to Euthanasia in Persons with Severe Dementia'. *Bioethics* 24(2).

Gaylin, Willard, et al. 1988. 'Doctors Must Not Kill'. *Journal of the American Medical Association* 259(14).

George, Katrina. 2007. 'A Woman's Choice? The Gendered Risks of Voluntary Euthanasia and Physician-Assisted Suicide'. *Medical Law Review* 15(1).

Gert, Bernard, Culver, Charles M., and Danner Clouser, K. 1998. 'An Alternative to Physician-Assisted Suicide'. In Battin, Rhodes, and Silvers 1998.

Gill, Michael B. 2009. 'Is the Legalization of Physician-Assisted Suicide Compatible with Good End-of-Life Care?' *Journal of Applied Philosophy* 26(1).

Gillick, Muriel R. 2000. 'Rethinking the Role of Tube Feeding in Patients with Advanced Dementia'. *New England Journal of Medicine* 342(3).

Glover, Jonathan. 1977. *Causing Death and Saving Lives.* Harmondsworth: Penguin.

Goering, Sara. 2007. 'What Makes Suffering "Unbearable and Hopeless"? Advance Directives, Dementia and Disability'. *American Journal of Bioethics* 7(4).

Golden, Marilyn, and Zoanni, Tyler. 2010. 'Killing Us Softly: The Dangers of Legalizing Assisted Suicide'. *Disability and Health Journal* 3(1).

Goodwin, Peter. 2004. 'The Distortion of Cases in Oregon'. In Quill and Battin 2004b.

Gorsuch, Neil M. 2006. *The Future of Assisted Suicide and Euthanasia.* Princeton, NJ: Princeton University Press.

Goy, Elizabeth R., et al. 2003. 'Oregon Hospice Nurses' and Social Workers' Assessment of Physician Progress in Palliative Care Over the Past 5 Years'. *Palliative and Supportive Care* 1(3).

Greasley, Kate. 2010. '*R(Purdy)* v *DPP* and the Case for Wilful Blindness'. *Oxford Journal of Legal Studies* 30(2).

Green, Michael, and Wikler, Daniel. 1980. 'Brain Death and Personal Identity'. *Philosophy & Public Affairs* 9(2).

Griffin, James. 1986. *Well-Being: Its Meaning, Measurement and Moral Importance.* Oxford: Clarendon.

Griffiths, John, Bood, Alex, and Weyers, Heleen 1998. *Euthanasia and Law in the Netherlands.* Amsterdam: Amsterdam University Press.

——Weyers, Heleen, and Adams, Maurice. 2008. *Euthanasia and Law in Europe.* Oxford: Hart.

Groenewoud, Johanna H., et al. 2000. 'Clinical Problems with the Performance of Euthanasia and Physician-Assisted Suicide in the Netherlands'. *New England Journal of Medicine* 342(8).

Hagelin, J., et al. 2004. 'Surveys on Attitudes towards Legalisation of Euthanasia: Importance of Question Phrasing'. *Journal of Medical Ethics* 30(6).

Hart, H. L. A., and Honoré, Tony. 1985. *Causation in the Law*. 2nd edn. Oxford: Clarendon.

Haverkate, Ilinka, et al. 2001. 'The Emotional Impact on Physicians of Hastening the Death of a Patient'. *Medical Journal of Australia* 175(10).

Heide, Agnes van der, et al. 2003. 'End-of-Life Decision-Making in Six European Countries: Descriptive Study'. *Lancet* 361(9381).

—— 2007. 'End-of-Life Practices in the Netherlands under the Euthanasia Act'. *New England Journal of Medicine* 356(19).

Hemmings, P. 2003. 'Dying Wishes'. *Nursing Times* 99(47).

Hendin, Herbert, and Foley, Kathleen. 2008. 'Physician-Assisted Suicide in Oregon: A Medical Perspective'. *Issues in Law and Medicine* 24(2).

Hertogh, Cees M. P. M. 2009. 'The Role of Advance Euthanasia Directives as an Aid to Communication and Shared Decision-Making in Dementia'. *Journal of Medical Ethics* 35(2).

—— et al. 2007. 'Would We Rather Lose Our Life than Lose Our Self? Lessons from the Dutch Debate on Euthanasia for Patients with Dementia'. *American Journal of Bioethics* 7(4).

Higgins, Philip C., and Altilio, Terry. 2007. 'Palliative Sedation: An Essential Place for Clinical Excellence'. *Journal of Social Work in End-of-Life & Palliative Care* 3(4).

Holt, Janet. 2008. 'Nurses' Attitudes to Euthanasia: The Influence of Empirical Studies and Methodological Concerns on Nursing Practice'. *Nursing Philosophy* 9(4).

Hurka, Thomas. 1993. *Perfectionism*. New York: Oxford University Press.

—— 2005. 'Proportionality in the Morality of War'. *Philosophy and Public Affairs* 33(1).

—— 2008. 'Proportionality and Necessity'. In Larry May (ed.), *War: Essays in Political Philosophy*. Cambridge: Cambridge University Press.

Hutchinson, Brian. 1995. 'Latimer's Choice'. *Saturday Night* 110 (March).

Huxtable, Richard. 2007. *Euthanasia, Ethics and the Law: From Conflict to Compromise*. Abingdon: Routledge-Cavendish.

Inghelbrecht, Els, et al. 2010. 'The Role of Nurses in Physician-Assisted Deaths in Belgium'. *Canadian Medical Association Journal* 182(9).

Jacobs, Sandra. 2003. 'Death by Voluntary Dehydration—What the Caregivers Say'. *New England Journal of Medicine* 349(4).

Jaworska, Agnieszka. 1999. 'Respecting the Margins of Agency: Alzheimer's Patients and the Capacity to Value'. *Philosophy & Public Affairs* 28(2).

Joffe, Ari. 2010. 'Are Recent Defences of the Brain Death Concept Adequate?' *Bioethics* 24(2).

Joiner, Thomas. 2010. *Myths About Suicide*. Cambridge, Mass.: Harvard University Press.

Jotkowitz, Alan, Glick, S., and Gesundheit, B. 2008. 'A Case Against Justified Non-Voluntary Active Euthanasia (the Groningen Protocol)'. *American Journal of Bioethics* 8(11).

Kagan, Shelly. 1988. 'The Additive Fallacy'. *Ethics* 99(1).

—— 1989. *The Limits of Morality*. Oxford: Clarendon.

Kamisar, Yale. 1958. 'Some Non-Religious Views Against Proposed "Mercy-Killing" Legislation'. *Minnesota Law Review* 42(6).

—— 1995. 'Physician-Assisted Suicide: The Last Bridge to Active Voluntary Euthanasia'. In Keown 1995.

Kass, Leon R. 1989. 'Neither for Love nor Money: Why Doctors Must Not Kill'. *The Public Interest* 94.

Kaveny, M. Kathleen. 2004. 'Inferring Intention from Foresight'. *Law Quarterly Review* 120.

Keizer, Bert. 1997. *Dancing with Mr. D: Notes on Life and Death*. New York: Nan A. Talese.

Keown, John (ed.) 1995. *Euthanasia Examined: Ethical, Clinical and Legal Perspectives*. Cambridge: Cambridge University Press.

—— 2002. *Euthanasia, Ethics and Public Policy: An Argument Against Legalisation*. Cambridge: Cambridge University Press.

Keyserlingk, Edward W. 1994. 'Assisted Suicide, Causality, and the Supreme Court of Canada'. *McGill Law Journal* 39(3).

Kimsma, Gerrit K., and van Leeuwen, Evert. 2004. 'Assisted Death in the Netherlands: Physicians at the Bedside When Help is Requested'. In Quill and Battin 2004*b*.

Kitching, Mark, Stevens, Andrew James, and Forman, Louise. 2008. 'Views Regarding Physician-Assisted Suicide: A Study of Medical Professionals at Various Points in Their Training'. *Clinical Ethics* 3(1).

Kon, Alexander A. 2007. 'Neonatal Euthanasia is Unsupportable: The Groningen Protocol Should be Abandoned'. *Theoretical Medicine and Bioethics* 28(5).

—— 2008. 'We Cannot Accurately Predict the Extent of an Infant's Future Suffering: The Groningen Protocol is Too Dangerous to Support'. *American Journal of Bioethics* 8(11).

Krahn, Gloria L. 2010. 'Reflections on the Debate on Disability and Aid in Dying'. *Disability and Health Journal* 3(1).

Kuhse, Helga. 1999. 'Some Reflections on the Problem of Advance Directives, Personhood, and Personal Identity'. *Kennedy Institute of Ethics Journal* 9(4).

—— and Singer, Peter. 1985. *Should the Baby Live? The Problem of Handicapped Infants*. Oxford: Oxford University Press.

—— et al. 1997. 'End-of-Life Decisions in Australian Medical Practice'. *Medical Journal of Australia* 166(4).

Laureys, Steven. 2005. 'Death, Unconsciousness and the Brain'. *Nature Reviews Neuroscience* 6(11).

Laureys, Steven. 2007. 'Eyes Open, Brain Shut'. *Scientific American* 296(5).

Law Reform Commission of Canada. 1981. *Criteria for the Determination of Death*. Ottawa: Minister of Supply and Services Canada.

—— 1983. *Euthanasia, Aiding Suicide and Cessation of Treatment*. Ottawa: Minister of Supply and Services Canada.

Lee, Melinda A., et al. 1996. 'Legalizing Assisted Suicide—Views of Physicians in Oregon'. *New England Journal of Medicine* 334(5).

Lemmens, Trudo, and Dickens, Bernard. 2001. 'Canadian Law on Euthanasia: Contrasts and Comparisons'. *European Journal of Health Law* 8(2).

Lesser, Harry. 2010. 'Should It be Legal to Assist Suicide?' *Journal of Evaluation in Clinical Practice* 16(2).

Lester, David. 2006. 'Can Suicide be a Good Death?' *Death Studies* 30(6).

Levy, Neil. 2008. 'Slippery Slopes and Physician-Assisted Suicide'. In Birnbacher and Dahl 2008.

Lewis, Penney. 2007. *Assisted Dying and Legal Change*. Oxford: Oxford University Press.

—— 2009. 'Euthanasia in Belgium Five Years After Legalisation'. *European Journal of Health Law* 16.

Lindemann, Hilde, and Verkerk, Marian. 2008. 'Ending the Life of a Newborn: The Groningen Protocol'. *Hastings Center Report* 38(1).

Lorber, John. 1975. 'Ethical Problems in the Management of Myelomeningocele and Hydrocephalus'. *Journal of the Royal College of Physicians* 10(1).

Lucretius. 1940. 'On the Nature of Things'. In *The Stoic and Epicurean Philosophers: The Complete Extant Writings of Epicurus, Epictetus, Lucretius, Marcus Aurelius*, ed. Whitney J. Oates. New York: Modern Library.

Luper, Steven. 2007. 'Mortal Harm'. *Philosophical Quarterly* 57(227).

Maas, P. J. van der, van Delden, J. J. M., and Pijnenborg, L. 1992. 'Euthanasia and Other Medical Decisions Concerning the End of Life'. *Health Policy* 22(1–2), *The Remmelink Report*.

—— et al. 1991. 'Euthanasia and Other Medical Decisions Concerning the End of Life'. *Lancet* 338.

—— 1996. 'Euthanasia, Physician-Assisted Suicide, and Other Medical Practices Involving the End of Life in the Netherlands, 1990–1995'. *New England Journal of Medicine* 335(22).

Macauley, Robert C. 2007. 'The Role of Substituted Judgment in the Aftermath of a Suicide Attempt'. *Journal of Clinical Ethics* 18(2).

McIntyre, Alison. 2001. 'Doing Away with Double Effect'. *Ethics* 111(2).

—— 2004. 'Doctrine of Double Effect'. In *The Stanford Encyclopedia of Philosophy* (Fall 2004 edn), ed. Edward N. Zalta. <//plato.stanford.edu/archives/fall2004/entries/double-effect/>, accessed January 2011.

—— 2009. 'Doctrine of Double Effect'. In *The Stanford Encyclopedia of Philosophy* (Spring 2009 edn), ed. Edward N. Zalta. <//plato.stanford.edu/archives/spr2009/entries/double-effect/>, accessed January 2011.

McLean, Sheila A. M. 2007. *Assisted Dying: Reflections on the Need for Law Reform*. Abingdon: Routledge-Cavendish.

—— and Williamson, Laura. 2007. *Impairment and Disability: Law and Ethics at the Beginning and End of Life*. Abingdon: Routledge-Cavendish.

McMahan, Jeff. 1988. 'Death and the Value of Life'. *Ethics* 99(1).

—— 2002. *The Ethics of Killing: Problems at the Margins of Life*. Oxford: Oxford University Press.

Maltoni, M., et al. 2009. 'Palliative Sedation Therapy Does not Hasten Death: Results from a Prospective Multicenter Study'. *Annals of Oncology* 20(7).

Mangan, Joseph. 1949. 'An Historical Analysis of the Principle of Double Effect'. *Theological Studies* 10.

Mann, J. John. 2002. 'A Current Perspective of Suicide and Attempted Suicide'. *Annals of Internal Medicine* 136(4).

Manninen, Bertha. 2006. 'A Case for Justified Non-Voluntary Active Euthanasia: Exploring the Ethics of the Groningen Protocol'. *Journal of Medical Ethics* 32(11).

Manninen, Bertha. 2008. 'Revisiting Justified Nonvoluntary Euthanasia'. *American Journal of Bioethics* 8(11).

Manson, Neil C., and O'Neill, Onora. 2007. *Rethinking Informed Consent in Bioethics*. Cambridge: Cambridge University Press.

Marcoux, Isabelle, Mishara, Brian L., and Durand, Claire. 2007. 'Confusion Between Euthanasia and Other End-of-Life Decisions'. *Canadian Journal of Public Health* 98(3).

Marquet, R. L., et al. 2003. 'Twenty Five Years of Requests for Euthanasia and Physician Assisted Suicide in Dutch General Practice: Trend Analysis'. *British Medical Journal* 327(7408).

Marquis, Donald B. 1991. 'Four Versions of Double Effect'. *Journal of Medicine and Philosophy* 16.

—— 1998. 'The Weakness of the Case for Legalizing Physician-Assisted Suicide'. In Battin, Rhodes, and Silvers 1998.

Mayerfeld, Jamie. 1999. *Suffering and Moral Responsibility*. New York: Oxford University Press.

Meier, Diane E., et al. 1998. 'A National Survey of Physician-Assisted Suicide and Euthanasia in the United States'. *New England Journal of Medicine* 338(17).

Miccinesi, Guido, et al. 2006. 'Continuous Deep Sedation: Physicians' Experiences in Six European Countries'. *Journal of Pain and Symptom Management* 31(2).

Michlowski, Sabine. 2009. 'Legalising Active Voluntary Euthanasia through the Courts: Some Lessons from Colombia'. *Michigan Law Review* 17(2).

Miles, Steven H. 1991. 'Informed Demand for "Non-Beneficial" Medical Treatment'. *New England Journal of Medicine* 325(7).

Mill, John Stuart. 1977 (original publication 1861). 'On Liberty'. In *Essays on Politics and Society*, ed. J. M. Robson. Toronto: University of Toronto Press.

Miller, Franklin G., et al. 1994. 'Regulating Physician-Assisted Death'. *New England Journal of Medicine* 331(2).

—— and Meier, Diane E. 1998. 'Voluntary Death: A Comparison of Terminal Dehydration and Physician-Assisted Suicide'. *Annals of Internal Medicine* 128(7).

Monti, Martin M., et al. 2010. 'Willful Modulation of Brain Activity in Disorders of Consciousness'. *New England Journal of Medicine* 362.

Morita, Tatsuya, et al. 2001. 'Effects of High Dose Opioids and Sedatives on Survival in Terminally Ill Cancer Patients'. *Journal of Pain and Symptom Management* 21(4).

Multi-Society Task Force on PVS. 1994a. 'Medical Aspects of the Persistent Vegetative State—First of Two Parts'. *New England Journal of Medicine* 330(21).

—— 1994b. 'Medical Aspects of the Persistent Vegetative State—Second of Two Parts'. *New England Journal of Medicine* 330(22).

Nagel, Thomas. 1979. 'Death'. In id., *Mortal Questions*. Cambridge: Cambridge University Press.

—— 1986. *The View from Nowhere*. New York: Oxford University Press.

New York State Task Force on Life and the Law. 1994. 'When Death is Sought: Assisted Suicide and Euthanasia in the Medical Context'. New York: NY State Task Force on Life and the Law.

Nuffield Council on Bioethics. 2006. *Critical Care Decisions in Fetal and Neonatal Medicine: Ethical Issues*. London: Nuffield Council on Bioethics.

Nuland, Sherwin B. 1993. *How We Die: Reflections on Life's Final Chapter*. New York: Alfred A. Knopf.

Nuremberg Tribunal. 1947. 'The Nuremberg Code'. In A. Mitscherlich and F. Mielke, *Doctors of Infamy: The Story of the Nazi Medical Crimes*. New York: Schuman.

Nys, Herman. 1997. 'Advice of the Federal Advisory Committee on Bioethics Concerning Legalisation of Euthanasia'. *European Journal of Health Law* 4(4).

—— 2003. 'A Presentation of the Belgian Act on Euthanasia against the Background of Dutch Euthanasia Law'. *European Journal of Health Law* 10.

O'Neill, C., et al. 2002. 'Attitudes to Physician and Family Assisted Suicide: Results from a Study of Public Attitudes in Britain'. *Journal of Medical Ethics* 28(1).

Obstein, K. L., Kimsma, G., and Chambers, T. 2004. 'Practicing Euthanasia: The Perspective of Physicians'. *Journal of Clinical Ethics* 15(3).

Ogden, Russel D., Hamilton, William K., and Whitcher, Charles. 2010. 'Assisted Suicide by Oxygen Deprivation with Helium at a Swiss Right-to-Die Organisation'. *Journal of Medical Ethics* 36(3).

Olick, Robert S. 2001. *Taking Advance Directives Seriously*. Washington: Georgetown University Press.

Onwuteaka-Philipsen, Bregje D., et al. 2003. 'Euthanasia and Other End-of-Life Decisions in the Netherlands in 1990, 1995, and 2001'. *The Lancet* 362(9381).

Orentlicher, David. 1998. 'The Supreme Court and Terminal Sedation'. In Battin, Rhodes, and Silvers 1998.

Otlowski, Margaret. 1997. *Voluntary Euthanasia and the Common Law*. Oxford: Clarendon.

Pallis, Chris. 1983. *The ABC of Brain Death*. London: British Medical Journal Publishers.

—— and Harley, D. H. 1996. *The ABC of Brain Death*, 2nd edn. London: British Medical Journal Publishers.

Parfit, Derek. 1984. *Reasons and Persons*. Oxford: Oxford University Press.

Pasterfield, D., et al. 2006. 'GPs' Views on Changing the Law on Physician-Assisted Suicide and Euthanasia, and Willingness to Prescribe or Inject Lethal Drugs; a Survey from Wales'. *Journal of General Practice* 56(527).

Pearlman, Robert A., and Starks, Helene. 2004. 'Why Do People Seek Physician-Assisted Death?' In Quill and Battin 2004*b*.

Pedain, Antje. 2003. 'Intention and the Terrorist Example'. *Criminal Law Review*.

Pellegrino, Edmund D. 1992. 'Doctors Must Not Kill'. *Journal of Clinical Ethics* 3(2).

—— 1996. 'Distortion of the Healing Relationship'. In Tom L. Beauchamp and Robert M. Veatch (eds.), *Ethical Issues in Death and Dying*, 2nd edn. Upper Saddle River, NJ: Prentice Hall.

Pereira, José, et al. 2008. 'Assisted Suicide and Euthanasia Should not be Practiced in Palliative Care Units'. *Journal of Palliative Medicine* 11(8).

Pinter, Andrew B. 2008. 'End-of-Life Decision Before and After Birth: Changing Ethical Considerations'. *Journal of Pediatric Surgery* 43(3).

Porta, Nicolas, and Frader, Joel. 2007. 'Withholding Hydration and Nutrition in Newborns'. *Theoretical Medicine and Bioethics* 28(5).

President's Commission for the Study of Ethical Problems in Medicine and Biomedical and Behavioral Research. 1981. *Defining Death: Medical, Legal and Ethical Issues in the Determination of Death*. Washington, DC: US Government Printing Office.

—— 1987. *Deciding to Forgo Life-Sustaining Treatment: A Report on the Ethical, Medical, and Legal Issues in Treatment Decisions*. Washington, DC: US Government Printing Office.

Printz, L. A. 1992. 'Terminal Dehydration, a Compassionate Treatment'. *Archives of Internal Medicine* 152(4).

Provoost, Veerle, et al. 2005. 'Medical End-of-Life Decisions in Neonates and Infants in Flanders'. *The Lancet* 365(9467).

—— 2006. 'The Use of Drugs with a Life-Shortening Effect in End-of-Life Care in Neonates and Infants'. *Intensive Care Medicine* 32(1).

Pugliese, Julia. 1993. 'Don't Ask—Don't Tell: The Secret Practice of Physician-Assisted Suicide'. *Hastings Law Journal* 44(6).

Quill, Timothy E. 1991. 'Death and Dignity—a Case of Individualized Decision Making'. *New England Journal of Medicine* 324(10).

—— 1993. 'The Ambiguity of Clinical Intentions'. *New England Journal of Medicine* 329(14).

—— 1998. 'Principle of Double Effect and End-of-Life Pain Management: Additional Myths and a Limited Role'. *Journal of Palliative Medicine* 1(4).

—— 2007. 'Legal Regulation of Physician-Assisted Death—the Latest Report Cards'. *New England Journal of Medicine* 356(19).

—— and Battin, Margaret P. 2004a. 'Excellent Palliative Care as the Standard, Physician-Assisted Dying as a Last Resort'. In Quill and Battin 2004b.

—— —— (eds.) 2004b. *Physician-Assisted Dying: The Case for Palliative Care and Patient Choice.* Baltimore: Johns Hopkins University Press.

—— Cassel, Christine K., and Meier, Diane E. 1992. 'Care of the Hopelessly Ill: Proposed Clinical Criteria for Physician-Assisted Suicide'. *New England Journal of Medicine* 327(19).

—— Lo, Bernard, and Brock, Dan W. 1997. 'Palliative Options of Last Resort: A Comparison of Voluntarily Stopping Eating and Drinking, Terminal Sedation, Physician-Assisted Suicide, and Voluntary Active Euthanasia'. *Journal of the American Medical Association* 278(23).

—— Dresser, Rebecca, and Brock, Dan W. 1997. 'The Rule of Double Effect: A Critique of Its Role in End-of-Life Decision Making'. *New England Journal of Medicine* 337(24).

Quinn, Warren S. 1989a. 'Actions, Intentions, and Consequences: The Doctrine of Double Effect'. *Philosophy & Public Affairs* 18(4).

—— 1989b. 'Actions, Intentions, and Consequences: The Doctrine of Doing and Allowing'. *Philosophical Review* 98(3).

Rachels, James. 1975. 'Active and Passive Euthanasia'. *New England Journal of Medicine* 292(2).

—— 1986. *The End of Life: Euthanasia and Morality.* Oxford: Oxford University Press.

Raz, Joseph. 1986. *The Morality of Freedom.* Oxford: Clarendon.

Reagan, Peter. 1999. 'Helen'. *The Lancet* 353(9160).

Rhodes, Rosamond. 1998. 'Physicians, Assisted Suicide, and the Right to Live or Die'. In Battin, Rhodes, and Silvers 1998.

Rietjens, Judith A. C., et al. 2004. 'Physician Reports of Terminal Sedation without Hydration or Nutrition for Patients Nearing Death in the Netherlands'. *Annals of Internal Medicine* 141(3).

—— 2006. 'Terminal Sedation and Euthanasia: A Comparison of Clinical Practices'. *Archives of Internal Medicine* 166(7).

—— et al. 2008. 'Continuous Deep Sedation for Patients Nearing Death in the Netherlands: Descriptive Study'. *British Medical Journal* 336(7648).

Rodrigue, James R., Morgan, Sam B., and Geffken, Gary. 1990. 'Families of Autistic Children: Psychological Functioning of Mothers'. *Journal of Clinical Child Psychology* 19(4).

Rosenbaum, Stephen E. 1986. 'How to be Dead and not Care: A Defense of Epicurus'. *American Philosophical Quarterly* 23(2).

Rosenfeld, Barry. 2004. *Assisted Suicide and the Right to Die: The Interface of Social Science, Public Policy, and Medical Ethics.* Washington, DC: American Psychological Association.

Rosner, Fred. 1993. 'Why Nutrition and Hydration Should Not Be Withheld from Patients'. *Chest* 104(6).

Rurup, Mette L., et al. 2008. 'The Reporting Rate of Euthanasia and Physician-Assisted Suicide: A Study of the Trends'. *Medical Care* 46(12).

—— 2009. 'Trends in the Use of Opioids at the End of Life and the Expected Effects of Hastening Death'. *Journal of Pain and Symptom Management* 37(2).

Schaich Borg, Jana, et al. 2006. 'Consequences, Action, and Intention as Factors in Moral Judgments: An FMRI Investigation'. *Journal of Cognitive Neuroscience* 18(5).

Schnakers, Caroline, et al. 2009. 'Diagnostic Accuracy of the Vegetative and Minimally Conscious State: Clinical Consensus Versus Standardized Neurobehavioral Assessment'. *BMC Neurology* 9(35).

Seale, Clive. 2006. 'National Survey of End-of-Life Decisions Made by UK Medical Practitioners'. *Palliative Medicine* 20(1).

——2009a. 'End-of-Life Decisions in the UK Involving Medical Practitioners'. *Palliative Medicine* 23(3).

——2009b. 'Legalisation of Euthanasia or Physician-Assisted Suicide: Survey of Doctors' Attitudes'. *Palliative Medicine* 23(3).

Select Committee on the Assisted Dying for the Terminally Ill Bill. 2005. *Assisted Dying for the Terminally Ill [HL]*. London: Stationery Office.

Shalowitz, D., and Emanuel, E. 2004. 'Euthanasia and Physician-Assisted Suicide: Implications for Physicians'. *Journal of Clinical Ethics* 15(3).

Shapiro, Robyn S., et al. 1994. 'Willingness to Perform Euthanasia: A Survey of Physician Attitudes'. *Archives of Internal Medicine* 154(5).

Shewmon, D. Alan. 2001. 'The Brain and Somatic Integration: Insights into the Standard Biological Rationale for Equating "Brain Death" with Death'. *Journal of Medicine and Philosophy* 26(5).

Sidgwick, Henry. 1907. *The Methods of Ethics*, 7th edn. Chicago: University of Chicago Press.

Siegler, M., and Weisbard, A. 1985. 'Against the Emerging Stream: Should Fluids and Nutritional Support be Discontinued?' *Archives of Internal Medicine* 145(1).

Silvers, Anita. 1998. 'Protecting the Innocents from Physician-Assisted Suicide: Disability Discrimination and the Duty to Protect Otherwise Vulnerable Groups'. In Battin, Rhodes, and Silvers 1998.

Silverstein, Harry. 1980. 'The Evil of Death'. *Journal of Philosophy* 77(7).

Singer, Peter. 1994. *Rethinking Life and Death: The Collapse of Our Traditional Ethics*. New York: St Martin's Press.

Slome, Lee R., et al. 1997. 'Physician-Assisted Suicide and Patients with Human Immunodeficiency Virus Disease'. *New England Journal of Medicine* 336(6).

Slomka, Jacquelyn. 1995. 'What Do Apple Pie and Motherhood Have to Do with Feeding Tubes and Caring for the Patient?' *Archives of Internal Medicine* 155(12).

——2003. 'Withholding Nutrition at the End of Life: Clinical and Ethical Issues'. *Cleveland Clinic Journal of Medicine* 70(6).

Smies, Jonathon T. 2003–4. 'The Legalization of Euthanasia in the Netherlands'. *Gonzaga Journal of International Law* 7 (available at <http://www.gonzagajil.org/>, accessed January 2011).

Sneiderman, Barney, and Deutscher, Raymond. 2002. 'Dr. Nancy Morrison and Her Dying Patient: A Case of Medical Necessity'. *Health Law Journal* 10: 1–30.

Special Senate Committee on Euthanasia and Assisted Suicide. 1995. *Of Life and Death*. Ottawa: Senate of Canada.

Stell, Lance K. 1998. 'Physician-Assisted Suicide: To Decriminalize or to Legalize, That is the Question'. In Battin, Rhodes, and Silvers 1998.

Stone, Jim. 1994. 'Advance Directives, Autonomy and Unintended Death'. *Bioethics* 8(3).

——2007. 'Pascal's Wager and the Persistent Vegetative State'. *Bioethics* 21(2).

Strubbe, Eva. 2000. 'Toward Legal Recognition for Termination of Life Without Request? Remarks on Advice no. 9 of the Belgian Advisory Committee on Bioethics Concerning Termination of Life of Incompetent Patients'. *European Journal of Health Law* 7(1).

Stutsman, Eli D. 2004. 'Political Strategy and Legal Change'. In Quill and Battin 2004*b*.

Sumner, L. W. 1987. *The Moral Foundation of Rights*. Oxford: Clarendon.

—— 1996. *Welfare, Happiness, and Ethics*. Oxford: Clarendon.

—— 2004. *The Hateful and the Obscene: Studies in the Limits of Free Expression*. Toronto: University of Toronto Press.

Swarte, Nikkie B., et al. 2003. 'Effects of Euthanasia on the Bereaved Family and Friends: A Cross Sectional Study'. *British Medical Journal* 327(7408).

Swiss Academy of Medical Sciences (SAMS). 2004. *Care of Patients in the End of Life: Medical-Ethical Guidelines of the SAMS*. Basle: Swiss Academy of Medical Sciences (SAMS).

Swiss National Advisory Commission for Biomedical Ethics (NEK-CNE). 2005. *Assisted Suicide: Opinion no. 9/2005*. Berne: Swiss National Advisory Commission for Biomedical Ethics (NEK-CNE).

—— 2006. *Duty-of-Care Criteria for the Management of Assisted Suicide: Opinion no. 13/2006*. Berne: Swiss National Advisory Commission for Biomedical Ethics (NEK-CNE).

Sykes, Nigel, and Thorns, Andrew. 2003*a*. 'Sedative Use in the Last Week of Life and the Implications for End-of-Life Decision Making'. *Archives of Internal Medicine* 163(3).

Sykes, Nigel, and Thorns, Andrew. 2003*b*. 'The Use of Opioids and Sedatives at the End of Life'. *Lancet Oncology* 4(5).

Tallis, Raymond. 2009. 'Why I Changed My Mind about Assisted Dying'. *The Times*, 27 October.

Thomasma, David C., et al. (eds.) 1998. *Asking to Die: Inside the Dutch Debate About Euthanasia*. Dordrecht: Kluwer Academic.

Thomson, Judith Jarvis. 1990. *The Realm of Rights*. Cambridge, Mass.: Harvard University Press.

—— 1995. 'Killing and Letting Die: Some Comments'. In Beauchamp 1996*b*.

—— 1999. 'Physician-Assisted Suicide: Two Moral Arguments'. *Ethics* 109(3).

Tolle, S. W., et al. 2004. 'Characteristics and Proportion of Dying Oregonians Who Personally Consider Physician-Assisted Suicide'. *Journal of Clinical Ethics* 15(2).

Tomsons, Kira, and Sherwin, Susan. 2010. 'Feminist Reflections on Tracy Latimer and Sue Rodriguez'. In Michael Stingl (ed.), *The Price of Compassion: Assisted Suicide and Euthanasia*. Peterborough, Ont.: Broadview.

Trammell, Richard. 1975. 'Saving Life and Taking Life'. *Journal of Philosophy* 72(5).

Tucker, Kathryn L. 2004. 'Legal Advocacy to Improve Care and Expand Options at the End of Life'. In Quill and Battin 2004*b*.

Twycross, R. 1994. *Pain Relief in Advanced Cancer*. Edinburgh: Churchill Livingstone.

Varelius, Jukka. 2007. 'Illness, Suffering and Voluntary Euthanasia'. *Bioethics* 21(2).

Veatch, Robert. 1975. 'The Whole-Brain-Oriented Concept of Death: An Outmoded Philosophical Formulation'. *Journal of Thanatology* 3.

Velleman, J. David. 1992. 'Against the Right to Die'. *Journal of Medicine and Philosophy* 17(6).

—— 1999. 'A Right of Self-Termination?' *Ethics* 109(3).

Verhagen, Eduard, and Sauer, Pieter J. J. 2005. 'The Groningen Protocol: Euthanasia in Severely Ill Newborns'. *New England Journal of Medicine* 352(10) (10 March).

Vrakking, Astrid M., et al. 2007. 'End-of-Life Decision Making in Neonates and Infants: Comparison of the Netherlands and Belgium (Flanders)'. *Acta Paediatrica* 96(6).

Vries, Martine C. de, and Verhagen, Eduard 2008. 'A Case Against Something that is Not the Case: The Groningen Protocol and the Moral Principle of Non-Maleficence'. *American Journal of Bioethics* 8(11).

Ward, B. J., and Tate, P. A. 1994. 'Attitudes among NHS Doctors to Requests for Euthanasia'. *British Medical Journal* 308(6940).

Wedgwood, Ralph. 2009. 'Defending Double Effect'. Unpublished MS.

Wijdicks, Eelco F. M. 2002. 'Brain Death Worldwide: Accepted Fact but No Global Consensus in Diagnostic Criteria'. *Neurology* 58(1).

Williams, Bernard. 1973. 'The Makropoulos Case: Reflections on the Tedium of Immortality'. In id., *Problems of the Self*. New York: Cambridge University Press.

Williams, Glenys. 2007. *Intention and Causation in Medical Non-Killing: The Impact of Criminal Law Concepts on Euthanasia and Assisted Suicide*. Abingdon: Routledge-Cavendish.

Wilson, Keith G., et al. 2000. 'Attitudes of Terminally Ill Patients Toward Euthanasia and Physician-Assisted Suicide'. *Archives of Internal Medicine* 160(16).

—— 2007. 'Desire for Euthanasia or Physician-Assisted Suicide in Palliative Cancer Care'. *Health Psychology* 26(3).

Woien, Sandra. 2007. 'Conflicting Preferences and Advance Directives'. *American Journal of Bioethics* 7(4).

—— 2008. 'Life, Death and Harm: Staying Within the Boundaries of Nonmaleficence'. *American Journal of Bioethics* 8(11).

Wolf, Susan M. 1996. 'Gender, Feminism, and Death: Physician-Assisted Suicide and Euthanasia'. In id. (ed.), *Feminism and Bioethics: Beyond Reproduction*. New York: Oxford University Press.

Wreen, Michael. 1988. 'The Definition of Suicide'. *Social Theory and Practice* 14(1).

Wrigley, Anthony. 2007. 'Personal Identity, Autonomy and Advance Statements'. *Journal of Applied Philosophy* 24(4).

Index